inexhaustible radio/TV
foot fall
immemorial past
exhibitionism of the soul
pungency

DIARY
1928-
1957

JULIAN GREEN DIARY 1928-1957

Selected by Kurt Wolff

Translated by Anne Green

Carroll & Graf Publishers, Inc.
New York

First Carroll & Graf Edition 1985

Carroll & Graf Publishers, Inc.
260 Fifth Avenue
New York, N.Y. 10001

ISBN: 0-88184-119-6

Manufactured in the United States of America

The excerpts from my diary were selected by Kurt Wolff with my approval. Had I made the selection myself, it might have been somewhat different, but the author is not necessarily the best judge in such a case, and I relied, wisely I think, on Kurt Wolff's critical sense.

Julian Green

1928

SEPTEMBER 17. PARIS. This diary, which I intend to keep as regularly as I can, will help me, I think, to see more clearly into myself. I expect to record my whole life in these pages, with complete frankness and accuracy. . . . How will the book turn out? I have no idea, but to know that it exists will be a source of satisfaction to me.

SEPTEMBER 18. If people only knew what lies at the heart of my novels! What a tumult of desires these carefully written pages conceal! I sometimes have a loathing for the furious cravings that give me no peace except when I am working.

OCTOBER 6. I want to begin reading the Bible again every evening as I used to, even if this only gives me a faint help against temptations; the least it can do will be to make me wish for better things.

OCTOBER 14. Have read a lot, dreamed a lot these days. Read *Mark Rutherford*, which I feel tempted to translate. What surprises me, when I come to think of it, is that there is someone in me who wants to write a book of this kind and I am obliged to oppose him. There is not a sentence here that I do not wholeheartedly agree to. I am familiar with these struggles and spiritual lapses. The beauty of this book fills me with a great disgust for this world.

DECEMBER 4. Have begun reading Pepys. It makes me sorry not to have better recorded the events in my own life. But he wrote for the pleasure of talking about himself. Now, I obey the incomprehensible desire to bring the past to a standstill that makes one keep a diary. And this desire came to me rather late. Why didn't I begin at eighteen!

DECEMBER 11. I was thinking today about my holidays at Savannah, in 1920 and 1921. I had fits of piety. I read St. Paul in a small, dark drawing room that looked out on an unpaved yard.

The Presbyterian church blocked the view and cast its shadow over the room; in order to see, I had to turn on the light in broad daylight. The heat was heavy and soporific, but I nevertheless pursued my austere reading. At my elbow buzzed a ventilator. From time to time I treated myself to a swallow of ice water. I believed that I understood every word I read. I had great spiritual yearnings, tried mentally to convey myself to a retreat in the desert where I could be a hermit, and felt happy even though my happiness took a strange form. A little of all this went into *The Pilgrim on the Earth.*

UNDATED. Went to see the Barthou collection this afternoon. I was alone in the gallery that contains fragments of statues, and these, I must say, do not appeal to me much. Yet, I stayed there almost ten minutes, seated on a straw-bottomed chair, before a large head of Bodhisattva that plunged me into a sort of abyss. The face is a fine, rather full oval and the brow a little too broad to seem to me perfect. Under the heavy drooping eyelids steals an almost sly glance. The mouth with deeply chiseled corners seems at times to smile, for if one looks at it closely, the face changes continually. What cannot be expressed is the superhuman intelligence to be read in the features. For a few seconds, I had the keen, disturbing impression that the stone head knew of my existence and that it was aware of the problems in my life. "Too many efforts," it seemed to say. "Too much disorder, too many desires." I left it regretfully, vaguely aspiring to better things, a fuller life, but I am too passionate to listen to Asia's teachings. We must, I think, accept the fate of our race and go up higher according to the spirit of our race.

1929

JANUARY 11. My fifteenth year was one of the happiest in my life. I no longer felt that I lived on earth. I can see myself once more, on a spring day, rue Raynouard, in Father Crété's room. We are leaning out of a window. Before us lie the Champ-de-Mars, Grenelle, and, in a sort of golden dust, the heights of Saint-Cloud.

Birds are singing in the mild air. On the terrace below us, an old blind priest walks up and down telling his beads and Father Crété talks to me about life after death. I am happy, but none of this can be expressed. The earth does not contain joys like these. It perhaps gives as powerful ones, but not of this particular quality.

JANUARY 23. A liver attack kept me in bed for three or four days. During this short illness, I thought my life was about to take a somewhat different turn, become more spiritual than it is at present. An absence of desires coincided with my body's weakness and the soul was allowed a free hand. How to make good use of sickness . . . It gave me a yearning for my stay in Brittany when I was nineteen, a time when I got up at night to say my prayers. Nothing impure in my life then. My visits to the Church of Saint-Melaine, to the cathedral at Rennes. Great spiritual longings and great joys. I was *aspirant* in the 50th Artillery Regiment. Later, I was sent to Alsace and to the Ruhr. Very gradually, a taste for living in the world came back to me and I gave up my plan of going to the Benedictines in the Isle of Wight.

FEBRUARY 10. An evening at Gide's. Present, apart from Robert and myself, were Malraux, Schiffrin, and Berl. A long discussion that I found a trifle academic about the small degree of actuality in contemporary literature. Good gracious! A book worthy of the name always belongs to its period on account of the spirit that quickens it. Descriptions of factory stacks and women with bobbed hair are not what date a 1928 book, but all that lies at the bottom of the book, uneasiness, a need to rebel, etc. When one of us said that in 1845 Balzac wrote novels that took place in 1820, Malraux exclaimed: "Don't let us talk of Balzac!" And everyone seemed to agree that it was impossible to talk about Balzac, without my understanding why.

MARCH 4. A great and furious desire to change my life, to be free, but there is no way out except in asceticism or in pleasure such as I used to know. I cheat the violence that forms the basis of my nature by writing my books. . . . It is madness to live like this, to warp my being.

APRIL 10. Gide wrote me such a nice note that I could not resist the pleasure of going to see him. I find him in his study. He tells me right away that he wants to have a straightforward conversation with me, as the others, those of his fellow writers, as he calls them, do not interest him. He has just finished reading my pamphlet (against French Catholics) and asks me how it should be interpreted. "You should see it," I reply, "not as a profession of faith, but as the expression of what I demand of Catholics." "In that case," answers Gide, "I agree with you wholeheartedly." Once more, he talks to me about the years of great religious fervor he had known and declares himself extremely sensitive to the charm of certain Catholic friends, but that he can resist them, when necessary. "Yet, I had warned Claudel . . . ," he says. Then shaking his head sadly, he adds: "All my friends have been converted: Ghéon, Claudel, Laurens, Copeau . . . this has made it impossible for me to talk to them. . . ."

A little later, I tell him how uneasy it makes me to be ranked among Catholic writers. Too many things separate me from the Church at present for me to call myself Catholic, but it would not enter my head to associate these spiritual difficulties with a novel. And even if I were Catholic, it seems to me that to be labeled a Catholic writer would always fill me with horror. It means cheapening religion. Should I express myself publicly on this point? "I should do nothing of the sort, if I were you," says Gide. "No, I have gone through the same experience. Better not open a debate that might bring you, in spite of yourself, to clearly state a profession of faith." "This would be all the more difficult," say I, "since I couldn't say exactly what I believe." "No more could I," says Gide, and he adds firmly: "At any rate, I know very well what I don't believe." We are silent for a few seconds. I think we both of us feel that this conversation is moving. "How painful it is," I say after a moment, "to feel embarrassed in the presence of people you respect and also love, but from whom you know that you may have to protect yourself some day, in spite of yourself. For some of our Catholic friends answer that description. . . . With the best will in the world, they never see you without a lurking idea of proselytism. They are worried about our salvation. They visibly have it on their minds, even when you talk to them of quite different matters. . . ." "Yes indeed!" cries Gide. "They will use every means to draw you to them. When you are with them, you find yourself in the situation of a woman faced with a man who would harbor *intentions*!" Intentions is said with a sort of emphasis. And Gide amusingly rolls up the collar of his thick black woolen coat.

He then talks to me at length about *The Dark Journey*. He seems to admire the whole of it, with the exception of Mme Londe, a character he finds untrue to life, but congratulates me on having continued to the end, in spite of this part of the book which he thinks unsatisfactory, "and at bottom, what I blame in *The Dark Journey* turns to your credit, for when all is said and done, what matters is to have carried a book like this to its conclusion, even with its defects. . . . It is a projection of yourself on paper." We next talk about what we have been reading. . . . Around four-thirty, he leaves me to order tea. I hear his voice at the end of the passage saying that he wants "the good tea." It is brought together with four crackers on a plate, and while we are feasting he asks me point-blank if I will entrust him with *The Dark Journey* to make a film of it. "I have searched vainly through the whole of contemporary literature for a book that could provide a script. One always reaches a place, a level place where the characters pause before moving on, but with you there is a *falling forward* that the screen would render wonderfully. For instance . . ." And he mentions some ten scenes in my book and then adds with a smile: "I hope you believe me now when I say that I know every hole and corner in your book!"

APRIL 11. I remember that my talk with Gide began by remarks about the present mania for classing the dead in one camp or the other, Catholic or atheist. "This is only of relative importance where the living are concerned," says Gide, "but not for the dead, who can't speak up for themselves. . . . See what happened in the case of Rimbaud, of Rivière. . . ." And he adds that for his part, he is taking precautions to avoid any misunderstandings after his death. . . .

APRIL 27. Plon offers me a contract that would bind me for fifteen years. How many wars and revolutions will have swept away contracts by 1945! It is already a great deal to live five years, ten years, without too much loss. Far from poisoning my life, this idea, which seldom leaves me, gives an extraordinary flavor to the present hour. Any plan for the future seems to me more and more futile. But let us behave as though everything were solid, let us go on working until everything crumbles.

APRIL 29. How I have suffered in this little room! What I took for a religious vocation was born here. The yearnings of my fifteenth year, those immense efforts to go to God . . . And here, too, the first desires and the terrible remorse that harried me . . . I used to mark my faults on the wall, behind a photograph of Murillo's Virgin. How many papers thrown into the fire, because of those small tragedies of conscience that make something so sad of our youth!

MAY 1.   Maritain to dinner. He is someone rare and exquisite, a truly Christian soul in Catholic armor, an armor that hampers his movements. Oh! I know he would protest if he read this sentence, but I can't express otherwise what I think of him. He stayed until eleven o'clock, talking about everything, passing suddenly from sadness to gaiety and from gaiety to an almost sorrowful tone. "Haven't I made a mistake?" he asks me. "Wasn't I wrong in busying myself with all those men of letters?" And, on leaving me, he looked sad and bewildered, although smiling.

MAY 25.   "Victor Hugo was a madman who took himself for Victor Hugo." Cocteau developed this paradox in the most brilliant manner, day before yesterday. How can what he said be said again? One would have to have Jean's voice and expression to bring all this to life. Certain proofs of the great poet's madness fill us with joy: "He wrote three hundred lines of verse at a sitting, swallowed oranges, skin and all, wolfed down lobsters, saying that the shell it was that made the sauce go down. . . . He made pieces of furniture with his teeth. . . ."

Colette listens and laughs with us, munching apples. She contributes her fund of anecdotes and tells about Victor Hugo's armchair that had various secret devices. . . .

As he came in, Cocteau showed us a sick bird he had found on the Champs-Elysées. Colette picks it up, examines it, and wrings its neck in the garden.

SEPTEMBER 24.   Gide came to see me yesterday. He talked about old age, about his in particular. "Sometimes," he says, "I have to look at myself in a mirror and tell myself: 'You are sixty,' for I don't believe it." And he goes on—not without a reminiscence of Goethe, I think: "I feel young with young people. They keep me from aging." Then he adds: "If it wasn't for Marc Allégret, I'd have already shriveled up completely." He then talks to me about my happiness and wants to know if I fully realize it. . . . I tell

him how much love made me suffer at the University, and he replies that he himself has never suffered from love, that he doesn't
know what it is, and I can't help thinking this a most extraordinary statement.

OCTOBER 3.   Lots of dreams, lots of meditations over the book I
am writing at present. The other day, in listening to the last movement of a trio by Schumann, it seemed to me as though the present were abolished and that the only thing that counted was the
music's extraordinary reality. Such a state of mind is impossible
to put into words. Everything fades away, everything appears
absurd and incoherent. There are times when I feel a great disgust for words. They continually show a man his limitations, and
I scarcely see anything but music that can carry him out of
himself.

OCTOBER 16.   For the last few days it has been impossible for me
to apply myself to work, and this for several reasons, the chief
being that I can't manage to *find* the beginning of my book
(*L'Autre sommeil*). This is extremely painful, for when I don't
work I have the impression that my life is useless. Yet, no effort
can make me find the first pages of this book if the time has not
come. What comforts me a little is that the same difficulties occur
with each book. Nevertheless, I go through painful moments of
discouragement.

OCTOBER 20.   A visit to the painter Vlaminck in his country house,
which is both like a farm and a studio. He is tall and heavy. In his
broad pink face, a beaklike nose and blue eyes with something
ferocious in them. But Vlaminck is extremely agreeable and brings
out some twenty pictures for our appreciation; I think them very
fine and he himself is quite proud of them. "You're going to see
surprising things," he tells us. "Now, isn't this beautiful? That's
painting for you! Look at this . . . and look at this tragic sky,
this road where something is going to happen. . . ." These comments exempt me from giving the usual praise. He then recites a
little poem he had composed and which he likes so much that he
recites it three times over, looking me straight in the eye the
whole time, and at the end of the poem an enormous burst of
laughter doubles him up. He next treats us to an essay on youth
and speed, where it is proved that the speed which characterizes

our times is a sign of decrepitude. Doesn't a child walk slowly, doesn't it take an hour to accomplish what it will do later in five minutes? The older it grows, the faster it gets about. . . .

A little later, he says abruptly: "My painting is the best." This I like, for that is the way he should think, in order to paint. But I regret his adding: "This probably seems idiotic to you, but if I admired M. Renoir, I could not paint. Douanier Rousseau was very stupid. He wanted to paint like Bouguereau, whom he copied, or thought he copied. . . ."

OCTOBER 29. Yesterday, lunched with Curtius at the café Voltaire, place de l'Odéon. One quickly feels at ease with a man whose manners are so simple. We talk of Catholicism and Curtius thinks me right when I say that religion does not provide the answers to some of the very serious questions that life asks us. I was thinking in particular about physical problems. "We are," then says Curtius, "the victims of political sexual morality, that of Israel, a morality that has passed into the mass of Catholic ideas through the channel of St. Paul. But," he adds (and this finds a deep echo in me), "whatever my attitude to Catholicism, there is a Christian element in me to which I could not be unfaithful without committing real apostasy." As a last resort, the Gospel. God is hidden to philosophers (even Thomists?). We then talk about several writers and Curtius tells me how much he admires Joyce, whom he considers the leading European author. "What about Gide?" I ask. "Gide lacks greatness." I have heard Malraux say the same thing, but in a more brilliant manner. As I tell Curtius of my difficulties in writing a novel, he answers: "You should have been a poet," little knowing how right he is.

NOVEMBER 13. Appendicitis on November 1st and an operation on the 2nd. (Dr. de Martel performed the operation.) The complete annihilation of the being by ether, a drop into a dark, sonorous chasm, a great noise of bells, like those of American trains, and above all, the impossibility of offering any resistance, of clinging on to anything whatever—there must be a little of all this in death. The minute before losing consciousness was, I think, strange but not at all terrifying. My first idea when I woke up was: "So. I am dead and, exactly as I foresaw, I still exist."

For a moment the body, the whole being, lay on some mysterious shore, waiting for the rising tide to carry it back. What was the soul doing, while this was going on? Where was it?

* * *

NOVEMBER 14. Today I can stand as straight as I did before my operation, and without effort. Desires, those tiresome companions, return with health. During the first days after the operation, the soul had little difficulty in soaring and I dreamed of a life where desires did not exist, where flesh was silent. Religion, I now see clearly, being made chiefly for the sick, could not fail to show itself to me under the most attractive colors, without its being possible to distinguish what part it could play in my life from now on. Religion has already succeeded in putting my life in such an alarming state of unbalance that I still fear it, although I have found my bearings once more. People think me pessimistic, but those who don't know that I am looking for happiness, the joy of living, yes, the holy joy of living, don't know me at all.

NOVEMBER 15. When I saw Curtius, I remember telling him of a bad dream I had had (I was being buried) and of my fear of dying in a few hours, of dying, for instance, of appendicitis. "Are you threatened with appendicitis?" he asked. "Not in the least." That was two days before my illness. How often have I noticed that we unconsciously prophesy, as though there were someone in us who knows far more about us than we do ourselves.

Have begun to write again with great joy.

There is someone whom I scarcely ever mention in this diary. Happiness is a story that cannot be told. Love is a story that cannot be told.

1930

MARCH 27. Lunched with Malraux at the Pergola, avenue du Maine. He thinks that I write my books according to plans, following a well-thought-out technique. Useless to explain. I prefer listening to what he has to say. He asserts that what he dreads is not death but the years around fifty and the sexual impotence of that age, an impotence which is a sign of death. We talk about the rising literary generation, the one between twenty and twenty-five, of how little interest their work presents. "What can they do?" asks Malraux. "They grew up in a peaceful era, without feeling the jolt of a war or a revolution that has proved so useful to us." And later he says this, which I find very striking: "Between eighteen and twenty, life is like an exchange where one buys stocks, not with money, but with actions. Most men buy nothing."

MARCH 29. Thought this morning about the story I am writing at present. I stand with my back to the wall. In hesitating to talk about the hero's love for a young man, I falsify truth and seemingly conform to accepted morality, I act with a prudence that will make me lose all self-respect. It is in behaving thus that one finally becomes a man of letters.

JULY 3. Read a life of Savonarola. The reformer is a most pathetic character. His affection for young religious, the games they played together in the country, his innocence. "You ought to play for salads instead of playing for money," he told the Florentines. His ferocity knew no limits where homosexuals were concerned. He talks openly of priests who spent the night with *ragazzi* and then went to say Mass. (*"Pensa come la va!"*) There are interesting details. Boniface VIII had to forbid priests to keep butcher shops, brothels, and to serve as go-betweens for prostitutes. . . .

1931

FEBRUARY 1. Reread Stevenson's *Suicide Club* with pleasure and admiration, but some of the author's literary mannerisms spoil the fine story for me a little. I cannot bear his irony, no matter how light, any more than his tendency to preach. This Scot always has a little sermon in his pocket and I think that, unfortunately, the irony is only there to make one swallow the homily. But the great writer is present at every page. Witness the speech he puts into a coward's mouth: "People trifle with love. Now, I deny that love is a strong passion; it is with fear that you must trifle, if you wish to taste the intensest joy of living. Envy me—envy me, sir . . . I am a coward."

*   *   *

FEBRUARY 7. Very much absorbed by my novel. There is a truth that must be reached at all costs, the one that lies in the heart "of every man who comes into this world." It is not the truth that can be found in a novel, it is not that air of likelihood that makes amateurs cry out their admiration. No, to discover that truth, one must work against oneself, against one's inclinations, against the skill acquired by habit, against success, against the public, one must suppress every page that has only the reader's amusement in view. Words form a sort of current that one must constantly swim against; whoever gives in to the temptation of following the current, goes straight to failure, for it becomes impossible, after long misusing words, to make them tell the truth.

FEBRUARY 14. This morning I decided to rewrite the second part of my novel. The pages lack intensity; the plot unfolds slowly and is not in itself very interesting. The lighting, that is, the play of contrasts, is too feeble, what the characters have to say does not come from their innermost self, and almost everywhere the deep truth is sacrificed to a conventional truth, the truth to be found in novels. I hope that all my efforts are not lost. I have gone through a painful time, I have had doubts about myself, about my faculty for invention and even the mere power of putting words together in a coherent fashion. I feel calmer and more confident today.

FEBRUARY 17. . . . When I told Gide that I was doing over the second part of my book, he said I was right. "I would have been worried if you had told me that all was going smoothly," he adds. "And you are right to fear habit. The dangerous moment comes when a book begins to move of itself." With a shade of bitterness, he then talks about an English novelist who, it seems, had plagiarized *Les Faux-monnayeurs* and had recently written an article about him entitled: "A Bogus Great Writer." "He is too clever," says Gide. "He gives in to success. He's one of those who should begin their books all over again!"

Regarding certain Catholic writers, he says: "One fine day they will annex Nietzsche. Everything that is tragic becomes Catholic. At any rate, they won't get anything out of Goethe. . . ."

FEBRUARY 18. Gide was telling me the other day that he would have liked to try his luck at publishing one of his books anonymously, but that such an attempt was impossible for his next work, because he had already talked about it, and to too many people. "Then you might put it off until the book after that," I then remark. He throws up his hands. "Do you think I have as many books as that in my brain?" he asks, laughing.

MAY 6.   Gide and Malraux have lunch with me. The subject of eroticism came up, I don't remember in what connection. Malraux talks about it brilliantly and maintains that eroticism really appears in full force only in countries where the notion of sin exists. Gide, Robert, and I say very little but listen with interest. A little later, Gide, who has been asked by Malraux for the definition of a Christian, looks at us, saying: "I feel I'm going to flunk it." But Malraux sticks to his guns. "Yet," he says, "you have touched lightly on the subject in your *Montaigne*." "Oh," replied Gide, "I touched lightly, I touch lightly on everything!"

After Robert leaves, followed by Malraux, I remain alone with Gide, who tells me about his plans in a friendly manner and—I think I can use the term—about his discouragements. He wants to write a novel in which he himself would be involved and seems unable to do so. He can only create a character that is exterior to his self, or else he falls back on his diary, but finds it impossible to write a novel of which he would be the hero. Proof being, according to him, that he is a real novelist and does not put himself into his books, as certain critics allege, critics whom he refuses to name. . . .

He talks about Bernard Faÿ's brother and quotes the admirable sentence pronounced by this youth who died at twenty-four: "I don't want to go on playing in a world where everybody cheats." "The fact is that you feel at times like someone waiting for a bus who has the last number," adds Gide.[1] "Then you say to the others: 'Go on! Get in!' " He says the last words violently, almost indignantly.

MAY 24.   This afternoon, at the Pré Catalan, I watched a young man whose maneuvers intrigued me. He ogled a very beautiful woman of an Asiatic type and, in order to get closer to her, changed his table. Finally, unable to contain himself any longer, although she was accompanied by an old lady, he went up to the

[1] In Paris, people take numbers to get into a bus.

woman and asked her for a dance. It must be said that she too had glanced at him. Yet she refused. He threw her a terrible look that she did not see and bit his lip. He was thin, very white, with a rather delicate nose, pale, staring eyes, an underhung jaw, a skinny nape, and his skull was hollow behind the ears. He did not blush, but moved slowly back, staring at the woman with an expression filled with hatred and greed. It is so rare to find anyone in Paris capable of suffering, or of feeling anything whatever, that the fact is worth noting.

JUNE 22. Finished writing the chapter in my novel: the nightmare of a guilty conscience. How often have I dreamed of a garden that never ended, of a street that continued indefinitely and led straight out of the world! As a child I sometimes felt angry at the idea of limits being imposed to space; a wall, a door, made me indignant.

JUNE 23. At the exhibition of Portuguese Primitives. In a troubled, uneasy period, this austere painting brings us back to reality. For what is called politics has no more reality than a nightmare, even when it is interpreted by uprisings and massacres. The cannon, that big fool, may perhaps kill me, without convincing me for all that of its existence, whereas a few notes of Bach's music seem to bear up the sky. Even if grossness triumphs in Europe, it will never be anything but a dreadful semblance. What is real is beyond all reach.

SEPTEMBER 6. Yesterday evening the fuse burned out and sent us to bed with candles; this reminded me of my childhood and of the terrors of that age, fruitful terrors. At our house in Andrésy, in summer, I dreaded the moment when, once in bed, I had to muster up the courage to blow out my candle. So I would sit on a step in the staircase, my candlestick by me and, on my knees, a shabby copy of La Fontaine's *Fables*. And as I read the little stories—some of which assumed a terrifying meaning to me—I tried to watch from the corner of my eye the fantastic play of shadows on the wall. (For me, the wolf in La Fontaine will always be a nightmarish character.) How wonderful it was to hear the drawing-room door open at last and my parents make ready to come upstairs! I scurried away immediately, having burned half my candle.

*   *   *

SEPTEMBER 16. As I woke early this morning, I thought about my childhood. There are memories that one scarcely dares touch. I remembered my room in the rue de Passy, at dawn. The sun came through the red cotton curtains and a blackbird whistled in the landlord's garden. I felt so happy that I laughed to myself, in bed.

Later, particularly from the age of fifteen on, I thought only of the future. Everything that I wished for, I located in the future, just as one puts away cherished objects in a cupboard. I carried everything toward a mysterious goal that I wished to reach. And then, when I was about twenty-five, the future suddenly vanished. I can't express this otherwise. Yes, nothing remained but the present. Happiness under all aspects had to be enjoyed right away. The cupboard grew empty.

SEPTEMBER 21. Sadness and disgust made me interrupt this diary. What a false idea it would give of me, if anyone chanced to read it. For there is everything in my life. . . . There is my work, the book that is being created in me at all hours of the day, there is what I read and the thoughts that I keep to myself; and lastly perhaps, what seems to take up such a great place . . . Where is this diary leading me? Toward what darkness, toward what death? What will I be writing in it, in a year? I am filled at times with a terrible uneasiness, but one must go straight ahead.

SEPTEMBER 23. Reading Havelock Ellis. How much more useful his works seem to me than hundreds of novels that teach us nothing about ourselves, that do not help us.

SEPTEMBER 27. In the Trocadéro gardens, I watched men felling a tree. One of them was superb, bare-armed, his broad breast swelling his striped vest. Perspiration glistened on his dark skin. Fine rhythmical movements, a sort of disciplined violence. The ax bit into the base of the trunk and small chips of wood began to fly. At last, the tree began to shake, two men with a rope made it fall to the ground with a great shuddering. The beauty of the scene was with me all that day.

OCTOBER 1. Maritain's visit depressed me. According to him, the world is nearing its end, nay, we are already slipping into the abyss, we are in it; all mystics agree on this point. If there isn't a war, a revolution will take charge and annihilate us. Everything is tumbling down. Germany will perhaps launch into a war without a hope of winning it: her way of committing a sort of suicide. Maritain then talks about Teresa Neumann, whom he saw in her village near Munich. He describes the blood that streams from the woman's eyes and coagulates on her cheeks during the night before Friday. In her visions of the Passion, she repeats Aramaic words that she hears without understanding them, and that specialists have been able to translate. She says that the Franco-German rivalry displeases God and she foretells a catastrophe if a reconciliation does not take place.

I am always moved by Maritain's presence. Everything that is candid and true in the man speaks from his eyes.

OCTOBER 5. When I think that a whole portion of my life has already disappeared completely from my memory, I tremble as though it meant the partial death of my being. Today, I was remembering my solitary holidays at Savannah, in 1920 and 1921. My room, described in *The Pilgrim on the Earth*, my forlorn walks taken with a beating heart under great oaks draped in veils of Spanish moss, my long fits of insomnia in the stifling night. Ah! if it had only occurred to me to keep a diary in such moments, what a liberation it would have been for me, what a benefit!

This evening, I put away old papers and old photographs, all that remains of a shipwreck. . . .

OCTOBER 8. At the Louvre, the "Rape of Europa" by Francesco di Giorgio. I have the impression that the world disappears before such a painting or, rather, that another world replaces ours. Here we step right into a land of dreams. As far as I know, none but the Sienese school can so perfectly achieve this sort of miracle (I am not talking about Oriental art, to which, as a matter of fact, Sienese art is somewhat connected). The Florentines do not take us away from earth, they even make it feel good to us, while Duccio or Sassetta leads us gently away from life. In the same manner, this picture by Giorgio is located beyond the world's borders. On a beach of mauve sand, where footsteps leave no traces, fawns and partridges wander along the banks of tender green water. Quite close to the river, groups of girls, pressed together like flowers in a nosegay, look at the great white bull that rears up majestically, a woven crown over one ear. Europa, in a gold embroidered gown and red stockings, reclines over the animal's flank and neck; she is not frightened, she seems as calm as Peace in Giotto's Good Government fresco. But what use is it to talk about this? It is as though one tried to describe music. Fifteenth-century Siena will always be the country of those who feel exiled in their own times. I regretfully left the picture, weary-eyed and a little heavy at heart. I don't know where we are tending, I don't understand the *usefulness* of what we do. Everything seems to me false and vain, except a few pictures, a few pages of music, and a few poems. I must try, by every means possible, to recover the lost country of which Siena gave me a glimpse today.

OCTOBER 21. For a novelist, there is a conventional reality and a reality that might be called a reality of vision. A man whose profession it is to write stories will conceive what I am attempting to express. Words sometimes gather together of themselves and form images that can have a certain appearance of truth and can take in a bad writer and a careless reader. Truth of vision demands a far more severe effort, a sort of gift of oneself. It is not enough to write, for instance: "She drew back before this look." One should have an inner vision of what these words describe. Otherwise, the following sentence will be a little less true (that is, it will not have the sound of inner truth, which is the only truth), and the sentence that comes next will be even less true and so on until the author has pulled himself together.

OCTOBER 25. I have been to the Louvre almost every day for several years; I have never met anyone there whom I knew.

I owe the Louvre an immense debt. I have the feeling of having been brought up and nurtured by it.

NOVEMBER 12. I am the man who wakes at dawn, his head still filled with the dreams of night, dreams of deliverance perhaps, and who walks to the guillotine; I am the man who leans from his window and sees his house caught in incandescent lava, like a vast stream of precious stones; I am the voyager who sits up in his berth and hears someone cry: "Too late!" on the bridge of a sinking ship; I am the woman who sees the murderer's revolver shine close to her temple, and I am the murderer, I am all that when I read a newspaper.

*   *   *

NOVEMBER 15. The exhibition of Italian drawings. It seemed to me as though an angel seized me by a fistful of hair and forcibly lifted me above my own self, beyond this world and into a universe where the marvelous reality of art reigned alone.

NOVEMBER 17. I have always admired French craftsmen, but recently my carpenter dazzled me! We had taken him to the Colonial Exhibition to show him a four-poster in Washington's house, a bed that Robert wished to have copied. M. Miot walked around the bed for a moment, looked at it from behind his pince-nez, took a few measures with a yellow yardstick, and without further ado went home. Three weeks elapsed, and this morning the bed is at Robert's. It is as though we had stolen the original at the Exhibition, for if there are any differences between it and M. Miot's copy, I can't see them. It is a great mahogany bed, light in spite of its size, with four very slender columns supporting a white linen canopy. It has the severe elegance of the eighteenth-century American style, that cold, well-bred disdainful some- ✓ thing that can be found in certain old houses in Richmond or Charleston.

NOVEMBER 25. Spent almost the whole day with Gide. Robert is with us. We all three have lunch near the Bon Marché and gossip gaily about this and that. Not for an instant did I feel that Gide is older than we are and would not even mention it if he himself hadn't alluded to being sixty. I can never rid myself of the impression that I am talking to a companion of my own age. . . .

As we talked about one of Baudelaire's prose poems, Gide, who happened to have a copy of Schiffrin's edition in his pocket, read aloud the first sentence of the poem and looked at us, his eyes shining with delight. . . .

Concerning *Hamlet*, Gide says that no one ever notices a question that Hamlet asks of Horatio and Marcellus: "And what make you from Wittenberg, Horatio? Marcellus?" A question, according to Gide, that calls for our thinking over the very German quality of the character. "To be or not to be . . ." is more or less Schopenhauer. And that continual hesitancy, that incapacity for action, that infirmity of purpose are neither French nor English, but German.

A little later, we talk about Shakespeare's sonnets and more particularly of the "Portrait of Mr. W. H." "This," says Gide, "is the sole interpretation not only plausible but possible of the sonnets addressed to an unknown man, which form the companion piece to the 'Dark Lady' sonnets."

He tells us of his fear of boring people (I think he said his terror of boring people), a constant anxiety that has led him more than once to shorten the end of his books.

Robert asks him what he thinks of a book that has come out about him and quotes from it an extremely funny sentence. "The author," says Gide, "came to see me just after the book was published and cried on my shoulder. Yes, I had to comfort him for having written his book!"

As I told him that out of carelessness I had left my diary open on my table and that the servants had certainly cast an eye over it, Gide says that the curiosity of servants flatters him and that he purposely leaves unimportant papers on his desk to satisfy their craving to know.

DECEMBER 1. Regarding inversion in literature, Gide talks about the difficulty there seems to be to approach the subject in a work of fiction. What results is more or less successful camouflages. Authors have always resorted to such stratagems. If that is the case, what a number of camouflaged books there is, what a number of semi-confessions that we no longer even understand!

DECEMBER 8. . . . I called up Roger Martin du Gard from Gide's flat, but the telephone rang in vain. "Yet he is there," said Gide, who was by me. "He is wonderful, he knows how to protect his privacy and not answer. . . ." I hung up, saying: "I couldn't, I think I would die of curiosity." "And so would I!" cried Gide. "I answer every ring of the bell!"

DECEMBER 27. This morning I went to see Roger Martin du Gard, who, apologizing for not coming to my house, asked me to call on him. We sit in a little room, forlornly heated by gas. We talk about Gide. I say at one moment in the conversation: "If I described him as I see him, no one would believe me, for his reputation shows him under such false colors." "Yes," replies Martin du Gard, "but he himself would contradict you and maybe prove your most skeptical readers to be right. For he isn't a miser, and yet he is. He doesn't lie and yet he does. . . ." But he asserts that in spite of Gide's being so shifty, he is a faithful and loyal friend. Out of weakness and also out of a desire to please, he sometimes tries to agree with whomever he is talking to, and the day comes when this person realizes that Gide has lied to him out of sheer amiability—and thus his reputation is firmly established. This, at any rate, is the explanation given by Martin du Gard. He also talks about Mme Gide. She has not left Cuverville for the last ten years and no longer reads a word of her husband's books. *Si le grain ne meurt* is a book of confidences, says Martin du Gard, and a book of confidences written for Mme Gide that is unknown to her. This is what he finds "pathetic." "And Gide wanted to talk to her, at a distance, as though he were telephoning, but she had hung up long ago." At Cuverville, Gide's attentions to his wife are "almost embarrassing." "You don't feel cold?" "Is the light just right?" etc. "She buries herself in domestic life, from despair. Gide adores her." Sadness (I think he said remorse) for having made her suffer spoils Gide's keenest pleasures, and if he thinks he has learned between the lines of a letter that something worries her, back he comes from the depths of Tunisia (or elsewhere) to be with her. Martin du Gard adds that Gide never talks of these things except to very intimate friends like himself.

DECEMBER 31. Everything I write proceeds in a straight line from my childhood.

1932

JANUARY 10. The other day, V. and I asked Gide to give each of us a photograph of himself. (V. had egged me on, for of my own accord—never . . .) "I'll think about it," says Gide. And suddenly: "Why, there's a very good postcard likeness of me. For my photograph is sold as a postcard," he adds. "There's real fame for you!"

JANUARY 19. Gide came to see me late this afternoon. Apropos of V.'s lies (childish lies, mere fibs), he talks to me again of truth, one of his favorite topics and one so often repeated that I end by feeling a little embarrassed. "We both have a Protestant heredity that explains this taste for truth," he says, adding that Catholics do not believe that truth is due to everybody and that such subtleness horrifies him. . . . A little later I tell him that I am not satisfied with certain things in the book I have just finished, and he nods approvingly. "Francis Jammes," he says, "is, on the contrary, delighted with everything he writes." This author is supposed to have said: "My *Georgics* are as superior to Vergil's as Christianity is superior to paganism."

JANUARY 21. What keeps me from talking about religion is the fact that in me there lies a fanatic dozing ever so lightly whom I particularly do not wish to rouse. . . .

JANUARY 24. Today I found some old negatives in a trunk. Printed a few snapshots. I saw myself again as I was at fifteen. On looking at a photograph taken at the foot of a big oak in our garden, I had the peculiar impression of being on the verge of remembering a thought that had crossed my mind at the very moment when the photograph was taken, and for a few seconds it seemed to me that a ray of light was about to pierce through the obscure depths of memory. I should have attempted to make my mind a blank, and perhaps, among so many others, that minute in my youth would have found its way to me; my efforts made it run away and fall back into an oblivion from which it was about to emerge. So much of us goes thus to nothingness, so many hours, so many years . . . It is an unpleasant and all but sinister sensation to feel oneself drifting slowly toward definitive unconsciousness, and I can only think with horror of the time when everything that I have known and loved will fade from my memory. What remains of my mother? A few letters, five or six photographs, and memories that will be with me till I die. When we die, my sisters and I, she will die once again and for ever.

JANUARY 28. "B. is a bad painter who someday will paint quite good pictures. They will perhaps be discovered a hundred and fifty years from now, in the depths of a museum in the provinces. Bérard has the charm of his race, and it may be that in constantly hesitating between beauty and fashion, he might finally choose beauty, but he is in danger of tumbling into fashion and staying there." Who says this? Gertrude Stein. She lies half stretched out on her black horsehair sofa, her hand buried in her poodle's white wool. She looks calm and strong as a monolith; she might be ten centuries old, that is, she has the youth and serenity of a mountain. She tells me that one day she opened a book of mine and saw that my sentences were really sentences; she adds that she read only one sentence!

MARCH 10. I have finished my novel. What am I to do? In spite of reading, my days seem empty. I dread wasting my time. Who knows how much of it remains to me? There is pleasure, of course, but I like it only when it is stolen from my hours of work. When it is just a way of filling in leisure, it no longer amuses me.

MARCH 15. Saw Gide this afternoon. He tells me that he can only think about Russia and Communism. What is the use of writing books? This scarcely has any meaning, on the eve of the important events that are taking shape in the world. "Does this disturb you?" I ask. "No, I find it stimulating!"

MARCH 25. This morning, rebelling against pleasure, which it seems to me impossible to do without, I tried unsuccessfully to read Pascal. One of Plato's Dialogues would have been as much help to me. The idea of a religious conversion appears to me at present as the falsest way of settling moral difficulties. To have recourse to God against oneself is an expedient for weaklings. What I looked for in Pascal was the sound of a voice that spoke to me of another universe than mine. What must be feared is that pleasure should harden the heart and endanger love.

APRIL 4. Pierre Bost came to question me about my attitude to politics. I tried to put together the substance of an answer, but all I think on the subject boils down to this: "I loathe politics. Because of politics, all that I love is in danger; it is a menace to individual liberty, a menace to happiness, it disturbs my work. I wholeheartedly believe in literature and works of art. This belief is entirely foreign to political preoccupations." Where can my place be in the present world? I have no idea.

APRIL 7. My book has only just come out and is already being trampled, as Flaubert expressed it. I went to Bagatelle the other day, with Robert. The weather was wonderfully fine and we were almost alone. The trees were not yet in leaf, but the lawns were thick with small white flowers. I wanted to be happy, to enjoy the lovely garden, but my book's failure made me a little sad. Why not look things in the face? It is a failure. This grieved me, for I am fond of success, like everybody else. However, I can say that I found something interesting in my very disappointment. I said to myself: "Ah, so that's the way one feels."

I had a good article by Jaloux, who generously defends each of my books when it comes out.

APRIL 29. A visit to Gide. He is back from Switzerland. I thought he looked badly and at first seemed a little weary, a little sad, but a few moments later all his gaiety returned and with it, that extraordinary youthfulness of eye and voice. He reads me most admirably a few pages of Sologub's *Démon mesquin*. His voice reminds one of a bird of prey; it suddenly pounces on a word, swoops off with it, and feasts on it. Then he lowers his book and smiles as though he had really eaten something delicious.

MAY 25. Gide told me the other day about the combined efforts of Jacques Maritain, Abbé Altermann, and Copeau to bring him to conversion. He says that at heart he appreciates this "sort of flirtation." He refuses his soul.

JUNE 13. Reread Renan's *Life of Jesus*. I cannot accept his calling Christ "the charming doctor," or that he should speak of "the orchard of an agricultural enterprise" when he means the Mount of Olives, for this is indeed an insipid way of describing the most sacred spot in this world. Closing the stout volume, I wondered what martyrs Renan's Christ would have called forth. Very few, I should think. The author wished to bring Him closer to us, but instead of bringing Him closer to us, he has lessened Him by wanting to make Him a kindly philosopher and, in order to have us accept Him, reduced Him to our level. I thought of what Blake says:

> The Vision of Christ that thou dost see
> Is my vision's greatest enemy. . . .
> Thine loves the same world that mine hates;
> Thy heaven doors are my hell gates.

UNDATED. Before the war, when I used to take walks with my uncle and when we passed by the Embassy where a fine star-spangled flag waved, I was told to remove my hat. I also tipped my hat to Washington's statue. My uncle bowed gravely. Not content with raising his hat, he held it at arm's length. I did the same, a trifle mystified. And what was more, I recited a few patriotic lines concerning the father of the country and the red, white and blue.

My uncle went back to America and I had almost forgotten the whole thing when one day, passing before the Embassy with my mother and recollecting my uncle's teachings, I ostentatiously saluted the flag. "What on earth is this freak of fancy?" asked my mother. "You've taken to saluting the flag? It's perfectly unnecessary." I tried to explain, but she stopped me by telling about my great-aunt who had braved Northern bayonets rather than bow to the Northern flag. How many times had I heard this story! Soldiers in dark blue surrounding the indignant crinoline, the flag stretched across the street, a bearded officer arguing with the "rebel" lady—this to me was one of the most important scenes in the whole of the Civil War. My mother's native town had been taken by Sherman in December, 1864. To subdue those Southerners who thought themselves superior to everybody, it was considered a good idea to make them pay their respects to the conquering flag. "I will not salute that rag," said my great-aunt. "Madam, you must pass under the flag." "Certainly not, sir!" She also said lots of other things that I have forgotten, but I know that she made such a fuss that she was let alone. . . .

JUNE 21. Saw Gide this afternoon. We had arranged to meet at the Picasso show and went through four rooms of paintings. Gide was full of enthusiasm. "It's amazing," he repeated. "Is there anything in contemporary literature to match this? No, nothing. No one has such boldness." He wants to see everything and does it a little too quickly to my taste, but nothing escapes him. As we talked of Picasso's baffling facility—for nothing seems impossible for the painter to achieve—Gide quoted what Ingres said, without adding any comments: "With talent, you do what you like. With genius, you do what you can."

We then went to the Bonney exhibit. Photographs of the 1900 period. Gide seemed amused at first, then ended by finding the show sad. Whereupon, in came Étienne de Beaumont, who tried to convince Gide that nothing could be prettier than the fashions of that period, but Gide kicked: "No," he said firmly, "they weren't pretty. They were ugly and sad."

We went to have tea, place de la Madeleine. Gide tells me that he has not yet read *The Strange River* but has seen the articles written about the book and in particular that by Th. I said that to my mind, Th. is to be distrusted for certain reasons. Gide immediately agrees with me and picks Th. to pieces. "Yet," he says, "some of the criticisms made about your book are right. You are blamed for creating an imaginary world." At this, I talk to Gide as I don't believe I ever talked to him before. "No one has the right to blame a novelist for creating a world for his characters. Quite the contrary. As regards my pessimism, the reading of any newspaper fully proves that life is at least as black as I say it is." On this point, also, Gide says I am right, perfectly right, and adds: "It is all to your credit that you have created this romantic world. Anyway, you are the only one who is able to do it. I have said so in my diary, but I am glad to hear you protest." He next tells me that the only fault he has to find with *The Dark Journey* is a "certain evenness of flow," due no doubt to its being written day by day. "To work daily is excellent, anyway," he murmurs. And so, if Gide is offered resistance, be it ever so slight, in a conversation, his line of defense breaks down completely, even though he may later fall back into some secret retrenchment or other. We shall see whether or not he will publish the passage in his diary concerning *The Dark Journey*.[1]

JUNE 23. As I was putting away my manuscript a moment ago, a question crossed my mind, one that I have often asked myself. If, instead of writing this morning, I had written after lunch, would I have written the same thing? If I set aside the beginning of this novel and took it up again in a month, would it continue in the way I intend to continue tomorrow? Does one page necessarily bring about another page written in such and such a manner, or does each page enjoy relative freedom that allows it to be what it is, independently of the page that precedes it? I could not but be bored by a book where all the pages would be determined by the first one, and yet I like a work of art to be governed by a certain fatality. The reader should, I think, have the impression

[1] The passage did come out in his published diary.

√ that things could not be otherwise, but in spite of this, something indefinable should hang over the characters, the possibility of something else, the thousand possibilities refused by fate.

AUGUST 1. BERLIN. The streets are perfectly quiet. Newspapers give the results of the elections: an advance for the Communists, and for the National Socialists a *Stillstand*. There had been some talk of a *Putsch* for today, but nothing seems to have happened.

Continued reading *The Master of Ballantrae* with very great admiration. If anything could annoy me in the book, it would be its perfection. I would prefer the author's skill not to be always so evident. He sometimes has the air of performing a very difficult task with professional ease.

AUGUST 8. Left Hamburg yesterday aboard the *Oceana*. I sat on the bridge and read *Almayer's Folly*, which disappointed me vastly, probably because I had heard it so highly praised. The most interesting part of its themes is treated very tamely. The author recoiled before a wholly sexual story that might have been magnificent: an unguarded reader can only understand just before the end what all this is really about. Does it require so much courage to say that a man wants to sleep with his daughter? As to the love affair between Nina and Dain, it is at most worthy of an operatic libretto. Some of the dialogues are rather absurdly lyrical, and certain sentences could have been written only by an ardent, ingenuous, and youthful author, such as: ". . . one of those long looks that are among a woman's most fearsome weapons . . . more deadly than a dagger thrust . . ."

As a compensation, I reread a few pages of Claudel's *Connaissance de l'Est*.

AUGUST 9. Around four o'clock this morning I woke and through the porthole above my bed saw the coast of Scotland shrouded in mist. I looked at it for a moment with deep emotion. Childhood memories, which I thought done away with forever, came back in a throng. Then I went back to bed and to sleep and, in one of the clearest dreams I ever had, saw my sister Mary. She walked from one room to another in a small, low, dark house. I remember that she bent her head with an anxious air and that she wore a gray dress with a small white collar of the kind in fashion around 1850. Seeing her dressed like that, I wondered if it were she that I saw, or someone in our family who resembled her. I could not talk to her and she seemed not to see me. The dream was short, but made such an impression on me that it cast a shadow over the whole of the following day.

AUGUST 12. I have no other ambition but to be a man. I rarely feel conscious of belonging to a race, to a country, and in such moments I behave and talk in an artificial manner that shames me. I cannot hate any people and nothing depresses me more than a patriotic ditty. However, this is a point where I have sometimes varied. On August 2nd, 1914, on hearing that day's news, I fell on my German grammar and tore it to pieces. I secretly hoped that the war would rid me of those fiendish declensions and that the enemy's tongue would no longer be taught in France.

SEPTEMBER 7. PARIS. I was thirty-two yesterday and it seems to me as though my life were only beginning. Worked today with great pleasure, but in spite of it, a renewed contact with my book after a rather long interruption makes things somewhat difficult. No one realizes the changes that take place in an author while he is writing a book, even if the book is short. Today, I don't feel quite the same as I did in July.

SEPTEMBER 11. At Souverain-Moulin, in the north of France. It is a seventeenth-century château, squat and severe as a fort, surrounded by water and great trees that stir softly in the gray sky. The wind thunders down the chimneys. I am writing this in a room whose windows look out on the gardens. With its long corridors that run into each other like the paths in a labyrinth, its big rooms with the lingering and delicious odor of country houses, the odor of childhood, this château rises to enchanted regions that one trembles to mention, for fear that the whole thing might vanish. A little while ago, I disturbed all this merely by walking about my room. I must remain completely still in an armchair, so that the magic may form around me once more; so that what lives within these walls may not be scared away.

As I did as a child, I amused myself in believing that I lived in 1700, that by leaning out of the window I would see a coach on the road and, for a few seconds, really thought to have succeeded. Some have a longing for future times; but I, more than thirty years old, still cherish an absurd regret for what will never be again, and what I like in Souverain-Moulin is that it belongs completely, not only to the prewar, but to the Old Regime.

SEPTEMBER 18. Around 1905, in the rue de Passy, we lived in a haunted house. You can shrug your shoulders! I remember that my mother's room included a sort of closet where clothes were hung. There, in my opinion, although I told no one of this disturbing secret, the devil elected to live. When I was alone in this room, I stood before the little closet, at a certain distance, and, half dead with fright, called the devil. For the first few minutes, nothing happened, and suddenly I saw something move among the clothes. How often did I indulge in this dreadful game! But I was never brave enough to stay until the end, and ran away howling as soon as suits and overcoats began to stir.

SEPTEMBER 23. I have moments of doubt that plunge me into the deepest gloom. There is really too much of a difference between what I write and what I would have wished to write. At times, when I hear very beautiful music, I imprudently weave it into the novel I dream of giving someday. This is hard to explain, but an author would understand me easily. I have the illusion of possessing tremendous power, until the last chord. Once back at my writing table, I sober up completely. Where are the impulses, the glow of enthusiasm I had a moment ago? I try to write, but have the strange feeling that words hate me and that I put them together against their will.

OCTOBER 3. In a world that goes too fast, I have decided to live slowly. I want to accomplish my task as though a long life were promised me. At table today, we talked about this, but in a vague, insufficient manner. To live slowly is not too easy. It means devoting a whole day to dreaming, when necessary, it means losing one's time to a good purpose. There are days when I long wearily for life in a country house, a life such as could be led at Souverain-Moulin. I would undertake lengthy studies, take up Greek again, I would idle along, I would carry my novels within me far longer, and they would be the better for it. Oh! how I hate the pace at which we all go!

OCTOBER 14. Yesterday, worked almost all day, from ten to twelve and from two to five. Wrote sixty-three lines in all, which is a lot for me. After that, I walked along the Seine as far as the Alexandre III bridge. The weather was delightful, cold with a faint mist and a fine pink sky. Thought the whole time about my work. When I read, I think about my book, when I walk, I think still more about it. Among all the paths open to me in this novel, I am trying to find the right one. I pass without transition from despair to hope. I often feel like giving up this book, then go back to it with a sort of furious rush forward.

NOVEMBER 19.   I have been thinking over the article I would like to write about an author's freedom. If a writer were free, would he accept a Rightist or Leftist dictatorship? Neither one nor the other. "But what party do you belong to?" "Not to yours." I am the kind of man who is stood up against a wall and shot in all revolutions. So much the worse. In all the political programs that are offered us, I find nothing that suits me. What sense does it make to call oneself a revolutionary and wish to be killed for a government that has its informers, its *agents provocateurs*, its bureaucrats, like all governments? No, the more I think of it the better I understand that a free writer has no place in the Europe that is being set up at present.

NOVEMBER 23.   Monday I went to the Lener concert to hear the thirteenth and fourteenth of Beethoven's quartets. The thirteenth is so full of sadness and sweetness that I am not ashamed to say that I cried. A madman, not far from us, conducted an imaginary orchestra. He had a delicate, sensitive face, red whiskers, hollow cheeks, a big hooky nose, and a famished expression. I watched him with great interest. He loved the music as much as I did and we heard it, perhaps, with the same emotion.

NOVEMBER 24.   A naïve, well-meaning person asked me today if there were rules for writing a good book. I answered that I knew of only one, which is to believe strongly in what one writes. And try as I may, this is the only rule I can find that holds good for all literary work. Truth belongs above all to an interior order.

NOVEMBER 26.   I listened to Beethoven's sixteenth quartet. Everything in this music seems strange to me. At times, one seems to hear in it the cry of a dumb man who wants to speak a new tongue, a tongue the like of which no one has ever heard. A little more, and wonderful dissonances would burst in these chords— for they are strained to a breaking point.

DECEMBER 18. A moment ago, under one of the Trocadéro colonnades, I paused to look at the Champ-de-Mars vista. The weather was like spring, with a luminous haze floating over the gardens. Sounds had the light quality that they possess only during the first fine days of spring. For two or three seconds, I lived over a whole part of my youth, my sixteenth, my seventeenth year. It gave me a strange feeling, rather more painful than agreeable. Yet I was in such deep agreement with the landscape that I wondered, as I used to, if it wouldn't be delightful to become part of all this and be reduced to nothing, like a drop of water in the sea, no longer to have a body, but just enough consciousness to be able to think: "I am a particle of the universe. The universe rejoices in me. I am the sky, the sun, the trees, the Seine and the houses that border it. . . ." This curious idea has never been very far from me. After all, perhaps something of the kind is what awaits us on the other side of death. And suddenly, I felt so happy that I went home, thinking that I should keep the memory of this great mirage as a rare and precious thing.

DECEMBER 21. Gide and his nephew have lunch with us. How awkwardly the writer behaves! Is this intentional? Or is it natural? He comes in and, I don't know how, makes us all feel ill at ease, for he is stiffer than he ever was. One tries to speak freely without paying too much attention to one's mode of expression, and Gide is there to pick out, one by one, any lapses in grammar, as an expert shot brings down partridges. The conversation wanders this way and that, as it does in *Paludes*. I feel that Gide is hostile today, but why? He sometimes reminds me of an old insect, well equipped by nature with defensive and offensive weapons, but an insect that nature has also deprived of wings, of color, of gracefulness. He highly praises Kurt Weill's *Jasager*, which he thinks very much in the U.S.S.R. spirit, and confides that after his "declaration of love" to the Soviets, he won't write any longer. After lunch, he becomes more and more grumpy. Seated before a self-portrait of Bérard, he asks "what it is," after staring malevolently at it for quite a long time, and declares that he doesn't

like it- which is what no one wanted to know. He irritates me a
little, does Père Gide.

DECEMBER 24. I went to see Gide, rue Vaneau, and there, almost
at his door, slipped and bruised myself in falling. Gide and Yves
Allégret dressed the wound. Gide was charmingly gay and made
me forget the bad mood he was in the other day.

Read Stekel's book on conditions of nervous anxiety, a book
that has taught me a lot about myself. May it cure me of a few of
the phobias that the author describes so well! On thinking it over,
I noted that the most troublesome and most harassing of my
phobias is that of death. It is in all my books. At a time when I
could call myself a Catholic, I did not fear death. I was twenty,
and at that age one doesn't believe in death, or one only believes
in it for others. One talks about it, pretends to fear or wish for it,
but there is nothing sincere in this, it is simply a literary attitude.
So far as I was concerned, the certainty of salvation sheltered me
from all the terrors that I suffered from later. My little *Pamphlet
against French Catholics*, which is a sort of farewell to the religious faith of my childhood, left me, so to speak, unprotected.
And so, the fear of dying immediately came to light in everything
I have written since, and bursts out in the novel I am engaged in
at present. I am at last tackling the subject that attracts, fascinates,
and terrifies me. I am like a man obsessed who throws himself into
the abyss that he dreads.

DECEMBER 26. My wounded knee obliges me to lie on the drawing-room sofa most of the day. I read *Sense and Sensibility* before
a big log fire. Delightful day! A feeling of deep security, very
near to that peace that passes all understanding mentioned in the
Bible. I put down my book, from time to time, to watch the flames
and smell the odor of burning wood. . . .

Jane Austen's method consists in contrasting one moral quality
with another—which quality she strives to personify—and although
I find the method a trifle mechanical, I surrender to the charm of
a writer whose smile is never a grimace and from whom emotion
never draws a scream, for well-bred people don't scream. Jane
Austen always remains a little within the bounds of what she
wants to say, with the exquisite reserve that she alone possesses,
but none the less her delineation is admirably clear. Compared
with her, Charlotte Brontë seems wildly disheveled.

1933

JANUARY 9. This morning, Gide paid me a surprise visit. He talks to me about Roger Martin du Gard, about his house at Bellême which has cost him a considerable amount and where he expected to write all the volumes of the *Thibault* series. A hill obstructed the view from one of the windows. He had it removed. Cost: one million francs. Then he grew tired of his book, of Bellême, and after ten years came to live in Paris. . . . Gide leaves me at twelve-thirty to have lunch with Lacretelle. And for the twentieth time since I met him, asks me on what terms I am with this writer, for Gide has lapses of memory. He declares himself delighted with Stekel's book on anxiety, which I had given him to read. Today, he made a curious impression on me. He gossiped without keeping watch over himself, and I suddenly had the intuition of being with a stranger. . . . He was probably quite different as a young man. But now . . . How is it that I inwardly shrink from him? He was most friendly. He questioned me about my work, but I couldn't help feeling that my answers did not interest him, and immediately talked of something else.

JANUARY 18. The exposition of Impressionist landscape painters; they are marvels at successfully catching the moment that will never return. A minute more and the sky will have changed, the surface of the water not be ruffled in the same way. On the other hand, the landscapes of Claude Lorrain and Poussin are, as it were, nature immutable.

JANUARY 20. In Renoir's painting, the obsession of a beautiful skin is so compelling that it can be found even in his landscapes, where the earth sometimes has flesh tints.

FEBRUARY 5. Read Dumesnil's book on Flaubert. I think it has taught me a lot. But the precepts set forth by Flaubert concerning the way to write a novel do not always seem to me right. What becomes of, not only inspiration, but mere inventiveness in a book where the least fact must find its counterpart in real life, in the author's personal experience? Beyond any doubt, a book like *L'Education sentimentale* can be written so, but you have to be Flaubert to do it. And at the cost of what sacrifices did he work according to such methods? I remember something that Henry James said about Flaubert; he compares him to a knight in magnificent armor, standing at the door of a great palace whose threshold he dared not cross. More exactly, James speaks of a sentry with shining weapons—these weapons must be taken further; there are other doors to open. Flaubert should at least have listened at the door of the soul. (*Essays in London.*)

The novelist invents nothing, he guesses. He will never be wrong if he obeys that inner voice that speaks in each of us and tells us whether we keep within the truth or if we step out of it. The inner truth is the only one that is really essential, the rest, no matter how beautiful, how tempting, is mere accessory.

FEBRUARY 8. Reading Walter Pater's *Plato* made me ponder greatly over myself, and these thoughts are not comforting. I would like nothing in me to obscure my love of truth. Now, pleasure is a danger and I have been carried down a slope where it is most difficult for me to keep from stumbling. That is what worries me, for I believe that the core of one's nature directly affects one's mind. A man who cannot resist everyday temptations can neither think powerfully nor even see things in their true light. I must write better books, I must never swerve from the inner truth. I think that by not giving in to the lures of an easy life, I will finally write a great book, and I hope someday to feel that I have not received more than I have given. I will find peace that day, but at present I am dissatisfied with myself. Who could imagine the difficulties I have encountered? Does one suspect, for instance, every time I describe an irresolute man, a man at variance with himself in my novels, that I have it in for myself? Some pages in my books are like an arraignment of myself.

FEBRUARY 10. Thought over and over a chapter in Pater on Plato's *ideas*. This is indeed a most appealing theory, for it is poetic, but it is also mystical. It affects the senses, but it is none the less spiritual. In my eyes, its attraction lies in admitting a mystery, and this mystery is that, among all *ideas*, beauty is the only thing in this world that is represented in a manner that can satisfy us. Never has physical grace been placed so high. A beautiful body partakes of the divine, but sensual love clouds and soils this divine reflection, and that is what should be told people who believe themselves to be Plato's disciples, because they are slaves to instinct. What appeals to me in this theory, and what holds my attention, is the seriousness of the role of love.

FEBRUARY 21. I am thirty-two, thirty-two times have I passed before the day and hour of my death, as one passes by the door of a house that one will someday live in, without even a thought of glancing at it. But I am getting used to the idea of dying and seeing everything that I love in this world die with me, for it seems reasonable to believe that we are nearing the end of a great ✓ cycle. How long will we sleep? It was only in 1900 that the remains of Cretan civilization were unearthed at Knossos. This vanished world had been slumbering for the last three thousand years. . . . Someday a man will stroll about a field and, turning over a clod of earth with his stick, as one sometimes does in country solitude, when the mind is absorbed in dreams, he will hit against a bit of metal and say to himself: "Why, there may have been something here." And if he is inquisitive, learned, and rich, he will excavate the site, and under eight or nine superposed cities he may perhaps discover Paris, as Schliemann discovered Troy. And if this bit of metal does not intrigue him, we will go on sleeping.

FEBRUARY 22. Last night, before going to sleep, I read a few of Milton's sonnets, those I am fondest of, the one where he speaks of his wife, who appeared to him in a dream, the one he dedicated to Cyriack Skinner, and the most famous one of all about his blindness. Around two in the morning, I woke up suddenly, with the feeling of having left a vast, deep, dark temple. The shadows were filled with a long murmuring, like the echo of a chant. All that day, I remembered it with strange emotion.

FEBRUARY 28. Day before yesterday, I went to Dali's to get my picture, as this is my month. (The painter being in financial difficulties, twelve persons had pledged themselves to make him a kind of annuity for that year, in return for which, each of the twelve was to receive a large picture, or a small one and two drawings. We had drawn lots to know which would be our month. To my great joy, I had drawn February, so did not have to wait too long.) I am given the choice between a large painting with an admirable landscape of rocks as a background, but with the foreground taken up by a sort of naked and whiskered Russian general, his head sorrowfully bent to show the shells and pearls that pepper his skull, and a small picture in wonderful shades of gray and lilac, plus two drawings. I choose the small painting. Dali talks to me about Crevel, who is ill, but "estoical." He enlarges greatly on the beauty of his own painting, carefully explains the meaning of my picture, which he calls the "Geological Transformation," and which represents a horse turning into rock in the midst of a desert. He is going to Spain and speaks with terror of the customs formalities and the thousand petty annoyances of a trip by *ferrocarril* (railroad), for he is a little like a child who is scared by life.

The other day, I was walking down a new avenue—mapped out but as yet unbuilt—that has been given the name of Paul Doumer. At the corner of this avenue and the rue de la Tour stood, only a year ago, a Louis-Philippe house that I described in *The Strange River*, a pension in my time, the Pension Mouton where I spent several months in 1914, then in 1916, with my father and sisters. It was in this pension, in the room I shared with my father, that I experienced one of the keenest joys that ever made a human heart beat. I was fifteen, I firmly believed in God and wished for nothing else on earth than to live for Him. When I said my prayers at the foot of my bed, I was carried away by such an outburst of joy that I wished I could die that very minute. Then, lying in bed and on my back, in a posture that I tried to make uncomfortable, I felt so happy that I simply could not sleep. But such feelings can neither be described nor explained. They have all the force of a first love. I was in love with God, with the Church, with the whole of an invisible world that became mine in attracting me to it. I think this happiness lasted almost a year, with intervals of lukewarmness. The first carnal sins and a deeper knowledge of myself put an end—and in the most heart-rending fashion—to the sort of ecstatic dream of my fifteenth year. In 1919, at Rennes, I was *aspirant* in the 50th Artillery Regiment. I had an extraordinary return to fervor, then in America, in 1920 and '21, and, since that time, nothing, but I distinctly remember those happy days, the happiness of a soul when it yearns for none but God.

MARCH 15. Gertrude Stein. She mentally turns over a consider-

able number of peculiar ideas and displays them forcefully, one
hand in the pocket of an ample embroidered waistcoat of the kind
worn by eighteenth-century financiers, the other twisting and
smoothing her cropped gray hair. Her eyes are large and beautiful,
there is something brave and *open* in her expression. She talks to
me at great length about an immense novel she wrote around 1907,
published in 1920, and which, she says, has been a source of inspiration for several contemporary American writers. And she
quotes several very well-known names. "It's a rather formidable
book," she tells me, "it moves rather formidably. It is an epic."
Her voice is deep and manly; when she laughs, she laughs in bursts
that show every tooth in her head. She speaks of Cocteau as an
important writer, some of whose work is bound to remain, but
what? She does not say, she does not declare herself outright
about anything in a precise way. She admires a large painting by
Berman that hangs in the sitting room, but does not even look at
the other pictures.

MARCH 21. A telephone call from Gide, who asks me to go to
see him as he has a curious manuscript that he wants me to read.
We were to go afterwards to see a film that a certain Mr. D. is
showing in his home. I think Gide looks worried. He hands me
two gray copybooks, tells me he will sit by me and write while
I read the typescript that has been entrusted to him. But he does
not write, he goes from one corner of the study to the other,
opens a door, talks to someone, returns, offers me a cigarette, and
finally says he is vexed because he has agreed to speak at a meeting organized by the *party* (the Communist party). Lots of German writers exiled by Hitler will be present. "But I am disturbing
you. Go on, go on reading." I feel that my very stillness annoys
him. He goes off again and talks to someone in another room and,
returning, says it is time to leave.

Off we go in the pouring rain. In the taxi, Gide talks about my
working methods. "One feels the influence of daily work in the
even flow of your books." But I haven't worked in this way for
several years. And also, infinitely more gifted authors than myself
have worked steadily every day. Dickens, for instance. And even
poets. "Ah? Who?" "Why, one of the greatest: Keats." "Only
once!" cries Gide with a defiant gleam in his eye. "When he
wrote 'Endymion.'" I was about to reply that, precisely, "Endymion" was a long and exacting labor and this strictly proves what

I wish to say, but feeling that Gide is so strangely, so inexplicably moved, I remain silent.

We reach D.'s house. He receives us in a vast, luxurious studio. Big couches strewn with white furs. On a wall, a wonderful Bokhara, the white ground scattered over with large red flowers. But this is only a sort of boudoir. In the studio proper, no other furniture but a sofa with a glass bowl of white lilacs by it, and that is all. Our host is dressed in dark red velvet. He is studiously affable. A Javanese servant appears, closer to a work of art, think I, than a human being; he wears a lovely gaudy costume and a sort of Highlander's cap and, under his sarong, show exquisitely delicate feet. This awe-inspiring person kneels and offers us cigarettes and candied fruits. I can't help smiling and Gide nudges me like a schoolboy. These refreshments over, we go into the next room to see the film, which we had been told about at great length. Not very well taken, but some of the views are excellent. In particular a scene where boys are seen dancing on the banks of the Indus, which is in spate. The river boils, white as the whitest smoke, and flows at a terrific speed. The tops of the trees rise above the waters. The dancers revolve slowly in a ring, in the meadow.

We leave at last. I dine with Gide at the Brasserie Lutétia. He seems once more very depressed. He tells me that Vaillant-Couturier has forced his hand, that he, Gide, had tried to retract his promise only to be informed that it was too late, that the posters were printed. This meeting is to take place at the (Masonic) Grand Lodge of France. Gide is so upset that he cannot eat. I don't think I ever saw him in such a state. He becomes a little livelier and his gaiety returns when I ask for some information about Tunisia, where Robert and I expect to go. In talking of Tozeur, his eyes light up.

MARCH 30. Those who have never waked up at dawn with the agonizing feeling that life is going by, those will not care for my book. I have attempted by means of hints to express the terror of death. In a book like this one, to allude to sickness and death heightens their prestige, if I may say so. I don't wish to know the exact nature of Amfortas' wound, it is enough for me to know that it killed him, and also, in retaining its anonymity, death seems to me far more imposing than if it appeared under a name borrowed from the medical jargon.

It so happens that by giving things a name, an irreparable blow hits them full in the heart. That, for instance, is what makes pornographic novels so poor; the contents of these books are self-destroying.

My last novel is the most extravagant of all those I have written so far, but if I didn't put this folly into my books, who knows if it wouldn't establish itself in my life? My books are perhaps what have allowed me to preserve a semblance of equilibrium. I was in an excellent mood for working this morning. A sentence that I had thought of, over a year ago, fell quite naturally into place; it had occurred to me one day as I watched the rain from my study window.

APRIL 4. In all my books, fear or any other rather strong emotion seems to be linked in some mysterious manner with a staircase. I noticed this yesterday in going over all the novels I had written. For instance, in *The Pilgrim* the old colonel walking up the stairs corresponds, in the hero's mind, to a sort of mounting fear. In *Avarice House,* Emily passes her father's ghost on the stairs. In *The Closed Garden* the heroine pushes her father down the stairs, where she spends part of the night. In *The Dark Journey,* Mme Grosgeorges, in an agony of distress, goes up and down the staircase. In *The Keys of Death* the hero thinks over the murder he has in mind on the stairs. In *L'Autre sommeil* the hero faints on the stairs. In *The Strange River* is a staircase where Philippe trundles his indecision and spies on his wife. Lastly, in the story I am finishing (*The Dreamer*), a staircase is the scene of a sinister and hysterical fit of laughter. I wonder how I could have repeated this effect so often without noticing it. As a child, I dreamed that I was being pursued in a staircase by someone. My mother had the same fears in her youth; maybe something of this has remained in me. I am sure that in many a novelist the accumulation of *memories beyond memory* is what makes them write. They speak for hundreds of the dead, their dead; in fact, they express everything that their ancestors had kept deep in their hearts, out of prudence or out of decency.

MAY 10. Yesterday I laid aside the novel I was writing (*The Dreamer*), to begin another. I am expecting a great deal from this new novel (*Midnight*), and wrote seventy-three lines by working all day. This is the upheaval I have been thinking of for weeks. I want to perform the impossible and finish this book by September 1st.

So-called love-making is the more often a caricature of happiness. Happiness is far greater, far deeper, and far simpler. And because it is simple, it can neither be described nor analyzed. Happiness cannot be told about and there are times when it swoops down on us, for no apparent reason, in the height of illness, or in a dark room where you are moping, or during a walk through the meadows; you suddenly feel absurdly happy, happy to the point of dying, that is, so happy that you would like to die, so as to prolong this extraordinary minute for ever. I felt this yesterday, in a tearoom on the avenue de l'Opéra, then once as I was reading *Sense and Sensibility,* and very often in my early childhood.

JULY 31. Continued reading *Nicholas Nickleby.* Except for the part about Squeers and Dotheboys Hall, genius appears very seldom in this first volume. The funny characters are not always funny and the gentlemen are awful, like most of Dickens' gentlemen. The author does not yet know how to give a clear idea of the spot where a scene takes place, except in the part mentioned above and where you really have a feeling of the country, of winter, and of solitude. Dickens' taste for cruelty transpires in the episodes at Dotheboys Hall, a cruelty that he toned down only too well for fear of his public.

AUGUST 12. Finished *Nickleby.* Squeers punishing Smike in the carriage is one of the most painful and most powerful scenes that I know of in fiction. The character of Nickleby seemed to me of small interest, and also those dreadful girls and their conventional virtues, but in Squeers is a depth of evil that makes up for the book's little imperfections. What wouldn't Dickens have done, had he dared!

SEPTEMBER 8. I often wonder what can be the meaning of life, if it has one, and above all, to what extent the material world exists. What can the present uneasiness of Europe signify, for instance—Germany's excitement, the anguish of so many men and women to whom the future appears black with threats? Obviously, no one can answer the question, but I often have a fleeting impression of living in a world that does not exist, or that does not exist in the way we imagine. Perhaps the material world merely has the value of a symbol. This idea has been familiar to me since I was fifteen. Thus, the universal uneasiness is perhaps the fictitious representation of your own uneasiness. The "crisis" is first of all in you. The disorder of the world corresponds to an interior disorder that you discover within your own self.

OCTOBER 20. After many a hesitation on my part, it has been decided that we will go to America next month. I resisted as I always resist the idea of traveling. How many times have I fallen ill just before going away! Packing my suitcases creates in me an uneasiness that I cannot understand, but that a Stekel would probably explain perfectly. It is perhaps, hidden under this symbolical form, the terror of dying that acts on me. To be afraid to die is absurd, and I know that very well, but my body does not; that is the reason why it conjures up a thousand difficulties at the proper time, does its best to simulate grippe or, as has been the case recently, more serious illnesses. I remember a doctor's exasperation as he said to me: "If you were really ill, I could cure you! But how do you expect me to operate on your brain?"

OCTOBER 28. Yesterday afternoon, at the height of an anxious state that had lasted ten days, I suddenly felt the indescribable presence of happiness. I went to my room, locked myself in, then returned to the drawing room, walked about the hall, and the house had never seemed pleasanter to me. From the windows that look out on the avenue, I watched the rain. The sky was a delicate gray and the light still strong enough to avoid turning on a lamp. Wandering from room to room, I examined the furniture as though I had never seen it before. This extraordinary state of mind did not last long. What curious stratagems things can invent when they guess that we are about to leave them, and when they attempt to detain us. The drawing room seemed unusually beautiful in the twilight; the furniture shone and glinted like metal, and the big prayer rug looked as though it had been laid on the surface of a lake.

OCTOBER 29. Have suffered a great deal these last days for fear of having, as I thought, contracted a disease. I went to see a doctor who said: "What do you want me to cure you of? There's absolutely nothing the matter with you." And off he sends me, but my imagination has broken loose and I return home in a state of mental distress that shames me. For nearly a week, I went through throes of anguish such as I had never yet experienced. Then, day before yesterday, as I lay on my bed a prey to terrible anxiety, I felt suddenly that there was someone in the room with me. Almost at once an inner voice said to me very gently, but with indescribable authority: "Be at peace. You are not ill." I got up immediately: happy, deeply, unutterably happy.

When I feel as heavy-hearted as I was for the last few days, I can only turn to God. But what does that mean? Who is the God that I believe in? I tried to speak to Him, a little while ago, in my room. Never have I felt surrounded by deeper solitude. Pray? I can no longer pray.

NOVEMBER 2. We went aboard ship yesterday at Le Havre. The boat is shaken by a violent pitching that prevents my writing legibly and upsets almost everybody. For my part, it delights me. The sea is a leaden gray; foam spreads its furbelows around the ship. I read Freud's little book on childhood almost at one sitting. Nearly everything in these astonishing pages should be underscored, but no matter how hard Freud tries to explain everything, the mystery subsists in its entirety. Once he has established that the child is in love with its mother, he has only moved back the limits of the unknown a little further, for I am still asking myself this question: Why? Concerning the essence of our being, Freud, like all theorists, is silent.

I had to wait until I was thirty-two before reading a psychoanalytical book. (Stekel's work on anxiety.)

NOVEMBER 28. NEW YORK. Since my arrival here, I have been living a little like a sleepwalker, surprised and often dazzled by everything. If I had time enough, I would talk at length about what I have seen. I will confine myself today to describing the extraordinary sight I witnessed three days ago. W., who pilots us around, had said: "You must go there tonight. I think something will happen." We went with him to Harlem. After a short walk, he takes us to a small bourgeois flat, its three rooms already crowded with men and women. If I understood aright, anyone can come, provided a dollar is paid. And so, we have a little of everything here, men in tuxedos, others in chamois jackets and corduroy trousers, which are the country's national costume since the depression. There are women here too, some of them rather smart. They have come to *see*; they hope, like everybody else, that *something* will happen, but that can only be after some drinking. So people drink and, from time to time, put down their glass to dance to one of the nostalgic airs poured out by the inexhaustible radio. But soon there is no longer room enough, as newcomers appear every minute. In the center of the smallest room, a gigantic sofa groans under the weight of ten or twelve persons seated cheek by jowl, all studiously serious, glass in hand. A young man in white velvet trousers comes up to our friend W. and speaks to him. Long fair locks straggle across his brow and, when he tries to push them back, fall over his nose. He is so intoxicated that one can scarcely hear what he says and his eyes can't focus. This is his first trip to New York. He comes from the West. The friend who made the trip with him is seated at our feet. He too is the worse for liquor, but a little less so. "I like all this," he says to me. "People smiling. Everything is all right." In the hum of conversation, I hear someone close to me say: "Oh, I get enough money all right, but I can't tell you how." Guffaws of laughter greet this semi-confidence. Another man says that the cost of *living* has gone down a good deal and that you can get rid of someone for less than a hundred dollars. I feel too hot and the cigarette smoke stings my eyes. When I suggest leaving to W., he begs me to stay a little longer. "You'll see," he says, "nothing ever happens till one in the morning. They haven't drunk enough yet."

Around twelve-thirty, something does happen. After a discussion which I unfortunately did not follow, someone dared one of the leather-jacketed boys to undress. How could he refuse? Everyone stared at him with a mocking, incredulous expression. If he hesitates, people will laugh. He is a big boy with a violent temper. He begins taking off his clothes, or rather, tearing them off as though they scorched him. As each garment drops, I imagine he will stop at that, but not at all, he even removes his socks and there he stands, completely naked in a circle of dressed people who look at him silently. After the first moment of amazement, a sarcastic voice asks the boy what he is going to do next. Without hesitating, he walks up to one of the women seated on the sofa; she laughs and pushes him away with the tips of her fingers. A man next her laughs louder, and a blow from the boy's fist immediately sends him sprawling on the carpet. This is the signal for an almost general fight. The women scream and faint.

The furniture is smashed. I see a small chair fly over our heads and crash against a wall. "Marvelous!" cries W. "They're sure to begin shooting." Vain attempts are made to separate the brawlers. The naked fellow is extremely powerful and fights everyone indiscriminately. The one I mentioned above, who was so happy, rolls at my feet with the boy in white trousers. The uproar is such that we can't hear ourselves speak. We go to the kitchen and deliberate. The police will be on the spot in a few minutes. Let's go. What surprises me no less than the rest is that the colored man in the cloakroom hands us our overcoats as calmly as if we were leaving after a concert. And as we drive through Central Park, W. leans over and says to me: "Some evenings, it's even more fun."

DECEMBER 1. From my bedroom window, I see Central Park. By night, it is studded with lights and seems like a great glittering river rolling its waters through the darkness. By day, with its network of long footpaths, its rocks jutting from the earth, and the delicate spread of its branchy trees, the park reminds you of a landscape in a primitive picture. Charming gray squirrels come up to you begging for the nuts they conceal in miserly hoards under bushes. It appears that around midnight, less timid beggars rove the paths and hold up rash pedestrians. I have also been told incredible stories of murders. . . .

Yesterday I went as far as Washington Square on top of a bus. Robert was with me. As we passed the Rockefeller building, all its windows ablaze, like a huge block of mica, we could not help exclaiming with surprise and admiration, like provincials. But any European arriving in New York feels a little provincial. In each of us, no matter how knowing, lies a greenhorn.

A little later we went to the Public Library, where illuminations ranging from the ninth to the fifteenth century are on show. A page by Girolamo dei Libri engaged my attention for a long time and I looked fondly at it. Mantegna's manner is perceptible everywhere, in the petrified draperies, in the little pebbles on the sand, in the curly waters of the torrent. I felt as though I had found a shelter in this landscape, yes, a shelter against all that overwhelms me in the monstrous beauty of this city. And as I stood before the wonderful Damascus plums by Jean Bourdichon, my heart beat as though the whole of Europe had been given back to me, Europe with its small houses on a human scale, Europe that we are in fear of losing at any moment, Europe with its museums, its cathedrals, its violent and shady politics, its grandeur and its baseness—how far away it seems and how little understood! I had lunch the other day with some New York writers and journalists. They discussed the international situation in an amazing way. Not that they were misinformed, far from it, they knew too much. But from all the facts stored in their memory, they drew conclusions, strictly logical ones, forgetting or not knowing that the gravest European problems present themselves under a supremely illogical form. There are unfathomable whims of fate, the *quid obscurum* that upset all observers' calculations.

DECEMBER 6. I have decided to go south. That is really why I came. I will go to see my friend Jim at Suffolk and we will return to the University. It has been eleven years since I left it, and I wonder if I will be sad or happy to see it once more. No doubt I did not know how to benefit from all it offered me; I did not quite understand the University, and it did not condescend to explain itself. It was only once I had left that I realized how deeply I loved it and was unknowingly immensely indebted to it. But in 1920 I missed France too much. At twenty, in one of the most beautiful landscapes in the world, without a worry for the future, I contrived every day to think myself unhappy. Ah! if everything had to be lived over again, with the experience that I have acquired since! How many friendships were offered me and discouraged by my lack of sociability!

DECEMBER 12. A little before Richmond, I woke in time to see a field of red earth under a pale blue sky and so many memories swept through my mind that I couldn't even begin talking about them. What makes my trip a little melancholy is that it is like a journey into the past. I remembered my holidays at my grandfather's house, a few hours from here. The house was far more than a country house; with the hills in the distance, the great trees that brushed against its walls, the place was, in my eyes, an ideal dwelling. It was a perfect world, locked within itself, carefully guarding its happiness and its peace, removed from the real world by invisible barriers. In summer, the house had a wealth of silence, of coolness, of shade. How good it was to read novels on an old tumble-down sofa in a library that smelled of old books! Gray, with a red roof, almost completely hidden by big firs, elms, and birches, it bore some resemblance to the country houses described by Russian novelists, or so I liked to think. It was built of wood and burned to the ground in one night, in June, 1922. Since then, I have mentally reconstructed it many a time, putting all the vanished objects where they belonged: in the dining room, a copy of Reynolds' "Winetasters"; on the second-floor landing, the big camphor-wood chest where the sheets were kept; in the drawing room, the backgammon board and the ivory hand used as a back-scratcher for the dog, and in the hall, under the stuffed horned owl, the shillelagh my grandfather had brought back from Ireland.

That stick was simply indescribable. One could give an idea of it by saying it looked like a gigantic corkscrew that powerful hands had twisted one way and stretched the other. I think this was the stick my grandfather asked for when, at the point of death, he got up saying he was going for a walk, he was going to Heaven.

There was fighting several times around the house during the Civil War. Bullets grazed the walls. Why didn't I note the stories my father used to tell me! When Virginia was invaded, my grandfather was arrested for helping the Confederates. He was imprisoned at Fort Warren and stayed there a few months. He would most likely have been shot if he hadn't been English. He owned no slaves except a sufficient number to do the cooking and housework and treated them better than a European treats his servants. I doubt for instance whether he would have allowed one of his colored men to sleep in winter in an icy room, such as those existing in almost all Parisian apartment houses, where nothing has been foreseen for the comfort of our servants. Owning slaves was a burden that is difficult to imagine nowadays. As they had no responsibilities, they had to be cared for continually, watched over when they were sick, their children brought up, and you had a whole black family on your hands, with its exactions, its whinings, its domestic feuds. So the abolition of slavery was greeted in the South with the same relief by whites and blacks, for in putting an end to an institution the very principle of which was intolerable, it rid slave-owners of a nightmare.

DECEMBER 14. At the University. She is the same as ever, cordial with that shade of disdain that gives her so much charm. Her vast lawns bordered by Greek Revival columns reflect a peaceful soul, perfectly satisfied with herself. You call on her, a hand is extended with a smile. If you turn away from her, if the whole of America forsook her at the foot of her hills, she would none the less pursue her quiet dream, adorned with classical literature, white frontages, black foliage. From North to South, what could there be for her to envy? Isn't she Mr. Jefferson's daughter?

I met almost all my old professors. The way they received me touched me far more than they could imagine. I believe almost all of them called me by my Christian name, which made me blush with pleasure!

Dr. Faulkner talked to me about the Negro question. He said, and I have always felt as he does on this point, that colored people are looked down on only in the North by whites. And he told me the following story. Four or five men are reading the papers in the lobby of a big hotel in Philadelphia or Boston. In comes a colored traveler who settles down not far from them and also opens his newspaper. After a look at him, all the whites leave the lobby, except one who gets up, goes to the Negro, and asks him where he comes from. "From Virginia." "So do I," says the white man. And they shake hands. What astonished me most is that the memory of the Civil War should still be so vivid.

1934

JANUARY 12. In Savannah. How strange it seems to be here! Last night, I was a long time getting to sleep. I lay in a gigantic bed, almost as big as the fabulous bed of Ware of which Shakespeare speaks. In the semi-darkness I could see the stout oak columns rise to the ceiling and mentally went over what my mother told me about her native town. In this great bed, my mother was born.

Yesterday, I went to see some friends of my family at Wormsloe, quite near here. Wormsloe is an old house hidden in the heart of a dusky park. It is protected by ghostly oaks; these giant trees are covered with Spanish moss that hangs in gray tatters continually stirred by the breeze, and nothing can be stranger than the light that filters through this sort of airy, funereal fabric. The house was built around 1780. Its name would have delighted **Poe**, its name and all the shadow that moves through the low-ceilinged, silent rooms. Noticed several fine Italian mantelpieces, mutilated by Sherman's soldiers as they passed this way.

Yesterday I showed Robert the house that my grandfather built shortly before the Civil War. To be accurate, it was finished on the day when General Beauregard shelled Fort Sumter, April 12, 1861. It is a vast Tudor house painted a tawny yellow. Sycamores border one side of it, and banana trees half conceal the Gothic porch. The effect is weird. To my mind, the house is both hideous and magnificent. It is one of those things where violent ugliness reaches peculiar beauty, and I think that Christian Bérard would faint with pleasure on seeing the semi-Gothic, semi-Louis XV drawing rooms! The room I prefer is the dark, warm library with its ogival mantelpiece with a blazing log fire, its portraits of Lee and Stonewall Jackson, its plaster busts, its pictures (all a trifle askew), its books in worn bindings. The Gothic moldings are disintegrating, the paint is scaling, and the whole thing remains splendid in a manner that seems peculiar to the Southern states. On the second floor, the room where Sherman slept. It was there, no doubt, that he wrote President Lincoln on December 24, 1864, to offer him Savannah as a Christmas present. It is not true that my grandfather offered the Northern general his house. Sherman exacted it because it was the finest (according to the taste of the period) and the roomiest in Savannah.

After supper, a long conversation with my Aunt Catherine. She talked to me about my maternal grandfather. He was a member of the Confederate Government and a price was put on his head by the Federal Government in 1865, which did not prevent him from dying a Congressman in 1879, aged forty-seven. He had a taste for parties, political activities, and eloquence. His wife is what is called a character in a novel. She spent most of her time in bed reading, believed herself to be ailing, and devoured a book a day.

JANUARY 13. Crossed the Savannah River. An immense river divided into five branches by islands. Its waters are clay red and reflect nothing. Its northern bank marks the boundary of South Carolina. I walked under big oaks draped in moss with its long, restless fringes. Impossible to describe the effect of poverty and magnificence produced by this parasitic vegetation. There is something disturbing about the very quality of its luxuriance. Its color hesitates between pale gray and a dull greenish white; it is both theatrical and sinister, lending a haunting melancholy to Southern landscapes. Seen from a distance, it reminds one of a head of hair. It comes from Barbados, a name that precisely describes its strange aspect. We call it Spanish moss.

Visited the ruins of Sheldon Church. An eighteenth-century church destroyed by fire in 1861. What still stands are the four walls and the brick columns of the porch. A great wood has to be crossed in order to reach it, you pass under giant oaks and there it stands, in a solitude where the only sound comes from a bird as it bursts into a sort of laughter. There stands a tree whose monstrous branches spread about ten yards from the trunk and sweep the yellowing brushwood with their gray fringes. I stood there for a few minutes, listening to the mocking, funereal chattering that came from a treetop. The sun shone at my feet. Never, beyond a doubt, have I ever been in a spot where I more keenly felt that we are nothing, that nature does not even see us. A vague, deep fear seized me suddenly and I ran away.

At the Tomotly plantation, I walked down an interminable avenue of oaks. Always those same long, torn curtains fluttering in the wind. Stout black branches writhe like great snakes inside this gray horror. These trees often give me such an unpleasant feeling that I am filled with a sort of anguish, and yet they attract me, for they seem to give the most beautiful picture imaginable of death. On this plantation, as far as the eye can reach, I see nothing but these huge black trunks raising to the skies arms laden with rags. You feel that by lingering in their shade, all things would become indifferent and that death would be easy. They are like so many old wizards watching over the soil of the South.

Returned to Savannah at sunset. The long avenues and squares seemed bathed in blood-red light. As I walked by the old pink and brown brick houses, I wondered how much and to what extent this town was part of me. I have lived here a lot in memory, but this is impossible to write about. A moment ago, I was obliged to ask my way. I comforted myself for this humiliation by remembering that even in Paris, and in my own quarter, I managed to get lost.

JANUARY 14. In the house where my mother spent her youth, I sat down to look around me and to pretend not to be just a

visitor. I am alone. From the window, I can see a pretty Colonial
house where Thackeray stayed when he came to Savannah and
where he wrote a few pages of *The Virginians*. On the other
side of the big shady square, the soft voice of a colored woman
selling fruit. Great silence in the house, where everything shines:
the tilted mirrors, the dark wood furniture, the black flooring.
Yet, thirty minutes away stand those pink columns in the solitude
of the woods, and those trees, like vestiges of prehistoric times
filled with dread, and at the top of the tallest tree, a bird from
the virgin forest laughing ominously in the sun. I don't know why
I think of this, seated by the innocent piano that played dances
for girls in hoop skirts. But it seems to me that in the South, a
barbarous and menacing nature marches almost to the threshold
of these frail white-columned houses. It is all around us, with its
buzzards and its snakes and its nightmarish vegetation. And a
melancholy that seems to spring from the beginning of time.

Yet my mother came from Savannah and she was gay. She was
a small woman, witty and good, whose footfall, voice, and peals
of laughter will be with me always.

JANUARY 28. Back in Savannah, this time under an assumed
name, in order to be free. I counted up that I am related to almost
two hundred people in this town. Dark glasses protect me pretty
well in the daytime. Yesterday, however, I found myself face to
face with one of my cousins at a street corner. I guessed from his
expression that he thought I bore a striking likeness to myself,
but without turning a hair I went on my way like a somnambulist.

FEBRUARY 4. The other day, to Cypress Swamp, one of the
strangest places in the world. Imagine a large wood of gigantic
cypresses tall and straight as the pillars of a cathedral and standing in ink-black water. On the borders of the pond, flowering
bushes with a heady scent. We rented a boat to go at random
through the trees. When we reached the heart of the wood, and
the banks were out of sight, I had the feeling of plunging into an
immemorial past. In this prehistoric setting, the silence itself
seemed filled with secret horror. Here, no bird sings. Their calls
could be heard in the distance. I was glad for a fine day, for the
sun to shine on my hands, and in spite of the light that pierced
the black foliage, I felt very much aware that we were in one of
those hidden spots for which death has a special liking.

On the banks grow crocuses and prodigious masses of pink and white camellias.

As we returned, I repeated to myself two lines of Poe's that kept their hold on me for the rest of the day:

> It was down by the dank tarn of Auber,
> In the ghoul-haunted woodland of Weir.

FEBRUARY 8. NEW YORK. The news from Paris has saddened me so much that I haven't had the heart to keep this diary. Hour by hour, during the whole of yesterday, I followed the movement of the riots, listening to detailed and I am sure very often most inaccurate reports in the local newspapers. We are leaving day after tomorrow.

FEBRUARY 13. This morning, I sat in the stern of the ship and looked at the gray sea, the white furrows we left behind us, the bridge glazed with spray and rain. It made me think of such vague, faraway things that I cannot describe them. By looking a long time at certain landscapes, I can sometimes conjure up from the depths of my memory certain recollections without my knowing where they come from. I have always had the power of doing this. It enchanted my childhood. Something of it, but very little, has passed into my books. These are memories beyond real memories, beyond those that can be located, dated, but how can anything so secret be expressed? The more one speaks of it, the greater the mystery. Lately, I mentally listed all the places I have known where these memories awaken. For instance, the charming, neglected garden behind Saint-Julien-le-Pauvre, or the room in the museum at Brussels where one has a view of gray and black roofs. I have never mentioned this to anyone. When I was a child, I used to listen to my sister as she played pieces by Schumann for me, and there was one whose title I liked almost as much as the music: "Distant Lands." Later, I invented a sort of geography of these distant lands. The East did not figure in it, but Edinburgh, Antwerp, and Friesland had a place of honor. Quite recently, looking at a map of the United States, my eyes fastened on Cascade Range, and for a few seconds I once more felt that bygone emotion, the absurd, delightful longing for distant lands. It would be hard to believe if I told what an influence this childish idea had over a whole part of my youth. What is certain is that the habit of situating happiness in distant lands ruled me up to my

sixteenth year, or thereabouts. I could not extricate myself from
my childhood; real life inspired me with deep distrust and I liked
the world only when it fitted in with my extravagant concep-
tions. Such and such an air of music charmed me because it substituted for the real world—where I could not manage to find a
place—an infinitely more real world where I strongly felt that I
would be happy. And behind all the ideas that I have forged of
death is this one, a remnant of childhood, that, in a word, death
is the most beautiful of distant lands.

Finished Woodward's *Life of Washington*. The humorous tone
of the book spoils it for me a little, but for all that, it is the work
of a man who searched for the truth behind the silly legends that
have cloaked the historical character. His Washington appears as
a man who was both empty and necessary, great on account of the
place he occupied. For it seems as though fate sometimes chooses
the most colorless men to assign them the most difficult task. The
interesting man, the one whom fate should obviously have selected, was Jefferson. But the fat, heavy, pompous boy called
Washington was chosen in preference to any other.

FEBRUARY 27. PARIS. "There will always be a France to love,"
said Renan. I am afraid that the France I love will end by disappearing. Each day seems to carry away a little of her. In the present commotion, an indefinable world is being born where I can't
find my place. A general sadness. I hear of nothing but people
who are frightened and want to leave the country.

MARCH 2. A long conversation with a Catholic writer who wants
me to see Father Altermann. I refuse. I refuse gently, but refuse.
We had been talking about the devil, whose presence I have felt
several times since 1923. The writer in question stared and mur-
mured: "But that is nevertheless a grace." A very strange grace
indeed. He added rather sensibly: "But where the devil is present,
Christ is also there." I thought over this conversation deeply. At
the bottom of my heart, faith still remains.

MARCH 14. Anguish. Whoever has not suffered from it could
not judge me. On leaving my publisher, where I had been to autograph copies of my book, I was suddenly seized with anguish. As
I walked down the rue Garancière, it occurred to me to go to
Saint-Sulpice, and there, in this church, I went and hid in the

darkest spot, in front of the Lady chapel. I thought as I knelt: "I have not come to make promises that I could not keep. There are things that I cannot give up. I simply want to receive *strength*. Heaven cannot refuse such a legitimate grace to any human being." I said my prayers as best I could and left.

MARCH 24. This morning at Passy, the thought came to me suddenly of all that is inexpressible in what we attempt to say, pen in hand. And this, to such a point that writing, for me, is no more than alluding to what one cannot express—because the words are lacking. . . . Try as we may, something always escapes us. The human tongue does not exceed certain limits.

MAY 2. Went to an exhibition of the Lord's Passion in French art. I was struck with respect and admiration for the stained-glass windows, although I know them so well. I remembered my bygone fervor, my great longing for a pure and Christian life. Have I gained much by rejecting all this? On the human plane, I have developed no doubt, but what of the spiritual? Compared with a saint, what am I worth? Very much moved by the great painted wood Christs from the Sainte-Chapelle. Pondering over all this a little later, I thought that our civilization is stranger than we realize. To see, from childhood to the day of one's death, representations of tortures in churches, in houses, and sometimes in streets, isn't that a really singular fact? A man nailed to two pieces of wood, that is what Christianity shows us at every turn. The Church was born in tortures. A fourth-century Greek child never saw anything in temples but statues of ideally beautiful and happy men and women, but we are offered images of a dying man. If a man who knew nothing of Christianity were taken to the Louvre, he might perhaps leave it, sick with disgust.

MAY 17. Gide looks sad and even a little scandalized on hearing that L., the writer, belongs to the Rightist association of the Croix de Feu. I tell him that for my part, I would never line up with any party because politics disgusts me and also because I know nothing about it. "Neither do I," says he. "I can't make head or tail of it. But if you don't choose, you end by being adopted by one or the other political party." And he talks of an anti-fascist league, among which figure Rivet and other scholars. He reads me a few pages of Kafka's *Trial*, which I don't know, and tells me the book seems most particularly designed for me, even more so than for him. He reads well, but in a theatrical manner, bringing out certain words with excessive emphasis. He tells me that Jouvet insists on my writing a play for him, a fact I very well know. We talk of the training necessary for writing for the stage, always a long process. According to Gide, a master stroke at the very start, so frequent in writing novels, is almost unknown in writing for the stage. As we part, leaning over the banister (I had been to see him), he talks about my drawing room, where he had waited for me day before yesterday, and sees in it a reflection of my personality: "It is an elusive one," he says with a smile and a nod, "and at the same time, a very intense one. Yes, that blue sofa and those red chairs . . ."

MAY 18.   Gide was telling me yesterday that he used to know the Uffizi very well. "I was even quite a dab at it," he says, smiling. "But now, this is no longer of interest to me . . ."

MAY 26.   How can the world's beauty be expressed? Some days, it crushes me like a tremendous burden. It delights me under every one of its aspects. I used to feel this so keenly that death appeared to me (this is horrible to say) like a sort of liberation from joy, just as sickness, according to Michelet, is convalescence in the opposite direction, and death a sort of recovery from life.

JUNE 1.   A lecture by Doctor Jung on the collective unconscious. Doctor Jung is a tall, ruddy-faced old man with a white mustache. He wears a dress suit and talks quietly about amazing things. According to him, we carry within us, in the deepest part of our unconscious self, certain ideas that are a remote heritage common to all races of humanity. Some of the sick people he looks after, on being asked to make sketches, have reproduced, unknowingly, extremely ancient symbolical signs that are familiar only to Orientalists. For instance, *mandalas*, or magic circles ornamented with crosses and snakes. Slides enable us to understand exactly what he means. Certain Tibetan or Hindu drawings correspond to sketches by children aged between seven and twelve.

Cassou and Jaloux were at the lecture. All three of us left together to gossip until 1 P.M. in a café on the place Péreire. They believe that *constants* exist in the human brain that would partly explain these strange drawings. Certain ideas, certain emotions always express themselves in the same manner. However, they make no attempt to explain, through reasoning, certain almost incomprehensible coincidences. For my part, I wonder if these mysterious signs are not an unconscious memory of an antediluvian handwriting. We inherit so many things from our parents and our great-grandparents. Why shouldn't this inheritance go very far back into the past, to the origins of humanity? We are steeped in memories.

UNDATED. . . . The children in my books—there are two or three of them—open their lips only with extreme discretion, and scarcely move, for the simple reason that the man who created them does not feel capable of making them talk, or even act, in a plausible fashion. Why is this? I don't know. I have always had the feeling that the "under sixteen" among my characters make fun of me. They bother me. I feel them watching me. They hope I'm going to make a mistake. It's a pleasure to send them packing. In *The Dark Journey* is a small boy that I chased from the book with a slap in the face.

Yet I am fond of children. I love my childhood and that of others, and I believe that I wouldn't be able to write another line if I lost the memory of my early years. How many of us who think themselves freed for ever of the terrors, hopes, and joys of their tenth year, live until their death on this hidden capital! The child dictates and the man writes.

JUNE 14. In my room, at the far end of the flat, I read the beginning of the Gospel according to St. John in the English version. I read it in a whisper. At the twelfth verse, I was blinded by tears. An extraordinary, unaccountable emotion seized me. I did not feel like kneeling. On the contrary, I got up, I tried to blot out inside me the image of the outer world. I think that in the depth of our being, at the very bottom of our heart, is a spring ready to gush forth. The Son of Man comes and sits by this spring and talks to our soul, the Samaritan woman. I have felt this keenly, at different times, for the last few years. Ah! may nothing ever destroy a love for the divine within us! This is what should survive all religions, whose forms are so often vain. To go through this life trying to establish a balance between body and soul is not enough.

AUGUST 4. I was tearing morning-glories out of a flower bed

when I was handed a letter from Gide about *The Dreamer*. It gave me such pleasure that, having read it once at a gulp, I went to a shady walk to read it over again quietly. Added to his letter was a very detailed list of the mistakes he had noted in the course of reading the book: three in all.

SEPTEMBER 2.   The other evening as I went to sleep, I said the prayer that Father Crété had taught me when I was fifteen, when a single impure thought had never yet entered my head: *"Jesu, mitis et humilis corde, fac cor meum sicut cor tuum!"* Never perhaps did I say that prayer with more faith than I did last night. But what is the good? In me is a great desire to change and, I can say so, strange as it may seem, a real love of Christ. However, I don't see how I will be able to undertake the struggle against temptations, since it all comes down to that.

SEPTEMBER 13.   In thinking over my life, I see that it has been a rather singular one, although nothing of this shows from the outside. I was very near to renouncing the world in 1918. I hesitated and stayed where I was. I believe I was right. I lost a great deal on the spiritual plane, but I think that a balance will be established someday. I am convinced that few men of my age are tempted as I am. This has already harmed me. I have allowed myself to be beguiled by the created world, but in me are elements of resistance. . . . I was brought to thinking all this by reading several books on Hindu philosophy.

OCTOBER 30.   Just a moment ago, we were in my study, having coffee and listening to one of Beethoven's quartets (the third of Opus 59). I was glancing through Father Bruno's book on St. John of the Cross, when I came across these lines, which were already familiar to me:

> *¿A donde te escondiste, Amado,*
> *Y me dejaste con gemido?*
> *Como el ciervo huiste,*
> *Habiéndome herido . . .*

I felt deeply moved, as though a powerful voice called to me in the stillness. For the space of a second, I had an intuition of what a mystical life can be, and what can also be, *seen from the other side,* the life that we lead in the world.

*   *   *

NOVEMBER 6. How can reading the Gospels be reconciled with a life where pleasure nevertheless plays a part? This does not seem to me possible. There are days when I can't open the New Testament without feeling a hypocrite, but should one, from hatred of hypocrisy, suppress all spiritual reading if one can't suppress pleasure, and can one go from one to the other without loathing oneself?

NOVEMBER 25. Reading the *Fioretti* makes me forget the present world and the dark future. I too have experienced the joy known to Brother Masseo, Brother Giles, and the other companions of St. Francis. No doubt this lasted but a few minutes in the whole of my life, but I know what it is, I have had those fervent moments when the world vanishes into mist, I have been in love with Heaven. A vague memory of it returns to me at times, but it is enough to make me happy. No doubt I had a calling.

At the Orangerie. A show of seventeenth-century painters. Dumesnil de la Tour. A marvelous artist, but his candle must not be taken away from him, or the reddish lighting that lends mystery to his painting. His "Nativity" is very beautiful. The Child is more touching than any Infant Jesus in the whole of Italian painting and more *real*. This is where France triumphs, she clings to the truth.

NOVEMBER 28. At the Orangerie. Dumesnil de la Tour delights me. He understood the magic of truth. Nothing seemed to him commonplace. To light a candle in the midst of four peasants was enough for him to enter an enchanted world, but an enchanted world where, by a miracle, truth remains truth.

DECEMBER 4. Yesterday, Raïssa Maritain was telling us what a short time had elapsed since the foundation of Christianity. What are two thousand years in the eyes of God? Scarcely an hour, perhaps. And she added that the coming of Christ was such a momentous event that its consequences are not yet apparent to us. I agree with her there. The Gospels are full of obscure sayings, and what we understand of these books, what we understand with our whole heart, can probably be reduced to a few verses. But I also think that the supposedly eternal churches will have to disappear and be forgotten before all the sayings of Christ find their accomplishment. . . .

* * *

UNDATED. Lately, Maritain, speaking of the Concordat between the Vatican and Germany, quotes Pius XI as saying: "If I had to, for the welfare of souls, I would make a covenant with the devil. . . ." As we were talking of "The Night of the Senses" by St. John of the Cross, I thought I saw an immense wall, such as was never built by man; it was perfectly white and rose into a black sky, where it was lost among the stars. This image engrossed me for some time without my finding it possible to divert my attention from it.

DECEMBER 12. Maybe I shouldn't breathe a word about the most beautiful, the most mysterious dream I ever had. I dream it once or twice a year. Suddenly, I see myself on a road that skirts the top of a cliff and I know that the dream is beginning and with it, a feeling of happiness such that human speech cannot give the faintest idea of it. Farther on, there will be a big iron gate, so difficult to turn on its hinges, then the long avenue of trees, then once again the cliff and I pause to look at the sea, but instead of the water I see an immense forest that stretches to the horizon and covers the whole countryside, and at that moment I feel as happy as someone who has passed beyond death. Is that all? It is.

1935

FEBRUARY 4. Read over the pages of this diary from 1928 to 1935. I think that the notebook I am finishing at present will show the signs of an inner change in me, although the circumstances of my outer life remain the same. There are, however, rather long periods of calm (how can this be expressed otherwise? The fever, the agitation sometimes drop) and then what is most serious in me strives for the upper hand. In such moments, these gray notebooks run a certain danger, but I think I would make a great mistake in destroying them, for they describe an experience of life that many people have not had.

FEBRUARY 16. At times I envy, and basely envy, people who can be converted, who throw themselves at the feet of a priest to get rid of everything that troubles them and makes them suffer. For me, this is impossible. To be quits of everything one has done, because one has confessed everything—no . . . Happy is the man who, without violence and without a struggle, manages to lull his desires and go higher.

FEBRUARY 28. I wrote forty lines this morning. . . . Last night, I wondered why I shouldn't portray my characters naked. Yes, that is how I would like to show them, in all their physical truth. As a rule, characters in a novel are reduced to a bust. They talk and wave their arms, but the lower part of their body, except in pornographic novels, is chastely concealed from the reader's curiosity. Yet the body speaks the truth just as much as the face, it has its own particular expression, it is humble, brave, contemptuous, cocky, joyful, pensive; courage can be read in the outline of the shoulders and of the breast, etc. This should be developed.

MARCH 15. These days are so overpoweringly mild that they prevent me from wanting to note the small things that make up my life. This is spring with its neurotic sky, its languor, its foretaste of death. Yet, I worked. There are one or two sentences in my book (*Midnight*) that made me laugh to myself, but I have such a reputation for melancholy that probably no one will notice that I am also fond of gaiety. And after all, maybe these sentences are not amusing.

MARCH 17. Yesterday, very near the Ides of March, Germany told the whole world that she was rearming. This must have been going on for years, or she would not have announced it so openly. So the Versailles Treaty is in shreds.

I don't very well see how peace can last. . . . It is not that I fear death. For the last few months, death has lost many of its terrors as far as I am concerned, but there is so much left for us to do and learn.

MARCH 20. I don't think I shall ever forget these days of anguish. There is an enormous commotion in the world, the repercussions of which make us all suffer. All I can hope for is that the storm will blow over. I dare not even say what I fear. England has just forwarded Germany the weakest of replies. Everything concurs to make Hitler certain that the whole of Europe is afraid of him.

The other day, in one of those moments of anguish that I cannot tell anyone about, I suddenly had an instant of overwhelming joy, a joy mingled with terror, because I did not understand its reason.

APRIL 14. ROME. At St. Peter's for the Palm Sunday celebrations. The clergy walks through the whole length of the basilica in a cloud of incense. Two choirs answer each other, one with the procession, the other from a gallery near the high altar. An admirable effect. The procession re-enters the nave after having gone around the portico. Suddenly, the choir takes up its chant from the gallery, as though moved by an unexpected inspiration and not according to ceremonial rites. In all this, I cannot help seeing a recollection of the Temple, for the Church is the memory of humanity. I don't mean to say that St. Peter's is a reminiscence of the gold and white building with which Herod the Great crowned Jerusalem, but the *effect produced* must have been the same.

APRIL 17. At St. John Lateran. The hymns moved me so much that I knelt with everybody else. Yet, an hour earlier, I was thinking of very different things. . . . I note this more in sadness than with irony. In church, I regarded myself as an awful hypocrite, but I had gone there to look at the gilt ceiling and the large mosaics, and the liturgy moved me.

APRIL 30. This morning, at four, I woke in a state of most painful anguish. I got up, went to the window, and leaned out. It was drizzling. The sky was a fine pale gray, and beneath me the tiled roofs formed a great confused mass of darkish pink. The birds sang in the Pincio gardens. There was such happiness in the air that I could not resist being infected by it for long. My sadness suddenly abated. I had the feeling that the day was dawning within me. These abrupt transitions from melancholy to joy are one of the traits of my character that intrigue me most, and the one that I put up with least easily. I would have liked to be more stable and, yes, more serious. I have moments of ridiculous frivolity, I mean that my sadness is often as frivolous as my joy.

MAY 10. Yesterday and the day before, I spent a long time in the Roman Forum and the Forum of Augustus. I found more beauty there than anywhere else in this town. These temples, torn to pieces, not by time, but by men, are a model of eternal perfection. No matter how small the fragment of a Roman work, it bears within it a world that to me seems unlimited. I mean that it contains art in almost its entirety where what is essential in art is concerned. After it will be nothing but repetitions, brilliant repetitions, no doubt, but also what a lot of trash! I sat before the bas-relief of the *Suovetaurilia,* where one sees a porker decked with fillets, more ferocious and more formidable than a battleship, a ram, then a bull laden with all the majesty of Rome. Lizards ran about in the sun at my feet. Raising my eyes, I could see the Arch of Septimius Severus and, toward the left, the Rostral column. How much more religious than St. Peter did this stricken landscape appear to me!

MAY 16. Just now, as I was filing some notes, I began to laugh. "What are you laughing about?" asks Robert. "I am thinking of Gide's rhinoceros." I had been to see Gide, a few years ago, on his return from Africa. Curtius was there. Gide talks to us a little about his journey, but briefly, and judging it would amuse us more than accounts and descriptions, he showed us a magnificent insect preserved in a small glass jar. We admire the big black scarab, whose head is provided with a horn, and this leads me to say that it looks like a rhinoceros. "It is not a rhinoceros," says Gide, "it is a . . ." (Here a Greek name that I have forgotten.) "I can see that it isn't, of course," I reply, "but don't you think that horn gives it a family resemblance to a rhinoceros?" Gide and Curtius look at each other. "My dear friend," says Gide, with a shade of surprise in his voice, "I assure you that it is not a rhinoceros." Curtius adds: "No doubt whatever on that score." "Naturally. I wouldn't dream of contradicting you." And I am silent, but think that if Gide were not born in France, he should have been born in Scotland, where every word is taken literally. Does he really imagine that I thought I had seen a rhinoceros under my very eyes, a rhinoceros in a glass container?

Months went by after this astonishing conversation, and someone informed me one day that there is a type of giant scarab called a rhinoceros. I felt relieved.

JULY 10. PARIS. Yesterday, a visit to Gide. I don't know how it was that we talked about our way of living when we travel and how impossible it is for us both to watch over our expenses and to keep accounts.

We go out and he talks of this and that. He tells me that what strikes him most in my books is that the pencil never leaves the paper, that the line is unbroken to the end, and that if he ever writes anything about me, he will stress this particular point. He also says that all that is true in my novels is true in spite of an appreciable disagreement with the reality of daily life. He adds that I have reached a turning point, that my real career will begin on the day when my public will desert me, when my books will be found too much unlike the naturalistic models that the public demands. "The public," he says, "wants novels that resemble those it knows." He further adds that I am not to flinch when the time comes, but to let myself go to my inspiration, to my real temperament—that of a visionary writer. In this regard, he resumes talking about himself and says that at bottom he has never found his real public. "What writer ever really finds his public?" I then ask. "Why, almost all of them. Look at Bourget!" I reply: "Let us talk of great writers. Didn't Charles Dickens appeal to a number of readers to whom he should not have appealed? His real public is being found at present." He agrees with me there and talks of the books he might have written and regrets not having written. "If seventeenth-century writers could have foreseen that they would still be read three hundred years later, they would have written quite differently. One can imagine their returning to this world and saying: 'If we had only known! . . .' For one feels that they could have done better and did not dare to." One can't help thinking of the preface to *The Loves of Psyche and Cupid*: ". . . No matter how little of an assurance a writer can have of talking to posterity," writes La Fontaine, "he should always have this object in mind and try to order matters for its use." I ask Gide what the books he did not write would have been like. "Oh," he says pensively, "works of imagination, novels . . ."

A little later, he tells me that so far I have had an exceptional place in literature, thanks to the element of unreality that is found in my books, "but," he says, "someday you will have to give up this position and take sides." (He is thinking of the great political conflicts that will probably split this country.) "Clashes between the Rightists and the Leftists are almost inevitable. Then you won't be able to confine yourself to literature. You will be forced to choose." "To choose?" I ask. "Choose between Communism and Fascism? And if I don't feel drawn to either party, what am I to do?" Gide shakes his head. "You will have to choose," he repeats firmly. (This from the author of *Les Nourritures terrestres!*) I ask him if he feels free, since his conversion to Communism. (He had said a little earlier that he had become "a representative person," with a slightly mocking laugh to show that he didn't take himself seriously.) He answers no and quotes what Barrès said when asked what irked him most in his parliamentary career: "To vote with my party!" We part soon after this. He asks me to think over the trip to America that we are planning.

JULY 13. Gide was telling me the other day that he did not know how to give an idea of the plots of his books, that he had never known how, and that he believed that people who can give a skillful account of such things are *worthless when they sit down before a sheet of paper.* (This because I had told him of sometimes feeling like acquainting someone with the subject of a novel I am writing and that, at the last moment, I had always changed my mind, for fear of not being able to do it creditably.) He added that when he narrates something, he is always afraid of not holding his audience's interest to the end. If, for instance, he is interrupted in the middle of a story, no one ever asks: "And what comes next?" when the interruption has ceased. He further says that in his books, the end is often unduly abridged; he wonders if this is not a "residue of his youth," the fear of not being listened to until the end.

SEPTEMBER 4. It has been a little over a year since I began to study Buddhism. Has this changed anything in me? Yes, I think so. What terrorized me formerly no longer touches me. I face the idea of death without a tremor, whereas the idea of dying used to be so painful to me that I dared not turn my thoughts in that direction.

SEPTEMBER 19. Once more those inner difficulties that I find so strange. I sometimes have the feeling of being a sleeper eager to wake who dreams of the day when he will be set free. There are moments when I imagine a voice calls me and the sweetness of its call makes me forget all that worries me in this world. What is best in us, in me, is love. Yesterday, in deep inner loneliness, I whispered: "If there is anyone close by who can help me, let him stretch out his hand to me!" But the voice must be obeyed when it orders you to listen. Often, in the midst of reading a book, one hears it with a beating heart, but out of laziness, or for fear of upsetting the whole of life, one waits like a coward for it to hush. That is what happens to me.

SEPTEMBER 24. A few minutes of deep joy lately at the thought that my liberation depended above all on myself and not on exterior circumstances. "Where lies the kingdom of God?" "Within you." (Ah! why don't we go there right away!) "Where lies Nirvana?" "Where the precepts are observed." So we are there, if we wish it.

Have read the *Gospel of Sri Ramakrishna.* It contains wonderful passages about the personal God and the impersonal God. How much more important this seems to me than the Anglo-Italian controversy!

The Police Department distributes booklets in apartment houses. So thus we know what precautions are to be taken in case of air raids (gas masks, shelters, don't get excited, everything is mentioned). I wonder when and how we will emerge from this hideous period.

OCTOBER 28. All five of us were seated around the dining-room table. A log fire burned in the hearth and it was so dark that we had to turn on the lights although it was not yet two in the afternoon. There were five of us and we laughed and suddenly I felt that we were far more numerous, that our gaiety had attracted all the missing ones, my father, my mother, and the two sisters I have lost; they sat by us and kept us company until the end of the meal, laughing with us all. I had an impression of great happiness, an impression of deep security, but dared not breathe a word of it.

DECEMBER 20. For the last few years, I have detached myself from many things. I sometimes feel like a man in a small boat. The boat moves away from shore. I have a clear view of the earth and its flowers, its houses, all that it has to offer me that is beautiful and good, but from time to time a powerful stroke of the oar removes me a little farther from it all. I then have a slight feeling of anguish followed by one of deep security.

The other day, as I listened to music, I had the delightful sensation of the proximity of another world. Behind the impalpable veil, there it is, the world of truth, that kingdom of God that intrigued me so much as a child.

On thinking about my life, I see very little progress. Yet there is a great desire in me to know the truth, but this means setting out on an adventure that requires lots of courage. If ever I get to know this truth, I will share it with those I love. The day will come when we will be ready. Then I will tell what I have learned and we will be far happier. We will know at last, all of us, that death does not exist and we will be together for ever. . . .

1936

FEBRUARY 5. How am I to change my life? From the inside. It is useless to burn books and manuscripts. Detachment is not thus obtained; a new heart is what must be asked for, and the rest is easily accomplished. I am always surprised and a little frightened to see people who imagine that they possess fine pictures, rare furniture, valuable books, whereas, it is just the opposite, I mean that all these objects are the masters of those who believe they own them. How many people might say: "I belong to a bronze by Pollaiuolo, to a couple of large sixteenth-century chests, to a sketch painted by Delacroix . . . etc." And the richer one is, the more tyrannical and numerous are these masters.

UNDATED. After an interruption of more than twelve years, I have gone back to the study of Hebrew. I had begun it at the University. A Polish Jew named Drabkin and I translated the beginning of the *Bereshith*, but I was too lazy to go on with it. What is more, everything touching the Jewish race gave me a feeling of inexplicable uneasiness. I had no hostility toward Jews, but our ground of mutual understanding was very limited and I saw very well that they did not think as we did. Scarcely anyone at the University spoke to Drabkin, aside from his coreligionists. This was the very reason why I tried to be friendly with him, in order to repair or at least lessen what I considered an injustice. But most surprising of all: Drabkin did not suffer at all from the ostracism to which he was subjected. I even wonder if he was aware of it. He laughed gaily over everything. He could neither be saddened nor offended. His ears stuck out on either side of a cap jammed down to the nape of his neck and he was completely lacking in elegance. I was fully aware of his ugliness, his barbarous accent, his contemptuous ignorance of our history, but envied him his knowledge of Hebrew. . . .

APRIL 5. At Ober-Lech, in the Arlberg. The hotel is isolated on a plateau surrounded by mountains. The snow has partly melted, but great patches of it remain. At the right, a wood of fir trees where I sit and read. I like these trees. From the window of my room, I look so long at them sometimes that they assume an indescribable aspect. A child would understand me. It is not that they change their shape or color, but they become different. In the morning, they rise from the valley of the Lech to the vicinity of the hotel, and at night they go down again, like a procession of pilgrims in their black capes. They do not move, but how clearly I can see them marching, swathed in mist! On and on they come, so numerous that some still remain in the darkness.

MAY 9. PARIS. Last Thursday, my first Hebrew lesson with M. Moses V., who had been recommended to me by a bookseller. With amazement, I saw M. Edme walk into my study. [M. Edme is a character in *Midnight*.] He is rather short, with very black hair, a carefully trimmed beard, a straight, delicate nose, shining eyes that look as though they were painted on enamel, thin cheeks, more like an Arab than a Jew. He makes me recite Psalm 23, which we then parse, but I was flurried, as much by the man's learning as by my own ignorance, so I answered wrong. We have begun reading Isaiah. I wondered that he did not make me begin at Genesis, but he probably thinks its Hebrew too easy. The tongue spoken by the prophets is infinitely more varied, with more nuances and more abstractions; the study will demand great efforts from me, but I remember properly only what I acquire with difficulty. At the University of Virginia, the *Iliad* was handed to students who could scarcely recite their Greek alphabet.

SEPTEMBER 20. LONDON. Long hours devoted to studying Hebrew. All that I know of this tongue I owe to M. Moses V., whose name I mention with gratitude. He it is who guided me through the labyrinth of the seven conjugations. The rest is a matter of vocabulary and I can now work alone. Took a great number of notes on Isaiah, also on Genesis. It is the most beautiful of all tongues, the one used by God to create the worlds and call His first servants. . . .

I think that what urged me to resume my study of Hebrew was the divergence of the English, French, and German translations, not to mention the Vulgate, which offers a particular problem. How is it, I wondered, that these translators do not always agree, since they all have the same text before them? Such uncertainties are not to be found in the translations of Homer. Could it be that the Biblical translators faced something untranslatable? I do not say that the essential part of the message has not come down to us, but what could not be rendered was the sound, the noise of the Hebrew sentence. Now, it is enough to read half a page of the Bible in the original to understand the capital importance of the choice of syllables in the drafting of this book, which is mainly a poetical book. A Hebrew poet has never resisted the pleasure of alliteration; it is for him a supreme way of expressing anger, indignation, joy, or fright. With a skill of which the best French translators can give no idea, he multiplies the sibilants and sets in motion the grandiose register of gutturals. The Almighty's powerful breath passes into this tongue and I am afraid that very little of it remains in Abbé Crampon's honest version. I will return to the subject later.

SEPTEMBER 25. Have read Gide's journal. How well I recognize him here, the Gide of 1925, the one we have lost! I continually feel like writing him, forgetting that the Gide who would read the letter would be the Gide of 1936, a Gide surrounded by new comrades; there are too many clenched fists raised around him for me to reach him.

OCTOBER 14. A *new beginning* of my book yesterday, another this morning. To begin a book used not to give me too much trouble. To a certain extent, I wrote what came into my head on the first page (from what depths does this come?), then I followed up this first page blindly to the end. At present, I realize that to go blindly along will no longer lead me anywhere, except to a trail I had already blazed and to a known objective. There is something in me that would drive me to repeat what I have already done, if I did not fight this instinct with all my might. One must carefully avoid being trapped by the snare of words. I ride a horse that knows his way to the stable only too well. If I wasn't more exacting, I would long since have slackened the reins; I try, on the contrary, constantly to set my horse straight. This is something that will be judged if ever these fifteen or twenty beginnings of novels are found among my papers. Some of them are curious.

OCTOBER 16. Dinner at Vyvyan Holland's. H. G. Wells and several less-known novelists were there. . . . As we talked about Germany, Wells says that the Germany of today is, in a way, the materialization of France's fears. . . . Around ten o'clock, after an excellent dinner, comes the time for port wine and limericks, and, regarding the latter, Wells asserts that this kind of literature was invented by Edward Lear around 1850, which surprises me, and he quotes, a little wrong, several of the best-known and most risqué limericks. Peals of laughter followed by long silences, those heavy silences peculiar to these parts and that are almost incomprehensible to anyone who has lived in France, where people practically snatch the words from each other's lips. . . . I have too much admiration for Wells' genius not to be a little disappointed, without quite knowing what I expected, anyway. I probably imagined that he would be brilliant, as brilliant as certain prominent authors in Paris, and now, on thinking it over, I like this great writer's simplicity (I don't say his modesty). As he talked about Lenin and Stalin, I asked him if Stalin spoke English. Not a word: an interpreter had to be called on. Stalin received Wells in a pullover, smoking a pipe, for which he apologized. What about Lenin? Did he know English? "Oh, perfectly. He had lived in London; he went every day to the British Museum. Why, the Russian Revolution was hatched at the British Museum!" A little later, I forget in what connection, someone mentioned the Bible. "A nefarious book," says Wells. "It has done the greatest harm to humanity and in particular to the Jewish race." I would have liked him to explain why. A good deal could be said on the subject, for I believe that a wrong interpretation of the Scriptures has given rise to innumerable false ideas. To quote one instance only among a thousand others, our conception of good and evil regarding physical love, the whole of our sexual morality originated by the Pentateuch and St. Paul . . .

* * *

NOVEMBER 7. At the National Gallery. What painter has expressed better than Rembrandt the majesty of the Jewish people? I am thinking in particular of the portrait of Jacob Trips, his severe face that of one of Israel's elders; a great skinny body wrapped in furs from which emerges a fine, dry, domineering hand grasping a long stick. I am also thinking of the portrait of the Jewish merchant (in this portrait the gray sleeve slashed with black is the finest sleeve I know in painting, even finer than Titian's sumptuous sleeves; yet, looking at it a little closely, one sees that it must have been made of rather poor fabric, although it gives an impression of richness that is difficult to analyze). Dreamed a great deal before these admirably dignified faces. Whether their business was explaining the Scriptures or selling cloth, these men had something royal about their brows and eyes. Yet it was perhaps these same Jews, these doctors of the law and these merchants from Amsterdam, who ill-treated Uriel da Costa. . . .

NOVEMBER 30. PARIS. Yesterday, for a moment, I had a great longing to talk confidentially to someone, to talk of my inner difficulties. For it is not good to remain silent always. But how can one speak of things that are sometimes beyond human speech?
. . . I have come to believe that death does not exist, that there is only a long development of life throughout the centuries, that the body's annihilation is a liberation, that a child at the time of birth imagines it is about to die because it leaves its mother's womb and that the same mistake occurs in our minds when we breathe our last.

DECEMBER 15. A telephone call from Gide. "Don't mistake my silence for coolness," he says. And he adds: "I sometimes dive under. . . ." I go to see him. He seems gay, younger than he has ever been since I knew him. He first talks to me at some length about *Midnight*, which he read at Cuverville. He likes neither the first nor the second part. . . . A little later, he expresses his admiration for English literature (this in connection with Shakespeare's historical plays). "We seem so dry compared with them," he murmurs. And he gives a nod, meaning "Yes, yes, we are!" as though I had protested. The conversation next shifts to politics, he congratulates me on not having made a choice between Communism and Fascism, "since," he says rather sadly, "they are the same thing." And he adds: "You are nonpolitical."

Stay so." He talks admirably of the *réfractaires*—the people who are opposed to the regime—whom he saw in Russia. . . . Portrait of a young German whom he met on a ship, during a journey on the Black Sea: a sort of Rimbaud, almost absurd if his face had not been so beautiful, wearing a leather jacket and carrying a small umbrella under his arm; with that, a wild unsociable expression. Gide asked him if he worked. Answer: "I don't work. I refuse to work." "But what do you do for a living?" "I manage."

Forgot to mention a moment ago that regarding the third part of *Midnight*, Gide reproaches me for having used the word *love* in every place where, according to him, I should have used the word *desire* "to express the panic frenzy in the story."

DECEMBER 21. Just realized that I haven't said a word about Edward VIII's abdication, which set England astir for ten days, but I keep my diary more and more neglectfully. This, I suppose, goes to show that I am gradually being detached from my former self.

1937

JANUARY 2. Long readings of the Bible in Hebrew. For the last months, I have been unable to think of anything but this book and fell gladly under its spell. . . . This immense wealth will probably never be exhausted and we are just beginning to have a glimpse of it, and yet it is ours, it constitutes the dowry given by humanity for its spiritual espousals. . . . Yet we must beware of the translators' counterfeit coins.

JANUARY 8. LONDON. Saw *Hamlet* at the Old Vic. It is at once the most beautiful poem, the most beautiful tragedy, and the most beautiful novel that was ever written. Certain passages, even the best known, appeared to me almost beyond what a man can do, and I left the theater dizzy and as though I were a little tipsy. The part of Hamlet is played by an actor who is a little too conscious of his handsome face, a little too athletic, a trifle too much given to leaping and bounding. Some of his attitudes are hard to excuse.

When he sees his father's ghost, he expresses terror by crawling on the stage and recites a rather long soliloquy on his stomach. An ultra-modern setting. An orgy of cubes and stairways and, in the second act, an endless vista of antlers. Are we at the court of a cuckold? None of these defects struck me during the play, but I had noticed them unconsciously. Shakespeare's lines do away with all that. And what Gide said came back to me: "How dry we must seem . . ." It might be.

JANUARY 26. I sometimes feel a sort of impatience with my body. If it could understand me, I would say to it: "What do I care if you are comfortable? Your happiness is an ever-recurring problem, more and more difficult to solve. Not a day goes by without your complaining. You are bored and you bore me. You have to be amused, taken here and there, your peace and well-being seen to. I protest against your whims but, like a coward, obey your tyrannical caprices, and if anything threatens you, I imagine myself to be unhappy and so I am. Your laziness, your constant kicking, your covetousness weary me. If I work too long, you take your revenge in headaches that oblige me to let you lie down after having drawn the curtains and turned broad daylight into night," etc.

FEBRUARY 5. Anne has been here for the last few days, and I have enjoyed showing her a few churches. These London churches are charming old ladies dressed with puritanical elegance, a white cap on their head, hands folded on their stomach. Thus they stand, lost in a city they can no longer recognize, aloof and disdainful. St. Bride's, which has to be hunted for amidst blackened houses, is one of the most engaging; a narrow garden, dying in the fumes of London, still protects it from the Strand's onslaughts, but the day will come when it will occur to someone that the ground on which the church stands is very valuable, and St. Bride's will give place to some skyscraper. Few strangers visit it. No Frenchman that I know of has mentioned it. Inside, it is white and gold and hesitates, without making up its mind, between being a house of prayer and a ballroom. It is austerely coquettish, with a leaning to Corinthian furbelows. If it followed its inclinations, the church would turn baroque, but it takes refuge in the well-bred graces of the neo-classic style. Its Greek columns relate themselves as best they can to great ogival windows; its height is cut in two by a gallery of black wood. Highly polished brass candelabra and golden flowers are sprinkled all over the church against a background of white walls. St. Bride's is more innocent than prayerful.

FEBRUARY 9. Last night we went to the Westminster Theater, where Chekhov's *Uncle Vanya* was given. I felt so full of bliss that, for a moment, I believed that *happiness* was near, the only name I can give to a mysterious event that has so little connection with what is usually understood by the word *happiness*. It is not human joy, but human joy sometimes leads to it. Impossible to explain what I mean. This inexpressible something is there, behind the denseness of this world. I did not strain to reach it, knowing only too well that in such cases one should keep a sort of interior stillness, a complete passivity, but the play began and the actors' lines dispersed it all. However, something remained to me of this great inner contentment, a feeling of absolute security.

Chekhov's play made me feel like going home to write. The author's beautiful expression, both sad and tranquil, shows in the matchless simplicity of the dialogue. Everything comes from the heart, from all that is common to mankind. What is human, all that is human in us, at the bottom of that heart of ours that we know so badly. Each is, in himself, the whole of humanity.

MAY 22. At the University of Virginia. I am writing this in the old library, where I like to think that Poe sometimes came to read and dream. Fifteen years ago, I worked at this very table. I tried to forget Paris and thought of it without cease, instead of profiting from all the happiness that was being offered me. I was in love and unsociable and made myself wretched to my heart's content. Is anyone ever stupider than at that age? I did nothing to discourage my own sadness but cherished it instead; it afterwards developed to an extraordinary degree, threatened to take possession of my whole life; I got rid of it by introducing it into my books.

Visited the new buildings, none of which are fine. The old University is intact, but while it used to be surrounded by woods, meadows, and ponds, as in Mr. Jefferson's time, it now suffocates within a belt of big, commonplace houses. Useless to tell me that the buildings were very expensive, that doesn't give them any more merit in my eyes. No, what happens to cities and universi-

ties is what happens to men: wealth kills something in them that
can never again be found or replaced. Now that the University
has become one of the big American universities, with a gym-
nasium the size of a railroad station, a dormitory as big as a bar-
racks, etc., it attracts an increasing number of Northern boys, and
I find no fault in this, but note that it is hardly any longer a Southern university. Its professors come from all over the country. . . .

MAY 26. Leaving the University, we passed through the finest
valleys in the world and I would have liked to linger there, but
time is short. Time is always short, from birth to death. Why?
Because we don't know how to stop. I scarcely had time to see
the Ragged Mountains again from a distance, the mountains which
are the scene of one of Poe's tales. It was, I think, during an
excursion in these mountains that he predicted to a few of his
companions that there would be a war between the North and
South.

The day before we left, around ten o'clock at night, in wonderful moonlight, I sat with Jim under the big trees that grow in
front of the library and, for a few minutes, I felt the sweetness
of living. Memories were perhaps a help, for I don't know what
alchemy changes yesterday's sadness into a feeling of happiness,
although it is a quiet happiness, a happiness of shades. I wondered
if there existed anywhere else in the world a landscape dearer to
me than the long stretch of lawn bordered by white columns and
black trees. Above whispered the breeze as it stirred the leaves
and, higher still, the great stream of stars.

> At midnight, in the month of June,
> I stand beneath the mystic moon . . .

I am sure that Poe thought of the place where I was sitting
when he wrote those lines. And yet, this wonderful night, these
trees, these white columns were to me the setting of a nightmare,
the nightmare of youth. In this very spot, the absurd and degrad-
ing thought of suicide crossed my mind. What a child I was!

JUNE 9. NAG'S HEAD, NORTH CAROLINA. Pleasure kills something
in us. I have thought this for several years and for several years I
have had moments of rebellion against myself, but cannot make
up my mind to talk to anyone about it.

. . . Last night, at supper, I suddenly experienced that strange happiness that I cannot define. Through the windowpanes, I could see the pale yellow sand, the turquoise-blue ocean, when something deep inside me told me to go to the beach at nightfall. My heart beat very fast and I could scarcely conceal my emotion. I returned to my room and waited until it grew dark. The sky was torn by long flashes of lightning racing from one end of it to the other. I took advantage of the fact that no one noticed me and went barefoot to the beach. The raging waves roared like a cannonade. Here and there in the darkness shone rotting fragments thrown back by the ocean, dead or phosphorescent fish, and I recognized the carcass of a shark that I had looked at that afternoon. I listened to the great call that came from the open sea and stayed there some time, my heart full of love, with a feeling of deep security. . . . But why talk of what cannot be expressed?

JUNE 24. I shall end by being completely detached from this diary, because I cannot succeed in putting in it what really counts in my eyes. Very few of my inner difficulties show in these pages; I can see very little in them of the constant debate that goes on between what is real (and wishes to rule me) and what is illusive (and fascinates me). In this world, I am like a hypnotized man attempting to return to wakefulness and to full consciousness. I have given in to the glamour of a pure and simple mirage; at present, it is difficult, it is painful for me to wake up.

JUNE 26. I read some letters from General Lee recently. In several of them, he mentions the old house I described in *Avarice House*. The house was really called Kinloch and belonged to my uncle Loughborough Turner. I spent a few days there around Christmas, in 1919. We used to get up very early when it was still night. In the big, dark dining room, my uncle read or recited long prayers, then we threw ourselves on the good, indigestible things that are served for breakfast in America: bread so hot that it burned your fingers, thick pancakes swimming in butter. You could see the bluish hills through the windows. But I have said all that in my book. How could I give that lovely house to a family of misers? I didn't know where to stick my characters, and then, I was tempted by the setting.

JULY 14. IN LONDON. 73 EGERTON GARDENS. Monday afternoon, just after leaving Le Havre, I was lying in my cabin, a little depressed, a little weary of not being quite well again, when suddenly in the heart of silence—for the sea's even murmur was like a silence that one might have heard, a scanned silence—I distinguished a very singular noise, which was like the very distant cries of a great multitude. Then I seemed to hear singing, thousands of voices singing in harmony, but singing one note only, always the same one, and there was an astonishing variety in this chant and such that words cannot describe it. At the same instant I felt carried away by immense joy, I had the impression that the whole of the universe was bathed in an element that I can only call happiness, and in this happiness everything was annihilated. For three or four minutes, I listened to this hymn of glory and suddenly it ended, but a very vivid memory of it remained in me. I have had experiences of this kind several times in my life. I don't know what to ascribe them to.

JULY 19. Spent the day with Gide, who is in London for a short visit. All three of us—Robert, Gide, and I—lunched at Kettner's. I was afraid that the place would not suit Gide, but he seemed to like it and admired the Caucasian scabiosas that graced our table. He is in very high spirits, which does not prevent him from being extremely pessimistic regarding Europe's future. "Too many reefs ahead," murmurs Gide, "too many reefs to avoid a shipwreck." He asks Robert a question which I try not to hear, but how could I manage not to? "What branch of the army do you belong to?" Then I hear Robert talk of artillery. "Anyway," says Gide, "a declaration of war would at once be followed by a revolution." An opinion that Robert does not share. Gide talks bitterly about the Communist party and the attacks aimed at him since the publication of his last book (*Retouches à mon retour d'U.R.S.S.*). . . . Robert leaves us after lunch. Gide and I go to Brompton Road on top of a bus. In the red and blue drawing room (where I recently resumed writing), I don't know how it came about, but we talk about the Bible and Gide tells me that he used to read it so much that it *bewitched* him. As I was remarking how sad certain of St. Paul's sayings made me feel, Gide quotes Abbé Mugnier's reply when he confessed how little he cared for the great apostle. Abbé Mugnier had looked at him for a moment with a smile and then said: "St. Paul is the backbone of the fish." Gide finds this answer admirable. "Don't smile," he says, "for it is indeed the backbone that gives the fish its structure, the ἰχθύς, it is the spine of Chris-

tianity." He then reminds me that St. Paul's epistles were of an
earlier date than the Gospels and I am very much struck by his
remark.

A little later, as we had gone back to talking about Christianity,
he tells me that, for his part, the expression to *seek God* seemed
too vague and did not correspond to anything much in his mind.
And he added, lowering his voice a little: "I feel far closer to
Christ than to God . . ." We parted shortly after this.

JULY 26. PARIS.   I remember an afternoon I spent in Brussels last
April. I was sitting by an open window on the top floor of a tall
house and looked at Sainte-Gudule as it rested over the roofs like
a great, dark bird; behind it, a gray-blue sky filled by the song of
a single lark. A view of such rare beauty, a beauty that went to
the heart, that I left it regretfully, like something that I would
never see again. We had scarcely gone down the stairs when the
sky turned cloudy. I will probably see Sainte-Gudule again, but
it will be another church. "One never dips twice in the same
river." I know that only too well. Only the Eternal really exists.

The Eternal is the most beautiful name that has been given to
God. You can think it over until you lose all feeling of the exterior world, and I think that, in a certain manner, it is in itself
a way that leads to God. If we seek what is eternal in the sensuous
world, all the manifestations of matter vanish from our sight, what
is most solid together with what is most ancient, until we reach
the limits of what is imaginable in all possible spheres. When I
was still a child, I used to think over occasionally the term *for ever
and ever* that Protestants add at the end of the *Pater,* and the
words finally gave me a sort of mental dizziness, as though by
continuing in that direction you would reach something inexpressible, an immense void into which you fell.

JULY 27.   Every time I open the Bible, I find an allusion to my
life, to my problems, to the particular form that moral weakness
assumes in me. That is why I consider the book a magical book.
For what does the second chapter in Jeremiah talk about? About
the reader, about no matter what reader who, having opened the
book at that passage, reads what I am reading about the wild ass
which is never sated, about Israel who prostitutes herself to the
baalim, just as each of us runs after pagan gods, that is, after all
the world's illusions, seeking our joy in what passes away, whereas

no joy is true or permanent that is not supernatural. Too many instances of this could be quoted.

Around my twentieth year, I wrote a page about reading the Bible. The page is lost, but I remember trying to point out, with the feeble means at my disposal, that the Jewish people was each one of us and that, in the great tragedy enacted between the Eternal and His people, the role of conscience is held by Moses and by all the prophets who came after him. And so, when the Israelites want to stone Moses, this is an image of human nature in rebellion against grace. The same is true when Jeremiah is persecuted by people at court who force him to go down into a well. . . .

JULY 29.   If one wished to be converted, churches should not be resorted to for that purpose, but places that are so-called haunts of pleasure. I scarcely know any but those in Paris: they are the saddest thing in the world, I think, and the ugliest.

OCTOBER 28.   A little while ago, I was listening to an air from Handel's *Hercules,* Iola's air, I think. The beauty of the accompaniment is so grave and so profound that I was suddenly startled, as though I had seen a ghost. "The tread of gentle night" coming toward us, walking down some mysterious staircase . . . step by step, the ear follows it in rapture. I wonder if music is not the easiest means of bringing us into contact with ourselves, with that secret part of us, hidden from us by the world—with God, perhaps.

NOVEMBER 8.   If we only knew that the whole of Heaven is contained within our breast, that the Eternal rests in us, that the voice of the universe speaks to us at all times, in the whispering of the rain, in the song of a bird, in a few lines sketched on a square of paper by an artist, in a prelude by Bach . . . Only the deaf and blind go through life without being overpowered by beauty ceaselessly renewed.

NOVEMBER 14.   In Achim Arnim's *Die Majoratserben,* I copied this sentence: "Each man begins the history of the world all over again, each man ends it." I wandered through the sentence as though it had been a great, shady avenue that led straight out of this life.

* * *

NOVEMBER 15. "Lamia." When I read Keats, I feel like a bear in a stream of honey, for everything there is delicious. I think that Keats, more than any other poet, has the extremely rare gift of conjuring up in a very precise fashion what he barely describes. The whole of the sensuous world seems contained in his verse, but, by looking a little closer in the hope of analyzing this magic, what do we find? A bare shoulder here, a lock of golden hair there, a narcissus . . .

DECEMBER 8. It is hard to work one's way to the top of the spiral that makes us pass so often through the same places. Yet it leads to death and illumination. Even in the darkest hours, when all hope of conquering oneself seems unreasonable, one should remember that above, very far away, shines eternal light. No matter what we do, we are going, sometimes in spite of ourselves, toward a happiness of which our mind can form no idea. What good is it to regret the shadows of this earth? We must think of death with hope and firmness, of the great, shining country that lies beyond the black gate.

1938

FEBRUARY. I think there is in each of us, not only the two men spoken of by St. Paul, but a good dozen persons who rarely agree among themselves and are almost always in contradiction. One of these persons is an eccentric—no, let us speak plainly—one of these persons is a lunatic. All of them hold forth in turn, and the lunatic also puts in a word. His presence is tolerated by his companions, whom he makes uneasy; he enjoys great authority and, in the case of many writers, he shows talent, I might even say that he is their talent.

MARCH 12. Since yesterday, Austria has fallen under German rule. It is the end, in sorrow and in shame, of Europe as we knew and loved it. The German armies entered Austria without firing a shot. Hitler was not put to the expense of a single shell. Neither England, nor France, nor Italy so much as budged. At the present time, it does not appear that a single man in the world dares say no to Hitler. Paris is dumfounded by the news. Each of us can share the general humiliation. Some people are afraid that Germany, intoxicated by her easy victory, will now turn her attention to Czechoslovakia. What would happen then? In spite of everything, no one wants to believe in a war.

MARCH 19. Saw Gide this morning. He looks very badly and the lower part of his face is now that of an old man, but his expression remains youthful. He tells me that he has never felt more alert, intellectually. He had nephritis in Africa, which obliged him to return to Europe. I made him read the parts of my diary that concerned him. He says he is glad that I mentioned his speech at the Grand Lodge of France and how much it disgusted him, talks of a novel that he began with a sort of enthusiasm and of an anthology of French verse he is preparing. It will have twelve hundred pages. He will give "nothing that is not exquisite." He scarcely mentions the European situation except to say that the annexation of Austria is the first chapter only and that it is absurd to talk about this country's rape when it gave itself joyfully to Germany.

MARCH 24. Read Jeremiah in Hebrew. How can I reconcile reading this book with my daily life? Here, in this world, no problem is given a solution. Everything will have to be settled elsewhere.

APRIL 13. Went to Gide's day before yesterday to give him some more of my diary to read, the parts where he is mentioned. He declares himself delighted. "If the whole book is like that!" he cries. Apropos of Victor Hugo, he tells me the story of the Guernsey hairdresser who stretched a sheet under the poet's arm-chair, cut his hair, and gathered together the locks to make them into a parcel which Hugo took away with him. In Hugo's house, says Gide, was a closet filled with packets of hair and of nail parings. Fetishism, thinks Gide, adding that as hair and fingernails play an important part in magic, the poet no doubt wanted to ward off any danger coming from that quarter. To my surprise, Gide seems to find this rather reasonable. We lunch at Michaud's, rue Jacob, where Robert is waiting for us, and Gide talks about Spain. He believes that once the Civil War is over, there may be a reconciliation between the governmental party and the rebels at the expense of the foreign volunteers, who will be accused of all the ills the country suffers from, and that there will be a crusade to chase out of the country Russians and Italians alike. He gives us an account of a meeting between the Pope and Cardinal Verdier (whom he calls Cardinal Mercier, for his memory fails him at times). Pius XI, it seems, regretted not having taken the hand held out to him by the Communists. "We have been lacking in love," he is supposed to have said as he burst out sobbing. "Ah, Christ would have taken the hand that was offered Him! He would not have spurned it!" At this, it seems, the Cardinal buried his face in his hands. Gide relates this scene with an emotion that makes him forget he is in a restaurant full of people, and he repeats over and over again the sentence about Christ in a manner that did not fail to touch me, and touch me deeply. Regarding the terrible difficulties with which present-day France is struggling, he says: "The men the country needs, well, those men lie in churchyards under wooden crosses." I ask him if this is not true of the whole of Europe. "No," he replies, "Germany knew how to preserve her elite during the last war, whereas France, with her extravagant generosity, gave everything she had, for the sake of the gesture. . . . And so did England. I remember Edmund Gosse speaking to me of England's youth, mowed down by the war: 'All our gallant youth . . .' " He looks old today. His face has taken a grayish tinge, his shoulders are bent, but in moments of emotion, such as he had a little while ago, a sort of flame returns to quicken his body and his features. As we were talking of I forget what passage in my diary, Gide says that I gave a very good sketch of himself and of me. As I hand him a page about Roger Martin du Gard to read, I tell him that I expect to suppress it. "Why?" asks Gide after reading it. "Martin du Gard knows perfectly well that I don't like his play." And the same held good for what he said about Claudel. He no longer withdraws. He does not refuse to see in print what he said in private. How many of us would do the same?

APRIL 23. Gide's wife died, I think, on Easter day.

MAY 4. Lunched with Gide day before yesterday. He is in mourning from his tie to his spats, for he wears spats. In a slightly lower voice than usual, he says a few words about his wife's death, a death that must have been a rather peaceful one. At Ferrari's, where we lunch, he talks on all sorts of subjects. He asks me whether I would write a preface to the French edition of the Bible that Schiffrin wants to publish, but I cannot consent to it. It would give a wrong impression of me, would make people think that I am taking a pious turn. Simply, I would feel ashamed. There are too many contradictions in my life and I don't want to be taken for what I am not. Gide presses me a little to accept, but indeed I cannot.

JUNE 7. That deep longing for happiness, that longing I have in me, as we all have, so much so, for instance, that I can't listen without melancholy to a bird singing on a too fine summer day in Paris, where does it come from? It is not merely the longing to possess everything, formerly so strong in me; it is a painful and sometimes pleasant nostalgic longing for a happiness too far away in time for our brief memory to retrace it, something like a recollection of the Garden of Éden, but a memory adapted to our weakness. Too much joy would kill us.

JUNE 10. Dined yesterday at Gide's. He had said to me beforehand: "Mme Van Rysselberghe will be there, and Catherine." "And who is Catherine?" I asked. Gide blushed a little (and this is the very first time I had ever seen him blush) and said: "Why, she's my daughter. I called her Catherine in memory of *Wuthering Heights,* but she doesn't like her name." He accompanies this with a pleasant little laugh. At dinner, Mme Van Rysselberghe talks about a writer and the articles he recently published against the Jews, and it seems that this same author is a trifle ashamed of his own anti-Semitism. Gide says that he has a regard for him without thinking him very intelligent. "Yet," replies Mme Van Rysselberghe, "you have to be intelligent to write as he does, with such a vocabulary. . . ." "Unquestionably," Gide answers at once. "You're right." How often have I seen him give way in matters of small importance, although he sticks to his opinion when the subject is worth while! Gide's daughter looks at us in silence. The upper part of her face is like Gide, but not the lower one. Her very black, very shining eyes are her father's, without, however, that attentive, ironical something that escapes words. She wears her hair in a net and hardly opens her lips.

✻ ✻ ✻

JUNE 20.   I try to read a page of the Bible in Hebrew every day. The Books of Samuel, which I am studying at present, scarcely offer any difficulties, but the Book of Job, which I read alternately every other day, is infinitely harder. I am speaking only of the style, of course, the obscurities of the poem itself being proverbial. I will return later to the enormous divergences I have found in the translations that have been made of it, divergences that I think due to the fact that the text suffered greatly before coming down to us. Generations of copyists have multiplied the misreadings of it. The letters that correspond to *D* and to *R* are rather easily mistaken one for the other unless perfectly shaped; the same holds good for *B* and *C*. The *calamus scribae velociter scribentis* of Psalm 35 is responsible for many an error. Doubtless, the context is there to testify, but no sooner is it a question of reestablishing the primitive text than modern translators no longer agree. This is where tradition is the greatest help. But which tradition?

JUNE 23.   I don't think anyone suspects what forms the substance of my sadness. How can I express it? It is impossible to say and would seem ridiculous, but I'm going to say it just the same. I wanted to be a saint. That is all. I can add nothing to this. A great part of my life does not resemble me. I am very keenly aware of constantly passing by the man that I wanted to be, and in a certain way he exists, he is there, and he is sad, and his sadness is mine.

JUNE 26.   Went to see Gide yesterday morning. He wanted me to meet a certain Mr. Cook, a colored professor who teaches at the University of Georgia. A man of about thirty, with a pale yellow skin and short beaky nose; his long feet are shod in white shoes; he turns the tips out widely, as do all the Jews I have known. For Mr. Cook is a quarter Jewish, as he himself informs us. He speaks French admirably, with an accuracy and animation that are far more those of a Jew than of a colored man. I think he gave us both an excellent impression of good will and intelligence. Once he has gone, I talk to Gide about the Negro question. I tell him that, with time, white America will have to absorb this black America whose existence is such a painful problem. . . . "But the Jews," says Gide, "America will never absorb the Jews! The Jews will have to absorb America. Yes, they will. And this will happen everywhere. In 1800, there was one Jew for every six thousand inhabitants in New York. Around 1890, there was one in every six hundred. Now, there is one in every sixty!" A little later, he tells me that he doesn't in the least believe in the superiority of a colored school child over a white school child, in the colonies. The colored child has a better memory, that is all. . . .

We leave the house together. In the street, I tell him that the movement for the abolition of slavery had originated in our Southern states and that, long before the Civil War. To which Gide replies that on his return from Africa, he had been tempted to write an ironical defense of slavery (what a subject for Swift)! He would have stressed the fact that a slaveowner took great care of what had cost him so much money, whereas a boss who directs free workers is far less concerned about their health. He knows that a sick or dead colored man can be replaced at a moment's notice, and cheaply. . . . We go to lunch boulevard Saint-Germain, at a small restaurant near the Légion d'Honneur, and have a rambling, desultory conversation.

I can't remember in what connection I ask Gide if he knows Asia Minor, and he tells me of a disappointing and rather dull trip he made there. "But the landscapes?" (I had in mind certain pages by Renan.) "Oh," says Gide, "a landscape is always fine. Those where there isn't anything to admire are very few. . . ."

After lunch, we walk toward the Champs Élysées. On the way, I ask Gide how his Anthology is getting on. He is reading over the seventeenth-century poets. "I hope you will include one at least of Racine's spiritual hymns," I say. And off we go, reciting verse as we cross the place de la Concorde under a broiling sun.

> *"De la Sagesse immortelle*
> *La voix tonne et nous instruit: . . ."*

"Ah! yes," says Gide and continues my quotation:

> *"Enfants des hommes, dit-elle,*
> *De vos soins quel est le fruit?"*

He considers these lines very superior to the choruses in *Esther* that are so much admired. For my part, I am weak enough to be fond of these choruses, but what is stiff and conventional in the age of Louis XIV is far from daunting me—on the contrary . . .

JUNE 30. We should make a note of the books we read. . . . No matter how much a writer thinks that he is not directly influenced by what he reads, there exists nevertheless a secret but unquestionable connection between the author's works and the books on which he feeds (as there is between our body and what we eat). It may be that such or such a page of a novel has been written in unconscious protest against a chapter read the day before, and this page can change the course of the whole book. We know what Poe read at the University by the librarians' slips.

JULY 2. Where the modern stage is concerned, I think Gide is more lenient than I am, or perhaps he isn't stirred by the wild hopes that seize me when I see the curtain part; consequently, he is less often disappointed. . . . Yesterday evening, we went to see *French without Tears*, or rather the French adaptation of the play, of which I believe it best to say nothing. Gide tells me the story of his gardener (at Cuverville) who threatened to leave him if X, the under-gardener, did not go. After a lengthy investigation, Gide finally learns that the under-gardener casts spells and that the cow had miscarried the very evening when he arrived at Cuverville. "What a subject for a novel!" cries Gide. "*The Outlaw* . . . Imagine the man's life, harried from one country to another because he has the evil eye. You could make something of it, Green. . . . Do you dislike being given the subject of a novel? Yet Pushkin gave Gogol the subject of *Dead Souls*. . . ."

After the play, we went off to drink beer. Gide talks about his diary, which, he says, has all but turned into "a graveyard for stillborn articles." He continues: "It gives a completely false idea of me, for I hardly ever keep it except in moments of discouragement. So I give the impression of being sad, and this is not so. I am neither sad nor unhappy." He tells me that the publication of my diary will have an important effect on me, but does not make himself more explicit. . . .

JULY 15. . . . We believe that we increase our happiness by multiplying our wealth, whereas we are also multiplying sources of suffering. By wealth I don't mean money only, but what money allows us to obtain and, generally speaking, what Satan offered Christ. But to leave this world for a life of contemplation means creating a new and as powerful attachment, an attachment to spiritual things. What then is self-detachment? Once, Maritain quoted to me what a mother superior of a convent said about a

nun who was too much attached to a strict observance of the
Rule: "She will remain a long time in Purgatory on account of
her virtues. . . ."

JULY 17.   Just had a telephone call from Gide, who wants me to
meet one of his friends. By some freak of fancy, he speaks English to me, as he does sometimes: "You will find him very interesting," he says, "yes, really. . . ." How I like hearing him speak
English! He is another Gide, a little uncertain of what he is about
to say, a little bashful; he must have been like that at twenty.
Noticing that my unsociability makes me hold back, he then says
in French, turning into the Gide I know: "Oh! I don't want to
bore you!"

JULY 18.   Lunched with Gide. He talks about Poe, says that in
England the poet's reputation is considered greatly overrated, that
he is a writer whose imagination is often "coarse and facile." I
find the opinion absurd and say so. "And yet," says Robert, "what
an influence he has had in France in molding certain poets!" An
indirect influence over Valéry, through Mallarmé. "Oh," says
Gide, "in the eyes of many Frenchmen, Valéry does not pass for
being a real poet . . ." And, guessing our thoughts, he adds:
". . . just as many people refuse to see a painter in Leonardo da
Vinci." W. F.'s son is also lunching with us. He is a silent, ob-
serving boy. After lunch, Gide, feeling tired, goes into the next
room to rest. Robert leaves, I remain alone with F., and we have
a little talk. He is a Communist, like his Papa. Seems deeply scandalized that I should think it doubtful that the governmental party
will win in Spain. "My father went over there. He saw the soldiers.
Their morale is excellent." He tells me that there will soon be a
"great uprising in Paris." "Who gave you this information?" "A
member of Parliament." I can't help thinking that in boys of his
age politics takes the place held by religion in many of the youths
of my generation.
   During lunch, Gide remarked that the past played quite a big
part in my diary. "In my case," he says, "when I was young, I
refused all links with the past, from self-esteem. I sold my father's
house for that reason. But since, with age, I have come to care
more for the past."

JULY 27.   . . . At Tournai, much admired the cathedral, but the inside, I think, shows too sharp a cleavage between the Romanesque and the Gothic, not to be detrimental to the latter which is frailer and less solid than the Romanesque. The ogival style seems stricken at birth by some mysterious disease. It visibly attempts to *escape*, like some neurotics. That way of sending vaultings higher and higher, in defiance of all reason (see Beauvais), is an act of deep nervous unbalance. In this sort of rush toward the sky lies a contempt for nature, a morbid defiance that the architect of the Parthenon would not have understood.

AUGUST 11. BÅSTAD, SWEDEN. We watch an insect, but does it see us? It is hardly conscious of a shadow in the light above it. We are perhaps unconsciously observed in the same manner by beings of incommensurate size. . . . Maybe there exists a spirit, an angel, a *power*, as the Greek Gospel says, who thinks, as it sees one of us: "This unfortunate insect has tried ten times, a hundred times, to climb that glass pane to find an outlet to the sun and the fresh air. It distinctly sees the sky through this transparent thickness that exists as though it were not, and yet keeps it prisoner, and it can't understand what prevents it from flying into space. Come, we'll open the window for it!"

For the last few years, the problem of the window that won't open has counted more and more in my life. It is, generally speaking, the problem of every life. To escape . . .

Last night, I walked along a road. Looking at the starry sky, I felt such deep joy that all the words I could use would express it badly. I paused, a prey to a mysterious happiness of which nothing can be said. It seemed to me that, very gently, the window opened a little. That is the way it must be at the last, when the body ceases to suffer and the soul stands on the threshold of night.

Night, night, I have always felt that night was favorable to me. For me, it indicates the vanishing of the world of appearances, the world lit up by the sun with its colors and its constant sound of words; in the material field of life it accomplishes what we should be able to accomplish in the spiritual field, and what it offers our eyes of flesh irresistibly attracts the inner eye. Before such a sight, all that has to do with our everyday life becomes insignificant. Our individual fate and the fate of nations are reduced to their true proportions, that is, to nothing.

SEPTEMBER 3. STOCKHOLM. At the Museum of Prehistoric Antiquities. All these vestiges of such a distant age made a curious impression on me, the impression that the whole of humanity marched through me, as though on a highway. It is all of me and I am all of it. I was born on the day when it raised its eyes to the clouds for the first time, I will be part of it to the end, if there is an end. I cannot die, its heart is mine, and this heart is only beginning to beat. What I call living is nothing else but the consciousness that humanity has of itself. I have felt this to such a keen degree that our fear of dying seemed to me suddenly one of the most tragic misunderstandings we have ever suffered from; it doubtless arises from that disastrous confusing of our bodies with ourselves. But how is it possible to talk about this? Such things appear natural to people who know what I mean, because they have *experienced* them. The others would take me for a madman. The characteristics of the thoughts that occur to me, as they will gradually occur to everyone (for nothing separates us from the other, just as nothing separates drops of water in the ocean), the characteristics of these thoughts are that their value is practically nil as long as they remain in the intellectual field; we will have to live them.

SEPTEMBER 12. COPENHAGEN. We are leaving Denmark by the next boat. Indescribable anguish broods over the world. I have my full share of this anguish, but in order to keep up my courage, I have taken my novel out of my suitcase and have set to work again. This does me more good than anything else. Have noticed that our agitation almost always lies on the surface. Deep inside us is a region of quiet, of happiness for whoever wishes it, particularly under such circumstances as these. "The kingdom of God is within you." If we believed this, we would go mad with joy, but our skepticism preserves us from this inconvenience.

SEPTEMBER 29. PARIS. I cannot bring myself to give a detailed account of so many hours of anguish. The most difficult day was the twenty-fourth. Returned on the twenty-fifth to Paris, where everything is in complete disorder. Everywhere, nothing is talked about but a mobilization, an ultimatum. On the 27th, news came that Hitler's ultimatum to Prague expired that afternoon at three. The war then appeared certain, but hopes revived this morning. Hitler, Mussolini, Chamberlain, and Daladier are to meet at Munich.

* * *

NOVEMBER 6. Last night, a familiar nightmare roused me from sleep, the nightmare of being pursued. I was in a rocky landscape. How well I recognized all those steep slopes, those almost vertical paths winding around the gigantic stones! I leap from rock to rock to finally drop shrieking at my enemy's feet. As I woke, it occurred to me that this enemy was my own self and that what my adversary pursued and wished to subdue was my body.

We must go beyond our conception of God, for God is eternally beyond all things.

On opening a window this morning, I breathed the odor of dead leaves brought by the wind. I can't express the happiness that these autumn days give me. It seems as though they brought me news of *elsewhere*, and then I immediately begin thinking that nothing that can happen to us on this earth is of much importance, since the mere idea of what is waiting for us later is enough, even at present, to overwhelm us with joy. "Eye hath not seen, nor ear heard, neither have entered into the heart of man, the things which God hath prepared . . ."

NOVEMBER 15. The other night, in one of the strangest dreams I ever had, I saw a lovely bird of paradise flying about my room and then alighting to walk slowly to the door leading into the passage. Its wings and tail were like sheaves of a cerulean blue. Someone above me said: "This is a bad omen, an omen of death." Then a long silence and another voice said, at a far greater distance: "Yes, an omen. The invisible world has parted open like a big curtain to send this magnificent bird into the lower world. How men fear death! The most comforting of omens terrify them and the messenger bird of joy brings sadness to their ignorant hearts." These words were not spoken; it was more like an exchange of thoughts; silence answered silence.

NOVEMBER 20. This morning I thought: A child in its mother's womb is snug and warm and most likely happy. It believes this small, warm space to be its universe, where it lacks nothing. What suspicion can it have of the world we know? None. Granting that one might enter into communication with an unborn child, what notion could be given it of a book, a house? None whatever. Our situation is the same in regard to the world beyond us, which stretches around us and which as a rule we reach only through death. In reality, we too live in a dark cavity which we like and will only be born screaming when we die. Then we will discover a universe of inexpressible loveliness and will walk freely among the stars.

DECEMBER 13. I saw Gide the other day and for the first time felt a kind of embarrassment in alluding to certain changes that have taken place in my life. I realized that the things I told him were said instead of those I wished to tell him and could not. This pained me. If he had been indifferent to me, I wouldn't have cared in the least.

DECEMBER 15. We were with the Suarèses the other evening and asked to see the cook's blackbird; someone went to fetch the cage and put it in the middle of the drawing room. The bird, disgruntled by being taken out of the kitchen where it was asleep, immediately ruffled its feathers and, when I went nearer to admire it, let out such a furious whistling that we were deafened. Not at all scared to see eight people around it. It leaves its cage in the daytime and wanders about the flat; it has learned the "Marseillaise," but that is a treat reserved to intimates. I would have liked to take it away with me. If the lease allowed it, I would fill our few rooms with animals. I would have several crows, blackbirds, and parrots; cats and dogs too, needless to say; no monkeys with their disquieting faces, but squirrels all free to come and go at will; the windows would stay open. Vasari tells us that certain painters of his times, Sodoma in particular, surrounded themselves with their favorite animals, but we have become so civilized that this is no longer possible.

1939

JANUARY 25. I showed Gide the parts of my diary that concerned him. When he read the account of our day in London, he nodded, saying: "Yes, that day, I felt that we might have talked to each other . . ." To get beyond reticences, what we lacked was not being together long enough. As regards myself, I can say that my talks with Gide are like the snatches of a long conversation that never took place. It is not from lack of confidence on his part or mine, but I require a lot of silence to be able to speak, and I think we are alike on that point. . . . On going home, I reread a part of *Si le grain ne meurt* with such pleasure that I felt like writing to the author as though he had just sent me the book. But I did not do so. I have always been awkward in showing affection.

It was at his house that I saw Gide. He wanted me to go to Egypt with him, but I refused. We talked over our day in London. He said to me suddenly: "You are fond of the mystics. Read Fénelon. Fénelon's letters." As we were about to part, I had a feeling of inexplicable sadness and I believe he had too. Something of it showed in his face and, I believe, in mine.

JANUARY 30. Came across some notes I had taken one day in May, 1938, after a visit from Gide. We were in my study, where I had collected a few books; a log fire brightened the room. I don't remember why we began talking of Flaubert's correspondence and I asked Gide if he recollected the admirable letter about Le Poittevin's death (and Le Poittevin's heart-rending cry as he lay dying: "Close the windows! It is all too beautiful!"). "No," said Gide, "I don't remember the letter well. It has been years since I read the correspondence." After hesitating, he asked: "Isn't the letter you mention the one where Flaubert says that as he watched over his dying friend, he read Kreutzer's *General History of Religions*?"

FEBRUARY 1. I have never had much faith in theories on heredity; their ingeniousness makes me skeptical. And yet, how much there would be to say about my ancestry. . . . I have been molded, at least apparently, by my adopted country, but there is something irreducible in me that comes from elsewhere. In putting away some papers, I found a sheet where I had noted, at a time when the person I am was still of interest to me, how much Irish, Scotch, and English blood ran in my veins and in what proportions. What is impulsive, dreamy, and also carnal in me, I owe to Ireland; to Ireland, too, the fact that I succeed one day and fail the next, everything that urges me to write my books, in a word, what is best and worst in me. I recognize the Scotch share in the religious crises—the most recent of which have not been the least painful—in a deep, unvarying love of the Scriptures, in a long perseverance that has almost always had the better of my innate laziness. From England . . . but this game bores me because of its artificial character.

FEBRUARY 5. I believe that one of the vainest worries for an author who publishes his diary is that of absolute coherence. For a reason difficult to explain, he likes to feel bound to his past, to establish a sort of resemblance between the characters he has successively *gone through* since birth. He tries to blend with them, he imagines that they speak for him, he scruples to disown what they have said for fear of being accused of vacillation. And thus in the heart of his being, slowly dies all notion of moral freedom, all aspiration to living, for the characters we were are now no more than ghosts, and a solidarity with the past is a solidarity with death.

In reading over this diary, I have often been surprised to see what I have put in it. How many gestures I will never make again! How many apparently definitive opinions I am now ready to find erroneous! But I appeal to tomorrow against yesterday, I appeal to the man I will be someday, I appeal to the man I am.

I have varied, I will vary again. At all times, I feel in me a deep aptitude for changing that mingles with the instinct of living. To remain where they are is an unnecessary martyrdom for many people. I am one of these, with all my heart I want to go forward. . . .

Baudelaire deplored that, among the Rights of Man, that of contradicting oneself had been forgotten.

Nevertheless, I won't keep this diary any longer. No sooner do I feel that I am writing for the printer than I wonder whether I would have written thus and so and not otherwise, a little less guardedly, a little more humbly. I regret the former free-and-easiness, and Gide's remark sounds dismally in my ear: ". . . a graveyard of stillborn articles." And then too, can one continue keeping a diary when the figure one cuts in this world no longer interests one? One should have Pepys' admirable lack of self-consciousness to keep a diary worthy of the name, to believe more than I do in the reality of what surrounds us. How remote the years when I wrote at a stretch the material for three or four printed pages of this diary, never tiring of the pleasure of telling myself all about myself! But all that is over now. I was someone talking aloud in his loneliness, it is no longer possible to me to continue if I know I am being listened to.

* * *

FEBRUARY 8. If the mystics are the lords of the invisible world, spiritists are its burglars. The kingdom of Heaven can be taken by violence but not by picking its locks.

What a Gospel could be written by gathering together the words spoken by Christ to His saints! If it belonged to me to do this book, I would give a prominent place to the word received by St. Francis de Sales one day when he was tormented by the idea of predestination: "My name is not the one that damns. My name is Jesus."

And also this to St. Teresa of Ávila, who was grieved not to be allowed the right of reading the Scriptures in the vernacular: "I will give you a living book."

The Gospel is a book that will never close and that is written each day in the heart of contemplatives.

Satan's masterpiece is to make us, of ourselves, tug at the rope until it breaks. To accomplish this, he puts it into our heads to read an increasing number of serious books until they sicken us. In his hands, the writings of the greatest ascetics become instruments of despair. It is easy enough for him to delude us. Who would suspect him of slyly laying on our table such and such a volume of *The Ascent of Mount Carmel* or *Spiritual Life* by St. Vincent Ferrer? Of course there is a certain risk in such expectations, but the old enemy knows only too well that he has little to fear, and he likes to fight Heaven with its own weapons.

The parable of the talents. As a child, not knowing that a talent was a coin, I imagined that this parable applied to writers, to painters, to all those who had received a gift, and today I doubt whether I wasn't right. The saddest thing is that having received a talent from God, we thank Him by paying Him back in false money.

The parable of the wedding guests. I can't help finding it most comforting. Of course, there are those who were bidden to the feast and who will languish in outer darkness because of their "great refusal"; but there are also the tramps who were forcibly made to enter the banqueting hall. *Compelle intrare* . . . Humanity saved in spite of itself.

When I think of my far-distant years of religious fervor, of those spiritual longings that I never mentioned, which all but turned my life in quite a different direction from that it has taken, I am surprised that the pendulum, having swung so far one way, should not have swung farther to the other side. But I was preserved from atheism, just as I was spared from walking on all fours and eating grass. . . . The idea that God might not exist has never so much as grazed me.

MARCH 15. There comes a time in life when you can't listen to music any longer, particularly if you have known years of great happiness and that the future darkens gradually. The other day, I stopped my radio when it gave out the first notes of a Beethoven sonata for piano and violin. "To suffer in that manner," I thought, "is really too stupid." In the same way, I don't wish ever to hear *Don Juan* again, for it reminds me too precisely of the time when I listened to it in the charming Residenz Theater at Munich; or Schumann's *Faust*, or his Second Symphony, and certainly not a single note of Schubert's. There may come a day when I may recover all this once more, but at present, music can only embitter a sadness I am ashamed of.

Thus ends the eleventh notebook of my diary, interrupted when I saw that the great European upheaval was about to begin again and that happiness was no longer possible.

Undated Diary

UNDATED. Although I learned English as a child and have never ceased speaking it, I can't write in that tongue without feeling that I am trying to put on a garment that was not made for me; this garment irks me and I am conscious of not wearing it as well as I should. It is a uniform that is too tight for me. My dressing gown, my everyday costume, the one I feel free and happy in, is French.

Vice begins where beauty ends. If one analyzed the impression produced by a beautiful body, something approaching religious emotion would be found in it. The work of the Creator is so beautiful that the wish to turn it into an instrument of pleasure comes only after a confused feeling of adoration and wonder.

Music is blended with my whole life and to such an extent that it is difficult for me to imagine one without the other. I am not sure that this is entirely good, but it is too late to change anything

about it. With time, I have learned how to free myself from certain musical influences and above all no longer to consider music
as a refuge in trying moments; on the contrary, I turn away from
it in such moments and don't wish to listen to it now except in
quietude and, if possible, in happiness. To coddle one's melancholy by feeding it with all the sadness of Chopin's "Nocturnes"
—no.

The first concert I ever heard was given in the old Trocadéro,
toward the end of the First World War. The famous echo in this
disastrous auditorium first played hide-and-seek with Berlioz'
"Hungarian March." Then a lady was heard in an air by Handel,
and with relentless fidelity the walls returned the singer's har-
monious bleats. The program was varied and copious. After that
came something I have forgotten, and next came the intermission.
After that, in a deep silence, rose a profound, even murmur and
the flight of a dark bird over an abyss: the first measures of the
Ninth Symphony, which revealed a new world to me. Until then,
I had believed that all religious emotion necessarily belonged to
Catholicism, but the voice I heard in this supernatural music spoke
to me of an infinitely larger universe than I had suspected; I admitted with surprise that the sense of the divine did not belong
exclusively to the Church. Less ignorant, I would not have been
so much disturbed. It was not that the Church seemed to me less
true, but she became different in my eyes, and the change worried
me, for I did not know what would come of it. The following
days did not restore my peace. Something worked in me for a
long time and suddenly, in an obscure part of my mind, something
exploded. The earth that I had learned to despise seemed all the
more beautiful and attractive since I thought of withdrawing from
the world, but I dared not acknowledge to myself that I had been
mistaken and the sufferings I then endured were such that I have
never quite recovered from them. What appears to me stranger
than all the rest is that having heard the Ninth Symphony time
and time again since, I have never been able to recapture the
religious character that I had first lent it.

UNDATED. Lunched with Stephen Courtauld at his house in Port-
man Square, in London. The decoration of the rooms is limited
to fillets of gold along the doors and ceilings. One would search
vainly for a house more elegant and more simple in the exquisite
delicacy of its proportions. Manet's "Bar of the Folies-Bergères"

hung in the dining room and I could scarcely keep my eyes off it during the whole meal. What held me was not only the quality of this marvelous picture but also the enigma of the mirror in which a person is reflected and whose back we should see and that is not there. . . . In the drawing room, the "Theater Box" by Renoir and five magnificent Seurats. After looking at the pictures as long as I could, I wondered what this painting gave me, apart from an immediate and very keen pleasure. Has it been a help to me as a writer? There are no colors in my books: nothing there but black and white, effects of light and shade, but they are the books of a man who would like to know how to draw with vigor. My admiration always goes to painters whose pencil stroke shows the most energy.

UNDATED. The other day I was talking to Gide about my diary and he advised me once more to publish it. "You will easily find a publisher for it," he says (the publication would have been, of course, that of the unexpurgated text). "You need only have ten or twenty copies printed," he continues. "That would be enough to preserve it. Think of what happened to Byron's diary. I thought that his sister had destroyed it, but the one who burned it was his *publisher*." "I will make several copies of mine myself," I then say. "It would be surprising if one at least were not preserved." "No," replies Gide, "that's not enough of a security. You have a family." "My family would not touch it." He makes a gesture, as much as to say: "Ah! you never can tell!"

Continued reading Flaubert's letters. After his twenty-fourth year, they lose all naïveté and become splendid, often harrowing. The little taste he had for happiness, his dread of the future, take on a tragic and sometimes disconcerting expression. I cannot imagine anyone writing to pass the time away, *to make life go by.* . . .

UNDATED. There are days when I think that I would have liked to know how to talk, and when I say talk, I mean putting words together in such a way as to close my opponents' mouths or to make them open in amazement, in fact to shine, to convince. Instead of which I sometimes mumble in a humiliating fashion. In short, I lack presence of mind. The strange thing is that I express myself with a certain ease when dealing with an absent-minded person; I sink below mediocrity as soon as I feel I am being listened to. So, for many a year, I blushed to the roots of my hair each time I thought of the telephone call the Governor of Virginia honored me with. I can laugh at the whole thing now. The telephone line connecting Virginia to France was to be inaugurated at Richmond, and two weeks before this ceremony I had been advised that the Governor would speak to me on that occasion and that all I had to do was to be at home and wait. There was something paralyzing for me just to imagine that thousands of miles away, such an important person would pick up the receiver and listen to what I had to say, but that would only happen in a couple of weeks. . . . Needless to say, I felt flattered. Soon, only one week remained. Finally came the day itself, then the hour, and the telephone rang. My throat parched, I took off the receiver. I then heard a great noise of water that sounded like the sea, or rather, a stage imitation of it. I was told that this was London. The sound of water began again and, at last, in a Judgment Day silence, the Governor's voice rang out: "Mr. Green?" "At the telephone." "Mr. Green, this is the Governor of Virginia. I am speaking from the Capitol, in Richmond. Can you hear me?" "As though you were in the room. . . ." At that moment, the Governor mentioned, one by one, the people who were with him, to listen to this telephone call from France; there were—can I ever forget it?—the president of a railroad company, the president of one of the large Southern banks, the president of something else that I can't remember, and with each new president (whom I imagined in a white waistcoat, holding a big julep), it seemed as though a little more blood flowed back into my heart. I believe I have managed to forget the sentences that fell from my lips, and the least I can say about them is that they must not have been very interesting, but I do remember sleeping very badly that night, kept awake by an imaginary conversation with the Governor, a conversation in which I shone. . . .

UNDATED. To be able to write a book, I must have an object to look at, a picture to place before me which I could *refer to*. Thus, for *Avarice House* I had the photograph of a room, taken at Savannah, in an unknown house, around 1880; in the center of an unpretentious drawing room, one sees a round table covered by a cloth and on this table, a closed book; torn leather armchairs; on the mantelpiece, a barometer; and on either side of the door, great solemn curtains drawn aside to allow invisible persons to pass. I think that almost all my characters have come out of this

room. In writing *The Closed Garden* I had before me the photograph of a painting by Utrillo.

1940

SUNDAY, JULY 21. BALTIMORE. Between the last copybook of
this diary and the page I am now beginning, the events we all
know of have taken place. I was in America when the war broke
out. I returned to France and stayed there until after the armistice.
Then I left Europe. I have been here a week. I will be forty in a
little more than a month and find myself in more or less the same
circumstances as when I was twenty—minus my illusions and minus
my enthusiasm—that is, most uncertain of the future. I am a French
writer, but cannot live in France, for the time being at least. So
consequently I must henceforth write in English. I am not unknown in this country no doubt, but fully realize that almost
everything remains to be done, to be done all over again. The
idea is more of an incentive than a discouragement. The despoil-
ment I must undergo is not granted to everyone, and it is sometimes a great and fearsome favor to be torn away from one's
possessions.

A long effort of liberation has probably been spared me because I was incapable of making it. During the five or six years
preceding the war I eagerly probed into all the sayings of Christ
regarding poverty. I used then to think that one could remain
spiritually detached in the midst of great wealth, that everything
depended on the mental attitude adopted toward worldly goods,
that the rich could be poor in spirit, and the poor eaten up with
avarice. I also wondered if I would ever be able to rid myself of
the possessiveness I felt within me. To this an inner voice invariably answered: "Leave that to me." I thought of that voice
as I crossed the bridge at Irún which leads from France into Spain.
But, no sooner freed from everything that might weigh me down,
how will I avoid thinking once more about making the future
secure? One earns a few dollars, first one buys a few books, then
two or three bits of furniture, then several little things one
imagines one wants, and the love of worldly goods is renewed

within us. But I have experienced the divine moment when such a love seemed dead in my heart.

JULY 24. There are times when I think that hopes of spiritual freedom are the saddest delusion that can torture the human brain. For I see only too well that I am not one of those who are able to do a necessary violence to their feelings and wonder that others can make such an effort. All I can obtain from myself is not to give up the idea that, when all is said and done, spirit is bound to prevail, but I am afraid that in my case its prey will be no more than a corpse. Perhaps the important thing does not lie in conquering but in fighting on to the end. How sad to think of being one of those who have only had a glimpse of the truth.

I am writing this in a small drawing room with French windows opening on lawns shaded by willows, cypresses, and oaks, and terraces where the grass grows between purposely uneven stones. Not a sound reaches me, barring the thrush's rather melancholy cry; the leaves hang motionless in the scorching air; at my feet pants a big black poodle whose yellow eyes watch my every gesture. Here, in this keepsake setting, imagination refuses to form an idea of the threat that hangs so heavily over the world.

I sometimes wonder what has become of our flat in Paris, and in particular of my study where I spent so many peaceful years without the least intuition of what was going to happen. However, I do remember that one day, as I stood before my bookshelves, I imagined a German officer reading the titles of the volumes and snickering at the fine Hebrew Bible in two volumes which I so much regret having left behind. But I immediately dismissed this premonition—if it was one—from my mind. Last winter, on a very mild and sunny day, I sat in a corner of this study, close to my books, whose gildings shone softly in a ray of light, and felt happy to be there, in my native city, a volume of poems open by me. I asked for nothing more. I could hear the birds in the Champ-de-Mars, the children laughing as they played in front of the house. Had I remained a few weeks longer, I would have heard the enemy dictator holding forth fifty yards from the spot where I sat peacefully drinking coffee.

JULY 25. I am copying, translating as I go into English, the narrative of what I saw in June, 1940, but the work is painfully slow. The English tongue has never prompted me to desire the linear perfection of form that French gives me, and I have the feeling of writing English with a hand that is always afraid of making the sentence run crooked.

JULY 26. The gardens under our windows cannot be discovered at first sight, for they are hidden under canopies of foliage; a network of green paths or grassy flights of steps connect with no other plan but one due to an intelligent whim. On a beautiful morning last winter, in the midst of a setting where nature had been chastened and reduced to a human scale, the finest of the oaks suddenly crashed down on the well-kept lawns; the air was still and unthreatened by the slightest breeze. . . . Although rotten at the core, the tree continued to put forth sturdy leaves and its powerful branches seemed to defy time.

Dined with the Garretts, who have a wonderful estate a few minutes from here. The great stone house is overgrown with ivy, much like a piece of furniture concealed by its loose cover; below it, vast lawns bordered by trees, a lake with a mist arising from it. We had dinner facing a rather fine but overwooded Italian garden; a too luxuriant foliage blurs the design of the paths and here, as in the real South, the virgin forest always tends to resume its rights and turn garden architecture upside down: shaggy nature, itching to go wild, needs a continual haircut. Nothing particular was said at dinner, or afterwards—we are not in France—not a thing to record, just a sort of well-bred good-fellowship. Nothing spiteful either and consequently, nothing amusing. . . . From time to time, the shifting outlines of the trees were etched against the background of a mauve sky shot by flashes of heat lightning. As my neighbor at table talked about the Frick collection, I could not resist saying a few words about the Barna da Siena that hangs in this museum, about the little picture hidden away in a small room, showing Christ in a red robe, bearing His cross. I had a reproduction of it on the mantelpiece of my study in Paris. I liked the mild, very reproachful glance that Christ turned toward me and also thought I read great affection in His eyes. A visionary's Christ . . . After dinner, went to a pretty low-ceilinged room in the middle of which shone a long polished wood table. All the men sat before a glass of brandy, and I with them, very much out of my element and not at all in my place. A bank manager questioned me about the political situation, and I tried to reply in a well-informed manner. . . . At such times, I always see myself as funny, but for one spectator only, myself. When I add up all that I can talk about to a fellow guest at a dinner, the total is small; no one ever asks me about *what I know*.

Most of the ten or twelve guests at this dinner seemed to believe in the possibility of a British victory, or at any rate that the German attack on England would fail; they hope that this country will be able to hold out two or three months longer, which appears interminable.

JULY 29. A chasm now stands between me and my youth: the war. This makes me feel I am aging. Before the war I went slowly toward middle age, and, instead of turning away, my youth continued with me. It followed me, as you go a bit of the way with a departing traveler. I would say: "Let's go as far as that tree together, let's go as far as yonder turning, let's go to the foot of that hill. . . ." It went as far as the Irún bridge, but did not cross the frontier with me.

Yesterday, happiness came in suddenly, as it used to, and remained for a moment in the great, dark, silent drawing room. We were standing by a window, looking at the rain as it spun its web in the lowering sky, and I felt, in spite of all the newspapers could shout at us, that happiness was close at hand, humble as a beggar, magnificent as a king. It is always with us (but we are unaware) knocking at the door to come in and sup with us.

My cousin, who has all sorts of plans in mind, wants me to spend next winter with her. . . . I dare not refuse anything that is offered me under present circumstances. Life is often given to fearsome acts of generosity and will not allow them to be scorned. It seems like a dream to see with what ease God has removed us from a long series of tight corners. I think that the most sinister hour of my life was the one when I burned a whole suitcase of papers at Bordeaux, in the bedroom of a small hotel. I threw bundles of letters into the fire, trying not to understand what I was doing.

JULY 30. Wasted a whole morning dreaming today, and in the worst possible fashion. Annoyed to feel hesitant, and to such an extent. . . . Read a few pages of Rothenstein's memories of life in Paris around 1890, a charming, rather foolish life, the description of which both saddened and charmed me. For I am really too fond of the pleasant side of life, I have none of the

Swift

American energy that blows up rock and uproots virgin forests! One of my greatest subjects of amazement is my love of a certain kind of stillness.

My cousin seems most mysterious to me, as mysterious at times as a character in a novel, mysterious as almost all women appear to almost all men. We see each other at meals that are cheerful and rather brief. She stays upstairs until dinner time and I on the ground floor which has been allotted to me. I can hear my cousin pacing to and fro above, and there is something indefinably pensive and preoccupied in her step. Two big black poodles keep her company; they sit at a window and bark deeply if anyone goes down the road, which is very rare, and—what is most curious —they sometimes bark for fifteen minutes without its occurring to their mistress to hush them, although they are so close to her; I wonder if she even hears them.

True order is founded on prayer, all the rest is more or less disguised disorder. The Middle Ages were a huge edifice whose foundations were the *Pater*, the *Ave*, the *Credo*, and the *Confiteor*. All that is built on anything else can only collapse sooner or later into blood and mire.

AUGUST 7. Worked pretty well at the book I am writing about my childhood. That is my way of returning to Paris.

Swift

MONDAY, AUGUST 19. Reread a few pages of *Gulliver's Travels*; its sinister beauty has always attracted me. Hatred of the human race gives the author a dark genius that scales the peak of disproportionate grandeur. Certain sentences make you shrink like a cut from a whiplash. A style both icy and vehement, a cold, clear-sighted fury, a scatological and gloomy humor all tend to show the deep, unruffled seriousness of an erotomaniac. When you reduce the whole of life to the performance of a few physical acts which then take on considerable importance, you end by having a view of the world that is, in a way, infernal, although not without beauty. But this beauty is of a terrifying order and not in the least appreciated by those who have never breathed in— be it ever so little—emanations rising from the bottomless pit. Sade is surely related to this great and melancholy author.

TUESDAY, AUGUST 20. A rule I have always tried to follow is to make each day a small life, as complete as possible: reading, writing, listening to music or looking at pictures. Not a bad rule, but one that has resulted in moderating my life's tempo. Thanks to it, nevertheless, I have been able to write more books than my innate slowness would have otherwise allowed. Yet, having formed the habit of building only by slow degrees, how am I to adapt myself to living conditions that suppose rapidly accomplished work, a book dashed off in a few weeks, lectures written in less than a month?

FRIDAY, AUGUST 30. Faces half seen, smiles understood too late, everything that passed me by from 1920 to 1940, and that I did not grasp . . . Yesterday, because of the date inscribed in a book, August, 1920, I began dreaming over my life, over what I was doing twenty years earlier. Have I improved? No. The liberation I vaguely counted on has not taken place. But the yearning for that never visited land should be kept within us, the journey should never be given up: that perhaps is the most important thing.

SATURDAY, AUGUST 31. Some Hindu writer, I cannot remember which, but think it is Vivekananda, compares the sexual instinct to a wild elephant tied down by one foot: sooner or later it ends by breaking its shackle. This instinct brings an element of madness into human life. Nothing indeed comes closer to a frenzied lunatic than a man in a paroxysm of desire. We are bound to earth by the middle of the body.

SUNDAY, SEPTEMBER 8. I was forty, day before yesterday. I am at the zenith of my life. This does not mean, or so I would like to think, that I will go downhill from now on. No, I hope for a long pause on a level stretch, a plateau on which I can stroll about, God willing. The wheat is stirring on this plateau and I may pass by with my sickle—but storms gather over harvests.

I should like to write the story of a man whose appearance showed complete serenity of heart, whereas, actually, this character's loneliness would be made tragic by carnal famishment.

TUESDAY, OCTOBER 1. NEW YORK. Tired of always being my same old self. Has anyone ever said a word about this particular form of sadness? Spiritual man dwells in the top of the face, in the lower part, the carnal man. The lower part of the face must not prevail over the top part, a small portion of the great universal dream should always be retained and nourished within the inner self.

THURSDAY, OCTOBER 10. I finally enjoy being in New York because the city is our last link with the Europe that has been taken from us. Our point of contact with the Old Continent.

FRIDAY, NOVEMBER 1. BALTIMORE. Today, I was foolish enough to go up to the attic where the volumes of my diary are kept, and to open one of the little notebooks bound in gray linen. I sat in a small rocking chair, by a window, and for an hour wandered through the streets of Paris, as I used to. The Paris of happy days, that of 1930. Once more I felt its sidewalks under my feet, heard the boats calling on the Seine, smelled the odor of its trees and its smoke, and hundreds of faces stared at me, as in a dream. I had a rude awakening. I must not read those diaries again, or else let it be over there, in a Paris from which Germany has been chased away. I have suffered too much and suffering wears the soul, just as fatigue exhausts the body.

THURSDAY, NOVEMBER 7. Someday, perhaps, I shall find peace, if not joy. Just as we did not know how happy we were before the war, in the same way we are ignorant today of the extent of our misfortune. I, for one, had placed my happiness in too many exterior things and realize it now. The setting and its accessories had passed on to the essential plane; I needed fine objects, amusements, I mistook pleasure for happiness, I was not sufficiently aware that true happiness takes shelter in an almost inaccessible region, as far as possible from the world.

WEDNESDAY, NOVEMBER 27. No matter how dark life becomes, the current of prayer must not be interrupted, for prayer it is that straightens everything out, even when the game seems lost.
    In spite of all weaknesses, we must believe that there is something great within us that will triumph someday, otherwise life would not be worth living. How could anyone wish to live for the pleasure of sending food to the stomach? Not I, for one. My ambitions are less modest.

THURSDAY, DECEMBER 19. My life has changed a little, interiorly. When did I make my choice? I no longer know. Perhaps, even, I never knew. One reaches a decision when the underground work *profligate*

nears completion, when the pros and cons have been weighed and counted once and for all in the mysterious region where such hidden operations are perfected. There came a second when I said yes, but my consent was obtained before I even knew it. And so we grope our way through a world of darkness. This frailty makes me skeptical as to the serious character of some of our errors.

MONDAY, DECEMBER 30. Does our body never weary of desiring the same things? For it always yearns after the same feast while our spirit continually demands something new. There are only two types of humanity that I have ever really understood: the mystic and the profligate, because both fly to extremes, searching, each in his own way, for the absolute; but of the two, the profligate is to my mind the most mysterious, for he never tires of the only dish served up to him by his appetite and on which he banquets each time as though he had never tasted it before. Probably because of this, I have always had a tendency to consider an immoderate craving for pleasure as an accepted form of madness.

1941

WEDNESDAY, JANUARY 8. It is sometimes more rewarding to watch a spot of sunlight travel over a wall than to write business letters, but who can understand that, of the two occupations, one is eminently beautiful and intelligent, the other perhaps base and stupid? A man who thinks thus is necessarily alone in the part of the world where I live, but he might possibly be better understood in China. How can one avoid being disappointed in talking to human beings? . . . In order to find yourself again, you must go to your room and close the door. In 1941, oh, how the outside world throws us back within ourselves, how much the invisible is present there, pleading with us just as angels glow in the night of the senses.

FRIDAY, JANUARY 10. On reading the beginning of the Book of Esther, I was struck by the sparkle of precious stones that dazzles the eye in the first chapter; each verse gleams like emeralds and sapphires. I do not doubt there is a hidden meaning in all this, but in growing older we lose the gift of understanding things with our admiration and thus passing through the gates of astonishment into Israel's great mystical dream. In my opinion, it is more important for me to know the cause of Vashti's fall from favor than to learn it is possible to breakfast in New York and sleep in London, all in the same day; each week finds me a little more deeply out of tune with my century.

SUNDAY, JANUARY 19.　In reading over Poe's *Metzengarstein*, I wondered why his country should have been so unfair to him. Over here, readers probably find him morbid and America does not care to be represented by such an unwholesome poet. She disowns him all the more violently since she herself possesses the lack of balance of which Poe's genius is like the dark blossom, the great night-flowering lily held in the hand of Death.

THURSDAY, JANUARY 23.　I am trying to write an essay on reading the Bible for Maritain, but such difficulties lie in store for me that I feel discouraged before even facing them. Before flinging oneself into an abyss, one must make sure of knowing how to fly. What I would like to say, in any case, is that the Bible has been a spring where I have drunk freely in times of distress and on the banks of these living waters have lain me down to dream of splendid *elsewheres*, from which all pain has been driven away.

JANUARY 26.　One of the secrets of real talent is to see everything *for the first time*, to look at a leaf as though one had never seen one before, for then only can it appear to us in all its *newness*. The power of marveling makes up the genius of childhood, so quickly blunted by habit and education, and no one will ever be able to fit words together in an acceptable order unless he knows a little how to see creation through Adam's eyes. In art, truth lies in surprising.

　　When one looks at a stone as though it were a miniature mountain, one begins to see it as it really is.

THURSDAY, JANUARY 30.　To be ready to die for someone whom one has never seen, whose voice one has never heard, that is the whole of Christianity. A man stands by a window watching the snow fall, and suddenly joy steals into his heart, a joy that has no name in any tongue. At the very depth of this rare moment, he feels a mysterious peace that no material worries can disturb; there lies the shelter, the only one, for Paradise is nothing else but loving God and there is no other Hell than not being with God.

FRIDAY, JANUARY 31. "I led you out of France so that you would come to me." How often have I heard these words in the silence! They have comforted me, may they not judge me!

WEDNESDAY, FEBRUARY 12. SUFFOLK, VIRGINIA. I am back again in a room where I suffered so much and where the hope of returning to France was the only thing that kept me from sinking. Do I still keep this hope? Of course, but what kind of France will I see again, and when? We are not people who have exile in our veins, like the Jews; it is hard for us to adapt ourselves to the presence of certain ideas. But then what could we dare complain of, we who have enough to eat and who sleep under roofs without a fear of their toppling over our heads? I took a walk yesterday afternoon in the surrounding country. The long, rust-colored plains seemed sad to me, but much in tune with my mood. The night before, on the boat that took me from Baltimore to Norfolk, I looked through my cabin window at stretches of water that shimmered milky in the moonlight, and it did me good. It was two in the morning and that night's supernatural peace went to my heart. Many of the sorrows we are sent can be soothed a little by a glance at the stars.

THURSDAY, FEBRUARY 13. Read St. John of the Cross. Very much struck by a passage where he says that as human nature yearns for God, it inevitably happens that this aspiration after good is simultaneously accompanied by a rising flood of carnal desires: as nature forms a whole, it is difficult to curb one side of it, in order to allow the other side to live. This explains why temptations can be so powerful at a time when our greatest impulses toward God are felt.

FRIDAY, FEBRUARY 14. It would require time and great freedom of mind to write a book containing the mystery of trees in a mist, the beauty of children's laughter, rain gleaming on the cobbles of a Parisian courtyard. Yet that was *my* book, the book I wanted to write; fragments of it strew all my novels. The war has brought about a deep and violent separation between the world and myself. Reading newspapers only adds to my confusion of mind each time I try to understand what is happening around us. No peace can be found at present except in prayer. The few minutes we give to God are like a fortress where we can take shelter and where we can be sure that the world will not reach us; no matter how much it roars and batters at the walls, angels are there, mounting guard on the battlements of the *Pater*.

FEBRUARY 28. On beginning *Varouna* in May, 1938, I was still influenced by a long series of books I had been reading as early as July, 1934. My object was the study of Hindu philosophies. India is a field of tares where wheat sometimes grows too. Two or three·years ago, I still believed in metempsychosis, one of the great heresies of our times, and the subject of my novel has no other meaning than that. But what took place with *Varouna* is what took place with other books of mine: I began it in a certain mood and changed in the course of writing. Around January, 1939, I happened on St. Catherine of Genoa's *Treatise on Purgatory*, and the work impressed me deeply. I have never believed in chance. The book answered many of the questions I asked myself and overthrew opinions that I thought deeply rooted in me; it determined a new current of ideas in my mind concerning man's spiritual destiny. Soon afterwards, a talk I had with Maritain about Aristotle and Plato dealt a crushing blow to such belief as I gave the dreams of Hindu mystics. This conversation pained me very much at first. Suddenly it seemed that instead of having thousands of years ahead of me to accomplish my salvation, I had only a few hours; it was a very rude shock but, at the same time, I felt that a whole structure of errors had crumbled. My conversion, which resulted from these facts and also from other more personal ones, took place in April, 1939, a few days before I left for America. About half my novel was written and I thought of laying it aside, but being curious to know how it would end, as well as regretful to leave it derelict, I felt I must go on with it. That is why, as early as the end of the first part, which must date from February, 1939 (the manuscript is in Paris), while I was slowly returning to the Church, an almost Christian tone is noticeable, or at any rate one very different from that of the beginning. The second part is already steeped with the spirit of

Ramón Lull, particularly the episode of the celestial lover, and the third is wholly Catholic. In a preface rewritten some ten or twelve times, I have also attempted to adjust inconsistencies that a careful reader might discover in these three narratives. I did my best to cleanse metempsychosis in baptismal waters and, its head covered with Manichaean veils, it looks almost Christian.

SUNDAY, MARCH 2. The other day I went to see Miss W., senior professor of English at Goucher College. I had to settle certain details of the course of lectures I am to give from March 24th on. Miss W. received me at the close of the afternoon in a small flat with windows opening on North Charles Street. On the drawing-room walls were reproductions of stained-glass windows at Chartres and shelves of most honorably well-thumbed books. In the fireplace, a couple of logs burned tidily, a gentle blaze, just the fire for a peaceful-hearted old spinster. Miss W. has a small grayish face, and her wrinkles smiled at me occasionally with a touch of mischievousness. She is learned and handles English cautiously, as though it were a rare and fragile object; one feels that she constantly minds her *p*'s and *q*'s. If a sentence begun seems to strike the ear harshly, she drops it and goes on to another. She told me that I would have fifteen pupils, but not to expect wonders of them, excepting for a little German refugee. "They keep their feet on the ground," she confided. "Then we will start from the ground," I said. What they lack most, it appears, is imagination. We will see soon enough, but how strange all this seems to me, even now!

THURSDAY, MARCH 27. My first class did not go off too badly. The classroom is on the second floor of the college, with two or three windows opening on the street. In the center of the room is a large round table at which eighteen people can sit comfortably. My pupils are between sixteen and twenty years old. Two or three are pretty. They all gaze at me with guarded curiosity. Feeling horribly ill at ease, I took a seat among them and after asking their names, began to talk, referring to the notes that lay in front of me, together with my watch. Contrary to what I dreaded, I was not afraid, but as I continued reading I wondered if what I said was worth while expressing, and this annoyed me. Putting my paper aside, I began improvising, saying with much emphasis several things I did not wish to say. In my flurry, I mentioned Uriah Heep as a character in *Martin Chuzzlewit*; a piping voice firmly corrected my mistake, and I laughed along with everybody else. I said a moment ago that this class did not go off badly, but that is not quite true; I went home discouraged, with a feeling of defeat and, worse than anything, a fear of having bored these children. I told them that they were to write me the beginning of a novel, and read amazement in many a face, but I know of no other rule for writing a novel than sitting down at a table and starting off with Chapter One. If a recipe exists, my pupils and I may discover it, but for the time being, I know of none. They were free to write what they pleased, I said, in the manner they understood best, but advised them to begin by painting a picture of the chief character. And if it suits them to first make a plan of the novel, let them; for my part, I never do. I felt that they were staggered by the latitude I gave them, not knowing what to do with it. I am curious to find out what will come of all this.

Another class on Tuesday. They have begun asking me questions. They cannot understand that I am not exacting a complete plan of the story they wish to relate. I tried to point out that the plot of a book is the characters' work, that the first thing to do is to create living, interesting characters, capable of action. So they must attempt to create a character and we would then see its capacities; the story will result from this. I am sure that they feel I am putting the cart before the horse, whereas it is exactly the contrary. I joked a little, they smiled politely. I asked their advice continually, to encourage them to speak. Have they *accepted* me or not? I would like to win their confidence and help them, teach them to use their brains. As to teaching them to write a novel . . .

FRIDAY, MARCH 28. Perhaps I ought not to write what I am about to write, perhaps it is wrong to preserve the memory of anguish for ever. Yet the moment I wish to speak of has had such a deep repercussion throughout my inner life that I want to mention it in this diary, which is an attempt to guess at the course my life is taking. So I see myself once more on the morning of the 21st or 22nd of September in a hotel bedroom at Rotterdam. The room is bright, commonplace, and white and gives on a street from which arises a ceaseless hubbub. By leaning out of the window, I can see sidewalks jammed with people returning from work, for it is past noon. Facing me, the jagged line of pointed roofs bites into the bright blue of a fine autumn sky. I open my suitcase, just to take out a Bible that I lay on the table and skim through to find words that will bring me peace, but turn the pages, unable to concentrate my attention on a single verse. My mind is like a bird, the terrified prisoner of a small room, my thoughts spin round and round; I kneel, try to collect my wits, but can only tell myself, forlornly: "It's all over, we will never be happy again: war has come." I get up and find I can scarcely stand. My soul does not know what to do with my body; yet I do not fear for myself. . . . A few hours before, I heard children calling out a strange word, whose meaning I finally guessed, for these same children pretended to shoulder a gun: war. It was at Dordrecht, at a canal crossing. War . . . Moloch has opened its nightmarish jaws, perhaps to devour what I hold dearest in this world. At that moment, in the hotel bedroom, my distress was greater than the religious feeling I had counted on to help me bear this trial. *I was not ready.* And the scene was so painful that today even, after an interval of more than two years, *nel pensier si rinuova la paura.*

SUNDAY, MARCH 30. There comes a second when our whole fate is decided, but that second is the fruit of a long series of actions and we do not realize that they are connected one to the other by secret links. I see well enough, or think I see well enough, the moment that determined my destiny. It was, I believe, in April, 1919, on a mild afternoon as I was returning home from Benediction. The ceremony had taken place in the crypt of the rue Cortambert chapel. Walking up the crypt stairs, I paused for an instant on a step, my heart brimming over with sadness at the thought of the world I was leaving, and also of all it might have given me and that I was refusing in order to enter a monastery. Heaven knows what took place within me at that moment. I felt suddenly that I had made the "great refusal" which was to give my life such a peculiar character. And at that same instant, a huge weight was removed from me: the weight of the Cross.

It seemed to me, in that second of time, that the whole earth had been offered me and, leaving the Middle Ages, I found myself in the midst of the Renaissance. Once more in the street, a street bathed in spring and full of provincial charm, I realized perfectly well that my life had just taken a fresh turn. . . .

I do not know why these memories come back to me. They hurt. The happiest years of my life have been so to speak embroidered on a ground of sadness. And yet, is this quite correct? Behind wonderful, carefree moments, when I was twenty-five, there lurked at times a shade of disquiet, but never of melancholy. Only after death will we know what our life meant.

WEDNESDAY, APRIL 2. Monday, I returned from my class with a headache. I had proved most inferior to myself, although my lecture had been carefully prepared. I intended making a quick sketch of a character as unromantic as could be, in order to show my pupils how to turn an unpromising subject to good account. A stationmaster. "Can you imagine a more uninteresting life than that of a stationmaster?" I asked the girls. "Why yes, we can," they answered, " a stationmaster meets all kinds of people." They were obviously right; my example was badly chosen, so I dropped it and tried my hand at improvising. The ringleader of the class, a plump Jewess, criticized my methods in such a manner that I blushed. "How can you expect us to write a novel? I think your idea is silly. . . ." Amazement kept me silent, but a little later, when I was talking about Jane Austen, my Jewess interrupted me again to inform me that this author's characters all expressed themselves in the same fashion. I then asked her to develop her idea a little and she gradually began to flounder, mutely begging for comments that I carefully refrained from giving. I finally showed her, with the most scrupulous politeness, that she did not know what she was talking about; she bit her lip and retired into silence. A few of the young ladies' papers are curious. One makes her character speak thus: "My father left me ten million dollars. My fortune now amounts to thirty-two millions. . . . I have had lovers. . . . I have loved love, ecstasy, and something else! I live in idle security" (that's easy enough, my girl, with thirty-two million dollars). One or two show a modest amount of talent. What a strange experience I am having!

MAY 20. A man can turn his room into a Paradise or a Hell without budging, simply by the thoughts he harbors.

MAY 23. Books, the exile's last resource. A book is a window through which one escapes.

* * *

MAY 30. On rereading *The Lives of the Desert Fathers*, I felt my fifteenth year thrill within me, a time when I was so madly in love with Heaven that I thought myself about to bound into the Kingdom in a single mighty leap. A recent Catholic, I imagined having a touch of the supernatural fervor that stirred the early Church. I wanted to go to Paradise at a full gallop. The memory of a winter evening has stuck in my mind more clearly than any other instance. It happened in the pension I tried to describe in *The Strange River*. My father and I shared the same bedroom. I was in bed; my father was saying his prayers. All of a sudden, I was seized with an unutterable happiness, a happiness of spirit that tore me free from myself. For a few minutes my soul was completely absorbed in God. I could not have said what was taking place in me, but my thoughts, instead of wandering here and there, as they usually did, came to a standstill in a sort of rapture that I have never experienced since. And the very words I use in trying to describe the indescribable only serve to confuse my memories. And yet, this is not so. What lives in my memory is the feeling of deep security—a little of which still remains—the inexpressible peace enjoyed by the soul when it takes shelter under the all-powerful wing of the Lord.

JUNE 12. Journey through Virginia. We left Baltimore day before yesterday for the Shenandoah Valley. The scenery strongly recalls certain chapters of the Bible: peace, the sweetness of wooded hills where the setting sun casts a pensive light; at the foot of the mountains shines the river like a great sword laid on the grassy meadows. What Nature says is unintelligible to those who are not fond of silence. Be it ever so loud, Nature's voice cannot be heard unless you listen close, and the least chitchat covers the sound of her words. There is a sort of *spiritual majesty* about these Virginia horizons that cannot be expressed. It is a setting for Ruth or the last chapters of the Pentateuch. Looking at the deep valleys where copper-colored beams of light seem to seek shelter against the night, one would like to be silent for ever, like Trappists. Human speech is almost always doomed to such failures and is so often inferior to what it intends to say that you wonder if this is not one of the consequences of original sin. Before that, there must have been other means of communicating thought, something less coarse. I have noticed one particular about human speech: the more it strives to clarify what is obscure, the more it confuses matters and increases chaos, unless inspira-

tion takes a hand. The real word, the word of words, can only
be sensed in the heart of silence, but all that I can say is mere
confusion.

At the University, toward the close of the same day. All the
students have gone; everything is given up to solitude and to
memory. We strolled on the big lawn that spreads before the
Rotunda: great trees whispered above our heads, rows of white
columns glimmered in the twilight, and I had never been struck
as now by the simple beauty of the "ranges." I would have liked
to linger there for years, but we had to leave, one always has to
leave, no matter what or where. And then, what would I have
done at the University? Where is my place? Where am I going
to live? Where am I going to die? Since Paris has been taken away
from us, I seem to wander about without quite understanding
what has happened to us all.

JUNE 13. VIRGINIA. Glanced through a copy of *The Strange
River*. It is my best book, my most grown-up book, the most
difficult to write, the most thoughtful, the richest, and also the
most difficult to read. Poor Crevel said it was a revolutionary
book; he was right, but what spoils the book in my eyes is that
in writing it, I did not see all that I should have seen and so very
nearly did. Philippe is a character that spells disaster, a bourgeois
who no longer believes in anything, not even in what he himself
stands for. In his permanent terror of a great social upheaval, he
should have foreseen the days of February, 1934. He should not
only have foreseen, but *seen* them, his fear could and should have
made a prophet of him. I might have written this and did not and,
for this sole reason, the book does not satisfy me, although I prefer
it to all my other novels.

JUNE 15. At Williamsburg, day before yesterday. A few years
ago, I smiled at it too easily. These brand-new houses mentally
and physically lack the film of age. They remember nothing and
want to look as though they belonged to a period of which they
are completely ignorant, yet they are sometimes beautiful and
curious and you wish to believe that the second capital of Virginia
was like that. A tunnel is almost finished and ready to whisk away
automobiles, whose presence destroys the illusion of being in an
eighteenth-century city. How soon will its inhabitants be forced
into wearing wigs and hoop petticoats?

To read over a diary is like turning over a sandglass; the sand

keeps on running through it, the sand is the same, so is the sandglass, and everything is different.

JUNE 20. Today, I spent part of the morning and afternoon at
the Library. Read the fourth canto of Dante's "Purgatorio" with
extreme pleasure. Here we are at last in the field of truth, far
from the hideous delusion so minutely depicted for us by newspapers every day! It is faith, an all-powerful faith that lends such
amazing density to the great Italian's words. In this immense poem
with walls as solid as those of a Romanesque basilica, there is
never a cleft in the rock through which doubt can steal.

JUNE 23. Sixth canto of "Purgatorio." One *sees* everything this
man says, each line strikes and arrests one's attention. His economy of words is so great that nothing could possibly be de-
leted, but his conciseness is surprisingly full of meaning. Certain
lines are haunting, such as Pia's cry: *"Ricorditi di me, che son la
Pia . . . , etc."* You walk into the terrifying world of *reality,*
where Maya ceases, where sensual illusions cease, where the setting of this life that conceals the truth vanishes; but in the kind
of spiritual landscape through which we move, souls are shown
us in such a manner that we see them—as though the poet lent us
his sight and we, in turn, saw into the invisible. If one could speak
thus without raving, you might almost say that spirit becomes
concrete in these verses.

JUNE 25. If we could live a life of holiness, death would no
longer be feared, for a holy life brings peace and deprives death
of its horrors. From the day—around my twentieth year—when
I realized that death would take me when my turn came, my life
was, so to say, poisoned. I seemed to see death at each bend of
the road, prowling around those I loved best.

Yesterday in Washington, where I spent a couple of hours in
the new museum of art (Mellon collection). Almost all Italian
painting is represented there. Overwhelmed by the beauty of these
pictures. It is a review of painting from Giotto to Piazzetta, and
in the unbroken connection of this great vision lies something inflexible, almost inevitable, even more moving than the perfection
of each individual work, for the painters probably had no more
than a rather vague idea of the continuity to which they all con-

tributed nevertheless. You can see the genius of the race pursue a dream of superhuman beauty.

Left the museum around two o'clock to sit on a bench in a wide avenue whose name I forget. I read a few *terzine* from the "Purgatorio." The day was very fine, I felt almost happy. If we were not wretched barbarians, what wealth life would ladle us by the handful!

A human being is separated from the rest of humanity by barriers that scarcely ever fall. That is the tragedy of one and all. Words betray us shamefully. We want to speak and no one is there to hear us, even though we talk to twenty people a day. What we think deeply is practically incommunicable. Love sometimes guesses our meaning, but that privilege belongs to love and to love only. God uses this agency to draw us to Him, for He alone understands us perfectly. Talking to a man is to throw a bridge over an abyss, but is there a road that continues the bridge on the other side of the abyss? Very rarely.

JUNE 27. Today I continued reading the "Purgatorio" with the same admiration and astonishment. There is great sweetness in the first *terzine* of Canto VII, an exquisite sadness that contrasts with the tone, so often hard and terse, of Dante's verse. I read and reread them with such keen pleasure that the trial we are undergoing grew easier for me. In Canto XI, the paraphrase of the *Pater* is of prodigious beauty; human speech suddenly rises to heights that we no longer reach; it seems as though this language was intoxicated by grace, but such an inebriation is divine and remains lucid. In Dante, there is no faltering, like that of a mystic coming out of ecstasy: he treads the air as though it were a road.

JULY 4. I went up to the attic the other day to take a manuscript out of a small trunk, an unfinished novel whose future has always appeared so doubtful to me: *The Transgressor.* I sat on the floor and read over several pages. A great many things had escaped my memory. How extraordinary to forget so much of what I wrote with such care. And as I read on, I could see myself doing so, and thought: "What a scene for a novel! To be sitting in a garret, reading a manuscript so peculiar that I do not quite know what I will make of it . . ." And it was really like a scene in *The Transgressor,* so much are our books part of us.

* * *

JULY 17. At Craftsbury Common, in northern Vermont, where we arrived yesterday around 7 P.M. in wonderful weather that reminded me of all the fine days in my childhood at Andrésy, at Conflans-Sainte-Honorine, at Poissy. As we came in sight of Craftsbury, the sun was imperceptibly, almost regretfully leaving the meadows and valleys. The earth seemed to laugh with joy in the golden light. As I gazed at one of the most beautiful landscapes in the world, one that made me think so strongly of France, I pondered over the deep mystery that war represents; it appeared to me in the light of a sinister game that humanity occasionally feels the need of playing, a game of violence and death, something like a *lust for unhappiness*, an irresistible need to suffer in order to restore some equipoise or other, the laws of which are unknown to us.

AUGUST 18. Reread Hawthorne's *Notebooks* sometimes with delight and at other times with boredom. A great writer, but the man himself seems a little slight. He lacked not living in a big city, or better still, in a capital. His generalities about life, the soul, good and evil are those of a provincial, but he is not short of genius. At times, he gives the impression of having taken long walks in the invisible whence he returns with an extraordinary booty of ideas that he expresses in two or three intensely deep phrases. He talks to us too often about his vegetable garden; you can be interested in green peas and salads but the subject is quickly exhausted. There is unquestionable beauty in the author's life, a studious life tinged with boredom, melancholy and austere happiness, but his taste for moral security and spiritual comfort disconcerts me. He fears evil and at the same time has a vague hankering after sins that he knows only imaginatively. I may be mistaken, although I do not think so. I have always felt that I guessed clearly enough the kind of man he was.

AUGUST 22. A curious study could be written about Hawthorne, with whom I have so much in common, as I now see on reading his journal closely. But his thirst for glory is very foreign to me. I have never wished for praise, nor done anything to obtain it (and this perhaps has gone against me). I would have liked Hawthorne to show more pride. "Will the world ever know me?" is a question he should never have asked himself (because he should have known the answer). What endears him to me particularly is

√ the value he gives to silence and all the invisible. His is a lonely and mysterious soul, nearer night than day.

AUGUST 25. Read Hawthorne's *French and Italian Notebooks.* A great disappointment. Hawthorne should have stayed in his pretty house at Concord or not told us what he saw on the other side of the Atlantic, for in Paris, Rome, and Florence this great writer becomes platitudinous. His admirations are often funny. In his eyes, the lounge of the Hôtel du Louvre is fit for a palace. (The whole passage should be quoted in all its delectable ingenuousness.) In Italy, he mistakes Giotto for Pinturicchio and, discoursing on painting, informs us that he prefers the works of the illustrious Mr. Brown (an American artist of his times) to those of Claude Lorrain. He blames Italian crowds for not being crowds but "a collection of individuals" (September 10, 1858), which is certainly the greatest compliment that could be paid a crowd. He is embarrassed by the nakedness of statues (this is rather touching although supremely irritating and ridiculous in a gentleman of fifty-four; I thought of my friend Benton, who would not read Baudelaire because he found him indecent and still remember with remorse his hurt look when I laughed in his face on that account, in 1922). Strange that Europe should have made a most experienced author write such nonsense. At the very bottom of Hawthorne lurked a provincial, brought to light by this journey. Noted a few passages where he talks at length of séances in Florence. Someday I will say more about this very poor book; there is something humiliating in reading it for those who, like myself, admire the author as one of the greatest writers of his time.

SEPTEMBER 8. NEW YORK. Spent the morning at the Metropolitan Museum looking chiefly at the Flemish primitives, and with such attention that I strained my eyes a little. What I particularly wanted to see was how they went about painting a tree. Gerard Dow gave me the best example of what I was looking for. The tree, of the horse-chestnut variety, is treated with the leaves in bunches, the top of each bunch edged with a thin line of light. So much for the general impression. In detail, each bunch forms a mass of tiny bright vermiculations on a dark ground, a process adopted later by Patinir, Isenbrandt and several others. The effect seems just right to me, showing a more scrupulous observation

than, for instance, the manner of certain Venetians in whose
painting trees are hastily sketched for the requirements of a background and look like sprays of feathers. I prefer Gerard Dow's
way of seeing nature, which is that of the Middle Ages, to the Impressionist method, in spite of Sisley's and Monet's great achieve-
ments, but then I realize more and more clearly that I often look
at the outside world with the eyes of a fourteenth- or fifteenth-
century man. . . . And it may also be that I sometimes look at
the inner world with the eyes of those who believe as people believed in the days of Tauler and Henry Suso. I was deeply moved
once more by certain pictures such as "Christ Appearing to His
Mother" by Van der Weyden, or the "Annunciation" by Petrus
Christus. [Since writing this, the painting has been attributed to
Van Eyck.] Such works would lead a man to Paradise if he could
listen to what they have to say; they create silence around them
(in the next room are the Italian paintings and their screams), but
what use is it to talk about what cannot be expressed?

I also wandered about in a landscape by Patinir, trees, meadows,
and blue rocks; I was happy for a moment, and that means a
great deal, nowadays.

SEPTEMBER 24. BALTIMORE. From my room, the eye looks down
into great masses of greenery where the sun touches a branch
here, the edge of a leaf there, as though to mark the stages of a
mysterious saunter. At times, I feel prisoner to the trees that
watch over the house in almost magical stillness; finally so still
that you would like the foliage to stir more often, the wind to
come down these airy steps, move about whispering through the
labyrinths of green. Sleepy nature is maybe more disquieting than
when in an angry mood. She is never man's accomplice, she dis-
likes his presence and would be glad for him to perish from the
face of the earth. Ivy's sole ambition is to bury our palaces,
churches, and factories under the sinister profusion of its small,
black, funereal leaf. The roots of the oak wish to shatter our
walls, its blind arms to pierce our roofs. Everywhere, the virgin
forest claims her rights to the earth desecrated by man; it was
there before him, and will survive the traveler whose passage in
this world offends it.

SEPTEMBER 26. What takes place in our brain in the space of a
minute should be recorded, if there were time enough to do it. But

indeed, there would not be sufficient paper and also, how could
the thread of such innumerable and rapid ideas be followed? You
might as well attempt to follow the flight of swallows through
the air. From one end to the other of life, a torrent of ideas runs
through us and only a few of these can be discerned with some
vividness. If this is the case, what is a diary, and how much truth
can a work contain? The amount we extract to talk about is just
an infinitesimal part of a sum that possesses its whole value only if
the eye takes it in completely. I am not, nor have I ever been,
quite the man of the diary I write. When I reread pages dating
back to 1928, or to 1935, or even to 1940, something in me raises
a protest. I am better and worse than I have implied, but I have
always wished to be truthful. Now, to be truthful is one thing ✓
and to be accurate is another.

OCTOBER 6. The story of the manna gathered and set aside by the
Hebrews is deeply significant. It so happened that the manna
rotted when it was kept. And perhaps that means that all spiritual
✓ reading which is not *consumed*—by prayer and by works—ends
by causing a sort of rotting inside us. You die with a head full of
fine sayings and a perfectly empty heart.

OCTOBER 16. Oh, when will the Seine be reflected in our eyes
once more?
    Yesterday I talked about death with someone. We were walk-
ing in a wood of firs, on a carpet of tiny, russet, needle-shaped
leaves; the setting sun blazed through the trees. We wondered if
such men existed as never thought of death. And although I myself so often think of death, can I even imagine the day when I
will no longer walk through city streets or under trees?
    I was about twenty when I first thought of death as inescapable.
It was in my uncle's orchard, in Virginia. I knew very well, of
course, that I had to die, but, as Bossuet said, I knew it but I did
not believe it. That day, I had a glimpse of what dying could mean
and was seized with a sort of terror. Until then, like all young
beings that life smiles on, I believed myself immortal, death was
for everyone else but me. It was a kind of interior revelation and
I do not think that I ever recovered from it.

OCTOBER 21. Listening to the *Kyrie* from the B minor Mass, I remembered the day in 1921 when I heard an air by Bach played for

the first time. Played is not quite the word for it. A music teacher sat at the piano to talk to us of Bach and with one hand ran over the first notes of that same *Kyrie*. It seemed, listening to this bare and unadorned phrase, as if I entered an unknown world. I had never heard anything like it, nothing that appeared more beautiful to me than the fifteen or twenty notes that rose in the silence; they made me think of footsteps, those of a numberless multitude marching along in a dim light, a humble, sorrowful humanity seeking its way through a great, dark country. It was as though music had been revealed to me in that single moment of time.

OCTOBER 27. It is growing dark. I place a lamp on the table and its light falls straight on the page of Homer with which I intend to fill my solitude. The window sash is half raised, night thickens behind it, but I can still see shreds of mist clinging to branches, and then comes the whispering of rain, a sound delicate as the patter of thousands of bird claws on the leaves, answered inside my room by my watch's tiny chatter. What silence back of all this! You would think that the water muttering in the trees and the ticking of the watch were the very voice of silence, rather than a noise that broke it. The little ebony elephant on the table watches my hand write these lines, and I want to note this peaceful hour as it passes from birth to death: it is five o'clock.

NOVEMBER 8. Some twenty-three or four years ago, in Rome, a friend put a volume of Bloy in my room. It was *Mon journal*, I remember. I was too young at the time to appreciate the merits of a book whose vehemence merely proved an excuse for me to laugh and jeer at it, although I was secretly perturbed by the serious character of its testimony. Such a voice echoes indefinitely through the years. All of us who have read Bloy and learned to love him do not rightly know what we owe him. I am not judging him as an author; he often ranks among the best, although at times he is also inferior to what he wished to be, and the reader suffers as much from this as he did. Nevertheless, he is the bearer of an immense message. In his letter about the conversion of Israel, for instance; the passage is one of terrible and mysterious beauty: a converted Jew is neither more nor less than the Prodigal Son who goes home to his Father, and no matter how he behaved, the Prodigal Son remains his Father's favorite.

*   *   *

DECEMBER 7. Today [Pearl Harbor], which should have been like all the other days created by God, with the sun triumphantly crowning a blue sky, today was in truth a day garbed in black to be mentioned henceforth with bated breath, as one used to mention August 2nd, 1914. It is a messenger of mourning, one of the veiled and masked ambassadors sent us by fate, bearing terrible and unknown credentials. But we must receive him calmly: "And when these things begin to come to pass, then look up and raise your heads," says the Evangelist.

DECEMBER 14. A moment ago, at the cathedral, I listened with great pleasure to an Advent hymn in which an entire civilization sprang to life, such as it was five or six centuries ago. No one will ever be able rightly to describe the peculiar effect of this music on the soul of a believer. It quickens echoes of a marvelous past that we remember deep within us, for it is our past and one common to all the men of our race. It should never be said that Americans cannot understand it. America stems from Europe, and it was the Europe of long ago singing this morning under the dark vaulting of a none too striking church. From the spectator's point of view, what improved things a little was the faded pink of chasubles striped with pale gold, the candlelight, the great copper cross and, in a word—apart from the spiritual side—everything that lends charm to the Church's ceremonies, everything that "appeals to the feelings," as monks would say.

1942

JANUARY 12. In New York, a few days ago. At the Franciscan church on 31st Street. Although not beautiful, it is really a Catholic church. The monks are responsible for this: their devotion attracts crowds who pray under the dark vaultings and pray kneeling for many long minutes. The crowd is made up of all sorts of people, many of them poor, as well as of cloaked somebodies with weighty Mass books, such as we have in Europe, regular attendants of the supernatural. Candles, barefooted, brown-frocked monks walking to and fro, continual prayer—I recognize

Catholicism in all this, what some would call the Catholic atmosphere, one I have always loved. The church copies one of the chapels at Assisi as best it can; horrible paintings offend the eye, but shadowy twilight improves things a little.

JANUARY 23. I have begun writing my lecture on Péguy. In reading over *Le Mystère de la charité*, I was most deeply moved by the fifteen or twenty pages about the Blessed Virgin at Calvary. It is the picture of the greatest grief that ever was, and one has to go back to the great French primitives to find it described with such power. I may perhaps attempt to translate these lines and read them at the end of my lecture.

FEBRUARY 14. Something new must be done; one's thoughts should not be continually sifted through the sieve of old books.

The Bible only is eternally young, like a mountain torrent that has been leaping down a slope for thousands of years. Not only is it the youngest of all books, but the most recent, it is in advance of everything that will ever be written. A man writing a thousand years hence is *already* behind Bible time.

MARCH 16. You cannot give an account of love, any more than you can give an account of misfortune. That is why there are so many omissions in my diary.

MARCH 17. Last night, to a performance of *The Magic Flute*, which I had not heard since 1925 or '26 and had then found a little boring. Yesterday, however, although the voices were middling and the settings hideously pretentious, I was thrown into a sort of rapture; it seemed as if all that we are in danger of losing had passed into this music, I mean that all the beauty of our unhappy planet had chosen this ethereal refuge against all our forces of destruction. One can, alas, blow up cathedrals and palaces with bombs: a little training, a gift for aiming straight, are sufficient for that, but Mozart's music is a sort of enchanted castle where a too unhappy soul can still find shelter.

MARCH 18. Alone in the house. I opened *Macbeth*, which I am to see acted tomorrow. The first act brought back all my former admiration—no, not quite; I began to jib at so much bloodshed and, on reaching the third act, closed the book. Psychologically speaking, it is one of the most *juvenile* of Shakespeare's plays. The characters' nature is given once for all at the very start, particularly as concerns Lady Macbeth, who will remain exactly what and as she is: she could pile murder upon murder during forty acts and still be the same. Macbeth, however, grows somewhat bolder, but his character affords no surprises. He and his wife are like steam engines driven full tilt along a perfectly straight track; crime never swerves them; from time to time a whistle shrills remorse, that is all, and on they go. And then, if you omit shrieks heard in the darkness, curses, the racket of a storm and daggers "breeched with gore," what remains is a singularly impoverished play. The action is, of course, carried out with great art and many of the tirades spoken by Macbeth and his wife are memorable, but I cannot believe that the weaknesses of this play escaped the author of *The Tempest*. I may change my mind tomorrow evening. In another fifty years, I think, *Macbeth* will have to be rewritten in modern English, otherwise no one will understand a word of it.

MARCH 19. *Macbeth* is more bombastic on the stage than when it is read. Yet the chief actor (Maurice Evans) is at least tolerably good. In spite of all, the mighty blast of genius pervades these horrific scenes, and the audience listened in perfect silence to lines that flew and bounded with all the vigor that was theirs three centuries earlier.

MARCH 24. The other evening, I read my lecture on Péguy to the nuns of Notre Dame (an Order founded by St. Pierre Fourier). I sat on a platform and, by me, Father Couturier in his white robe. Facing me, some thirty nuns in black, and a few pupils. I read distinctly and noticed that almost all these women were in tears. What moved them was the passage about the Blessed Virgin in the *Mystery of Charity*. And so, it suffices to read these few pages for their eyes to water. How happy you are, Sisters! I walked home in the beautiful moonlight. As I reached the house and paused to enjoy the quality of silence in the countryside, I understood suddenly that for years, perhaps, a divorce had been pronounced between my daily and my inner life, I mean that I no longer have a hold on what mankind calls real life. I felt this very strongly as, so to speak, I faced the revelation of an obvious fact. This is what I might call my problem, and that would not be a problem if there were not a war. I know only too well that the *emergency exit* is within us.

MARCH 31. The state of Christianity in 1942: English children "evacuated" from the coast inland are questioned by grownups. The latter ask them who is Christ. Answer: A swear word. That is all they know. All they know of Christ is this blasphemed name. The real causes of the war are perhaps to be found in facts like these.

APRIL 26. Finished *Memories of Happy Days* yesterday evening at seven. I wanted to call it *Before the Evil Days* (a quotation from the last chapter of Ecclesiastes), but my publishers convinced me that this title, far better to my mind than the former, would create a bad impression on account of the word *evil.*

MAY 11. So here you are, almost forty-two . . . If he could judge you, what would the boy you were at sixteen think of you? What would he say about what you have become? What secret hopes have you not disappointed, hopes you do not even remember? How passionately interesting, though sad, it would be to confront these two beings, one so full of the promises that the other has so little kept. I can imagine the youth harshly scolding his senior: "You've deceived, you've cheated me. Where are all the dreams I gave you to keep? What have you done with all the wealth I so foolishly handed you? I vouched for you, went pledge *for you.* You have gone bankrupt. Far better would it have been for me to leave with what I still had and that you have wasted. I do not admire you, far from it." And what would the elder man say in his defense? He would talk of acquired experience, of useless ideas thrown overboard, he would bring forward a few books, talk of his reputation, look feverishly through his pockets and desk drawers for something to justify him. But he would defend himself badly and I think feel ashamed.

JUNE 6. All the dead are our elders. When a child of ten dies, he is my elder because he *knows.*

JUNE 11. Read Stekel's book on anxiety again. There is a certain amount of uneasiness in the admiration I feel for this work. For these brilliant pages simplify our personality to the extreme, and

I really mean simplify, whereas, conversely, the author forms an exaggerated idea of our mental subtlety. This transformation of "slight repressed desires" into anxiety, in spite of such complicated processes, reduces our physical and moral nature to the role of a machine, or almost. Our brains—I do not say our souls, as this word has no place in these gentlemen's vocabulary—our brains, as well as our hearts, are so many factories where desires of all kinds change into I know not what that is atrocious as well as forbidden. The instinct of murder, or theft, or incest struggles desperately to come into the open and bring about the act of liberation. The borderline between good and evil vanishes, or if it remains it is only at the cost of physical and mental torture. Can it be that the human being is a monster? The answer might perhaps be yes, were it not for grace. One puts the book down with the feeling that we are even more mysterious than we thought, and that is no doubt what is truest in this stout volume—but the truth is there, unbeknownst to the author: it is a valuable one. No sooner does a man imagine that he knows himself, that nothing escapes analysis, than he heads straight into darkness. The sense of mystery should always be retained.

JULY 19.   I would like to be able to tell the truth about myself. I know this is very difficult, that it depends not only on an honest purpose, that a particular form of talent is requisite, and above all, a determination to avoid being ensnared by words. I would like to tell *my* truth one day, one hour, or only for a few minutes. . . . The only means I can see of managing this is to write a novel.

JULY 22.   If the war ended tomorrow, I would no doubt find myself much the same as I was in 1939, and the fact worries me, for in the spiritual order, this war is meaningless if it does not help part of humanity to improve. And if the operation fails, if the few million men and women whose duty it is to shake themselves free refuse the opportunity offered them—an opportunity that is perhaps a formidable godsend—the war will have to continue or to start up again. Just as each of us is the cause of the war, in the same manner each of us has the power to stop it. As soon as one tries to find the real causes of this war elsewhere than in our innermost selves, one gets lost in the chaos of human reasoning, for war is above all a spiritual tragedy.

* * *

AUGUST 10. This morning's mail brought me a letter from President Roosevelt. It begins with these words: "President Roosevelt to Julian Green, greetings." (This is the usual formula.) It then enjoins me to report at the York Road office in Baltimore, with a three-day change of linen, for, the document goes on to explain, I have been called up and found fit for the army.

AUGUST 26. NEW YORK. I have just had lunch with Saxton at the Century Club. He had a letter from Thomas Wells in Paris, saying that the city was more beautiful than ever. Could he have any suspicion of the way this remark affected me? In the twinkling of an eye, I saw the Seine once more, Notre-Dame, our deserted flat. . . . After lunch I went to Harper's with Saxton and he presented me with a copy of my book which is to come out in a few weeks (*Memories of Happy Days*). Is it absurd to own that I felt a childish pride as I went off with the book under my arm? That I skimmed through it in the bus that took me home and, what is more, stopped in a tearoom on Fifth Avenue to read over a few chapters?

AUGUST 28. I went to see Maritain yesterday evening. We spent an hour and a half chatting in his flat on Fifth Avenue. He talked to me about Bloy and Péguy. I wanted to know if Péguy was not a little boring, a trifle too didactic in his conversation, but it seems not, that on the contrary he had great charm, that what he said had none of the labored, determined quality of his written style. I asked Jacques why Péguy had never answered Bloy, who had written him after reading one of his books. . . .

Péguy thought it strange that anyone should live in Montmartre, as Bloy did. To Péguy's formal mind, Montmartre was the equivalent of a night club.

I felt very close to Jacques during our whole conversation. I said that God would overthrow empires to wrest an assent from a soul, and that we see only dimly the spiritual side of great catastrophes.

He told me of an English Carmelite nun who had been ordered to ask that special worship be given the Blood of Jesus, and that as this worship had been refused by mankind, the threat of very great misfortunes had grown more definite. A little later, I said that the supernatural was like an element whose laws we knew badly, that by calling on its intervention, terrible *disorders* might take place—disorders that are really attempts to restore divine order—that those among the bourgeois who knew this, instinctively and by every means protected themselves (by the refusal of all poetry, of all religious mysticism).

SEPTEMBER 7. CAMP MEADE. I would like to note a few aspects of the days I am going through, so that an experience that has been forced on me may be turned to the best account, be it ever so small. I am writing this at the close of a cold, rainy day, seated on a campbed in the tent which I share with my four companions. The place is very badly lighted by a single electric bulb. On a canteen, a little radio plays one of those melancholy airs that the American ear never seems to tire of. The Spaniard, a nice, stout boy, has gone to bed, from despair. The Chinese traces beautiful characters on a sheet of paper, and the curiosity with which I look at them certainly has nothing indiscreet about it; he is a slim, reserved youth, given at times to fits of mysterious laughter. The Canadian, with bulging blue eyes, is probably the most touching of all in his childlike sadness and perfectly helpless attitude toward military life, which he cannot get used to. The American is a very silent, strapping fellow given to sudden fits of expansiveness, when he lets out rather unfortunate things: liquor makes him talk so. He is skinny and ugly, not as bad as might be thought and as he leads one to think. For my part, I am overwhelmed by boredom after a long, perfectly empty day. I talked this morning to a young Jew from Palestine who recited several passages of the Bible to me in Hebrew. A moment ago, I lay on my bed, wrapped in a blanket, and read the New Testament (Segond's translation), which I keep in my pocket. I wonder what meaning my present life can have.

SEPTEMBER 30. Yesterday, I held my first class for officers. There were twenty of them, not counting twenty soldiers and noncommissioned officers I have mentioned elsewhere. My heart thumped as I began to talk, but, as always, my "double" spoke for me. . . .

OCTOBER 7. There is nothing difficult about getting up when all the stars are shining in the black sky. I think, on the contrary, that to see the stars helps me to bear the whole day's burden, but what hurts is to be parted from those I love. However, I believe that if everything that happens is accepted as coming from God, life is wonderfully lightened. I wonder that men can accept a military life, that they see it only as the consequence of a certain policy, without realizing that beyond it all are a will and an intention superior to humanity's tragic whims. And this will must be appealed to, so as not to give in to sadness and fatigue.

OCTOBER 21. I could not sleep last night. Too many thoughts struggled in my mind, and it seemed as though my whole life came back to me in great fragments, like some landscape lit up by sudden flashes of light, in deepest night. At three in the morning, I got up and walked about outside the tent. The sky was a very dark blue and the stars spoke a tongue that words cannot express, a tongue that will always move me, for it appeals to what is truest in us. I lose myself in contemplation of the night sky, as some throw themselves from a bridge, to end it all, but in my case it is to find what I have been seeking since childhood, and when I look at the stars I can never be completely unhappy.

DECEMBER 1. Dog-tired. I don't know how many generals from Washington are coming here for the day, to see how we are doing. I am supposed to hold a four-hour class, so that if the generals happen our way, they will be certain of finding me at work with my pupils. Have just been told I will have to lecture before the Secretary of War. The subject I have chosen is the geography of France.

Moments of horrible sadness. Particularly in the morning, when whistles make us jump out of bed and a phonograph with a loud-speaker blares *gay* tunes of heart-breaking melancholy. I wonder how long I shall be here. I think they are keen on keeping me, alas, although the O.W.I. in New York has asked the army to *lend* me to it.

DECEMBER 31. Demobilized. Returning to Baltimore.

1943

JANUARY 4. NEW YORK. I often wonder how they live, those blameless ones! A pure soul is so mysterious! As I was thinking things over, the other evening, it seemed all of a sudden as though I saw a mental picture such as I have seen several times during the last five or six years. My mind's eye showed me a great city built like a fortress, but low and squat, on a vast plain at twilight. A hazy light rose from the city, and after a time I understood that this city was our soul and the light was the light of grace. A man in armor walked along the ramparts, and this man was human will, which mounts guard on the ramparts of the soul. And in the shadows of darkness, all around the city, was a great ragged mob of dismal faces, moving furtively. When a prowler came near the walls, the armed watchman thrust him aside with his sword, but could not prevent one or two of them from finally gaining entrance, nor could he prevent others from following, nor, after an hour, the whole city from falling into the hands of these ragged prowlers who represented in my mind thoughts of pride and covetousness.

JANUARY 16. Reread St. Augustine's *Confessions*. He seems to have conquered the frenzy of sensual desires at one blow, after his conversion. He talks admirably about these terrible chains he had dragged after him with such delight. During my whole youth, I was obsessed by the thought of an ideal life in which anxieties of a sexual order would not exist, because the pain they continually bred seemed out of all proportion to physical pleasure. It is not by chance that love is called a passion.

A verse from Ecclesiastes has haunted me all day: "God has put √ eternity in the human heart." [The author here follows the French translation from Crampon, 3:2.] Yesterday, I went to the little church on 62nd Street. It was nine at night. The church was empty; just two women whispering in a corner, a couple of Italians, their heads covered by scarves, and there was also, in the middle of the nave, a dead man in a coffin, under a black drapery. I tried to imagine that I was a corpse and my entire life took on a new light; struck by the smallness of our efforts to go to God, to respond to continual appeals.

JANUARY 24. Reread a few pages of *Le Rouge et le noir*, and in particular the chapter entitled "Le Séminaire." I used to admire this piece more than I do now, when I mostly see in it a sort of frantic dryness that is not unlike Sade. I quite see the beauty of these pages, but no longer enjoy it. It enraptured me formerly, but at present all I see in l'Abbé Pirard is a cassocked scarecrow and he no longer interests me. What a strange seminary the author takes us to! It gives the impression of a seminary for lost souls.

JANUARY 27. The Casablanca Conference. An offensive in Tunisia is expected, perhaps a speedy invasion of Europe. (The word *invasion* is frowned on over here.) The O.W.I. spreads the news throughout the world in twenty-two tongues. . . . How little I feel part of all this! I write my paper every day and take it to 57th Street, where I read it before a *mike*, in a small, empty room. Strange to talk daily to someone who, alas, cannot answer and maybe does not even hear.

FEBRUARY 2. Looking at a photograph of Gattamelata, I wondered how a blind face could be stamped with such strength of character, but that is the way with almost all of Donatello's portraits. Now, what expression can an eyeless face have? The truth is that the eyes are usually what lie in a face: they try to mislead an observer as to the meaning of the long, sad tale told by the lips, the nose, the curve of the cheeks, the lines and wrinkles, in fact the whole of a mask that cries: "I am the face of a miser, of a hypocrite, of a coward, of a pleasure-loving man!"

I recently bought Vigouroux's Polyglot Bible. Yesterday, in the preface to Ecclesiasticus, I read a sentence that plunged me into an endless reverie: "The four manuscripts that have gradually given us these fragments" (this concerns the Hebrew text of the book in question) "would seem to have come out of the *guenizzah*, or storeroom, of the Moses Synagogue in Old Cairo." Oh, the power of the simplest words! This sentence took me into an unknown world, yet one where everything seemed familiar. Thought of the term *Consul romanus*, which stirred Thomas de Quincey's imagination so strongly.

FEBRUARY 20. At Robert's flat on 62nd Street I can look out of the window and, with a slight stretch of imagination, think myself in Europe, in a bygone Europe—but there, in the 57th Street building, what I have at my door and see through the large bay window is my own century with a vengeance. A huge steel bridge, two gigantic gasometers, and a couple of factory smokestacks; so much for the foreground. In the distance beyond, skyscrapers. But in some strange way, the view is tolerable, I mean that these hideous objects compose into a sort of beauty. And in this hell of stone, brick, and metal, with never a leaf to gladden the eye, each morning, a bird sings: not for long: just four or five notes, that's all, but this single trill contains a world of solitude.

APRIL 7. Words cannot express the loneliness created in the soul ✓ by sin, for it estranges God from us, and in the absolute the only true presence is that of God and real loneliness exists only where He is not (if these words can have a meaning). Love and sometimes friendship stave off ordinary loneliness, but God alone can do away with supernatural loneliness.

APRIL 15. I gave a lecture yesterday at a large college for girls. I was shown a suite of drawing rooms all in the 1860 style, all very solemn, with heavy curtains and tufted furniture that people would fight over at the Flea Market. Talked with the professors until it was time for my lecture; we gravely exchanged platitudes about the temperature and the war; I have learned to do this with all the soberness expected of me. Formerly, when I was younger and less patient, I refused to take part in this make-believe and lapsed into haughty silence. I read my lecture before two hundred girls whom it could only have bored to tears and who none the less applauded vigorously, as one girl, delighted, I imagine, to be free to run away at last. Never have I felt so gauche. There is so little reality in my present life, I mean so little that corresponds to what I am, to what is like me. . . .

MAY 2. I have always dreamed of a life where sensuality would be absent, not by reason of ascetic discipline, but from the very nature of this ideal existence. However, doesn't this mean dreaming over the happiness of childhood? If I said this, I would have psychiatrists against me, I know, for they claim that childhood is a period of great sexuality and no doubt they are right, but a child does not suffer from sexuality; he is not even conscious of it, virtually it does not exist where he is concerned and so he is able to enjoy the happiness I mention.

(AUGUST, 1948. *Yet who would wish for such questionable happiness? It stands to reason that the sexual instinct is a cause of much suffering, but apart from purely physical manifestations, it is also an element of essential activity that is to be found every-* ✓ *where, in my opinion, as much in the field of intellect, in literary creation, as in spiritual life itself. The odium cast on it by Catholic and Protestant writers is one of the saddest errors of puritanism, the origin of which is far earlier than the seventeenth century. And, moreover, a very difficult error to get rid of. Right in the twentieth century, our ideas of religion are so peculiar that one is not religious, in the eyes of the world, without also being ever so little of a puritan. For the devout, enemy number one is the sexual instinct; the only thing he forgets is that this instinct comes from God.)*

MAY 3.   There are people who suddenly cease believing in God. Speaking for myself, I am aware of gradually ceasing to believe in humanity. It impressed me for a very long time by its speeches, its laws, its books, but I am beginning to see it in a true light—a very sad one—for humanity is an old lunatic whose fits of cruelty alternate with smiles. Humanity thinks itself majestic and venerable, forgetting its constant taste for blood and an immense thirst for calamity. Do not tell me that it seeks happiness; humanity, and this is only too clear, loves rows and ructions.

MAY 4.   Thoughts have wings, words trudge afoot. In this lies the whole of a writer's problem.

MAY 8.   I have never looked at Dürer's seated Christ without feeling heartsick, for it seems to me that if He is in such grief, it is particularly on my account. To whom would I dare say such a thing without feeling very ridiculous? Yet the little drawing really gives me that impression, and I wonder if this is not the very one it should give. Otherwise, in thinking that such terrible sorrow is caused by the whole of humanity, the sense of personal responsibility is considerably lessened. And as regards this question of salvation, I wonder if God does not wish it to appear to each of us like a great debate between Himself and "me," between Himself and every human being, as though each human being were alone on earth or, better still, as though each human being were in himself alone the whole of humanity.

MAY 25.   Read and reread the metaphysical poets: Donne, Herbert, Crashaw. I have a great feeling for Herbert's subdued poetry, for those nocturnal dialogues with Christ, in an old English vicarage: one can imagine the table with its lamp and papers, hands dropping a quill pen to fold in prayer. This is one of the sweetest and most peaceful moments in the history of the human conscience. When a recluse talks with God, how little does he know that such an hour of recollection sums up the aspirations of a world and that what he is doing perhaps surpasses in importance the clash of armies battling over a province.

JUNE 3. A spiritual void cannot be filled by reading the mystics; that would amount at most to staving off one's hunger. What induces us to buy so many books on religion? This is no doubt a "leaning," but shouldn't it worry us to see so many books around us, so little Christianity in us? I secretly think that a well-prayed *Pater* would teach us as much as the works our curiosity battens on, leaving our hearts thirstier than ever. We wish too much to know for the sake of knowing, instead of knowing in order to improve ourselves. What good are all those books of ours if they do not teach us to love our neighbor?

Taking up Chaucer again. His is the morning freshness of medieval times. In his world, already an old world, he was new. He discovered spring and all its scents, as though it were the first of all springs. We are too weary, too surfeited to pick a rose and smell it with the simplicity of a man of those times. But it must be said that we have also been too much bombed, torpedoed, and exiled. . . .

JUNE 8. Spent yesterday evening at the Maritains'. Lourié and his wife were there, Paulding of the *Commonweal*, Father Couturier. Jacques talked about Father Lamy. He told a number of very beautiful stories, such as the one about Father Lamy climbing a hill with a statue of the Blessed Virgin in his arms that he means to place in his chapel. All the village saints accompany him, climbing with their bare feet a few inches off the ground, passing through trees whose branches remain motionless; all of them have halos differing as to size, and talk to each other, saying: "He is going to send us away. . . ." In the course of conversation someone remarked: "There are no saints nowadays." Father Couturier answered rather gruffly: "Madame, St. Catherine of Siena's mother used to say: 'There are no more saints.' There are, on the contrary, a great many. We have all known some." Followed a discussion on art and religion. I said: "One can imagine a saint painting a picture (Fra Angelico) or composing music. Can one imagine a saint writing a novel?" "Why not?" they asked. "Then name one," I replied. So far, a novel written by a saint remains a sort of theoretical case. I even wonder if the fact of writing a novel would not curb serious spiritual efforts.

JUNE 11. I was saying the other day that in novels virtue is usually shown up in a ridiculous light, no matter what the author's intentions. What could be more frightfully bungled than Little Nell in Dickens, or Balzac's virtuous young ladies? The most remarkable exception, to my mind, is Mme de Tourvel in *Les Liaisons dangereuses*. What part does irony play in this woman's portrait? I have no idea, but it seems obvious that the character *escaped* Laclos and lives independent of the author. White is a color (if it is one) that novelists use clumsily; they are far more skillful in using black, which is, according to Tintoretto, the most beautiful of colors (if it is one).

JUNE 17. Wandered around Times Square and its vicinity the other evening, giving in to the longing I sometimes have to mix with a crowd, to be lost in a multitude, for no definite reason. Not that I get tired of books, it is a sudden craving for the streets. To my knowledge, Poe alone has described this feeling well; however, either from innocence or a sense of decency, he does not explain it. With me, it is perhaps the counterpart of a too regular life; a minimum amount of disorder is perhaps necessary to afford a certain balance, or, if the word *disorder* is too extreme, let us replace it by the *unforeseen*. The best that streets can offer is the unforeseen. But I hate crowds and after a few minutes drifted into a movie.

JUNE 18. My edition of Mallarmé is incomplete (a selection of poems published by Perrin); I am completing it by using a copy of the N.R.F. edition belonging to Robert. Took the greatest pleasure in copying the whole beginning of *Hérodiade*. One cannot imagine how words could say more, or better; with Mallarmé, speech possesses a peculiar quality of extreme transparence combined with great inner complexity; it is like a block of cut crystal that revolves on its own axis; its outline can be seen at times and suddenly the pattern disappears, the sharp edges crisscross and seem to multiply in an apparent disorder out of which light unceasingly flashes. It has been wrongly said that his language is obscure. It is anything but an obscure language, it is a language without the ghost of a shadow and whose mysteriousness seems to be woven with light.

JUNE 30. Writing letters has always bored me to an incredible degree. The shortest note obliges me to make one and sometimes two drafts, which is ridiculous. A letter begun is often set aside, and sometimes for ever. In my drawer are numerous sheets of paper with just these words under the date: *Dear Mr. . . .* or *Dear Mrs. . . .* and that is all, because I have stopped, discouraged by the intense futility of the whole business. I have great difficulty in expressing myself in a letter. I say too much or too little, and the too little does not seem worth while continuing, whereas the too much always exceeds the limits of what was expected. I think I have unfortunately lost more than one friend by not having written a necessary letter in time, but then, what is a friendship that hangs on a letter? I want stouter friendships that stand up better before a trial by silence.

It so happens that one thinks so often and so habitually of God in set phrases that this great reality, which is the only reality, is obliterated by conventional words. We should try to think of God in His *newness*, in His eternal freshness. From time to time, but rarely, we have a confused impression of a huge mystery and then falter a prayer, at times the best of all possible prayers. How many of us have ever had a feeling of the presence of God? We take refuge in the most familiar forms of our religion, I do not simply say of religion, but what we make of it by a daily refusal of holiness . . . We fumble our way along without knowing what we are, or what we are doing, without knowing what is happening within us, because the world has put our eyes out. Money, sensual pleasure, ambition, success, kill in us all feeling of the mystery that surrounds us from birth to death. . . . This feeling should never leave us, the voice of silence should never cease to echo within us, the voice that says: "You are mine, I shall never let you go."

JULY 4. Human speech. Its imperfections are what intrigue me; to realize such insufficiency, it suffices to compare the swiftness and clarity of our thoughts with the heaviness and slowness of the words we use to voice them. There must have been a time (before original sin?) when human thought flew from one brain to the other without the help of this clumsy go-between.

* * *

JULY 11. Read Joergensen's *St. Francis*, which impressed me very deeply. There would be a great deal to say about it. St. Francis' struggles to preserve the original character of his Order seemed most pathetic to me. He failed, he saw his work changed, become jeopardized (some would say: succeed), and that, under his very eyes. The great good period was that when the brothers slept under the stars and all but starved. Later came money, came a desire for knowledge. A school was founded at Bologna, in spite of St. Francis' explicit wish, and he *cursed* the founder. The question would be to know if the first Franciscans were not really the only true evangelical Christians that the earth has seen since the apostles.

JULY 12. My mind is still taken up with Joergensen's book, for I see clearly enough that it passes judgment on our own way of living. We are so far removed from the Gospel that at first sight, one does not quite see how we could return to it. I know that when we kneel to say our prayers we are (in a certain way) with the Gospel, but the rest of the day we are separated from it by chasms. We open our lips, it would seem, only to deny it. We have lost the way to happiness. The life of a Franciscan around the year 1200 appears a martyrdom to us, because we see only its more difficult aspects, against which our idea of *well-being* rebels. We cannot conceive the unutterable interior joy that formed the counterpart of terrible privations (terrible in our eyes). Joergensen says that the English Franciscans, on meeting again after all sorts of difficulties, felt such great joy that they could not speak intelligibly. St. Francis danced as he talked to the Pope. We know that he sometimes pretended to play the fiddle with two sticks of wood and sang until rapture overcame him. These were men intoxicated with joy and such a joy that our wretched pleasures can never come near it. St. Francis was certainly one of the greatest of all poets and to such a degree that we wonder if holiness is not poetry under an absolute form, and if human poetry, even when it crawls on a level with the ground, is not the reflection of spiritual splendor such as we are incapable of imagining. What would sleeping on a board matter to us if Christ and Mary came to visit us? One is appalled at the thought of all we need to spend a short day without discomfort. A gloom is cast over some people by a bad meal, or what they call a bad meal. I have wondered for the last few days if Christ did not offer us His Gospel a *second* time during St. Francis' life. I know, of course, that He offers it to us every day and at every hour of the day, but that time was, if I may say so, a special time, a more particularly pressing exhortation. The world, the whole Christian world, should have followed. It does not appear that this took place.

JULY 20. Reread a few of Whitman's poems. He is an American after my own heart, a grand person, ignorant, crazy, generous, and inspired. There is something barbarous about his intemperate speech, but a deep feeling for human fellowship and a contempt of all meanness rank him among the very first. When he lays a branch of lilac on President Lincoln's coffin, the gesture is most important, because of the man who makes it and because of Lincoln. Whitman possesses the enormous immodesty of a child, and I am afraid that America is secretly ashamed of the *enfant terrible* she has given the world. Stevenson has written pages of facile irony about this great poet, whom the Scot refused to understand, for it is easy enough to make fun of Whitman's absurdities, which are numerous. His greatness covers it all, his long cape, his vast and so bravely "artistic" sombrero; but in Whitman lies a sort of childlike nobility that Europeans cannot appreciate because a certain type of ingenuousness irritates them. I know very well that Whitman's extravagances can raise a smile, but who could resist his way of clapping you on the shoulder and calling you Camerado!

AUGUST 2. It is always rewarding to read Stekel, and what I have said in this diary about his book on anxiety calls for several things to be set straight. We should see where he is right in simplifying our nature, in considering it as a mathematician studies a problem in algebra. It may indeed be, as the author says, that a transmutation of feelings is effected in the secret regions of our moral being, but the deep, supernatural causes of our actions cannot but escape an observer such as Stekel for whom the supernatural is a fabrication. Stekel would have challenged the possibility of such a theory as that of God working in us, unbeknownst to us, but we can resent a man of his intelligence denying the reality of religion without even having attempted to experience it; that is what irritates the mind in an otherwise stimulating book. I readily admit that "syphilidophobia" is a disguised fear of moral impurity, that the phobia of poverty is, also in disguise, the fear of not being loved (a fine, deep explanation), but these so-called elucidations only increase obscurity, for when all is said and done, we always end by asking: Why? Why is it so? Why this transformation of one thing into another? The answers he gives to such questions are inadequate, for they do not explain what prompts us to act. The mystery is not even touched on.

AUGUST 11. It is sometimes enough to pray fervently for ten minutes to feel that something is happening, that the soul is struggling to free itself from the world—but the powers of imagination are terrible. All one can hope for is to keep faith to the end, as best one can, as one would shield a lighted candle from the wind with a cloak—but one can never forget that at sixteen, one simply wanted to become a saint; one was right, then: that is the only honorable ambition.

AUGUST 19. John Donne's sermons fill me with great aversion for his doctrine, steeped as it is in death and damnation, but the writer is great. There is something both ringing and low-pitched about his sentences that strikes and arrests attention; they are often affected and grandiloquent, but they have a way of suddenly struggling loose from their draperies, and you feel as though Lazarus stood before you in all the horror of after-death corruption and talking with remarkable authority. Donne seems almost hypnotized by the more brutally painful aspects of death. To say it attracts him is putting it mildly—he is in love with it. There is a sort of firm, icy despair in him, hardly tempered by faith, having more in common with Seneca than with the Christianity that this ex-Catholic claims to be his. A strange character, haunted by memories of his youthful errors and to such a point that one wonders if he is not vulnerable at heart and, in spite of himself, in agreement with this disclaimed part of himself—a great sensualist who somberly and deliciously relishes a regret for his sins, failing sin itself. He shows a frightful zest in talking of moral evil, or the effects of the plague, or the pangs of death.

AUGUST 23. I was at the Co-ordinating Council a little while ago, to hand in a paper I am to read there day after tomorrow. Nailed to the wall of one of the offices was an immense plan of Paris, in admirable detail: every house could be seen; one might almost have counted the windows and chimneys. I immediately looked for and recognized our house on the avenue de La Bourdonnais and the one on the avenue Wilson. All that is over there, and I am here. The thought, so simple that it might seem absurd, plunged me, nevertheless, into a deep melancholy. I looked at that map with an outburst of love, for Paris is in us, in a way that I cannot express: the streets, the lines of the river correspond to something interior. All that has become part of our consciousness, but I think one would have to be deprived of Paris for a long time to understand what I have just written.

OCTOBER 15. I wonder if I shall ever be able to define what I call happiness. I don't mean a feeling that everyone knows, or has known, or thinks he has known, but something else more particular, something almost religious—a paralyzing emotion. I think that I must have been about eight when I experienced it for the first time in a classroom of the Lycée Janson. By looking out of the window I could see the gabled roof of a covered gallery that connected the small lycée with the large one, and it was when I was looking at this roof that a mysterious joy swooped down on me. I think that I remained in this indescribable state for several minutes, no longer quite aware of what was happening around me and, above all, not knowing why I felt so happy. Today, I feel that this unreasoned happiness is perhaps the normal state of humanity when it is torn away from evil, I mean the happiness that humanity would know if it returned to God. Several times later I have known moments such as I have just described and *that never depended on outside circumstances*. This is exactly what distinguishes them from moments of ordinary happiness. I was not happy just because the day was fine, or because things went well, it was because of other things that I could not understand, that I still do not understand. And I have always been struck even by the slightness of the connection between this happiness and that induced by love, for instance. I call it religious on account of its extreme graveness and on account of its mysterious origin.

NOVEMBER 20. Very much struck by reading Hopkins. He wanted to be a saint before being a poet. He believed that a good Jesuit glorified God better than a great poet, and he was both. He attempted to exorcise nature, to see God through it, to separate it from sin and discover it as it was before original sin. His curious, beautiful, forceful language tries to express what lies beyond human speech; a language that seems close to ecstasy, that tries desperately to see what man saw in the Garden of Eden, and that the poet *remembers*. Around 1875, this Jesuit, practically unknown to almost all of his contemporaries, leaped ahead of the most modern of our present poets, who seem to follow after him.

NOVEMBER 27. A little while ago, I was looking from the window of my room at the little gardens back of the house and saw, seated at the window of a small house that faces this one, an old gray-haired woman sewing diligently. I watched her for a few minutes, my head full of childhood memories brought up by the tiny gardens and the woman's even movements, which reminded me of Mlle Goudeau, our old seamstress; and I was anxious to retain all that was true and singular about this moment: the unknown woman wrapped in her little mystery, I in mine, and between us, a sort of bridge thrown from my window to hers by memory.

CHRISTMAS. To the Manhattanville convent yesterday for midnight Mass. The great freezing avenues in this part of New York, an unlovely night in a setting of sordid houses, shattered silence, blown to pieces by passing cars, drunken laughter, hostile colored faces, and then the convent in the solitude of a large park on top of a hill. A sung Mass, like those I used to hear in the rue Cortambert, but this one sung by more proficient voices, disincarnate voices that seemed to pass above humanity rather than mingle with it. About fifty of the black-gowned nuns went to communion; they walked up to the altar and returned with an admirable slowness that showed how little they lived in our times and that their life, wholly turned inward, already partook of eternity; their gait, in an indescribable manner, had the slowness of smoke rising from a wood fire into motionless air. They appeared to float, like people in a dream. It is religious life that teaches such slowness in a world basely enamored of speed. Nothing was more beautiful than these very deliberate and very simple attitudes, this refusal of all haste.

DECEMBER 28. I said good-by a moment ago to my O.W.I. colleagues, for I am going back to Baltimore. We had a farewell glass of port in Lazareff's office. I am writing this in the sitting room of the 62nd Street house; I have had pleasant times here, but it is

already taking its place in the past, as one leaves a house long
before crossing its threshold for ever, and it has been some days
since I really felt present in this place. The flowered curtains are
drawn, the large room is quiet, a little mysterious—it has always
appeared so to me—the fire glows in the mock-marble fireplace
and the wood crackles softly. From time to time, I hear the distant
rumble of a train as it thunders by, but night muffles sounds and
throws a man back into himself. . . .

1944

JANUARY 12. BALTIMORE. Spent three hours last week in the
Washington art museum. Intensely weary, but hope to derive
some benefit from this. Thought about what painting says to each
of us. It bears witness to the world's beauty, raises a great and
violent protest against habit, which gradually blots out from under
our very eyes the wonders of daily life. It is the Fountain of
Youth where our imagination bathes. Between 1850 and 1900,
French painting unconsciously and unceasingly took up St. Francis'
"Praises unto the Lord of His creatures": Sister Water and
Brother Sun constantly being honored.

FEBRUARY 7. Reread the *Aeneid* in the train that took me to
Washington. I found too keen a pleasure in the book not to attempt to discover what it is made of. For months I have lived shut
up within myself, and the verses I am reading seem to lend a new
radiance, a new force of persuasion to the outside world, and at
the same time revive a universe in which grace apparently plays
no part. Every one of us is so permeated by Christianity, even
unbelievers, that the ancient world always appears more remote
and more peculiar than it really was. Some feel a longing for it
that is akin to the regret one might have in leaving a country for
exile. What takes away from the happiness of some among us is
that in the world such as they know it, there exists a book called
the Gospel. A book that takes up very little space, that each of us
is free not even to open, but it remains none the less true that the
book is there, and that the presence of this slim volume causes

several to be not so easy in their minds as they would like. They would be far happier but for the few hundred pages that may very well end by keeping them from sleep and disturbing them to the depth of their beings.

FEBRUARY 19. Continued, not without hesitation, *If I Were You,* the novel I began a while ago. What always makes me pause on beginning a novel and what makes me go back on what I have written and start off afresh, is that once the first pages are written, I have to live with the characters described, live with them for three hundred pages, with them and the manias, faults, and pieces of furniture I have bestowed on them.

Read *The Rock,* by T. S. Eliot, with great admiration, particularly the first page and its masterly statements on our ignorance. And these questions: "Where is the wisdom we lost in knowledge? Where is the knowledge we lost in information?" One would like to see such lines inscribed on the fronton of every university in the world.

FEBRUARY 28. A visit from Robert. We walked together on the road. We talked of what we were reading, of the books we would like to write. I told him that he was the only person in the world to know me perfectly and that I could, in consequence, say everything to him and be certain that he would understand. He is always present, whereas most people are partly elsewhere when you talk to them, even if they are fond of you. The head is there, the heart is far away, or the heart is close at hand but the head travels.

MARCH 23. WASHINGTON. Six P.M., a time when children call out to each other in a manner different from that of noon, I mean that their end of the day voice is softer, gentler, touched with unconscious melancholy. It seems as if everything tried to harmonize: the light and the street noises become more subdued, silence itself changes quality.

MARCH 29. Read Dorothy Hewlett's book on Keats with passionate interest. I marvel that, having been dead more than a hundred and twenty years, he should still inspire the reader with love. A boy with cheeks too pink, with black hair, shiny and soft as feathers, they say, whose hazel eyes had "a winelike luster." I like to think that he once crowned himself with laurel, that he put a wreath of bay leaves on his lovely head for fun and kept it there in the presence of visitors, refusing to remove it, in spite of smiles and raised eyebrows. It is said that his ecstatic gaze made people pause in the street. Beside him, Byron, who insulted Keats ("that dirty little cad," he called him), Lord Byron was nothing but a coxcomb who smelled of cigars, who dreaded getting fat above all things, a lady's man, a success, a poet who sold well. Whereas Keats, Johnny Keats, once upon a time advised by a weighty critic to "go back to the shop, Mr. John, back to plasters, pills, and ointment boxes," bore within him all the poetry in the world.

APRIL 9. Thought this morning that, of the two men living within us (the two men spoken of by St. Paul), each wants to fulfill his destiny and reach a sort of perfection, the highest possible for him to attain, but for this to take place, one of the two must kill the other, as there can never be a lasting peace between them. There can be truces, but with time the truces become shorter and shorter and more and more difficult.

Felt depressed this morning on account of the problem I have just alluded to. Worked hard to forget it and the war as well. I have counted up that a fifth of my life has already been spent in war-times.

APRIL 21. Impossible to say everything in this diary. . . . I have tried to recover a balance that is more and more endangered by my dual nature. Hosts of questions crop up incessantly. Perhaps such uncertainties form part of my fate, teach me something that I must learn. . . . What I lose in all this is my past buoyancy. My heart is no longer so light, nor my head. I keenly feel the hypocrisy there would be in attempting to reconcile a life of pleasure with religious practices. Yesterday, because of a long-standing promise, I was obliged to go and read a lecture on Péguy to the Jesuits at Woodstock. I read four poems ("The Holy Innocents," "Sleep," "Innocence and Experience," and "Leprosy and Mortal Sin"). My audience listened in deep silence; I was afterwards told that it had been much struck by the *newness* of Péguy. Before reading these poems, I was taken to a room to prepare, to *recollect* myself, I suppose (a *prie-dieu* under a portrait of Newman in his old age, a desk, a fine view of the large park). . . . What is strange and that I note carefully for future reference (such landmarks are useful) was the effect that reading Péguy's poems aloud produced on me: I was deeply moved, far more perhaps than the "theologians" seated before me (there were also a few "philosophers"). Something told me: "Maybe this is for your own good rather than for theirs" (that is, the journey, all this traipsing)—but could I not have just as well read or reread these poems at home? No, the circumstances I mention lent them a particular quality.

APRIL 24. Once more, I pulled the volumes of my diary out of their box. I should not have done so: it is a mistake that can result only in immense sadness and most useless regrets. Of course, so long as I read them, I am back in Paris, but I wonder if I will keep this diary or if I will not burn it someday. I have always had a mania for flinging troublesome manuscripts into the fire. No one will ever know how many papers I burned in my youth. Nine times out of ten I was sorry for it, but it was then too late.

MAY 6. God should not be sought in books—except in the Gospel, which is not "books" but the book—He should be sought within us, for God is within us long before He is in books, and far more so. He is the one who must be eternally rediscovered, and I say eternally, because our eternity will no doubt be spent in doing this. The definitions given of Him are often obstacles to the knowledge we might have of Him; spiritual books, no matter how excellent, build systems, and not one of these systems is God, but is too often a substitute for Him, in the reader's mind. The feeling that an ignorant man can have for God is sometimes more exalted than what professors of theology say about Him in their books. More and more I distrust people who cannot talk of God without quoting texts, as though a historical character were being discussed.

MAY 8. BALTIMORE. Yesterday, went to St. Mary's, the Sulpician seminary near here, in the country. An immense, very majestic building with an important façade; severely plain except for a great doorway flanked by massive columns and surmounted by a heavy balcony, the whole edifice in the seventeenth-century Spanish style. Finished, I am told, in 1927. It is the finest thing I have seen in America, as far as modern architecture is concerned. A seminarian, Mr. Prime, had invited us to Vespers. So I sat by

Mr. Prime, who wore a surplice over his soutane. The chapel is a long room lit by tall windows. Two rows of stalls faced each other; there were over two hundred pupils and ecclesiastics, all in surplices. I had an extraordinary feeling of happiness when the Psalms were sung, the *Magnificat* and particularly the *Jesu dulcis memoria.* The sun shone softly in the long chapel where the many surplices lent a snowy whiteness. . . . I was no longer in America, I was in France and even in a seventeenth-century France. Very much struck to see how successful the thought of the founders of the Order had been in creating such a powerful illusion thousands of miles away from Paris and at a distance of three centuries. What I had before my eyes was a reflection of the Saint-Sulpice seminary in Paris, or at any rate of something that must have existed over there and been preserved intact through space and time. Perhaps the correct manner in which Latin was pronounced by young and old may have had something to do with it.

MAY 13. Never has the light seemed more beautiful to me. It is like a great hoard of riches tossed by handfuls into the depths of the foliage, depths all a-rustle with cries, songs, and calls. Can it be that I have never looked at it before? It turns the shade into a servant that follows it step by step in wonderful humility. I look untiringly at the lawns where a pattern of branches shifts amid pools of gold; now and then I leave my books and papers to walk on the road and in the woods to watch daylight triumphant.

MAY 24. It is cooler, after last night's storm. Robert, who had never been to Mount Vernon, took me there. For about ten minutes we drove through a vast garden; a wood bordered by lawns. I had been to Mount Vernon ten years before. Memories filled with melancholy came back to me, memories of a time when I knew I would be back in Paris in a few weeks, a time when my life was not, as it is today, sadly unmoored. We sat on the porch behind a row of slender columns. At our feet, beyond great stretches of green, ran the Potomac shrouded in bluish mist, a huge river with straggly shores that could easily bear whole fleets on its titanic shoulders. Indoors, I was once more struck by the countrified look of small rooms indelibly stamped by the simplicity of eighteenth-century American life such as is found almost

everywhere from North to South. I think one should have stood
within these walls to understand a certain America, for Mount
Vernon is like the mother cell of a great hive, of ever increasing
proportions. Looking at a rather dark little parlor whose tiny
window offers an immense view, I dreamed for several minutes,
as though something had at last been explained to me, I imagined
all the reveries, hopes, disappointments, and courage the room
had contained. Walls painted a dull green, polished wood furniture, silver candlesticks, the carpet with its bold floral pattern,
and, in this triumphantly conventional, honest setting, confined in
the narrow window and shattering the whole house, the landscape
like a large gap, and the vast blue river. I would have liked to
make all this perceptible, but such a twofold and contradictory
impression escapes speech; what can be said of it is inadequate
and can only be alluded to.

MAY 27.   Read Browning's "Songs from Paracelsus." Beyond a
doubt, these lines were written for me:

> Yet we trusted thou shouldst speak
> The message which our lips, too weak,
> Refused to utter . . .

That is one of the greatest mistakes I will have to answer for
someday, a far more serious mistake, to my mind, than everyday
covetousness. I have held my tongue when I should have spoken
out. And I could have spoken; I had the means, I still have them.
Browning says elsewhere that an artist saves or loses his soul
inasmuch as he uses his gifts. I feel keenly that God speaks to us
through the mouth of those we see every day and through the
mouth of books that fall—and never by chance—into our hands.

Thought today of what D. H. Lawrence said in a sentence that
contains all this writer's eccentric violence: "We are crucified in
sex." Strangely true of many among us. It used to humiliate me
to have this problem in my life. I supposed that the great men I
admired had not had these difficulties. They simply did not mention them. The sexual question did not fit in with the idea I
wanted to form of myself, a somewhat foolishly solemn idea.

JUNE 6.   Heard today that the Allies have landed in Normandy.
It took me some time to believe it or even understand the news-
paper headlines. They are fighting between Trouville and Caen.
We returned to Washington last night.

Passing through Gainesville, we went out of our way to see "The Lawn" (my grandfather's estate). The house, rebuilt after the 1922 fire, looks very good among the old trees. The big cedar, the one I described in *The Keys of Death,* is still there, an old crippled giant still defying storms. All the windows were shut, and I understood that everyone was away. Robert climbed the bank that borders the great lawn and looked over the fence, which is covered with honeysuckle. A moment I shall remember. A vast blue sky, a deep silence, the late afternoon silence in the country, and the trees that talked to me of my twentieth year, of my father with whom I had strolled around the house one day in 1921. I was happy then, a little on account of the absurd, enormous confidence I had in the future.

JULY 4. MILLS COLLEGE. I held my first class yesterday. Spoke without notes for almost an hour, to my own surprise. I sat down at my desk much as one would fling oneself into the water, but with the first words, my anxiety gave way to self-confidence. After an hour of this, I was spent. I talked about the novel, brought up the question of knowing where books come from, but without providing the answer (how could I?). The class listened in admirable silence. A couple of nuns took notes. About twenty people in all.

Went to see the Milhauds after dinner. . . . Darius talked about Satie and his mania for collecting. After his death, ten unused and moth-eaten suits, hundreds of brand-new handkerchiefs, dozens of umbrellas were found in the composer's room. Cocteau is said to have seen him come out of a department store in a shower, an umbrella thrust inside his coat to protect it from the rain, looking up at the sky with hatred. No one ever entered Satie's home during his lifetime, says Milhaud. In front of his house at Arcueil-Cachan is another house, a deserted one on the wall of which some hand (Satie's hand?) had written: "The devil lives in this house."

JULY 20. At table today, several students asked for my views on education. I laughed and answered that I hesitated to tell them, as my views were unconventional and we were in a college. "Oh come!" they cried, "we aren't children!" "Well," I said, "they stuff your heads full of facts, without teaching you to draw useful conclusions from them. Education consists in rousing intelligence, in stimulating it rather than burdening memory. It doesn't matter much that you have read all Spinoza and all Plato (as you are forced to in some colleges) if you don't know how to reason correctly. And rather than make you swallow all these books, it would be far better simply to give you a taste for reading (which you have lost through enforced reading), etc." It was all they could do to keep from applauding. What I said was so unlike what is usually told them.

JULY 21.   If everything could be said . . . But Poe is right: *My Heart Laid Bare* will never be written. "No man dare write it. No man will ever dare write it. No man could write it if he dared. . . ." Or, having written it, he wouldn't dare not throw it in the fire.

AUGUST 5.   Mrs. Stein tells us that she has a great number of letters from Matisse and that she burns them as soon as she reads them over, which makes us all protest in horror. What can be done to prevent her from destroying the letters? She shakes her head, only promising to save one letter which she hands us and that contains the account of a visit Matisse paid Renoir in 1918. I remember this sentence of Renoir's: "I'm just an old fellow who hasn't done much, but what I've done is really mine." Speaking of his painting, he says: "Yes, but it's *not enough like Courbet.*" Mrs. Stein tells us there is too much about stomach-aches in these letters of Matisse. "How could all this interest the public?" How? Of course it would! She smiles and shakes her head. She is going to burn the whole lot, except that single letter.

AUGUST 13.   At Birmingham, Michigan, with my brother Charles.

AUGUST 17.   Yesterday, I walked by myself in the gardens of Cranbrook. I looked at Milles' big, innocent statues mirrored in the water. Also looked at boys and girls bathing in a little lake: that was more beautiful. America's masterpiece is youth: its body is a hymn of glory.

Had a long talk with Charles. He looks very much like my father as I knew him around 1920. My father was forty-seven when I was born. I particularly remember him when he was fifty-five or sixty. Charles' big gray eyes have Papa's kindness. And he has also inherited my father's courtesy, the meaning of which is scarcely ever understood nowadays, or appreciated. Charles thinks the war is about to end, but he has two sons in the army and I am afraid this influences his judgment. He has had a hard life. His courage and, above all, his extraordinary trust in God make me feel very close to him. When in difficulties, he is always convinced that God will "straighten" everything out. And, of course, that is what happens. The other day, a neighbor said to him with a smile: "Everyone knows that God protects the Greens in a special way!" I laughed with him, but have always thought so a little too.

AUGUST 23. BEAR TRAP FARM, VIRGINIA. Today, at breakfast, a woman at a table not very far from ours said it would be a good thing if Paris were razed to the ground so as to be done for ever with that impure city. Her neighbors calmed her down at once by remarking that if people began razing all impure cities, they would have to raze Washington, New York, etc. And the lunatic said no more. In this curious hatred of Paris lie so much sensual deprivation, years of repressed desires, frustrated pleasures, longings. . . . This is not the first time that I have noticed the manifestation of a puritanical conscience. "We are at war because of Europe's sins" is an argument that leaks from the talk of the calmest and best-informed people. No one can understand anything about an American unless he remembers that even in a lack of religion, the reactions of a religious man still linger in an American. The old yeast of puritanism is still what makes the dough rise sometimes.

AUGUST 24. In Hawthorne's diary, his "day-book," as he calls it, I noted this which enchants me: "In an old house, a mysterious knocking might be heard on the wall, where had formerly been a doorway now bricked up." And this too, extraordinarily penetrating: "A person to be writing a tale, and to find that it shapes itself against his intentions; that the characters are otherwise than he thought; that unforeseen events occur; and a catastrophe comes which he strives in vain to avert. It might shadow forth his own fate,—he having made himself one of the personages." (Pages 15 to 20 in Houghton Mifflin's edition, 1910.)

I am writing this in my room. The wind blows with a great murmuring that passes through the whole sky. Silence over the countryside, silence spread over the countryside like a sheet; yet if one listens closely, the locusts' chirp can be heard in the meadows and the distant creak of a cart going up the road. In the little house where I am staying, the hour is so deeply peaceful that one would like to spend it only in doing beautiful things, in writing, or in praying (if one could). The crowing of a rooster rises from the bottom of the valley, but over all this is silence that masks every noise. I must also note, for memory's sake, that the blue of the hills verges on violet.

AUGUST 26. Yesterday evening, at seven, I heard an American correspondent in Paris; he was speaking from there. His voice was indistinct, but around that voice was the hum of Paris. All I understood was: "This is So-and-so in Paris." And that sentence was enough for me. I listened without catching a word, but delighted and more moved than I can express. And so Paris can be heard once more. The odious gag is off. . . . At supper, in the lovely dining room where old furniture gleamed softly and candlelight flickered on the rafters, ten or twelve of us sat at the long table. Through the window, I could see bluish-gray clouds sail through a pale green sky, chased along by a cold wind from over the hills: there was something violent and gloomy in the great picture that contrasted with the restfulness of the room where we sat, with the soft, peaceful candlelight. After the soup, a maid came in to place a glass of white wine before each of us, then a graying gentleman rose and said a few very simple words; he said: "We must not speak of the fall of Paris, but rather of the rise of Paris," and raised his glass to drink France's health. Someone else added—an old white-haired man: "And we are also thinking of our boys who are fighting." And that was all. After supper, I thanked the man who had spoken. He smiled; he said: "It's three in the morning in Paris. I don't think there's much sleeping there tonight."

AUGUST 27. Reread *King Lear*. When I was twenty, in Virginia, an hour away from the place where I am now, I used to turn storms to account by reading over certain scenes in this play which is, sure enough, the story of a big storm, whose hero is a storm; Lear himself is that storm; all he can do is to rage or weep, he's not a man, he's an element. From the very first scene on, he is mad or doting, but he is a dotard of the violent type. What bothers me greatly is the counterplot of which Edmund is the chief character, for Edmund is a conventional traitor and, owing to him, *King Lear* is a magnificent poem and at the same time a

melodrama. The scene where old Gloucester is tortured is almost
unbearable, but contains this unforgettable line: once the old
man's eyes have been put out and he declares that he wishes to
go to Dover, Regan cries with terrible brutality: "Go thrust him
out at gates, and let him smell his way to Dover." (Act III, scene
7.) Very much struck by marvelous scene 6 of Act IV, where
Edgar is seen as he pretends to lead blind Gloucester to the edge
of Dover cliff, whence the old man wants to throw himself, but
they stop long before. "You are now within a foot of the extreme
verge," says Edgar. Gloucester flings himself forward and falls
on the ground. Edgar then feigns to be someone at the bottom
of the cliff and congratulates the old man for having fallen unhurt
from such a height, and Gloucester believes this fable. The scene
is strangely poetical; it is, unless I am mistaken, the one Keats
liked so much and that he used to read over on the Isle of Wight.
Particularly the passage containing the word *samphire*, a rather
mysterious word.

AUGUST 28. I don't want to drop *King Lear* without noting several things that have struck me. Act V, scene 3: this which is important: "And take upon's the mystery of things, As if we were
God's spies." The idea was taken up by Browning. A poet is
God's spy.

And this also: Act V, scene 3. Regan has just been poisoned
by her sister Goneril. She is in great pain and cries: "Sick, O,
sick!" Then Goneril, in an aside, makes a comment that cannot
but be found extremely comical in its cruelty: "If not, I'll ne'er
trust medicine."

Shakespeare often gives his language a familiar turn, not unlike
current American speech. For instance (to be found in *King
Lear*): "Shut your mouth, dame." And this, which is very fine,
at the very end of the last act (Kent speaking): "Vex not his
ghost. Oh, let him pass! He hates him That would upon the rack
of this tough world Stretch him out longer." There would be
better examples to find, however.

SEPTEMBER 4. BALTIMORE. Translated seven or eight pages of
Memories of Happy Days, but don't know if I will go on with it.
Certain naïvetés pass in English but would not be tolerable in
French. This is because I am not the same person in both tongues;
I knew it, I said it throughout a lecture.

* * *

SEPTEMBER 17. Read Auden's *Look, Stranger*, with deep admiration. Some lines make you feel like clapping your hands (I realize that a critic might say: That's just what we find fault with! but that is not the way I take it). I do not find in them the facility he is accused of, what I see above all is a certain contempt for pleasing everybody, of being understood by the many. He teaches near here. If I followed my lead, I would go to see him. As it is, to have a great poet in the vicinity is a great deal. I cannot resist the pleasure of quoting a few lines where singularly beautiful images remind one of Blake at his best:

> That later we, though parted then,
> May still recall these evenings when
> Fear gave his watch no look;
> The lion griefs loped from the shade
> And on our knees their muzzles laid,
> And Death put down his book.

SEPTEMBER 22. Read some of Auden's poems. They have a touch of the Byronic irony adopted nowadays by so many English poets with a sort of fervor. The pietism of unbelievers. It is characterized by complete nihilism, by contempt for everything that has been handed down by parents, that is, for the nineteenth century, for the Victorian era, a rebellion against venerable commonplaces, against everything that has so long confined us in our political errors and that produced moral circumstances apt to hatch wars such as that of 1914 or of 1939. It must of course be admitted that they are right, nine times out of ten. But also to be included here are the snickers that greet the testimony of mystics ("night of the soul, dry as a bone"), in short, the great desert known as "the clean sweep."

There is a fact in my life that I have never so clearly understood as today: for the last four years I have been running away from the book I want to write. How can I not understand the meaning of all those numerous attempts that were cut short so abruptly? The reason is that I have not published *The Transgressor*. Writing a book is not enough to set an author free, the public must read it, the public must know. Everything that I have written for the past four years, memoirs, diary, prefaces, lectures, has been written *instead of something else*.

*   *   *

SEPTEMBER 23. Reread Stekel again. The conclusions of his book on anxiety are fascinatingly interesting. Enough material there for ten novels. There is an excellent passage about the havoc created by tenderness in the souls of beings thus made incapable of facing life. But I can never reread Stekel without saying to myself as I close the book: "Yet the Church is right: sin is a terrible reality." It remains nevertheless true that what he calls repressed sexuality can be dangerous to a degree not always suspected, when a very strongly organized spiritual life does not provide the necessary counterweight, does not restore equilibrium. Wouldn't insisting on repressing sexuality, in a very moderately religious person, mean exposing him to serious accidents, body and soul . . .

Beyond these things is the world of mystics. I was struck by what I read in Eckhart this morning: a priest said to him: "I wish I had your soul in my body." And Eckhart replied: "That would be useless. A soul can save itself only in its own appointed body." (Fénelon said something similar: to save oneself by means of one's own particular temperament.) And so our instincts, which vary so much from one individual to another, would be the particular instrument of our salvation. Can one imagine, however, a part of the human race banned by society in the name of divine laws, and that on account of instincts which this banished minority cannot help? Must it go in a body to a convent? This seems absurd. And what does the Church say about this? The Church is silent. Mauriac, to whom I submitted these difficulties, merely shrugged his shoulders as much as to say: What can be done about it? An answer most Catholics make. And this argument: You wouldn't have the Church allow such things, would you! I note that in this case the Church follows the example of Jesus, who was silent. St. Paul expressed himself long and furiously on the question we are discussing. Christ did not say a word about it that has come down to us, and yet, in Judea, at the time, under Roman rule, in a great city like Jerusalem, the question must have been asked Him, anxiously asked Him. What did He say? He kept silent, as the Church is silent. This is in itself a sort of answer, but what an obscure one!

OCTOBER 1. A moment ago, I listened once again to George Gershwin's *American in Paris*. The opening theme, a young American on the boulevards around 1920, is so good-natured and at the same time *so faithfully observed* that I felt a little heavy-hearted. The Paris of 1920 (for me of 1922) is so far from us and seems so lovely and carefree that it is almost painful to remember it. Nightly walks along the Seine or the Champs Élysées, street lights shining through the horse chestnuts, mystery, gaiety, the smiling quality of it all, the absolute confidence in the future that swept me onwards, the exhilaration of being alive in the most beautiful city in the world and at the finest moment of my youth —I felt at times that my heart was not big enough to hold such happiness. This pretty theme, a trifle waggish and a trifle sad, brings it all back to me now. I hope never to be the man who thinks the Paris of his youth more beautiful than the present one, but it seems to me that between 1920 and 1928, life had a certain sweetness never since recovered. I feel heartily sorry for the boys born twenty years after me.

OCTOBER 8. Read *The Tempest* for the sixth or seventh time, but was never so much struck as now by the character of Caliban. We are so used to seeing in him a brute in the state of nature that the author's intentions are obliterated by this preconceived notion. Trinculo and Stephano are just plain out-and-out drunks, but Caliban, with all his coarseness, often expresses himself exquisitely. It was Schlegel who noticed that he always speaks in verse. What Caliban says about the sounds heard on Prospero's island is exceptionally beautiful, and one feels keenly that it is not just a fortunate accident in Shakespearean poetry. No, Shakespeare wanted the lines to be beautiful because they were Caliban's:

> Be not afeard. The isle is full of noises,
> Sounds, and sweet airs, that give delight, and hurt not:
> Sometimes a thousand twangling instruments
> Will hum about mine ears . . .

And what follows. There is a delicacy in this conception of a completely and deeply natural being that could only be that of genius. Therein lies the surprise. A savage who talks of music like Byrd or Purcell! A second-rate author would probably have given him a base, rude speech. What makes me feel ill at ease in this play (although the defect is less apparent here than in many others of Shakespeare's plays) is the triumph of commonplaces, the royal vestments that clothe hackneyed ideas. But the music and color of the verse rank it among the finest ever written.

* * *

NOVEMBER 8. Yesterday evening, Father Couturier came to see me. I no longer remember in what connection I said that sin gives an experience of life that can be turned to immense advantage, spiritual advantage; that sin educates the individual, is a sort of school where he learns to know humanity; that God allows souls that have lived in sin to escape from it and then grow closer to humanity than souls that have never lost their innocence. He allowed that I was partly right, remarking however that the danger of remaining in sin is far too great, and that very spiritual souls intuitively know sin to such a degree that it amounts to a perfect knowledge of all aspects of the problem. Such intuition, I said, would be tantamount to genius, that is, extremely rare. . . . At one moment, I seemed to justify sin and wish to prove the usefulness of evil, but Father Couturier understood me. I was thinking of a certain young priest whose complete ignorance of worldly matters turned him into a sort of child; I know perfectly well that the confessional is an admirable school of psychology, but before he has learned his lessons, how many souls will the young man have rebuffed and discouraged by his uncompromising harshness!

NOVEMBER 20. As we walked in the woods just now, I was telling Anne, in connection with an invitation I had just refused, that I never felt quite at ease with rich people. I have been like this since childhood. It is perhaps because I was brought up very simply; something in me disapproves of luxury (as much as it nevertheless admires it). To dine in a dining room that looks like a dining room in a palace plunges me into a sort of stupor that quickly turns to melancholy. Sumptuous surroundings depress me and I never feel quite happy with a gold plate before me.

In the life of the poet Hopkins by Eleanor Ruggles are quotations from letters exchanged by Hopkins with an Anglican divine, also a poet, but a completely unsuccessful one. Hopkins tries to comfort him. He tells him first of his own lack of success, then says this which I find deeply touching, because one feels he believes it (and also because it is true): "The only just literary critic is Christ, who prizes, is proud of, and admires more than any man, the gifts of his own making."

Reading the book on Hopkins reminds me of certain questions I have sometimes asked myself about physical beauty. Is beauty a sign of latent spiritual perfection, like the mark of a superior vocation? I have always thought that a faultlessly beautiful being who commits an evil deed betrays the man who is himself as he should really be, whereas an ugly being (of a particular ugliness, however, for there exists an ugliness that is almost a form of beauty) who perpetrates an evil action only makes the inner man conform with the outer one.

NOVEMBER 26. Read some of Yeats' poems with delight. An Irishman has a mysterious understanding with nature; you might think he had made a covenant with her, and when he talks about the country, the trees and the grass and the sky do the talking.

Reading the life of Hopkins, I can't help feeling that his personality was crushed by the discipline of the Order to which he belonged, but that is perhaps the impression that the author wants to give. Be it as it may, I wonder to what extent Hopkins accepted his vocation. He remained faithful to the end, but admitting that he never entertained doubts about the wisdom of decisions taken, he would never have fallen back, would never have owned up to a defeat, for to flinch in the face of a decision that involves a man's whole character would not be like an Englishman of his kidney. And in any case, there is no serious reason to believe that he was not an excellent religious although one suspects him of lacking enthusiasm.

NOVEMBER 29. Have thought a great deal about the beauty of human beings (perhaps Hopkins roused these thoughts in me, although I must say that they were only dozing). It seems to me that the beauty of the human eye alone is beyond all possible speech; and I remember that Father Couturier, who was very austere but most intelligent, once said to me: "Nothing in the world is more beautiful than the human body."

DECEMBER 15. At the theater last night to see *The Cherry Orchard*, a play that I admire deeply and whose meaning is more clearly apparent than ever over here, in 1944, for I think that America contains lots of cherry orchards, ready to pass from hand to hand. Behind me, a nasal voice said in an important, well-informed tone: "The play was written to show the corruption of the ruling classes." (!) Keenly sensitive to the beauty of certain scenes where, as in Shakespeare's theater, the characters seem suddenly *larger than life*. At one moment, the limits of sadness are reached when, in the big, bare room, empty of furniture and the large wooden shutters closed, the old, white-whiskered servant comes in and, finding he has been forgotten, lies down on a sofa that has been left behind and very simply dies while the cherry trees are being cut down in the orchard. I know of no one but Chekhov who could have produced such an effect; one almost resents such a form of cruelty even though it is accompanied by the most moving tenderness. The comic scenes I thought overstressed, but that is life's way of being funny, and life does not always have a light hand.

DECEMBER 30. On reading a book like the *Imitation*, I am always struck by the intense reality of the spiritual world; a reality so powerful that it seems to shut out any other possible reality; it consequently appears quite natural to be captivated by an invisible world that offers us the only lasting goods. Things become more difficult later, once the book is closed and other realities present themselves. The answer could be, of course, that compared with spiritual realities, those of the physical world are scarcely more than shadows that seem terribly lifelike at times. The opposite phenomenon then takes place, I mean that the reality of our world of flesh is so commanding that it excludes even the idea of a contradictory reality.

1945

JANUARY 18. WASHINGTON. I have often wondered why the sun makes me feel so sad. That is not the way it usually affects people. There are days when great splashes of light on a wall fill me with dreadful melancholy! People would probably cry out in horror against my irreverence if I said that I almost always feel happier when the sun disappears from the sky, and the time when lamps are turned on in cities has a very special charm for me. "Busie old foole" [1] gives me a headache. I never go out in the morning if I can avoid it. In my mind, everything tragic takes place in full

---

[1] See Donne's "The Sunne Rising."

sunshine. "The night shall be light around me." How often has that sentence from the Psalms come back to me! Night is to some extent my home. I have always noticed in my books that when some calamitous event is brewing, the weather is almost always fine.

FEBRUARY 1. . . . I ask this without being able to answer: Does religious indifference afford a novelist greater freedom? What scruple can arrest him in creating the world contained in the pages of his book? A book without mortal sin? You would have to be Péguy to write such a book, and Péguy was not a novelist. Now, a real novelist does not reign over his novel, he becomes his novel, is immersed in it. The connivance between himself and his characters is even deeper than he thinks, and if they sin, he sins too, in a certain way. He is all that his book is, if he believes in it, if he allows himself to be caught; and if he does not allow himself to be caught, if he is not under the spell cast by the monstrous thing that issues from his brain—for a novel is a monster—he no longer writes novels, he manufactures them. Supposing this is the case, and it is, beyond the shadow of a doubt in my mind, I would like to know if the fact of writing a novel is consistent with the state of grace. I cannot and will not answer this question. I am above all afraid of the answers that could be given me, the ingenious solutions. A scrupulous man will never produce a great novel. For fear of offending God, he will write prudent platitudes and who knows if God does not wish a risk to be taken? Who knows if this is not the way to please Him and to fulfill one's vocation?

JULY 19. I stopped just now before the stall of a man selling magazines and candy in the doorway of a building. I bought some magazine or other. The young man in a white coat who stood behind the counter looked smiling at his open hand and I held out a quarter, but he did not take it, went on smiling and looked down. A little surprised, I said then: "This magazine costs fifteen cents, so you owe me ten, as I gave you a quarter." He immediately handed me a dime without a word, but still smiling. He was blind. I had a strange feeling of his moral superiority over me, although it was impossible for me to explain why. Perhaps on account of a verse in Job that has played such a great part in my life, and where I cannot help seeing the solution of certain problems: "I have made a covenant with mine eyes. . . ." This blind

salesman was safe from the weaknesses usual in those who see, he does not sin with his sight, and if ever he made a covenant with his eyes, he is now certain of keeping it. He looked joyful; a handsome sixteen- or eighteen-year-old face. An indefinable quality of poetry surrounded him because of his infirmity, he was *apart.*

JULY 22. Asked Father Couturier the other day if he had ever thought about the happiness of medieval men who lived in a world with so little room for doubt and where, generally speaking, everybody believed in the same thing. But all of us who live in a world where doubt is, to a certain extent, the general opinion, how can we not feel isolated and like lost children in modern civilization, we and our singular ideas about the incarnation and the transubstantiation (singular in the eyes of the world, but as natural to us as the sun in the sky)? He said that he too had had that feeling of solitude, but I did not encourage him to say more. I could have added that this feeling of spiritual isolation, so painful at times, historically precedes the joy of universal belief, for the first Christians, lost amidst Roman civilization, must have felt a little the way we feel today.

JULY 27. BALTIMORE. I have a passport and will soon leave America. These last days in Baltimore have been difficult. To go away is almost always for me an uprooting, even if it means leaving a place where one has suffered, and I was not always unhappy on Blythewood Road, far from it, in spite of the war. I have known moments of hope and real happiness, thanks to my cousin's kindness. . . . So the other day, I packed my trunks and watched a man put my books into crates. The room where I worked for four years has that look of disaster peculiar to moving, and the heat has added to the sadness of my preparations for departure. And yet, isn't this the moment I have been waiting for since 1940? It is, of course, but I can't help it; I am not leaving in high spirits.

AUGUST 7. CRAWFORD NOTCH. Day before yesterday, looked long at the sky, which happened to be exceptionally transparent. Except in Tunisia, I have scarcely ever seen so many stars and such bright ones, although they seemed larger to me in Africa. What could ever be said of such a sight? It reduces human speech to nothing. Even the effect it produces in us is beyond words. A great inner happiness, a deep feeling of the world's vanity, a more mysterious feeling akin to that of the presence of God, an enormous silence within us, like an echo of Heaven's silence.

AUGUST 14. NEW YORK. Took up *Romeo and Juliet* again. On reading it afresh, I discovered a wealth of beauty that had escaped me in the past. The love scenes are among the only convincing ones in the whole of literature or are even the only readable ones, because a love scene is what we anticipate in dread as it is almost invariably a flop, even with the greatest writers, even with Balzac and Dickens. Here love itself speaks its genuine, inspired language; it is really the heart's outpourings, the inimitable freshness of youth and its faltering amazement. There are strange weaknesses toward the end of the play, such as Juliet's soliloquy just before she drinks the sleeping potion; a few extravagances, one of which at least is funny; she is in a funeral vault and threatens to break open her head with the bones of a deceased relative!

AUGUST 28. At Suffolk, where I wanted to say good-by to Jim before leaving for Europe. He is married. I had scarcely sat down in the drawing room when he told me that he had had a letter from France and wanted to read it to me, in order to dissuade me from returning there. I answered, with a sharpness at once regretted, that I knew beforehand what the letter had to say, that I was as well informed as anyone in America of the state France was in. I refrained from adding: "When you love someone, you don't say: 'I'll come to see you when you're quite well again.'" But Jim was most hospitable and affectionate. There is a world of memories between us.

SEPTEMBER 19. AT SEA. To leave those we love is horrible; it is almost like dying. The last words exchanged, hands waving as the train slowly leaves the station, I can hardly bear to think of it and remain perfectly calm. We should never say good-by. I stayed in my cabin on the boat while New York grew distant and disappeared in the mist.

SEPTEMBER 29. AT SEA. Around eight this morning, my first sight of the coasts of France. They are a dull blue against the almond green of the sea and a smoke-colored sky. I was moved by these soft, mellow shades, for they seemed like the mellowness of France herself. In America, the sky has an empty transparency, the sea the hardness and sparkle of precious stones; nothing over there of the tender, misty effect I have before me, one so conducive to dreaming.

OCTOBER 6. PARIS. At the American Embassy, Keeler Faus, extremely agreeable as always, tells me he has just seen Gide, who talked to him about me. Would I like to speak to him? I should be delighted, and a minute or two later Faus hands me the receiver with Gide at the end of the line. When I gave my name, I heard, and everyone else in the office with me, a great cry, an "Ah!" that enchanted me and then this sentence: "Wait till I bring my armchair closer. . . ." An appointment is made for Sunday. "Now I recognize the sound of your voice, Green. It moves me, you know."

OCTOBER 8. I found Gide much the same as when I had last seen him. I say much the same, because, for all that, there was all the weariness of five hard years. He held my hand in his for a long time, made me sit facing him. The expression in his eyes is the same, an expression that portraits do not quite succeed in conveying, for they always give him a sharp look, whereas Gide's is above all attentive, with a depth of feeling. He wears a black cap, shaped much like those of Neapolitan fishermen. He talks to me about Paris, says I am going to suffer from cold and hunger. He himself is going to Egypt. Then he asks me what I have been doing and I mention my translation of Péguy, but he jibs at Péguy—although he used not to—and thinks his poetry bad. Is that his exact term? It seems to me it was. . . . He then tells me that Gabriel Marcel had talked to him about his own conversion in 1916, and also of mine. According to Gide, Marcel is mistaken, but what about my conversion? I tell him it is perfectly true that I was converted in 1939. He listens silently, nods, then reminds me of his "hostility" toward the Church. I have long known of it, but my friendship for Gide has never changed. I often thought of him in America. He answers by laying his hand affectionately over mine and says: "I knew it."

OCTOBER 11. Long walks through Paris. Very depressed by the thought that I have no place to live.

* * *

OCTOBER 15. I sometimes feel like Rip van Winkle, who slept a hundred years and returned to a changed world. The coin I hand a newspaper vendor is given back to me because she thinks it spurious. Yet the coin is like those now in circulation, with this slight difference: it is made of silver; I found it in the pocket of a prewar suit.

OCTOBER 16. Have just been to see Gide. He received me just as someone was leaving, someone who had helped him "revise his translation of *Hamlet*." Once alone with me, he complains of the innumerable difficulties he met in this work. *Antony and Cleopatra* was far easier. Shows me a passage where Hamlet says he killed Rosenkranz and Guildenstern "with these hands." For all the French translations render the word "arm" by "hands," whereas Gide is certain that the meaning is not hands (literally arm, in English) but a weapon. The English friends he has consulted think him right! But in the same passage, I notice the phrase "he whor'd my mother" that Gide translates by "he has dishonored my mother." I can't help saying that dishonored seems a weak term and smacks of high-flown speech. "And how would you express it?" I feel very much at loss. However, I hunt for a sentence and find this: "He turned my mother into a whore." That is literally the English meaning. . . . Gide then goes and sits in a corner by the window, exactly between the piano and the window, separated from me by a small polished wood table. How often have I seen him thus, huddled in a corner of the large room, talking in a subdued voice and listening as only a very few know how to listen!

He talks at some length about the attitude of all and sundry during the occupation. . . . Finally, as he hands me a copy of *Attendu que . . .* we speak about the *lama sabachtani*, which I refuse to interpret as he does, and later, concerning the mysterious sayings voiced at times by men and the irritating quality of these sayings because we are uncertain of having understood them right, he quotes these words of Valéry's, found among his notes, the last one he ever wrote. "By chance the last one," says Gide and then, correcting himself, adds: "We must not say by chance." Valéry said: "The idea of love in the divine was introduced for the first time by Christ." (Not at all sure of quoting correctly; this should be checked, but if the sentence is perhaps not exactly as he said it, I believe the meaning is just as I have given it. . . .)

As he asks me certain questions about my religious opinions, I reply that, maybe on account of my Protestant upbringing, I will always find it difficult to talk of religion, or rather, of *my* religion. Our personal religion is more of a secret than anything else. And then, my case is not such a rare one that much need be said about it. I am sure that God acts differently with each of us; yet, in one of George Herbert's poems, I find all that is essential in my conversion, even down to several very precise details. Wouldn't it be enough to read the poem? So Gide and I look it up in the *Oxford Book of English Verse* but, to my great surprise, without finding it; it was perhaps judged to be too well known; it is "The Collar." . . .

I said to him: "Whatever arguments can be opposed to Christianity, this is perfectly unanswerable: 'You spoke and I heard your voice' . . ."

As we were parting, he said: "So you have never been able to find your balance? I have always maintained that we must allow everything we have in us to develop freely. The crises you go through show how youthful you have remained, and to what an extent. I too have had such crises, but put a stop to them. They only tear you to pieces. I said to myself: 'Oh well, it can't be helped!' and ended the whole thing."

A little earlier, he told me that he had spent ten days with Mauriac at Malagar, and that the two of them read aloud to each other, Mauriac reading Racine and Gide the Bible. "I read the historical books, the story of David. . . ." We then launch forth on the subject of Catholics and the Bible, a subject I will return to some other time. "It should be admitted in exoneration of Catholics," said I a moment later, "that they have no fine French translation of the Scriptures. The equivalent of the English Bible does not exist: the Bible, in France, has never been the literary monument it is in England and in Germany. And this is most serious: it is not *quotable* in the French translations. When an Englishman quotes a verse from the Scriptures, he repeats the words and the order of the words with scrupulous respect for a translation that is a work of genius. In France, the words that come to one's lips are a more or less faithful recollection of . . . Crampon."

Gide makes this striking remark: "Even when faith changes or disappears in a Protestant, something remains of his early formation. When faith disappears in a Catholic, everything gives way." To which I reply that this may be true in France, or even in England, but not in America. I don't want to generalize, but it seems to me that over there, it is Catholics who are uncompromising and Protestants who are slack, because Catholics have the minority spirit, the "little flock" turn of mind that makes them hold tight. Puritanism has changed camps.

I don't think I ever saw him more alert, or more like himself.

OCTOBER 18. May the world not destroy what is valid in us. I came home this evening to read the Bible, to try to shed some light on my darkness. There are times when you cannot help but have a horror of yourself, when you are in agreement with those who would condemn us, if they knew. But what the world knows least is what takes place in a soul, and I think that if I were to be judged by the world and not by God, I would be damned. Reread four or five times the poem by Herbert that I mentioned to Gide.

Gide was telling me this morning of a Catholic boy, a very pious and horribly deceitful boy, who serves Mass, goes to confession, etc. (by "etc." I suppose Gide means that he goes to communion) and whose confessor, "one of those holy, short-sighted souls," does not see his baseness. Gide is too ready to hold the Church responsible for such isolated cases.

OCTOBER 19. Nothing leads me to believe I will find a flat. This is becoming a rather painful problem. I am thinking particularly about the moral aspect of the question. Last week, at the theater, I was overcome by the idea that I would not be able to find a roof in my native city; this aroused my indignation—rather briefly, to be sure—but violently. I might be told that I was unreasonable. I can't help it. I find it hard not to be able to say this simple thing, in Paris: "I'm going home." Yet I looked at a flat yesterday that had been offered me and refused it. It was almost out of town on the quai de la Gare, in a house that was to be torn down before the war and that will cave in of itself if steps are not taken to prevent it. One walks up a black and evil-smelling staircase that yells of crime. The view of the Seine is splendid, but would be ruined for me by the continual roar of trucks rolling past the windows. And then, a house that looks sinister in broad daylight must be inexpressibly sad when night falls.

UNDATED. I sometimes hear it said: "Where there's a will, there's a way." But this is said thoughtlessly, as the minute one begins to will, the problem is solved, no matter which way. So the real difficulty must be, not to will, but to have the will to will. For it is so true that back of the will is another will that sets it working. ✓

Thought a lot about physical pleasure and the way it attacks faith. No theologian has ever been able to explain to me how the errors of the body can reach the soul. The truth is that the body is not the guilty party, but the soul that consents. There lies the mystery. How, being spirit, can it consent to what it hates? But the fact is there: a voluptuary makes a bed for the unbeliever.

OCTOBER 23.   I found Mauriac in his study. You reach it by means of a very steep inner staircase. I ran down it, both he and the maid cried: "Look out!" I went up to him and kissed him. . . . He talked about my diary, saying that he had valued it during the occupation, but reproached me with having said too little. "But you can't tell the whole truth!" I cried. "People wouldn't tolerate it. . . ." In the dusk, his head seems quite white; he coughs. Talks about "this poor country," of an exhausted France, of fears for the future, and drops the word *revolution* (under his breath, as though to keep it from waking up). . . . Later he mentions the articles I sent the *Figaro* from America. "Of course your idea of France was right, of course it was right, in spite of all these changes." I understood that I had been mistaken. "Of course it was right" informed me better than a long speech.

NOVEMBER 25.   I wanted to hear Mass at Notre-Dame and went there this morning. Strange to be forced to write that on seeing the great, stark cross that is to be erected in the center of the Weimar-Buchenwald camp, I was gripped by an unexpected emotion, more violent than any I have felt, it seems to me, since 1940, for it was as though the France I am looking for said to me suddenly: "Here I am." This cross must be eight or ten yards high. A French flag hangs from the crossbar so as almost to conceal the foot. It is set in a heap of sand and gravel under the big rose window on the right-hand side of the transept when you face the high altar. I don't think the Middle Ages would have devised anything different. This cross will replace all those that could not be put up over the tombs of the fifty-one thousand dead at Buchenwald and the annex camps for the simple reason that there were no tombs, the disorder in which the victims' remains were found allowing only for a single, mass burial.

*   *   *

NOVEMBER 29. I was telling Father Couturier how disappointing it is to meet certain authors, although their work is most deserving, because they appear to live on a lower level than their work. "The reason for that," said the Father, "is that they put all their spiritual energy in their books and that there is not enough left for them to live on a higher level." If this is so, it would account for the fact that so many conversions are paid for by an apparent decrease in talent. What should have gone into books pours into daily life. Let us hope that good authors who are bad Christians will find salvation through the books they write!

DECEMBER 5. Yesterday I took a young American officer to see Gertrude Stein, as he wanted to meet her. I am anxious for him to admire the quays at twilight, the rue des Grands-Augustins, the rue de Savoie, all the old houses. Why? I really don't know, but have always felt this to be a moral obligation; one should pass on what one has received. Be it as it may, we reach the rue Christine. A wide staircase for sedan chairs. A barking behind the door: Basket, the white poodle. We find Gertrude Stein and Alice Toklas in a room hung with Picassos and Francis Roses, the portrait of Gertrude Stein by Picasso placed over the mantelpiece mirror; near it, Picasso's young nude girl holding a bunch of flowers. A tribute to Le Nain by Rose: the portrait of a young ragamuffin in gray and black, rather fine, but when all is said and done, Le Nain directed the Englishman's hand. Gertrude Stein makes me sit by her on a big black horsehair sofa. She tells me that one day at Belley (not sure it was Belley) she turned on her radio "by chance," just as it was announced that I was going to speak and that it moved her to hear my voice. It was in 1942 or 1943. I sit and look at her. Her face, which is carved in rock, has become very beautiful; a great spiritual force has modeled the nose, mouth, and brow. Her very large, very black, very deep eyes sparkle with intelligence. She wears a gray skirt and a grass-green sweater. Her hands are short, square, and strong. Turning to Captain X., she asks him several questions and ends by making a big speech that is singularly like a dressing down. "Our soldiers like you so much," he says. "Yes, because I am frank with them and don't tell them lies. They have been told too many lies. One said to me: 'We have lost our illusions about the war and the newspapers, because we know what they make of the news, we have lost our illusions about ourselves, we have lost our illusions about God. . . .' " (Not to have any illusions about God would be the beginning of wisdom!) She continues: "It is very serious. They have lost faith. They are devitalized. All you Americans are devitalized, you have lost that something that drove the pioneers onwards, the founders of the United States. What's the reason for this? All Americans are job-minded, they think of nothing but their job. A job is the answer to all their problems. The soldiers go home with the fixed idea of finding a job. That is what is weakening the whole nation. What America needs these days is martyrs. Go home and be martyrs!" "But, Miss Stein, why don't you become our first martyr?" "No, I've shown my mettle, I've proved my courage."

1946

JANUARY 3. It is owing to Jacques B.'s great kindness that all my books were safe during the occupation. While I was far away, he had them placed in a small room, on the fifth floor of an old house in the rue Saint-Augustin. I found them there the other day. Many of them were piled against the walls, others lay flat on the long shelves that run around this strange library, and at first, I dare not put a finger on anything. If I pull out a book, twenty topple over. There must be six thousand of them and the room is not large. I recognize a book I often thought of in America. I take hold of it, pull at it very gently to extricate it from a tottering pile, and the whole thing slips down slowly, the whole thing collapses. Soon I am in a sea of paper. At my feet suddenly appears a great bundle of letters that I thought I had destroyed, and I throw myself on it to read the letters over, standing, in this icy room. How many memories throw me back into the past! A moment ago, I was almost happy. But not at present. With gloved hands, I replace the letters in their envelopes and go toward the door, for I have spent at least an hour stirring up the past, and wonder once again why we are always so eager to keep what can never be anything but a pain to us, after having been so much of a joy. To forget is no more, no less, than a grace.

* * *

JANUARY 14. I went to a Dominican convent today to attend a taking of the habit. André and I get there around half past six and are made to wait in the visiting room with some twenty people. At the far end of the room, double doors flung wide open allow a complete view of a rather vast room (the chapter hall?) that looks like a drawing room that has been turned into a chapel, the walls painted white, and a very plain altar with a great Christ above it. Four tapers have been lit. Silence. Along the walls, two rows of motionless monks face each other, and some seem to be praying. They all wear a black cloak over their white robe. I don't know if they realize the aspect they offer. With a complete disregard for size, the big ones stand with the little ones, the very tall with the very short, as though it had been done on purpose. They do not move at all, they even move so little that, in a few minutes, everything begins to look unreal to me. I myself stand among the others without budging, and the prolonged stillness finally produces a most peculiar sensation verging on dizziness, I mean a sort of fascination, like dizziness. It seems to me that I am gradually becoming a figure in a picture. I would like something to happen, I expect a great deal of what I am about to witness, and at the same time I dread this silence, this immobility, coming to an end. After ten minutes, a great clatter of shoes and two boys dressed like scouts pass among us to go toward the altar. We are then introduced into the chapel. The subprior is seated in an armchair, his back to the altar, an embroidered stole around his neck, and I see, stretched out before him, their brows touching the floor, the two scouts. "What do you ask?" says the subprior in Latin. They murmur something I cannot catch. The subprior then says: "*Levate!*" and they get up. Both are young, not over twenty, and one seems handsome. The subprior then makes a little speech, reminding both of the days they spent in a prison camp during the war, and talks very simply to them about their vocation, as though the three of them were alone. The boys then kneel and a white wool robe is slipped over them. I was very much surprised to feel a sort of indignation at that moment. To see such youth disappear under that wool, those slim, lithe bodies buried in stony whiteness, all that seemed terrible to me. I expected and secretly hoped for an exactly contrary emotion. I counted on some indefinable but great yearning for religious life, instead of which I experienced a spiritual withdrawal. Meanwhile the two novices embrace each of the monks with a tenderness both spiritual and human, recalling for me a picture of medieval times that I thought gone for ever. Next, all the monks go to another chapel and we follow, walking behind them in the corridors. The subprior once more addresses the novices, saying this in substance: "In two years, if we are pleased with you, and you are pleased with us, we will keep you, otherwise you will be free and so will we." I admired the clarity of the contract.

After Compline André and I meet the subprior, who takes us to his cell, which is large, well lit, full of books. He motions to me and I sit on his bed, which, to my surprise, is made of planks with a blanket thrown over them. A few minutes' talk and we go down to dinner. Here we are, in the refectory, a long white hall in the center of which some forty monks sit at a table that seems immense to me. Along the side walls, two other tables of the same size, with a row of monks on one side only, their backs to the wall, on an interminable bench. All their hoods are pulled down almost to the eyes. At the end of the hall, a lector stands reading a life of the curé d'Ars in a completely colorless voice. From time to time, a monk corrects him: "Pronounce your words better. Don't say tirrible. Say terrible." As for me, I sit on the subprior's right, near one of the two doors that face each other at either end of the refectory. We are served a good soup, a dish of rice, some hare pâté (for André and me, not for the others), an apple, and a biscuit. I am forgetting the beer, which would have had the greatest trouble in intoxicating a baby. So much for the fare. From time to time, a monk enters the refectory, flings himself down before the subprior, who raps on the table with a small gavel, and the monk gets up and goes to his seat. I cannot help finding great beauty in this thirteenth-century life, kept up in the heart of the twentieth. I stare, try to remember everything, I also listen. The lector's voice is so intentionally toneless that it requires an effort to follow it. I recall this: "An unbelieving woman once said to me: 'If I had faith, your breviary would burn my hands.' Brothers, does your breviary burn your hands?" Such fine and vehement words spoken *recto tono* produce a strange effect; you have the impression that the lector strips the clothes off the text and offers it naked to the listeners' intelligence. I keep wondering what all these men think. The monks who serve us come and go in their wonderful white robes, as in Fra Angelico's predella at the Louvre. When the meal is over, the subprior raps the table with his gavel and the lector stops. Everybody gets up. André and I are asked into a drawing room with some ten monks and seat ourselves in armchairs. As could be reasonably expected, the conversation turns on literature and I wonder what meaning literature can have for men in black and white robes. Perhaps they pretend to be interested in it out of courtesy, but what can it matter to a religious if such and such a novelist does or does not go through his little tricks? This struck me as a sort of revelation. It seemed that each book discussed was, at one fell swoop, emptied of its contents. I wished I had been able to say something worth saying (and also worth listening to); no indeed! As ever, under such circumstances, not a word passed my lips. And then the others, all the others, are so delighted to talk that I would hesitate to deprive them of this pleasure. I prefer being silent. There are enough people in this world who give tongue for one of us to keep quiet and no harm done.

A little later, the subprior speaks to a brother whose innocent face is truly that of a child and wishes him a happy fête day. The subprior says something like this: "We all love you. You're like a little boy." At which the brother nervously wiggles his fingers under his scapular. That very morning, it seems, his companions, in kindly fun, had slipped a bag of marbles into his shoe as a fête-day present. André and I leave shortly after.

I could not get to sleep this night before two o'clock. I thought about the refectory, of all those cowled heads and then of the after-dinner conversation. I should have said something, but what I heard disagreed too strongly with what I was thinking deep inside me. And also, if I had spoken, they would probably have listened, and I can't talk if people listen to me. This sounds like a joke, but I can't help it. If I find a man driving nails into a bit of wood, or shining his shoes, or laying colors on canvas, I can easily tell him what I am thinking about, if he appears more attentive to his work than to my talk. In any case, when more than two people are present, I am dumb. Yet I have talked to almost a thousand people, and that, several times. But it was not at all the same thing. To begin with, I read my text, and to read before a thousand people is as good as being alone in a desert. What seals me up tighter than anything else is to see three or four people looking at me and waiting. Why is this so? I have never known. I believe I much prefer saying what I have to say in writing.

JANUARY 16.   Heard a priest discuss the Christian idea of love.

He said some very fine, very bold things on the subject, but what
he lacked—and I say this very gravely—was physical experience
of love . . . and of sin. A virgin soul that is called on to direct
men and women can lead them to disaster through an ignorance
of the passions. Theoretic knowledge, even accompanied by
prayer, is not sufficient. Among the American clergy, I have seen
boys fresh from their seminaries, with resolute faces and heads
full of answers. A contempt for the flesh could be clearly read in
their eyes; if they had tried to understand, these alarming children
would have believed themselves lost.

JANUARY 20.   Late this afternoon, I went to see a friend who lives
on the boulevard Beauséjour. The dining room is packed. The
guests throng the buffet showing all the less shame because, the
electric light having failed, no one can see them. A candle or two
shed a poor light on all these people chattering unceasingly like
children at playtime. Someone pushes up to me: "Do you recognize me?" Do I! It is Gaston Gallimard. A stage director assures
me that he wants to put one of my novels on the screen, whereas
in 1930, he told me he was waiting for the first snowfall to film
Leviathan, for he *had* to have real snow. . . . A former comrade
also looms up in the darkness. He was redheaded, still is, and his
voice has not changed. I feel a trifle bewildered by all I see, by
all I hear. Can all this be true, can this crowd, lit up by flickering
candles, be the Paris I used to know? Isn't it a dream from which
I'll wake up in a moment? But also present is a Paris I do not
know. In the half-light, youngsters with carefully tousled hair
talk in lisps about their poems. A young man who was at Buchenwald for months tells me that the prisoners belonged to different
categories. The old ones, those of 1933 or '34, had a right to the
movies and . . . to the brothels. The last-comers are regularly ill-
treated by the earlier prisoners. To be told of all these horrors
in a drawing room has an extraordinary effect on me. The same
man told me that he had known Father Leloir very well; he had a
respect for him but thought he showed immoderate zeal for conversions. According to him, the Father talked a great deal about
marriage and in such a manner that he seemed to have an unconscious yearning for matrimony. I think this true of a certain number of monks. Sealed up inside them is an excess of tenderness that
their words unwittingly betray, and in a most pathetic manner.
Went home tired and exasperated. I was told lots of things that I

could not hear, but no sooner am I in a drawing room than I seem to go deaf and my sight dim. I was like that at eighteen and am still so today. The very word *drawing room* has something about it that makes me feel depressed and gloomy.

JANUARY 24. It sometimes occurs to me that all I receive in this world, my relatively comfortable life, the pleasure I take, for instance, in reading in bed before going to sleep, all that is perhaps my *reward*, in the sense given it by the Gospel, when it declares that those who have been favored in this world will be told: "You have had your reward." And so, no Heaven. Or rather, I will have had my Heaven, and what a shabby, stupid heaven! So much so that I write it without a capital. Yesterday, in the subway, I read almost the whole of St. James' epistle, where I stand condemned thirty times at least. "Thou shalt love thy neighbor as thyself" is called "the royal law" (2:8). Struck by verse 19, Chapter 2, which I should have used as an epigraph for my pamphlet against Catholics: "Thou believest that there is one God; thou doest well: the devils also believe, and tremble."

What really counts is to fight, even if it means being defeated each time: to accept, to knuckle down, is horrible. Something inside one should say no, even if the body says yes. And how could the body say anything else but yes? That is its language. It is acting true to part. But the soul's silence can only be the silence of death. Spiritually, my life is a disaster. I insist on writing this sentence down in black and white to see how it looks. Yet I wonder who would have the nerve to write: "Spiritually, my life is a success." One would have to be an idiot. However, I stick to what I have said.

FEBRUARY 1. Lunched in a house on the faubourg Saint-Honoré. Bénouville was there. Nothing particular to note, but in ten years, how interesting a conversation I have already forgotten would seem! What wouldn't I give to know the trifles that a few people discussed at dinner, for instance, in this same house, around 1780 . . . or 1900!

At the British Embassy day before yesterday. Much admired the great drawing rooms, particularly the white and gold drawing room where dinner was served. The house once belonged to the duc de Charost, who was reading a book when he was taken to the guillotine and marked the page by turning down a corner

guillotine

before having his head cut off. I sat by Louise de Vilmorin, who was at her loveliest. She and Lady Diana Cooper discussed Bresson's *Anges du péché*, a film that they had just seen. The scenes of convent life enraptured them and, not content with describing them, they decided to act one for us. Louise was the mother superior and Lady Diana threw herself down flat on her stomach to ask forgiveness for her sins.

Had lunch with a young painter yesterday. Éluard was there, tall, almost majestic. He speaks slowly and gravely, with a courtesy that we are beginning to forget. His face is the face of a poet. Around him spreads a zone of solitude that I did not attempt to breach; people talked to him a great deal, but it seemed to me that even the most talkative were never able to get at him, and I admired a haughtiness that managed never to lack politeness.

FEBRUARY 2. I never meet anyone without being told that we are racing headlong toward an era of fresh disasters. I had a long fit of insomnia last night, during which many thoughts stirred in my mind, most of them very gloomy. Then I remembered St. Teresa of Ávila's prayer: "Let nothing trouble you, let nothing terrify you. God only." And I once more found peace. The wish to leave the world has crept into my heart again, but what would I find in a convent, seated in my cell, in a black or white robe? Myself. Yourself is the one that you must cast off.

FEBRUARY 10. Mass this morning at the Benedictines', rue de la Source. The church is bare, gray and pink, not too ugly, and the monks' black robes create a great impression. The beautiful hymns have a beauty that wishes to please God alone. They really turn away from the world and are intended for God. None of the operatic cooing and winking of music for degenerate times, like ours. The liturgy, gestures, and minutely ordered movements, all this is for God. Then what am I doing here, what is this crowd doing here? A low Mass would be far better for us. Aren't we in this church to feast our eyes and ears rather than to pray? Why trick ourselves? Let us leave the monks to their business, which is to praise God by singing true, with a pure heart, and let us go elsewhere to pray.

FEBRUARY 12. A young man, both very handsome and very ugly, sometimes the one and sometimes the other, was talking in my

presence of his conquests in Stockholm and Copenhagen. This re-
minder of an easygoing, delightful, and poisonous life made me
very sad and I wondered whether it were possible to be saved
without withdrawing from the world. No doubt one can. The
world is a sort of novitiate for many people who will pronounce
their final vows in Heaven. Thought of the wonderful youth I
had. We did not have the frantic excitement of the boy I have
just mentioned, but we had joy. There wasn't that confusing of
pleasure with happiness then. We were happy. What more could
we wish for? I think that if these people had *one hour* of the unutterable happiness we then enjoyed, they would never forget it
and would remember it as the supreme event in their lives. No one
suspects that during the years when I was writing those inexplicably gloomy books, I was so happy that such bliss sometimes
kept me from sleeping and I wept with joy.

"From disaster to disaster, we are heading for victory." This
sinister 1940 saying came back to me. I believe that this is just
simply the way we are heading for Heaven. Thought a lot of a
sentence by Father Lallemant: "God is more interested in governing a single heart than in governing the whole of the natural universe." I have been upset by so many things these days, the rue
de Presbourg lunch, for instance, and, that same day, what an unknown priest said to me with extraordinary simplicity, after hearing my confession: "You are saved." "How does he know?"
immediately asked the inner voice I know so well. But he may be
right, after all. If I believed the opposite, I would go mad.

FEBRUARY 18.   Disturbed by the problem that I am in the habit of
calling the problem of two realities: the carnal reality and the
metaphysical reality. Am I to be their battle-ground to the end of
my life? So that is to be my fate, the fate I so often speculated
about around my thirtieth year: the particular question that will
have been asked me in this world and that I will have to answer.
But in what way do these difficulties differ from those of all
human beings? In a great many ways. Each of us is a special case.

MARCH 22.   Yesterday afternoon, at Saint-Médard. The air was
inexpressibly sweet and the doors of the church left open to let
in the warmth, although the apse still held a little of winter's cold
mingled with the first breath of spring and the peculiarly heady
odor found in very old churches. Lots of memories came back

to me, memories of walks through the old parts of Paris when I was twenty and crazy to improve my mind. At that time, the idea of pleasure did not even occur to me. I was so ignorant of sensual matters that a nun could have given me pointers! None of that interested me in the least; I imagined, for instance, that men and women came together only once a year. School had not taught me anything; I found out only much later what took place there when I was a student. This protracted innocence seems disastrous to me, in many ways: it is always paid for very dearly later.

APRIL 10.   I went to see Lucien Daudet yesterday afternoon. He received me in his little, dark, low-ceilinged room. Both legs paralyzed, he sits at a table littered with books and papers. Over his shoulders, a shawl and a black *veil*. His delicate, suffering face is wasted, but his expression gentler than it used to be; the bitter lines at the corners of his lips have disappeared. On the mantelpiece, a gilt wood statue of Mary, and facing him, on a level with his eyes, a photograph of his father, Alphonse Daudet, whose face is ringed with a sort of fur made up of his hair and beard. All around, portraits, souvenirs, knickknacks, a horribly melancholy little world—all that remains of happiness. He talks with admirable preciseness. I remember what he said about the youth of 1946: "They don't know what life, such as we knew it, is. They don't even know what a good cake tastes like, but they don't care, they are happy, they don't care a fig for anything." He also said: "I hear of nothing but sprees and roistering." I maintain that we were happier. "And yet," he said, "you never knew the days before 1914." And to give a good picture of these times, he adds: "Times when shops did not shut between noon and two!" Nothing could be more like an episode in one of his father's books than this life ending in an old Paris house. As I was getting up to go, a lady just back from Switzerland entered. "How is her Majesty?" asks Lucien Daudet. He was speaking of the Queen of Portugal. It was like an echo of *Kings in Exile*, one of his father's novels, and on that echo I took my leave. A stifling sadness falls over one in this little room pervaded by the heavy odor of the nineteenth century. In the hall, before shutting the front door, I glanced at a fine photograph of the Imperial Prince (Napoleon III's son).

MAY 4.   I thought I knew this Beethoven quartet (Op. 59, No. 2) by heart and yet was upset last night by all I found in it: such splendid violence, such explosions, such sudden tenderness, the beauty, the tangled network of its themes, the quivering of wings, the throbbing of fountains. Debussy's quartet moved me on account of the happy memories it recalled, the inexpressible happiness that was mine around 1930.

MAY 9.   Alone in a chapel at Saint-Sulpice, a young man kneels on the edge of his *prie-dieu*, arms crossed, body erect, a big black rosary mended with string and hanging from his elbow; very simply, almost poorly, dressed in black, a very handsome face, pink shading into brown, tousled hair with a lock sweeping his eyebrows, large, deep eyes. He yawns from time to time and, when anyone approaches right or left, turns his head sharply in that direction. After a while, he grasps his rosary, carries it to his lips with a sort of violence, crosses himself, puts his rosary in a pocket and, always very straight, continues praying. His distractions, his weariness, his good looks all made him a very mysterious person and as passionately interesting as a fictitious character. And there was this too: faith, the strange spectacle of faith. I went out of my way to leave without going past him.

JUNE 10.   I went to Gide's day before yesterday as he wanted to see me alone. He talked to me about religion, in connection with Bloy's book (*Ici on assassine les Grands Hommes*). What struck him particularly in the passages about Hello were those relating to the writer's last days and, at the very end, this pathetic cry: "Make the little ones pray!" What disconcerted Gide more than anything was the despair that appears to have attended the poor man's death, but what do we know about it? Who has ever been able to tell what takes place in the soul of a dying man? He then talked about a mother superior ("Is that what they are called?" he asked), a relative of Edmond Jaloux, who also died "in despair" among her nuns. But the temptation to despair almost always lies in wait for a believer on his deathbed. I see very clearly that that weakens religion in Gide's mind, for he seems to believe that the object of religion is to give unshakable confidence to whoever is about to cross the great borderline.

JUNE 14.   Sins of the flesh teach some people what they would never have otherwise known, and I mean this in a widely human fashion and not only an erotic one. Experience of physical love goes far beyond the body; it includes a world of valuable knowledge, where much good mingles with much evil. I sound as though I were justifying pleasure, which is not at all my intention, but I have known very sensual men and women with a far more developed sense of humanity than souls obviously more virtuous and innocent. To know, in the physical meaning given the word in the Bible, is no vain term.

UNDATED. The more improper parts of an intimate diary are far less the erotic passages than the pious ones. A Carthusian monk would understand me! Exhibitionism of the soul is more difficult to admit than that of the body. I have that feeling each time I go into a so-called religious library and am so disgusted, not only with all those books, but with myself, that nausea does not seem too strong a term to describe it.

JULY 13. When I hear certain Frenchmen talk—among those I value most—I feel a little sad not to be as quick-witted as they are. No doubt I have been given gifts they do not possess, but there is something wonderful about their nimbleness of mind. They cut figures of eight on the ice with the greatest ease. But when I cut figures of eight, I almost always hear the ice cracking ominously. Yet these men can be reproached on two scores: firstly, they think too fast; they are deeply ignorant of the fact that the shortest way from one point to another is not always the straight line. Secondly, they can see only in broad daylight and go all but blind at twilight. This said, I have said about all there is to say.

JULY 21. Read Auden, at first with admiration, then with a certain weariness. His extraordinary felicity of phrase reminds one of a man who always wins in a lottery. There is something about this that annoys and finally irritates me. He is so obviously proud of his verbal nimbleness; he says all he wants to say with never a stammer, he says everything one thinks and was on the point of saying, and saying far less well than he does. He rarely shows emotion, but when he does it is exquisite (in the poem about the two refugees, for instance).

AUGUST 4. The day when a man realizes that he will never be able to know everything is a day of mourning. Then comes the day when he vaguely suspects that he will not even be able to know much, and finally comes the autumn afternoon when he sees that he never even completely knew the little he thought he knew.

AUGUST 22. Worked as usual this morning, but felt discouraged. Who will like this book? Thought today that one of the only things I am proud of is never having written a quarter of a line for money, nor even tipped my hat to obtain a prize.
✓ How vain everything is but love! Just as a sailor senses a storm in a clear sky, I feel that my life is about to change.

AUGUST 25. A moment ago, read André Gide's *Theseus* at one sitting. It gave me a feeling of irritated pleasure. How can I deny my admiration for its style and, to begin with, why should I deny it? But this goes much further than style, for here style clings to something very precious, which is human flesh. Most beautiful and noble is Oedipus, who puts out his eyes to see more clearly into the inner world, more noble perhaps than Gide himself thinks; and at the end, Theseus takes leave of us after a wonderful speech which might be, I believe, the author's last will and testament. . . . What a jumble he makes of all the judgments one is tempted to form of him! I think him mistaken as to the meaning that his work will have in the eyes of posterity, those distant generations that he strives to reach beyond present generations (and this is precisely what I would most admire in him: the care he takes to find words within the knowledge of those who will come later).

AUGUST 26. Robert lent me a copy of *André Walter* with a photograph of Gide at twenty, a long rather full face, long black hair, the eyes of a Chinese, a drooping lily attitude, a somewhat "arty" pose. I was staggered by the changes time has wrought in him. I think I could have talked to the youth he was then. I would have discussed things with him. We had a few uncertainties of opinion in common, but now it is sometimes difficult to talk to Gide. As Americans say, he knows all the answers, and what attracts me is indecision, a certain wavering, a "well, I don't know . . ."

AUGUST 27. A long, passionately interesting conversation with Béguin. He talked about death, and when I said that all the dead I had seen looked as though they knew something we don't know, he made a remark that I think extremely curious: "No one can have any idea of life without having looked at the face of a dead man."

SEPTEMBER 23. The man I am will always raise a protest against the man I wanted to be and the two will live together to the end, but the man I wanted to be will be the one on whom judgment will be passed.

OCTOBER 1. Dropped in on Gide late this afternoon. I said in substance: "Although I am far from sharing your views in *Theseus*, yet I don't think I ever read anything of yours that I thought finer as to style." . . . He told me he had written the book in two months with a glad heart. The simplicity with which he talks about it appeals greatly to me, and I went so far as to say that Theseus' last soliloquy left me with a feeling of melancholy as I could not help but seeing it as a sort of farewell, like that of Prospero in *The Tempest*. "Why yes," says Gide, "it is a farewell." However, he adds immediately that he wants to write "one more book" and the words are said with a sort of enthusiasm that take forty years off his age at one go. He then declares himself sick of our present world and of the growing flood of totalitarianism, which he loathes. A moment later, he tells me confidentially that he is going away in January. "To Egypt?" "Much farther." "To America?" He looks at me for a second. "To Tahiti," he answers finally, stressing each syllable. "And it might be," he adds, "that I will never come back. . . ." As he talks about my diary, where "too many things are passed over in silence," I ask if he means physical problems. "Yes, those," he says. I then ask: "But do you know of a diary, of a single published diary, that is not silent about these questions?"

OCTOBER 16. Spent the day in a large monastery near Paris. . . . I was left by myself in the library for a moment and asked for a book written by Melchor Cano for Philip II of Spain, who wanted to have him as his confessor. The author very simply states his own defects. I read for half an hour. I was to be fetched at five, but at six I was still alone in the vast room into which night was slowly creeping. Yet outside, the sky was still light, a pale blue. Workmen were hammering in the vicinity. Immense sadness of the countryside at that hour. I felt cold. I wondered if I could bear shivering twenty years in a monastery for the love of God. Suddenly, I fell into a sort of despair. I thought: "If the religious life is not true, nothing in this world is true, and then it's finished, I have nothing left." I stood motionless, horrified by the great black tide that rose toward me. Doubt went through my mind and I was frightened. I did not move, but all I felt capable of doing was precisely not to move and to remain as I was. It seemed to me that death itself could not have been sadder or blacker than this exceptional moment, one that I believe unequaled in my life. I had a violent distaste for religion, for myself, for everything. This lasted about half an hour, but it was only some time later that I grasped the reason for all this and the presence of whom I had felt within these walls.

DECEMBER 3. Last Sunday, to the Latour-Maubourg convent to hear Camus. There are far too many people and the two drawing rooms on the second floor are crowded. We are placed in the first row. Camus is seated a couple of yards away from us and faces us at a small table. By him, Father Maydieu in a white robe. In the next room, a Dominican stands *on* the mantelpiece, peacefully smoking his pipe. Ill and visibly weary, Camus talks however in what I think a most moving manner about what is expected of Catholics in the France of 1946. He is moving in spite of himself, without the least attempt at eloquence; his integrity is what stirs one. He speaks rapidly, simply, with notes. In his rather pallid face, his eyes are sad, his smile is sad. The lecture over, Father Maydieu asks me if I have anything to say, and I shake my head, unable to answer without a few minutes of reflection. A few in the audience ask questions, but such blundering ones that it would be better if they had held their tongues. One of them, an ex-revolutionary with an ingenuous face, says this and it makes us all start: "I am in a state of grace and you, Monsieur Camus, I tell you very humbly that you are not. . . ." Camus's only answer was the smile I have just mentioned, but he said a little later: "I am your Augustine, before his conversion, I am struggling with the problem of evil and can't get to the end of it." Indeed, one is reminded of Augustine by this Latin from North Africa who is trying to find out how we would behave in the presence of the Vandals. Someone else in the audience who had listened attentively to Camus gets up and says: "Monsieur, I can't make up my mind in forty seconds about the way I would behave if the

Church were persecuted. I want to think it over all my life."
"Monsieur," replies Camus, "you are just about five years old."

DECEMBER 6. Many a time since childhood I have tried to seize
upon the moment when I fell asleep, when I could tell myself:
"I'm going to sleep." I have never succeeded, but the instant just
before the sort of drop into unconsciousness is marked by a phenomenon which I call the dissociation of mental pictures. For no
sooner do I put out the light than I begin to see. This is one of the
only gifts remaining to me from a time when I could scarcely
talk. To imagine, for me, is to see pictures, and when I am not
able to see, I won't write any longer, for it seems to me that the
starting point of all my books is the bolster where I lay my head,
but I find it impossible to say how I see. At any rate, there comes
a second when these sometimes startlingly clear pictures suddenly
dissolve and slide into one another. There results a sort of chaos
that invariably announces sleep.

DECEMBER 9. Yesterday, I was quoting this saying of Father
Dehau's to Robert: "Faith is the cross where intellect is cruci-
fied." And I said that Bossuet would have liked this sentence.
Robert asked me if I was sure of this. For Bossuet, faith continued
intellect in an unbroken line. And he quoted this sentence of St.
Augustine's: "Faith is the fruit of intellect."

DECEMBER 27. It was thirty-two years ago this morning, St.
John's Day. I thought once more of my mother's face as I saw it
on her deathbed. Twice I went to look at her, staying each time
for a few minutes that have meant a great deal to me. She seemed
far from this world, far from us all, with the air of having been
entrusted with an uncommunicable secret and of moving away,
gliding straight toward unknown spaces. Her extraordinary grav-
ity made an impression on me that the years have not obliterated
and that has marked me for ever, I think. It was then that she
really taught me all she knew of the invisible, of religion, and she
pointed it out far better then than when she taught me the cate-
chism. Her face was extremely noble, particularly the high,
rounded brow, the somewhat mysterious mouth that smiled, it
seemed to me that morning, *but intermittently*. Around her, an
enormous silence; yet she did not frighten me. The dead do not
frighten.

1947

JANUARY 8. Lunched with Cocteau. Talking about the theater, he said that it is always a curious thing to watch the audience, particularly "at the moment of hypnosis" which comes sooner or later. The moment when everyone is spellbound, a rather brief moment, "for," he says, "in France the house is always empty. Everyone is on the stage. Everyone is the queen." One feels like applauding when he says such things. Struck by what he says about "the conspiracy of the plural against the singular," signs of which he sees everywhere. Extremists have told him that his play was *insulting*, because it did not conform to the pattern approved in their set. "Your books are insulting," he told me. "*Midnight* is an insulting book." (I am truly thankful that it is.) He talked to us about his house at Milly, the so-called bailiff's house, which he is already attached to; says he wants to be buried in the garden, "and may the dogs piddle on him, if they feel like it!" Talks sadly of France, which he finds so changed, of its wretched and ambitionless youth. . . . Nowadays, he thinks, holiness is the only thing that creates a worthwhile ideal. Monasteries have taken all that was best. . . . Struck by his pessimism: "We are like the people who used to say: 'Ah, if you had only known that great actress, Rachel!' We say: 'Ah, if you had only known 1920!' And we are right."

JANUARY 9. The carnal man lives with the spiritual man. One tries to slit the other's throat. To give up pleasure means throwing the carnal man into jail, but none the less, he goes on living, tied up, and gagged as tightly as you please; yet he is there, and what is strange, he changes, follows a completely personal evolution. What he longs for today is no longer what he longed for at twenty, or at thirty, or even at forty. An inflexible determinism forces those furious appetites to *develop in nonsatisfaction.* Thought sadly about all this. How is it that we are what we are? We scarcely ever know it. I am completely ignorant about my great-grandparents; even my grandparents never told their secrets (they had some, we all have some). Between these unknown people and myself, my exceptionally good parents formed a sort of moral barrage, but behind them, some way behind them, what a number of neurasthenics walled up in their *idée fixe,* and to put it more frankly, what a number of lunatics! Often thought that I have kept my balance by writing my stories.

UNDATED. I was talking to Robert about the irritating problem of translations. Sticking to the literal meaning is the more often a mistake, as the author who is being translated would certainly have used other words and said different things if he had written in the translator's tongue. So you should try to discover the book he would have written in that language. With a swiftness of thought I have always admired in him, Robert summed up the whole question in a single sentence: "A good translation is not a glove turned inside out; it is another glove." Nothing could be better expressed.

JANUARY 28. Yesterday to Véfour's, where a farewell party was given for the ballets that are leaving for some place or other. I went there to see Bérard, who had agreed to illustrate my diary.[1] An enormous mob under the charming painted ceilings, and in the mob, two or three faces I thought handsome. Bérard took me into a corner, sat with me at a table, and talked about this edition of my diary: "I thought at first of featuring American soldiers. That would have been very pretty. Then I had the idea of showing Paris as seen through your own sadness." His beard is touched with silver under the chin. His fat pink face is at times extremely dignified. I thought of the dreary day when I looked at a self-portrait of Bérard in a New York hotel bedroom. The painting stood on the floor, propped against a wall, a picture in exile that looked as though it knew itself to be in exile. If I could have been told then: "In six years, at Véfour's, Bérard will tell you how he expects to illustrate one of your books," I would have taken many a trial with a lighter heart. Around us, lots of very smart people, what is called society. I did not stay long. I wanted to talk to Laurence Olivier, but could only have made myself heard by shrieking, and felt so ill at ease that I went away.

FEBRUARY 4. . . . I have been reproached for what are discreetly termed my reticences. Yet, to give the public my intimate

[1] This illustrated edition of my diary never came out. Bérard assured me that the publisher had kept the gouaches; they were exceptionally fine.

diary is an idea that has never entered my head. One would have to be crazy. . . . I notice, however, that the most impatient, the most eager, the most vexed not to *know,* those who most loudly accuse me of not having said enough, are always the most guarded and the most timorous. The zeal for truth burns them up when it means having others speak it. "Come on, be bold! Go ahead! Go ahead!" they cry, shoving one by the shoulder. And then, they sit down.

FEBRUARY 20.   I finished my book at midnight, yesterday. Three full pages in two hours, which is not my usual speed, but I was determined to end it that night. Around eleven o'clock, I felt my room grow cold and threw a log on the fire. I don't know why I note these details, except that the very last hour devoted to a book nearing its end is a specially grave one in the author's eyes. The book does not finish at all in the way I imagined it would. The idea of Fabien wrapped in his sheet and going to answer a knocking at the door is probably an unconscious reminiscence of the episode where John-Mark, clad in his *sindon,* runs away naked when he is arrested (Mark, 14:52).

APRIL 24.   Today at last I am back again in the setting that our furniture creates for us, the setting of my whole youth, which I regard all the more fondly because I have been deprived of it since 1940. Impossible to write for more than a month. Worked from morning till night to put a little order in this flat, to attempt to bring it out of chaos. For we were obliged to move in with workmen on the premises: masons, plumbers, painters, electricians, locksmiths. An indescribable disorder. Gaping floors, torn partitions, plaster everywhere, and a fine gluey dust that stuck to fingers and went down our throats. No baths. Meals hastily eaten in a room that looked as though it had been shaken up by an earthquake, bits of furniture piled one on top of the other, all the suitcases heaped in a corner. . . . All that is over now. I am writing these lines in my study, the window of which looks out on Embassy gardens. Deep peace.

MAY 21.   At times I have such a keen feeling of the world's emptiness that it seems as though my mind will not be strong enough to stand the weight of such a truth. This sounds a strange thing to say, and I think very few people ever think of it. Some days, I can't open a book, even one of poems, without saying to myself: "What's the good?" God alone exists, He is the only one that *is*, and to feel separated from Him is horrible, for apart from God I can see nothing but vanity. If such is the case, how can I be interested in what interests the world?

JUNE 20. Someone just back from the United States tells me that America is recovering from the war "like a giant from a scratch." So much the worse and so much the better. It means that the lesson has not been learned.

JULY 12. The inexorable reality of the material world, its stones, its voices, its faces, its great beauty, its thought even, everything that, in a certain way, *seems right when spirit seems wrong*, because this world offers nothing that is not provable and almost tangible, whereas the world of spirit, of faith, remains interior, mysterious, *nonprovable*—how would it be possible to avoid suffering from this eternal contradiction? A man who lives by his faith is necessarily isolated. At every hour of the day, he is in acute disagreement with his century; at every hour of the day, he is alone and, in a certain fashion, appears to be mad. This is one of the most peculiar aspects of the tragedy our conscience is going through in Europe. No matter how numerous Christians still are in this world, no matter how close their mystical union, they cannot help but have at some time or other a feeling of terrible solitude. . . .

JULY 19. A feeling of nothingness. Indescribable. It is familiar to those whose lives have been bared of all *divertissement*, in Pascal's sense of the term. For to certain souls, no longer to believe in the need for *divertissement* means losing their mainstay. There is nothing like it to make you rush to God, as you would cast yourself into an abyss, for the problem that now faces you is: God or nothing. Living in a large, well-furnished room does not alter the question in the least. Comfort, music, books, the pleasures of conversation change nothing and, above all, add nothing, because it is impossible to add an iota to nothing and that *nothing* remains all-powerful back of all the appearances that it destroys. But what is instructive in such contacts with nothingness is the growing conviction that the sole possible reality is God. One knew it, of course, but not in this manner, not to the marrow of one's bones.

JULY 21. Went to see Gide. He had written me a most cordial note, but I thought, for the first time, that nothing good would come of this visit. He received me in his little bedroom, where he was at work writing. Above his bed, a mask of Goethe. Gide wore a green-checked thick woolen shirt. Almost at once, he talked about my novel, which he judges very unfavorably. "You want to save your soul," he said, "but just look at what a cost!" I then replied: "You oblige me to quote the Gospel: 'For what is a man profited, if he shall gain the whole world . . .'" "Yes," he answered rather quickly, "but in spite of that, see . . ." He next developed the idea that a convert loses his talent and that the Church is responsible for this. Suddenly, he seemed furious with me, as though I were guilty. "Wait until I have done wrong before judging me," I then said. "But you'll never do wrong, Green!" he cried. "You are far too honest for that, and it's because you are honest that I am fond of you." So he has it in for the Church. He flew at her again. He had seen Curtius in Germany, and the latter is "more of a Protestant than ever since seeing the evil done by the Church." I must say that this argument does not move me, but the following remark seemed graver: "I find that converts are never bettered by their conversion. The proud remain proud, etc. There is no improvement." And he asked me point-blank: "What about you? Do you feel you've improved?" As though anyone could answer yes to such a question! "Copeau," he went on, "is what he was before his conversion, only more so." He dwelt at length on this point and, pursuing his criticism of Catholics, reproached them with always having a ready answer for all occasions, like the Communists. (I myself have always raised the same objection, but did not breathe a word of it this morning. The replies they furnish to all problems deprive them of any feeling of mystery, to my mind, but that was not what Gide was talking about.) When our conversation was almost over, he began luring me with a magnificent literary future: "You are capable of great things. You have behind you a whole series of remarkable books. . . . You carry a heavy responsibility. You will cause many people to draw away from the Church, once they see what harm she has done a man like yourself." (Why so anxious for the welfare of the Church?) He showed me the place I could occupy and suddenly darted this question at me: "Why don't you have *a try at the devil for a while?*" I told him that I would never be on the devil's side. And then, this from Gide: "You could pretend . . ."

Once more, I said no. Going back to my journal, which he had mentioned a moment before together with my novel, he told me that my diary was full of reticences, that I had only recorded "*proper* things." "Yes," said I, "but the omissions are very clearly indicated, as well as the nature of what I have omitted. Now haven't you yourself published a journal that contains many blanks? What a lot of things you don't say!" "I'll see to it that the blanks are filled in," he replied simply. An hour and a half had passed. I thought we had said all we had to say to each other that day and stood up to leave. At that moment Gide did something that went straight to my heart and far more deeply than he believes: he also got up and kissed me.

JULY 22. That conversation with Gide stirred me so deeply that I had to lie down when I reached home. My heart thumped for almost an hour. And now, I wonder if his kiss did not mean that he was saying farewell to me. He told me confidentially that he thought "constantly of death" and watched it approach "with serenity." One sentence in particular comes back to me: "I think of death with complete indifference, if that is understood as serenity." Regarding the Catholic faith, he said that he could see nothing in it but a phenomenon caused by autosuggestion and heredity. Forgot to note that at one moment he asked me why I did not write a book anonymously, as Jouhandeau did in the case of *De l'Abjection*. (That, I imagine, meant having a try at the devil for a while, but a try without too much of a risk.) "That is impossible," I replied, "my books are of such a particular nature that their author would be immediately recognized." He agreed with me on this score. I have also forgotten to say that at the beginning of our conversation he asked: "Why don't you take holy orders? How is it you haven't left the world?" I answered that one doesn't take holy orders without a vocation. "That's just it," he continued, "with your Christian vocation, I don't see why you don't go into a monastery." "But a vocation is something very definite," I replied. "You can be a very earnest Catholic and not have one." I was convinced as I listened to him, and am still more so on thinking it over, that he talked to me as he did because he thought it his duty, an imperative, inescapable duty.

JULY 24. Yesterday morning, in the faubourg Saint-Honoré chapel of the Dominican Fathers, Anne abjured the Anglican heresy at the hands of Father Couturier. A very long, meticulous, but beautiful ceremony. First came the exorcisms at the side door of the church, not the main one. Anne could not enter before the *spiritus immundus* of heresy had been driven out of her. I thought this a little hard. When I was converted in 1916, the heretic that I was entered the rue Cortambert chapel without any ado. Nor was I made to read the act of abjuration on my knees, as took place yesterday. It was standing, and my hand on the Gospel, that I read Pius V's confession of faith (in a loud, ringing voice, I was told later). Yesterday, I could not help protesting in my heart, for to see her kneeling, you might have thought poor Anne was accusing herself of a crime. Is that the way one knocks at the door of the Father's house? The Church behaved more leniently to me. I was moved, however, and very much moved, as I am always by the presence of something real in violent contradiction with the world: water, salt, an immense sign of the cross that seemed to cut the sky in four, beyond the walls of this sorry chapel. . . .

AUGUST 26. BERNE.   Arrived here at twilight. It is the best time. To slip into an unknown town at the moment when the light begins to waver and soften, not quite at dusk, but just before it, gives a secret joy: I don't know what I am hoping for, but my hopes are high. . . . After dinner, a walk down a long and beautiful street, probably one of the strangest the world affords, lined with old houses whose ground floors jut forward a little, like the roots of very ancient oaks, and whose roofs have the outlines of hats; and the street is so long that it resembles those one walks down in dreams and that never end. In the middle of the street, at intervals, are fountains with Renaissance figures. A setting that could not be used in a novel: too fine. One would have to be Hugo or Hawthorne. Strolled around the cathedral this morning. Market day. Fruit, vegetables, cheeses, delicatessen, an overabundance here of what is cruelly lacking in other parts of Europe. There is so much of everything that it doesn't seem true. One has the impression that what is true, what is serious, is misery and that the happiness seen here is an illusion.

AUGUST 29.   Last night, one of the most curious dreams I ever had. I had gone to sleep in anguish. . . . After a moment, I saw myself (which never happens to me in dreams) in our rue Cortambert flat, the one where I spent part of my youth. In the hall was a glass sentry box, very much like the telephone booths to be seen in the streets here. Motionless in this glass sentry box was a man in a raincoat belted in at the waist; his hat was pulled down and almost hid his eyes, but his expression could be guessed. His face expressed nothing but extraordinary brutality, with something blind about it that made him most alarming. I knew that he had been living with us for years and years and that he usually stayed in his sentry box. . . . I also knew that he possessed superhuman strength but had only the intellect of a child of five, a brute who had always obeyed me, although he had obeyed less perfectly for some time, because it had dawned on him that he was stronger than I. If I told the man to go here or there, he carried out my orders, but with an ever-increasing and threatening sullenness. Usually, I chased him from my room and he returned to his sentry box, but I was afraid of him and my fright grew greater by the second. Finally, I saw him coming toward me, to kill me. Having taken refuge in my room, I turned the key in the lock, but when I awoke, my heart thumping, he was already shaking down the door with his powerful shoulder. How can I see anything in this brute but the personification of instinct? The whole dream was intensely real, far more so than everyday life because nothing besides action was given any importance. This confirms my belief that a man who dreams is sometimes a far more gifted artist than the man who is awake. Words cannot express the length of time passed in a vision that lasted a few seconds. Years of horror followed one after the other.

OCTOBER 8.   There was a brief moment in my life that I have never told anyone about, although I think of it at times, and it still remains perfectly mysterious to me. It must have been in 1932 or '33, at the end of a very fine afternoon in May. The sun cast spots of light on the wall at the far end of my study and I watched them as I lay on a sofa. There came a moment when these spots, which moved very slowly, reached the edge of a frame. I don't know why I then had a feeling of the world's immense sadness; it was like a kind of revelation. What meaning can such words convey to anyone who has not felt exactly what I felt then? But I can add nothing to what I have just written except that I was seized for *the first time* with a melancholy I have never been able to shake off entirely. Since then I have sometimes said that a spot of light on a wall seemed to me one of the saddest things in the world; but who could understand such a peculiar remark and one so apparently unreasonable?

OCTOBER 25. At Solesmes Abbey. Very deeply touched by the hymns I heard in the chapel. An *Ave, maris stella* that, according to Father X., goes back to the twelfth century, makes you feel like leaving the world then and there. But what century are we in here? Certainly not the twentieth. The monks in their black robes seem to glide over the surface of the floor like ghosts. On their faces, *pax*, as everywhere in this place. Peace and joy. On this cloister's threshold, the hideous agitation of the century dies away. It seems to me that Benedictine life is one hymn of happiness and love, in a rather slow mode, true enough, but what charm in this slowness and how precious it is to me in a world that a passion for speed has made almost idiotic! A hymn, that's what it is. All these hours, from Matins to Compline, are sung softly, almost tenderly. And how carefully the music is handled by voices that are so humble and so true! *Bis orat qui cantat*, says St. Augustine. It occurs to me at times that these monks live in a sort of great liturgical dream, whereas, in reality, they are the ones who see things as they are, and we are the ones who live in a dream always on the verge of turning into a nightmare.

NOVEMBER 3. A young author has sent me a copy of the work he is writing about me, in which he believes he can prove that all my novels have been written under the devil's influence! This view seems to me very systematic. . . . But what is true is that my novels allow glimpses of great dark stirrings that I believe to be the deepest part of the soul—and that always escape psychological observation—the secret regions where God is at work. These books could not have been otherwise than as they are. I could not rewrite them and change them. I think that each is in itself a chapter of a very large book that I will never end writing. If I must be judged, I should be judged by my work as a whole.

NOVEMBER 5. Excellent remarks about the translations of the New Testament, in Goodspeed. What he most clearly brings out is this, which I knew but had forgotten because I wanted to forget it: the King James Version is difficult to accept, as much on account of its mistakes as of its obscurities. The English public, which continues to prefer it to the Revised Version in which all

the errors were lopped off at the end of the last century, understands it all the less for knowing it almost *by heart*. We should
pause before this term whose magnificence is hidden because it has
become a commonplace. A Protestant knows his Bible by heart,
he knows it from the heart, from love. This bond of charity exists
between himself and his Bible: it is really *his* Bible and it is his
because he loves it. A Catholic, when he reads the Bible, when he
happens to read the Bible, reads the Bible and not his Bible. In
general, he does not read it at all, he prefers to believe that the
Church forbids him to, which is false. But to go back to Goodspeed, he thinks that a too literal knowledge of the Scriptures is
an obstacle to understanding the texts; you end by never asking
yourself the meaning of the words you quote—and which sometimes have none in the old translation I am discussing. (The only
example I can remember at the moment is not the least picturesque: it is found in Matthew 23:24, where a misprint that makes
the sentence incomprehensible has passed, together with the context, into the memory of English readers. I have never heard this
verse quoted, and it is among those most often quoted, without
the mistake turning up, doggedly faithful.) Goodspeed is in favor
of putting away the 1611 translation among the great literary
works of the past, and reading the Scriptures in modern versions
that are more literally accurate. Knowing all this, a sort of instinct
makes me revert to the book that revealed the word to me when
I was a child and whose old language will always move me. I have
this to say in its defense: every time it agrees with the original,
it is admirably faithful and is, I believe, unequaled in English;
where the Old Testament is concerned at least, it does not seem
to me possible to translate better than when the translation is
good, I might even say that it does not appear possible to translate
in a more Hebraic manner (it has introduced Hebraic construc-
tions into the language). And then, it will always be right in my
eyes because it is the most beautiful.

NOVEMBER 8. Yesterday and this morning, spent my time arranging books in the large cupboard that I have turned into a
bookcase. One of these cupboards has already been converted to
such a use in my study. Now there are two of them, side by side,
forming a single wall of books, facing a longer wall. So one of
my oldest dreams has come true: to work surrounded by books.
One always ends by getting what one wants, one gets it a little

late, more often too late, when one scarcely wants it any longer, but one gets it. Those rows of old bindings made a brave show in my eyes, but as I displaced all the books and replaced them on other shelves, I heard the voice, the mental one we all possess, ask the eternal question: "What's the good?"—a question that darkened part of my youth. What's the good since nothing lasts? What's the good since we have to die? A question asked repeatedly that sometimes directs us toward the absolute; and that perhaps comes to us from God.

NOVEMBER 25.   Anne was talking to me yesterday about one of our sisters, whom we lost in January, 1918, and the circumstances of her death. "Why, didn't you know?" (In 1918, I was on the Italian front.) "She suffered greatly" (meningitis), "but always smiled when anyone joked before her. This lasted two weeks. The time came when she seemed very low. I felt her pulse and knew her life was ebbing away. Perhaps she realized it too, for suddenly in a loud, clear voice, she said: 'Now I lay me down to sleep . . .' " (I knew the little prayer that children are taught:

Now I lay me down to sleep,
I pray the Lord my soul to keep.
If I should die before I wake,
I pray the Lord my soul to take.)

"She only managed to say the first line and died. She did not know many prayers." She was very beautiful, a little silent, but not sad; she was twenty-three.

DECEMBER 8.   I don't know of a prettier landscape in Paris than the one I see from my windows. A moment ago, under a stormy gray sky, I had a glimpse of the little Dutch Embassy through black trees and, suddenly lit up by a last sunburst, these colors began to shine softly behind a faint mist. I looked long at the narrow gardens that can be picked out here and there, with their lawns, ponds, flower beds all so discreetly designed; one makes out a touch of green that stands out faintly against the pebbled walks, the whole effect being one of faded, washed-out colors, like the wools in an old carpet. I don't think a sheerer quality of melancholy could be found anywhere. At the far end of a murky, rainy sky—for here comes a shower—the twin steeples of Sainte-Clotilde seem to waver, then grow dim, and the squat little dome of Panthemont gleams softly like a big black pearl.

DECEMBER 16. . . . Some days, life appears to be a very thin and yet invincibly opaque veil behind which roars a huge fire, but this is not only hell-fire. The veil I speak of is everything that the senses teach us: the color of the table on which I write these lines, the cheeping of birds under my windows, the sound of a neighboring convent's bells, the gardens I catch sight of when I look up, and the noise made by this pen as it runs over the paper, all that I see, hear, touch, and taste all day long, and not only that, but the thoughts of people who talk to me, and also my own thoughts, in fact everything that is not God. When the veil's appearance is too beautiful, it forms a trap where souls are snared (*"Species decepit me,"* says one of the elders in the story of Susanna). Men spend their time in "agreeably blinding themselves," as Pascal has it, and hide from the immense fire of God's charity.

1948

JANUARY 18. Speaking of false memories (the impression of having seen a place where one has never set foot, the impression of having lived in a house whose threshold one has never crossed), I told someone that this must be a manifestation of hereditary memory. The idea was once developed by Jung. I remember the lecture he gave around 1935 about the drawings of madmen, many of which bore traces of millenary memories: an illiterate patient, for instance, produced an extremely complicated drawing whose equivalent could be found only in Tibetan art. It is highly probable that in writing the preface to *Varouna,* I recollected this theory of humanity's memory, the great common source at which we all constantly draw. I wrote the preface in an attempt to make it clear that my novel was not a story about metempsychosis, but what use has a preface ever been? About twenty years ago, I was in a small Austrian town for the first time. As I was about to go by a large house with an open gateway, I thought suddenly: "A little uphill street and at the end of the street, the sky." This was

exactly what I saw less than a second later. The house bridged
an alley, a rather usual thing in Austria, and this alley climbed
steeply to a flat piece of ground where the sky was visible from
top to bottom. The shock this gave me made me feel pensive for
the rest of the day. Unquestionably, I had never set foot in this
street, and all the fables about the transmigration of souls returned
to me. The truth appears simpler to me now. Humanity is but
one man and is to be found in its entirety in each of us. For a
second, in an unknown town, I had memories of this town. I had
lived there with generations of men and women. How and why
we are suddenly enlightened as to the past, I don't know, but the
experience is profoundly disturbing.

FEBRUARY 9.   The silence of the room where I write is one of the
greatest treasures of my life; it is also a luxury, and I wonder if
I won't be one of the last men to enjoy it. In a quarter of a century, will a writer's life such as mine be possible? I sometimes feel
as though I already belonged to a bygone age.

FEBRUARY 20.   Had lunch in a restaurant with about ten people.
Camus sits facing me and I try to talk to him. I am deeply touched
by his very sensitive, very human face. There is such obvious integrity in the man that it almost immediately inspires respect:
simply, he is not like other people. Malaparte and his book *Kaputt*
are discussed. Mme X. tells us that on meeting the author, she said:
"I have read your book. I would have very much liked to read
the other." (That is, the one he would have written if Germany
had won the war.) Mme X. says that Malaparte did not reply.
Whereupon, Camus exclaims: "If you had said that to me, Madame, I would have left the room!" "Oh! the French are so sensitive," answers Mme X. "Italians aren't like that."

FEBRUARY 22.   I was told of a recent convert who exasperates
everyone around her by her uncompromising zeal. Any conversion is, in fact, a tacit reflection on one's neighbor, but who would
not lose patience on seeing these proselytes monopolize St.
Thomas, put on deep airs to which they have no right, because
their wisdom is a brand-new wisdom, much like a borrowed garment obviously not custom made. At fifteen, I used to see a mounting fury in people's eyes when I brandished some scarlet sentence
culled from Bloy's diary.

* * *

FEBRUARY 28. An ever-increasing horror of the spiritual indis-
cretions such as are published nowadays, unasked-for confidences,
illuminations, ecstasies! The "humble" tone—which saints, real
saints, have never had, theirs is different—the dull, pious chatter
that tends to be "edifying" and is simply scandalous. And if ever
I have been guilty of this—I hope not—I here pass final judgment
on myself! For this is not true religion.

MARCH 4. Paris this morning was wrapped in a pure white mist
behind which shone the spring sun, and the mist was like a veil of
snow stretched across the sky in front of a huge, blazing diamond.
In writing this, I remember something I saw in a small château
in the north of France, in 1935. I was in my room at three in the
afternoon of a very fine summer day, watching tiny specks of
dust pass slowly through a sunbeam. One of them, caught in the
rays of this dazzling light, began to shine like a tiny sun; this did
not last long, but when the diminutive star was extinguished, it
was replaced by others that glittered in their turn. This sight held
my attention for some time, but if it seemed beautiful to me then,
in the sky of memory, today, I find it richer still, decked out like
a constellation. The soul must shine like this in the presence of
God, for it is a mere speck of dust compared with the great sun
and the light in which it moves is what gives it life. I remember
having read in St. Teresa of Ávila that a soul in a state of grace
is so beautiful that anyone who could see it would, if that were
possible, take it for another God.

MARCH 10. Very much struck by one of Keats' letters in which
he describes a trip to Scotland and particularly Fingal's Cave,
which he talks of enchantingly: "Suppose now that the giants who
came down to the daughters of men, had taken a whole mass of
these columns and had bound them together like a bunch of
matches; and then, with immense axes had made a cavern in the
body of these columns." How well one sees what he means. . . .
He has the precision peculiar to poets that novelists possess only
inasmuch as they are poets. On reading these pages, I was seized
with a renewed love for Keats, whom I consider pre-eminently a
poet and place ahead of all the others, with Hölderlin. But it is
not only the poet, it is the man himself who fascinates me. I like
to think that a young man who was anything but a softy, and even
proved pugnacious and a little rough at times, should have written

the woman he loved: "The world is too brutal for me—I am glad there is such a thing as the grave." During his last illness, he said: "I can feel the cold earth upon me—the daisies growing over me."

MARCH 18.   Read a most informative article by Father Bouyer about psychoanalysis in Switzerland. One passage was like a flash of light. I formerly taxed psychoanalysis with suppressing the freedom of the individual by making him the tool of circumstance and, above all, of heredity; now I understood suddenly that circumstances and, in particular, those caused by heredity are like a sphere of action chosen by God, where our freedom is exercised in a measure known to Him only. ("Circumstances are God," a Dominican father once said to me.) This tallies with the thoughts suggested to me by Gide's remark about faith, "the result of auto-suggestion and heredity." Although I know very little about psychoanalysis, what has always seemed curious and attractive about it is that it penetrates to the core of the soul's mystery without throwing much light on it; the further it advances, the more things become obscure; once a question is solved, another appears behind it and the newly revealed question hides an even greater one.

MARCH 29.   Have thought a great deal about the problem of the novel, lately. A fact of cardinal importance is that I no longer feel like writing one. Why is that? I am discouraged, perhaps, by the threat of another war. But that threat will always exist, even if war does not break out. We should behave *als ob*, as Adler says. But there is something else: fighting oneself, fighting against the physical instinct, paralyzes a novelist's imagination, for the simple reason that the talent of a novelist is rooted in sin. The source of a novel is impure. I am summing up and, in summing up, simplify what would be very lengthy to say and also very complex.

APRIL 12.   A novelist is like a scout commissioned to go and see what is happening in the depth of the soul. He comes back and reports what he has observed. He never lives on the surface but only inhabits the darkest regions. Such has been my experience. I admit that it is not necessarily that of other novelists. Thought about it this morning in connection with the ties that exist between the novel and faith. The idea of writing novels in defense of

Christianity has something about it that horrifies me. I would rather give up writing than trump up a piece of fiction tending to prove anything whatsoever.

MAY 21. A long conversation with Father Couturier on the subject of the novelist. The latter feeds on everything he sees, on everything he reads, on everything he hears. If he is a believer, the difficulty begins when he sits down at his table to write, for he is obliged to become each one of his characters and plunge with them into their sins. I used to think this a false problem, but the fact is that no novel worthy of the name exists without a complicity between the author and his creatures, and far more than complicity: a complete identification. I think that is why no one has ever heard of a saint writing a novel. When I read novels whose source has been "purified," I marvel at the wealth of poisons to be found in each character! Delete the poison and you kill the novel. And if God wishes works of art to be created, as Father Couturier said to me, would one dare to condemn *Les Liaisons* ✓ *dangereuses*? Once expurgated, what would remain of literature? Depressed and annoyed by this question.

MAY 30. Called up Gide yesterday morning: "Why, of course, come to see me. You are always welcome." I suggest tomorrow: "That's too far off. Come this afternoon." He wanted at first to come to see me in my new flat, but was afraid to climb my four flights of stairs. I dropped in on him around six o'clock. He is in the usual corner between the window and the piano, and each time I see him there I am reminded of a great bird in its eyrie. He is dressed today in white flannel and wears the black cap so amusingly described by Guth ("a photograph where he is seen wearing a convict's cap and gaily playing the piano"). I have brought him a present which I put on a table, and he gazes at it, in his own words, "with emotion and devotion." For it is a cast of Chopin's hand. He looks attentively at the plaster hand, turns it over, regrets the lack of lines in the palm, admires the extreme slenderness of the fingers, the vigor of the wrist; while the hand is delicately feminine, the wrist is a man's wrist; the whole strength of the hand is sheltered there. Besides, says Gide to me, it's not the hand of a pianist: the stretch of the fingers is not wide enough. Listening to him, I am struck by his pallor, but he holds himself very straight, his eyes shine, and both his speech and thought are admirably clear. Conversation glides from one topic to another, and I can't remember in what connection he asks me if I know about the Kinsey Report. I was about to say that I was ill informed about politics (he knows that, anyway), but something held me back and I simply answered: "No." Great amazement, a rather scandalized amazement. "What! Then I'll go and fetch it for you." He leaves the room and returns a few minutes later with a thick volume, crammed with notes, and makes me read several passages, in particular a series of questions put to twelve thousand Americans by three professors over there. I marvel that such answers could have been obtained, for the questions concern sexuality and acts, certain ones of which are punishable by the laws of the country; now, Americans as I know them are somewhat reluctant to tell such secrets, dreading above all that people might *know*, but it would appear that the professors in question knew how to go about it. According to the author, says Gide, seventy-five per cent of Americans should be in jail, if the law were applied. Interesting. As to American women—for the first volume is about men alone—the women will also have a Kinsey Report, and I don't think they lose much in the waiting. What annoys me a little about this bulky volume is, I must say, the mania for statistics. I refuse to believe that twelve thousand Americans, no matter how skillfully chosen, can inform us accurately about the mentality of the entire male population. "Figures don't lie," as people so often say in the United States. That remains to be seen.

JUNE 9. Yesterday, a visit from Béguin. He talked about Bernanos, who is very ill and had had his gall-bladder removed. I remember how generously the man behaved to me early in my career and how much he encouraged me then. He suffers greatly from being unable to write novels. "I have a dozen novels to write," he told Béguin. And if he does not write them it is because he wastes his energy on magazines and newspapers: the times are responsible for this. He suffers from not being able to be Bernanos. . . .

JUNE 10. I sometimes wonder if it is possible to work out one's salvation while remaining in the world. Some heretics have thought not, but the starting point of almost all heresies is a truth misunderstood. Day before yesterday, Béguin talked to me admirably about the grace of sin. I always benefit by listening to him. When he left, I thought about this: some people go naturally to God, and those are the saints. The rest can only return to God, and that means all of us, but in a certain way, those who return to God know a little more than the ones who have never done anything but go straight to Him; they are infinitely poorer, but have received a special grace that saints have not had. "Return . . . Return . . . Return . . ." is the word continually found in the prophets. The gold ring, the best robe, and the feast are for the soul that returns.

JUNE 13. There is a curious letter of Voltaire's about instinct. The following sentences throw a wonderful light on a great problem: "It must be admitted that, in art works of genius, everything is the work of instinct. Corneille wrote the scene between Horatius and one of the Curiatii as a bird builds its nest, save in this particular: a bird always builds it very well, whereas we weaklings do not." Too many authors nowadays build their books with their brains, at the expense and to the detriment of their instinct; now, instinct in many cases is genius, but they dare not give in to it. Fear of being ridiculous.

I saw a bird build its nest. It happened in Baltimore. A blue jay lodged in a corner of my cousin's window. One day, she came to fetch me, opera glasses in her hand, a finger on her lips. I approached on tiptoe and looked at something five yards off, my eyes glued to the glasses. To be truthful, the fat bright blue and light blue bird had already built his nest, but he shaped it, trampled it, rounded it out, and—I almost burst out laughing—accomplished this last feat with his cerulean bottom. For he stood in the center and turned around slowly, pushing at the edges of the little skiff. This took a good fifteen minutes, but the bird was finicky and patient. Finally, he sat down, looking extremely satisfied, made himself as large as possible, and filled his home to a nicety.

JUNE 15. I was in a bookstore a little while ago and skimmed through a reissue of Gide's diary, which I had never read entirely, but after a few pages I was once more convinced that I would never be able to finish the volume. Why? I am not quite sure why. He writes beautifully and every page is crammed to overflowing with a wealth of ideas, yet, while he gives all he has to give, he chills the heart, and the more you read, the less you believe, the less you hope, and—I say this regretfully—the less you love.

UNDATED. At times, I remember an unkind, lucid sentence of Stendhal's: "In a seminary, there is a certain manner of eating a soft-boiled egg that denotes the progress made in religious life." I care so little for this man—although I can never open one of his books without falling on a few pages and devouring them—yet how much I admire him, in spite of my dislike!

JUNE 21. Saw Gide, a moment ago, in his little study. He offers me a tumble-down armchair over which he has thrown a folded blanket. Removing the blanket, he shows me that the armchair is losing its horsehair stuffing. "I sometimes think of having it repaired, then I tell myself that it will last out my time, so what's the use?" He says this gaily. I don't believe I have ever seen him downhearted. . . .

JULY 10. ASCONA. Perhaps it may do me good to write down what is worrying me. But indeed I can't. I am ill. With every appearance of health, I am ill. Yet this is where everything will be decided, I know it for certain. However, you know perfectly well that nothing is ever decided. The final assent is never given in this world, excepting in the ear of death. We never are, we continually become. And how could this conventional setting be the one for a tragedy? From my window, I see a garden and at the end of the garden mountains, and in the garden, a gardener. Can everything end in a postcard?

JULY 12. These hideously memorable days . . . The religious crisis I am going through began on June 30th. I wonder how far one can go without losing one's mind. And in the midst of all this, a strange happiness. Drove to the Madonna del Ponte, which is almost on the Italian border. The waters of the lake are two sharply contrasting colors: turquoise and navy blue. A clump of huge cypresses, some so old that they are dying and only remain standing thanks to props of masonry.

Felt very sad to hear that Bernanos had died. He knew all the things that grieve us. And it was this very fact that made up his greatness. No matter if we saw him dressed in a suit like the rest of us, he was a man out of the invisible.

* * *

JULY 22. MERANO. I spent a couple of hours dreaming in the big public bathing establishment. Above the cabins, a purple mountain wore a thick bonnet of white clouds. As I saw all those bodies running about happily, or loafing in the sun (none was very beautiful except those of children), I was struck once again by the chastity of nakedness and, in a roundabout way, returned to the irritating question of soul and body. People talk about the body *and* the soul, as though the body were the container and the soul the contents, as if the two could separate at will, be distinct, whereas more often they mingle, a little as earth and water mix in mud. There is no perceptible borderline between the two, or at any rate no borderline that is not breached continually at every minute, as though it did not exist. The soul is reached through the body and the body through the soul, and therein lies the whole tragedy of the human lot, which makes us such deeply mysterious beings. "Oh, body, thou art the soul!" cried Whitman.

AUGUST 8. PARIS. We all have a dark angel with whom we must struggle. Yesterday, I was seized once more with a wild desire for earthly happiness because a lunch with friends, a walk with Paris as a setting, everything talked of my too happy youth, too happy for me to bear remembering today. In my Jansenist moments, I come to wonder whether one can live a Christian life in the world and if an insuperable contradiction does not lie there, but it is impossible that Christ should have come to save only the religious in their convents. I have known men who could not accept the fact that they were sinners, and even great sinners, and who were furious not to be saints.

AUGUST 20. Writing books comforts the author for everything that life has refused him. It might even be that an overgratified, successful life could have proved a sterile one for him. A surfeited man does not write.

AUGUST 23. I woke this morning at dawn and *saw* my book [1] from beginning to end. It roused me from sleep. Facing me, in the darkness, stood that motionless character. As though the whole thing had been given me, as though the whole thing had been given back to me. Not much in common with the story of Célina

[1] *Moïra.*

as I had intended writing it. A moment ago, I really recovered my taste for work, for life, and felt the pen between my fingers racing over the paper, as if it wrote of its own accord. Happy in spite of the physical problem that darkens my life, but all that will also pass into my book.

SEPTEMBER 25.   I was sent into this world to write. Not to write would kill me by slow inches. To say that this book helps me to live would be saying very little—it helps me to breathe.

SEPTEMBER 27.   Yesterday evening, I read the second chapter of the Epistle to the Ephesians. It contains this strange verse: ". . . and sins, wherein in time past ye walked according to the course of this world, according to the prince of the power of the air . . ." What echoes this rouses from the depths of the reader's soul! There are times—I hesitate to say so—when I resist a temptation to open the Bible, because I know the power of its spell. For me, it is far more than a book, it is a voice and a person.

Thought over my novel at dawn this morning. I must keep it from tending toward eroticism—it is only too eager to do this of its own accord—because the spiritual counterweight will not be strong enough to assure its balance. What should not be too clearly expressed is that everyone is in love with the hero. What I have against eroticism is, above all, its facility. It is no longer daring now, but a sort of triteness, and that it has become fashionable is enough for me to loathe it.

There are strange remarks in Havelock Ellis about the connection between religion and sexuality. Did we ever wish for such a thing? I should think not! If the religious element in us heightens the sexual one or, to talk like bygone moralists, if what is good heightens what is evil, where is the solution of the problem?

OCTOBER 6.   A long fit of insomnia last night, during which I thought about religion. That is the other side of my nature, the stronger. I have taken a loathing for books that speak of God as though He were someone who could be questioned and who obligingly satisfies our little curiosities. God likes this, prefers that, thinks such and such a thing. The truth is that we know practically nothing about this. What, exactly, God wants of us, why we are born in this period and not in another, why here and not there, are so many mysteries. No one in the world has ever shared God's secrets. Religion should be brought back to something very simple, to the Eucharist and the Scriptures. To abide by the articles of faith, no more, no less. All the rest is conjecture. Three lines of Dante come back to me, the Italian so clear that one might be reading French:

> *Avete il vecchio ed il nuovo testamento*
> *ed il pastor della Chiesa che vi guida:*
> *questo vi basti a vostro salvamento.*

OCTOBER 19. I said to a religious: "Chastity is the body's nightmare. The soul is certain of its vocation, but the body's vocation is physical love. That is its mode of expression, the way it fulfills its part; that is all it thinks, that is all it thinks about. How can you expect it to understand the soul's cares? That body and soul are forcibly wedded is a mystery. The body hates the soul and wants it to die." I add this: "To remain chaste does not necessarily make a saint of you, but chastity is one of the hallmarks of holiness, and if you wish to be chaste, you also wish to be holy, without daring to admit it, perhaps."

OCTOBER 24. I said to myself this morning, in church: "Listen to what your conscience says." But my conscience said nothing. I thought about the book I was engaged in copying, of my early diary whose fate seems so doubtful. I think that four religious out of ten would have told me: "You are committing a great sin." Yet, at certain times, I hear a voice deep within me that urges me to continue. I cannot express this otherwise. The voice is not like those we hear *through memory*, it is something both silent and confused. This strange book will cease someday from appearing to be so, and will accomplish its mission, which is to be useful to a few people, to guide them, to teach them to avoid certain mistakes, to help them to a better knowledge of a lonely man's heart. Of course evil is mixed into this work, but it cannot exist without evil. That is where it is human. Evil, in the present case, is like a vehicle for the good contained in the book, and what is good in this book—which I will never see in print—is an endeavor for a truth which is my truth. I have tried to tell the truth at all costs.

NOVEMBER 9. Read some of O. Henry's short stories. They are written by a semi-barbarian, fascinated by words, who handles them much as a savage would turn over a handful of bits of

colored glass. His stories are very ingenious, but as they are invariably written in view of a final surprise, you must wait until
the very last lines to judge of the merits of what has preceded—
and this is a most questionable form of literature because of its
mechanical process. O. Henry has had enormous influence over
American short-story writers and appears to have broadly out-
lined a model for their tales. He has a wonderful imagination.

NOVEMBER 13. I wonder where I get this passion for telling the
truth honestly, without choosing or altering. As a rule, one doesn't
say everything, one tries to obtain a certain unity of character,
but on what plane will such unity be carried out? On the spiritual
or the physical? Whichever the plane chosen, one will cheat: one
is willing to tell the truth about the soul, but not the truth about
the body; or that about the body and not . . . etc.

Read the Book of Esther in my Hebrew Bible. What confusion
there is in my life! If I were to put all that into a novel, people
would think it impossible, would say I had invented it.

NOVEMBER 20. Called up Gide's number. Great difficulty in ob-
taining it. The person who finally answers is incomprehensible
and, what is more, does not understand me. I was about to hang
up when Gide comes to the telephone: "I was told that M. Scribe
wanted to speak to me. I hesitated to answer!" Tells me that he
is too ill to see me, that he had left his bed to come to the phone
when he realized it was I, but that he is going back to bed and
hopes to be "fit again" in two or three days.

NOVEMBER 27. In Jefferies' *The Story of My Heart*, there is a
very curious passage on the feeling of worship that the sight of
a beautiful body arouses in the author, who is intensely pagan.
I have often experienced this and said so. Something religious. And
I believe that Jefferies is right in saying that ascetics are the real
impure, although I would have preferred him to say the puritans.

DECEMBER 19. Had a friendly telephone call from Gide, this
morning. He receives me a little later in the small room where he
works. A big leather cushion has been thrown over the broken-
down armchair that he has given up all idea of repairing. On the
mantelpiece, a bronze head of Gide on which is tossed, no, most
carefully placed, a fine green velvet beret. Gide himself wears a

fisherman's hat under which his face seemed to me extremely pallid and his eyes a little weary behind his spectacles; his voice is softer, lower than usual, but as clear and distinct as it was twenty years ago. I give him the passages about him in the fourth volume of my diary and ask him to read them. He reads the first page and declares himself touched that I don't think he has a sharp expression—such as photographers give him—but an attentive one. When he asks for the following pages, I tell him that I would prefer to leave them with him: "You can return them to me later. I would feel cheated if you read them now; I would much rather talk to you." He laughs and agrees. Tells me he is going to publish his correspondence with Claudel. . . . When he asks me what I think of *Le Partage de midi,* I make no bones about expressing my admiration for the play. "But," he says, "the text has been modified in the name of orthodoxy. . . ." I left soon afterwards.

DECEMBER 20. Gide said to me: "Claudel is a man who thinks one can go to Heaven in a Pullman."

DECEMBER 22. Read Thomas Merton's autobiography with great pleasure. He is a young poet, now a Trappist, in Kentucky. Almost all his loathings are mine, but his led him to a convent. He talks roughly and brutally of worldly life and of all the foolishness that amuses us. He is often right, but it seems a little easy to be right in this manner, I mean in exposing the inaneness of worldly pleasures. Intelligent worldlings are perfectly aware that all this is vanity, but nevertheless enjoy it. "Turn away from it all," they are told, "for everything will pass away." They think this the best possible reason for hanging on to it! However, the book is a great fisticuff through a papier-mâché setting.

DECEMBER 30. What meaning can I give to this dream and what does it want to tell me? I was in a vast Romanesque church and, holding a child by the hand, led it to the doors of two adjoining prison cells, each with a grilled peephole in its door. I raised a lighted candle and said to the child: "Look, this is for your good." The tortured faces of two men appeared at the peepholes. I then said: "These two men are going to be burned on Tuesday. . . ." The whole thing is all too clear, down to the detail of the peepholes, but why two men? They are my own self. Perhaps a tendency to see myself twofold. And who is the child? Myself also?

1949

JANUARY 2. Two forces face to face and equally formidable: spiritual energy and sensual emotion. There is sensual emotion in everything we see, and in everything we don't see, spiritual energy, but in everything we see, spiritual energy penetrates like the waters of a river that bursts its barrages and overflows into the meadows. And in everything that we don't see, sensual emotion rises like a great overwhelming flood. There is sensual emotion in a prayer so innocent that a child could not pray it better, and in the transports of physical love enters something like a blind longing for Paradise lost. Nothing is quite pure, just as nothing is quite impure. A Sister of Charity's humble heart may be swollen with sensual emotion, which our Manichaeism alone prevents us from seeing, because we will not admit that sensual emotion is also a work of God, and that it is essentially many-sided. In the same way, a frenzy for pleasure does not take on its full meaning and cannot be wholly understood, unless one recognizes that it contains something divine, a nostalgia for holiness.

JANUARY 16. A Catholic talks to me about what he calls the delights of communion, but I know him to be very sensual and, like many men who are more or less allured by mysticism, he transfers his sensuality, bag and baggage, to the religious plane. He has no idea of this, but I see it so clearly that I cannot help dropping a hint about it, as discreetly as possible; I have known him long enough to do so. . . . He tells me confidentially, a moment later, that he has never experienced remorse for carnal failings. And what true-hearted man would talk otherwise? Remorse of this kind is almost always obtained, I was going to say trumped up, when conscience stings us—if it still lives in us—as soon as we sin against love.

FEBRUARY 2. What a strange profession is mine. I am working well, with a passion for forgetting, plunging into an imaginary world. And what do I meet in this imaginary world? My own problems immeasurably enlarged to the point of reaching terrifying proportions.

*　　*　　*

FEBRUARY 5. Worked a lot at my novel. How alive that Joseph is! He fascinates and at the same time horrifies me. What a monster of sensuality one must be to possess such modesty, such outrageous modesty!

FEBRUARY 12. Had a long talk with Elie-Anne about Marcel Proust, who sometimes came to see her with Lucien Daudet. "He always seemed self-conscious and said very little. His appearance was so queer that Lucien had to assure us that he was really somebody. When we read his books, they irritated us. They were so wrong and at the same time contained enough truth to make them plausible, but we knew very well that things were not at all the way he showed them, because he had never known *the real dukes and the real duchesses*. He had only second-hand information. The people he should have known would never have received him, because they lived in a closed circle and never saw outsiders."

FEBRUARY 26. The truth I have reached, after years of struggles and thought, is that I hate the sexual instinct. I recognize its importance, I admire the gigantic force that has achieved so many works, but hate desire, that force that throws so many wise beings at the feet of fools and makes them rave, like lustful children. I wish it was not so.

Devoured Gourmont's *La Physique de l'amour*. Chastity, "the strangest of all sexual aberrations," he says. The amours of moles, tragic amours, of a surgical character. Frightful the hit-or-miss methods of nature, "that good mother," Gourm' nt says with a snicker.

FEBRUARY 27. Just as I returned from Mass this morning, I had a telephone call from Gide asking me to see him. I went at once. Gide is better, after a heart attack. I find him at his usual place, in the library. The small table he sits at is littered with books and papers. An open copybook where I recognize half a page of his handwriting and a volume of his collected works. He stoops a little, his face very gray, his cheeks covered with a white stubble, for he seems not to have shaved for two or three days. Shakes hands and makes me sit opposite him. "You're going to find me intellectually diminished," he says, laughing. I laugh too and reply: "You say that very friskily!" Turning serious, he answers: "No, I feel diminished." "No one would think so . . ." "But I am." "Yet I find you working." "I'm just pretending to. See, my pen is dry." (He points at it.) It takes a lot of courage to talk so about oneself, to be so clear-sighted. A little later, he tells me that he has received a *thirty-word* cable from America (his voice supplies the italics), asking him to go over there to receive the Goethe Prize. "What's the Goethe Prize?" "I have no idea. I've been offered five thousand dollars and all my expenses paid." "How magnificent they are!" "Yes, magnificent, but I'm not going, I'm too tired." He speaks of a letter from an American called Henson, who mentions me. "But who is he?" asks Gide. I tell him. Henson has a great admiration for Gide, and I speak highly of the young man, whom I met when I served in the American army. "Yes," says Gide, "there are some very fine people, no matter what is said to the contrary. There are lots of them. I don't care for people who run down this one and that and who play the pessimists. I'll leave this earth thinking that there are very fine people in this world. I say this without sadness. There's no sadness in me. No, I don't like people who take pleasure in spitting in the soup." "Oh, neither do I!" I answer, disgusted by the picture conjured up. "Neither do you, I know it. That's why we see each other. And then, have you noticed that it's always in other people's soup . . ." But I have been with Gide for half an hour and must go. In connection with Scandinavia, where I intend to go this summer, Gide asks questions and sighs: "If I followed my inclinations . . . No, it's impossible. You're going there this summer? Well . . . I can't." That was the saddest thing he said that morning. I get up and he shakes my hand. As I am about to cross the threshold of the library, he asks me what I am reading at present and if I know of a book to recommend for Catherine. I think for a moment. The books I read are so serious that I hesitate to mention them. However, I have been rereading Montaigne and say so. "Ah," says Gide, "what edition are you reading?" "The small Jouaust edition that gives the 1588 text and that of the second edition." "I am asking this to know if you have the variants. That is most important." (Forgot to say that when I mentioned Montaigne, Gide exclaimed: "That surprises me, from you!" "Because I'm a Catholic? Why, Pascal read and reread him." "Merely to refute him." That remains to be proven. Pascal admired and hated him at the same time. I might have answered, but thought of it too late, that St. Francis de Sales took the keenest pleasure in reading the *Essays*.) Gide is near me, asks me to take down one of the four big volumes he points to on a book-shelf. It is a magnificent Montaigne with broad margins. The variants are in italics. "You know the famous sentence about La Boëtie . . . Well, 'because it was I' was added later." "Yes," I replied, "it doesn't figure in the first edition." "The sentence is held up to us as something wonderful, coming straight from the heart," continues Gide. "But it took thirty years to come straight from Montaigne's heart!" He suddenly becomes the Gide I used to know, and during those last few minutes I find him exactly as he used to be. He shakes my hand again. "It was nice of you to come over right away." I don't think he ever showed himself more affectionate than in that little sentence. What I admire in him is a never-failing lucidity, a desire to see things as clearly as possible, not to be fooled by his own self.

MARCH 20. Father Couturier called me up the other day and said: "I want to *reassure* you about Hell." I had to make him re-peat the sentence, which I didn't catch at first (surprised as I was by the word *reassure*). He reminds me that last week, during lunch, he had expressed doubts about the large number of lost souls. I had said: "No one ever preaches any longer about our latter ends. The clergy dares not speak of Hell. All the saints believed in it and talked about it." Today, he says: "I want you to know that I believe in it, like all good Christians." "But, Father," was my reply, "I believe exactly all that you believe." Strange to think that he should have said that to me, of all people. My very first book was partly based on this subject. He had much better talk about Hell to such Catholics as seem not to believe in it at all, but this trait in Father Couturier's character pleased and touched me. It is truly that of a spiritual man, centered on the invisible world, and a conscientious one. Nevertheless, it made me laugh.

APRIL 10. Claudel was told of Gide's witticism: "Claudel is a man who thinks one can go to Heaven in a Pullman." To which Claudel replied: "Well, Gide is going to Hell in the subway."

APRIL 18. A visit from Father Couturier. He came to ask for some information and has no idea of the extraordinary impression he made on me. One dares not write the word *holiness*. Do I know what a saint is? Yet I thought that it must be something very much like this. There was an inimitable radiance about him, a real humility that seeks neither to hide nor to show off, a gentleness that is the gentleness of a violent man. At one moment, I could not understand what he was saying and thought I saw him through a sort of shining mist. . . . Thought of the tomfoolery I hear. Writers outdo themselves at it: "My customary sincerity . . ." "My honesty . . ." "My terrific modesty . . ." Poor things.

Listened over the air to Messiaen improvise. Music that sounds as though it had been composed *after* the end of the world. It has monstrous beauty, makes you see vast caverns where rivers flow, where piles of precious stones glitter. You have no idea where you are—in India, perhaps. The composer was playing the organ in Trinity Church. Never have the vaultings of that hideous building heard more disturbing sounds. You have the impression at times that Hell yawns open. Cataracts of strange noises *dazzle* the ear.

APRIL 24 OR 25. AT SAINT-NICOLAS-DE-VÉROCE, IN SAVOIE. Read the *Introduction to Kierkegaard* by Jolivet. Few books have upset me so much since I came into this world. It is horrifying at times to discover oneself in another man, and this happened to me when I read this book. But isn't it the role of very great men to reveal us to ourselves? I mean that they teach us what we knew without knowing that we knew it. In this sense, Kierkegaard's sentences are like so many magic mirrors where the soul is reflected and sees itself for the first time. Thought once more about Descartes's dream, which has engaged so much of my attention lately. Are books merely an aspect of this dream? Wouldn't it be, rather, that the reader imagines what he reads, or thinks he is reading? In the flashes of Kierkegaardian thought, one has glimpses of great depths that are singularly like a revelation. "Christianity has not materialized," he writes.

MAY 2. As long as something inside us protests against ourselves, there is room for hope. It is when one accepts oneself as one is, and gives up, that the game is in danger of being lost. In other words (if I wanted to be funny), one can set one's mind at rest so long as one feels uneasy!

MAY 5. Alone today. I took a path that runs down into a valley, through the meadows. I followed it to a wood of fir trees where

I spent the better part of the day, for this is one of the most beautiful spots in the world. One finds oneself there on a sort of spur that advances to the middle of the valley and cuts it in two. Thicknesses of moss and fir needles give the ground a wonderful springiness, as though the soil bore one up. Inside the wood, the ground goes up, goes down, with green-carpeted ravines from the bottom of which loom very straight firs taller than the pillars of Notre-Dame. A dim light, a silence broken only by bird songs, a complete stillness everywhere and solitude are what is found in this spot. I dreamed, I thought of our life, of what Robert said to me about Kierkegaard the other day, on the road: "The older one grows, the more one wants to provide for one's inner life." Thought about what the philosopher says concerning the necessity of "choosing your choice." He sums up almost all my problems in three words.

MAY 21. PARIS. Read Kierkegaard's *Fear and Trembling,* which affected me like a thunderclap. I know what faith is, I have grown up in its shadow, for, seen on this side of death, it is a shadow. My parents handed it down to me, by God's grace, and it goes so deep within me that it lends its color to everything, to good and evil alike. Without a feeling for the absolute, we would sink like a stone. We are all like the church of Philadelphia, in Revelation: weak, but protected on account of our weakness.

MAY 22. If few people go to Heaven, how will *you* go there? How would you form part of the elect? What is duty? To count on a miracle. I am not afraid of Hell and never was, in spite of desperate efforts to obtain this fear, but I think that what would be more grievous than going to Hell would be annihilation after death and not to see God. I must admit that reading a sermon by Newman on the small number of the chosen disturbed me very greatly.

JUNE 15. The other day, as I was tidying a large cupboard, I found a plaster cast that I used to be very fond of: the head of the charioteer of Delphi; and next it was the cap I wore in the American army, and I put the cap on the charioteer's head, just to see; the effect was so likely that it made me laugh. Nothing more Greek than a young American's head, when he is handsome.

* * *

JULY 1. . . . AT VERRIÈRES.   I enter the world called real as one
enters a mist. I would like to pause and explain what I mean, what
I believe I understand. It takes very little for the outside world
to lose its reality in my eyes. No doubt it is not with impunity that
since 1924 I have thrown myself deliberately, and at the price of
great effort, into a state known only to novelists, in order to believe and *see* what I describe. Following which, the world does
not always appear to me as something completely real, and there
are moments when I clearly feel that I'm going to lose my footing. Consequently, when I see a large number of people who have
to be talked to, I shrink back and don't quite hear what is being
said to me. I take refuge in temporary deafness. I am present, but
like a somnambulist. I may perhaps seem at ease, but a somnambulist also gives that impression. . . . I went the round of the
guests, I saw a splendid garden in the sunset, very big trees, long
stretches of grass, and, in a setting fit for childhood memories, lots
of very well-dressed men and women, society in fact, what is called
society. I looked at the bright pink sky beyond black trees. . . .
During dinner, I talked to my neighbor about this feeling of unreality. She was English, she understood. I told her of having seen,
in an American university, sapphires and rubies lit up by "fluorescent" light, and that these precious stones were just pebbles picked
up on a road. It might be that this light showed them to me as
they really are. God, perhaps, sees them so. Poets and saints are
the only ones to guess that a veil is stretched between us and the
world (I kept these ideas to myself). Then I talked to my left-
hand neighbor. Her Christian name, Evangeline, is written on a
cardboard four-leaf clover, but the name only suggests to me
Longfellow's poem. She speaks French, and so well that I wonder
where she comes from. She is interested in literature and asks lots
of questions about my work (this happens only once every ten
years); I am amazed to be sitting next to someone who forgets to
talk about herself. I ask her if she writes, but she waves aside the
question as though what she did had no importance, and asks me
about a book that I wrote in English. We talk about America.
One of the most beautiful streets in the world is the main street in
Salem, where Hawthorne lived, and it is now exactly as it was two
centuries ago, with its large eighteenth-century houses set back a
little from the road behind rows of trees. Does she know it? Why
yes. She also knows Concord, where Emerson, Thoreau, Hawthorne, and Melville lived. She has seen everything that Europeans

never see, they who form such a hasty and often oversimple opinion of the United States. She smiles when I mention Baltimore
and gently says that she is Dr. Fisher's niece. Now I lived for three
years facing Dr. Fisher's house, and my cousin and sister know
him well. I suddenly emerge from my haziness. My neighbor is
the wife of Ambassador Bruce.

JULY 2. To know everything no longer interests me. To know
everything is a young man's dream. What interests me passionately today is to understand, and I no longer wish to know except
for the sake of understanding more clearly. Anyway, what value
has knowledge in itself? What Bayle knew over two centuries ago
seems debatable to us. How much error can be found in Erasmus'
knowledge! In fifty years, our books will make schoolchildren
smile.

JULY 17. Yesterday, an exceptionally happy and beautiful walk.
We went to Versailles and at once walked to the Grand Trianon
and passed through it to see the gardens, delighted by their design
and color schemes, and from there to great empty avenues, overgrown with nettles, grass, and brambles, but still most majestic
between rows of huge trees. We were quite alone, and I had a
feeling of indescribable happiness, a human but not carnal happiness, a happiness free from shadow. . . . I would have liked the
walk to continue till nightfall, but everything always has to end,
we must always go farther on, we must always turn back. No
doubt there will be other walks like this one, but not quite like it.

JULY 18. Novel. I must not allow the action to bog down in
conversations, as it might have done in psychological develop-
ments. As soon as a character listens to himself talk, he must be
made to shut up. From time to time, I take up the book from the
beginning, that is, I skim through it to look over the contents of
each page in a few seconds. In this way, I can see if it is making
headway, if it is moving, or if, on the contrary, it is marking time.
The beginning of the second part, which I am tackling today,
must have the same impulse as the beginning of the first part had.
The characters themselves furnish the action and I leave it to
them. As soon as I try to direct the action myself, I am almost sure
of making a false move; they *know*.

* * *

JULY 19. Last night, listened over the air to a part of *Don Giovanni*, which is being given at Aix. After an hour, I went to bed, no longer *hearing* a music I know too well and am so deeply fond of. I might almost say that I was familiar with the leading airs before knowing how to read, for my sisters used to play and sing them in our old rue de Passy flat. All my life, these delightful themes have been with me, following me in joy as well as in sadness; they have already lost their novelty for me, and it is a pity; I fear to hear them too often, not to find them each time lovelier, fresher; I dare not write that I fear to tire of them. The passages that touch me most are in the second part and reach one when the ear is already a little weary. What wouldn't I give to hear *La ci darem* for the first time! That intoxicating *first time* that in all spheres gives us something we will never find again . . . I have always thought that our joy in Heaven will be made up of this, that we will see God for an eternal *first time*; there will be a one and only time that will never cease, there will never be the sad thing linked to duration: repetition.

JULY 20. How keenly one feels whether a book is necessary or not—and this holds good less for the reader than the author! Is the initial impulse powerful enough to carry the story to its end? At every page, one should have the feeling of an irresistible pressure from within; instead of which, more often one has an impression that the author is ridding himself of a chore. It sometimes happens that the book undergoes this mysterious pressure at the beginning, but that the pressure loses vigor on the way and stops short, leaving the book to follow as best it can. Those sluggish words that cover page after page, those long sentences written by a man in a hurry to get through with it all . . . I have always had the greatest distrust for an overlong book, because it is often the sign of a lack of energy and not, as is thought, the mark of great labor.

AUGUST 10. Violent efforts to learn Danish.

Read John Addington Symonds' *Michaelangelo* with admiration. It now appears obvious to me that the man had the same horror of the sexual instinct as is found in Leonardo. Perhaps he dreaded the very thing that attracted him. His work is not that of a satisfied, surfeited man. It is in itself one of the most powerful sexual acts ever produced by art, but would seem to be that as an act of compensation. I can easily imagine that this somber, violent, timid man was chaste. None of his contemporaries, so far as we know, ever definitely proved that he was not. I believed the opposite for a long time, although without the least proof.

AUGUST 15. . . . What meaning can there be in all this? Our life is a book that writes itself and whose principal themes sometimes escape us. We are like the characters in a novel who do not always understand what the author wants of them.

SEPTEMBER 24. The carnal episodes I sometimes describe express a part of the truth that I carry in me and that is my truth, but they weigh on me and I hate them. All this will, one way or the other, get into the novel I am writing at present. Thought once more about the problem of sentences among which one must choose, those it is necessary to discard, but whose presence must make itself felt. All this subjacent, nonwritten book . . . the mistake that many transatlantic authors make is precisely to want to write it. Most of them do not choose.

A religious upbringing has shown me only too clearly the vanity of the world. That is what paralyzes ambition in me. I have never quite believed *that the game was real*. I would die of shame if I were to push myself forward as some people do. And let's not talk of modesty. It has nothing to do with the matter. I work exactly like a bird or a bee, because that is what I was made for, because it is my instinct and I would suffer too much in going against this instinct. I don't believe there can be the least question of literary fame nowadays, on the threshold of such a strange world as opens before us. I am completely indifferent as to whether my name will be remembered or forgotten. In eternity, this will not be of the slightest importance, but I want to fulfill my destiny, which is to express what is in me.

SEPTEMBER 28. Marveled as I read the Book of Esther in Hebrew. A reward for more than ten years of effort. I can at last get at the text that is back of translations.

SEPTEMBER 30. Sometimes I feel so happy to be alive that I sing when I am alone. I even think I would be perfectly happy were it not for the sexual problem, which I don't want to talk about. This morning, I was obliged to stop working on my book after thirty minutes. No one will ever know until after my death how much

I have had to fight in order to continue being myself, to be present until the end.

OCTOBER 1. Read Lafuma's *Études Pascaliennes.* I always find it moving to be with Pascal again; he has had such an influence over me that I cannot even imagine what I would have been if I had not read him. His terrible sentence about sensual pleasure has sounded more than once in my ears this entire summer. "May they get drunk on it and die."

OCTOBER 5. . . . As we were speaking of applause, of the sound of applause, I said that I very much disliked this violent, brutal noise, and Mme Bourdet, a theater fan to the core, exclaimed: "Oh come! It's the most beautiful sound in the world!" I stuck to my guns, I said that nothing was more beautiful than the silence that follows a Passion by Bach, at a concert of sacred music, a silence through which linger the last chords, the very last note where music dies away and disappears as into an abyss, instead of shattering against the sort of resounding wall built by hand clapping.

OCTOBER 9. Abbé Omer Englebert's book on St. Francis of Assisi contains interesting remarks about the Poverello's virginity, a virginity very delicately questioned by his latest biographer. The first ones had rather clearly pointed out the sensual nature of the failings of the youthful Francis. After the saint's death all this was quickly glossed over and we were led to believe that his errors consisted in singing and dancing farandoles through the streets of Assisi. Farandoles indeed! I would much rather know that Francis made a few mistakes. He becomes all the dearer and more human to those who love him and his merit can only be that much greater. But I have always preferred saints of fire (such as St. Augustine) to saints of ice whom temptation did not even graze. That St. Francis of Assisi should have stumbled, revives our hope. There he is, very close and very vivid. As the Lord liveth, he sinned like the rest of us.

OCTOBER 12. A priest who is enamored of mysticism tells me of his horror of theology: "It's nothing but straw! And who said that? St. Thomas. What do you say to that?" And speaking of St. Clara, who instructed her daughters to admire creation and look at the trees when they left their convent, he makes this remark: "What she really said was: 'Look at men and look at trees,' but the author of the book you mention did not think fit to say 'men.'" It seems, however, that in a future edition the quotation will be given in its entirety—and in Latin. A fine saying of St. Francis', who, when he once heard himself called a saint, exclaimed: "Don't canonize me too quickly! I am still quite capable of begetting children!" When I ask my visitor if he thinks that the Poverello's spirit is still extant in his Order, he replies shrewdly enough: "It's as though you asked me if the spirit of Christ still prevails among Christians." We next talked about Father Damien. My visitor had been to Molokai and told me that one day he had been to visit the lepers at Saint-Louis, in Paris. There were about ten of them. The nun said: "Don't let them touch you." A missionary from Molokai came up to him and, holding out his hand, said: "As you see, I haven't got leprosy." "And yet," continued my visitor, "the lower part of his face was eaten away by this terrible disease. But I shook his hand. Could I have done otherwise?" This is very much in the manner of the first Franciscans.

OCTOBER 16. I write what I see. If I had to sum myself up as an author, I think this sentence would say all there is to say. If I don't see, I can't write, I mean that if my mental eyes do not have a very clear view of the scene I want to describe—I designedly say scene, as one speaks of a scene in a play—I can do nothing. I am not like writers who can invent at will, without seeing anything, who invent with the help of words and not with their mental eyes (and this ends by being felt). I have said in the past that all I could do was to invent, but I had not sufficiently thought over the problem when I expressed myself so inaccurately. The truth is that I do not know how to invent. There is something or someone in me that makes me see my characters and makes me see them in action. In my case, such intensity of vision has never been greater than when I wrote my first three novels. It decreased in *The Strange River* (the influence of surroundings and an incomprehensible desire to go against success). The gift was given back to me in *Midnight* and *The Dreamer*, almost totally failed me in *Then Shall the Dust Return* and in *If I Were You* (excepting the scene with the child and perhaps also the one that takes place in the passage du Caire). In the novel I am writing at present, the vision is so clear that it prevents all explanations of a psychological order; so much the better.

* * *

OCTOBER 21. Reread Rilke's *Notebooks of Malte Laurids Brigge*, but am going back a little on my former admiration. Too many pages are spoiled for me by an obvious desire to intensify the author's native melancholy, to "pile it on," to make a show of anguish in and out of season, about a woman who sells pencils, a building that is being torn down, about some word pronounced in a certain fashion, about a draft. I know, unfortunately, what anguish is. It is not gratuitous to that extent and, when it appears, has solid reasons for doing so. From subtlety to subtlety, one becomes the prey of literature, literature of the most spurious kind. But there are passages of outstanding beauty (a description of the reading room at the Bibliothèque Nationale, for instance). I admire this great artist, but don't like his way of telling us: "Look out, I'm going to suffer, and you're going to see in what a subtle fashion."

OCTOBER 24. Once more obliged to reconsider my opinion of Rilke. Having opened his *Notebooks,* I happen on the wonderful story about the epileptic man. There is so much sympathy in this account—I give the word its literal meaning—such a great and genuine compassion that I scarcely see any but a Russian writer capable of approaching love of such quality (how can this be expressed otherwise? It is really a question of love, the gift that distinguishes saints from the rest of humanity). Yet I was exasperated a little earlier by the list of fears that the author says he feels or has felt: fear of a small woolen thread, fear of the button on his nightshirt, fear of a crumb, but in order to judge him, one should remember what he had set out to do, namely, "to discover among visible things the equivalents of interior visions."

. . . Reading Rilke enchants me. Almost everything in these extraordinary Notebooks should be quoted: the sentence about his dead father's face, which looked as though it "remembered out of politeness"; the description of the Reverend Jespersen, the portrait of Margaret Brigge, the piercing of the father's heart and the wound that lets out two drops of blood, like a mouth pronouncing a word of two syllables. I take back everything harsh that I may have said about this great writer, not without maintaining a few reservations about certain mannerisms such as the hypersubtleness that spoils for me the first thirty pages of the book. Among the letters that I have received is one written fifteen years ago by a friend of Rilke's; someone will find it someday; it said that he had liked my first book. I realize today the very great value of such a testimony.

OCTOBER 29. My novel is getting on slowly, too much so perhaps, but it seems to me that clearness of vision is obtained at that price. I could cover a larger surface of paper each day, but then I would be *inventing* and, to a certain extent, lying instead of describing as truthfully as possible whatever it is that I see. Often it seems to me that I see only a bit of an apron, a gesture, the lower part of a face, and can only catch a word or two; at other times, I am given a whole scene, with a superabundance of details, details that I don't know how to dispose of and among which I must choose. Anyone examining my manuscripts would notice that all the suppressed passages were invented in order to hurry on to reach the real truth that I knew was waiting for me further on. Who works in this manner nowadays? The other day, that was the question I asked a young Belgian critic, M. Théo Louis, because I thought it interested him. He said that, as far as he knew, the fact of visualizing characters does not seem important to present-day novelists, who are far more preoccupied with ideas than with images, "but," he adds, "although it is true that your characters rarely express ideas, your books hold a view of the world, a philosophy." I replied: "If you like. What I have against certain novelists of today is not that they make their characters express ideas. No, what I have against them is that their characters' ideas are not part of those who voice them, but part of the author. When a character in a great Russian novel confides his ideas, what speaks is his flesh and blood and we believe what is said, but how is it possible not to see that the characters of such or such a modern writer are no more than his mouthpieces and that their speeches are interchangeable?"

. . . Jacques Maritain has always maintained that my books were those of a man living on the mystical plane (he means this in the broader sense), and I think, as a matter of fact, there lies in all my books a deep uneasiness that an irreligious man would never have felt. I am not trying to say that my books are Catholic novels. The very idea appalls me. But I believe that all my books, no matter how far they may seem from an ordinary, accepted religiousness, are none the less essentially religious. The anguish and loneliness of my characters can almost always be reduced to what I think I called a manifold dread of living in this world.

NOVEMBER 1. I have spent many an hour reading that I could have given to my books, but that is my way of building what I call the dike and holding fast. Studying too much is laziness, said Bacon. Not in my case. I devote three hours a day to reading, plus an hour and a half to studying the Bible. To my novel, about an hour and a half; that is all I can do, I mean that what I write after an hour and a half invariably has to be rewritten the next day. Twenty lines, sometimes thirty, that is all. I write only in the morning because my critical sense is most wide-awake then. The evening is a time for a lyrical frame of mind. I write letters only when obliged to and consider the practice a mere waste of time. What I have to give, I would rather put in my books; my books are my letters.

NOVEMBER 4. I asked Father Couturier: "If you were a pagan, would you let yourself be converted by Claudel?" He started: "I should think not!" We were talking about the correspondence between Gide and Claudel that is now appearing in the *Figaro.* Even when Claudel is right, he is right in an aggressive manner. With him, goodness assumes a condescending air, and in spite of oneself one is tempted to side with his adversaries. And yet, I repeat, he is right, but how often have I noticed that the more zealous the defender, the more clumsily truth is defended. . . . You could swear that truth does it on purpose. What can be said about the effect such bludgeon strokes might have on an unbeliever? However, the poet of genius appears here in some very fine passages.

NOVEMBER 6. Today, as so often happens, a fit of indescribable melancholy as I walked about the rooms I have taken such pains to furnish. What is the origin of this sadness? I don't know. It is the sadness of being in this world and of feeling the threat that hangs over all that one loves. I can never be completely happy in a world where death always has the last word and where it can step in at any moment. And even at that, if I were the only one concerned . . . I marvel that we can laugh so often, that we can behave as though *it* were not there.

Gide once told me that if he ever wrote anything about me, he would stress the fact that I draw without ever allowing my pencil to leave the paper. This unbroken line is plainly visible in the novel I am writing at present.

NOVEMBER 10.   Somerset Maugham's *The Summing Up* is a book
that delights me. The author's honesty and common sense make
the work rare and unexpected, and he talks of his profession with
a deep understanding of all its difficulties. What he reveals of himself is all the more arresting since you feel it is true. Nothing
extraordinary; his experience of life does not differ much from
what we all know, but he says things as they are, very simply,
with a first-rate choice of words, and that is enough for each
sentence to hold one's attention. The recipe is so simple that I
wonder why it is not used more often, but then I think that the
sort of parade called literature would no longer exist. And yet,
how interesting truth is, and that solely because it is the truth!
Even in small things, it has an inimitable ring, it has a charm and
a strength of persuasion that all the trickeries of style can only ape.

NOVEMBER 11.   I was thinking, a moment ago, that certain difficulties would not have existed in my life if I had not been subject
to ungovernable fleshly appetites. My books would have been
quite different. Better? I don't know, but different. My books
are the books of a prisoner who dreams of freedom. . . . The
novel I am writing is one long cry of anger against instinct. . . .
I am not saying all this to complain but to put the question correctly. I think that my case will appear very strange someday,
when all is known, and yet I am inclined to believe it is a com-
moner one than would be supposed. Faith is the cause of this
bitter conflict.

Reading Maugham. I can't always find him right, particularly
when he says it is stupid to reread books, that to learn languages,
dead or living, is a waste of time; but I agree with him when he
writes that England and France are the only countries to own a
literature: the others only have great writers. True enough, these
two countries are the only ones where one finds an unbroken line
of great works, the river that runs flush to the brim without
ever drying up.

NOVEMBER 16.   In spite of feeling so weary tonight, I want to try
to give an account of my visit to Gide. I went to see him this
morning to ask his consent for Biblio-Hachette to publish a letter
he wrote me in 1934 about *The Dreamer*. He showed me into the
little room where he works, which has a view of roofs. We sat
down opposite each other; between us, a small table covered with

books and papers. Gide's face looks pinker than I have ever seen it since my return from America, and he seemed young and alert, just as he was before the war. He was never so charming to me perhaps, so simple in manner, so cordial. I believe he was really happy to see me, for he said so several times as though he were bent on convincing me of the fact. When I told him why I had come, he appeared a trifle surprised, which leads me to think that people do not always behave so scrupulously with him. He read the letter, his letter, most attentively and paused once to exclaim under his breath: "Why, my letter is very good! I'm glad to have written it!" I then handed him a rather long, separate postscript, which is a list of errata he had noted in my book. "Have that printed too," he said good-naturedly. "It will show up my school-marmish side! . . ." We had a rambling conversation and I can't remember in what connection I told him that I don't sleep well. "Do you know Descartes's letter on insomnia?" I do not know it. He led me to his study and, taking out the Pléiade edition of Descartes, sat in a corner by the window. The letter is addressed to his friend Guez de Balzac. Gide read it slowly, in a beautiful, distinct, sonorous voice, not at all like the weary, toneless voice he has at times over the air (I am thinking of his radio conversations with Amrouche); on reaching the passage where Descartes talks of his dreams and says—I am quoting from memory—"I walk through formal boxwood gardens, enchanted palaces . . ." he lowered the book and looked at me with an enraptured smile; he felt an almost sensual joy in reading this beautiful language.

NOVEMBER 17. . . . This too I did not mention in the account of my visit to Gide: as we sat facing each other, he told me that he was reading the last volume of my diary and, owing to this, thought of me every day and talked to me (those are his very words). Told me again how very much touched he had been by what I wrote about him in 1944. He made several unsuccessful attempts at lighting a cigarette, holding the lighter far too much to the right. Yet he reads with ease.

NOVEMBER 21. Perhaps God wishes certain souls to live in a state of unbalance. There are times when I believe that a great many men will be saved in spite of their faults, and even through their faults, because they remained steadfast in faith and charity, amidst the most violent crises.

* * *

DECEMBER 3. Simone Weil. I knew very little about her works and am reading them at present with astonishment. She touches on all the subjects that move me most and seeks what is deepest in us. Her passion for the absolute makes her kin to the best, and her contempt for what is relative is, I think, unequaled except by St. John of the Cross and Pascal; they are the ones she reminds one of sometimes. How many books that were mere literature does she convict of vanity! How many things does she outmode and reduce their contents to nothing! Robert tells me that her conclusions are nonhuman, and I think so too, but that means she climbs to heights where we find it hard to breathe. A monster of intelligence. There is something about her that horrifies.

DECEMBER 4. Too sensitive to the voice of human beings. I think it reveals them more than their expression or their hands, although the latter own up to almost everything.

DECEMBER 8. Reread in Harris the (authentic?) account of Wilde's frightful death, the body that burst open, and later the disinterment. Wilde seen in his coffin with a beard, still recognizable in spite of, or because of, the quicklime that merely succeeded in drying the flesh instead of devouring it, and Ross' wonderful charity, waving aside the gravediggers and their shovels to go down into the grave himself, to pick up the horrifying remains with his own hands and reverently place them in a coffin. Ah, how glad one is that such a gesture was made, that there should have been one Englishman to make it, that not everyone should have been hardhearted, and that a really Christian soul should have been present at that moment, by the grave!

1950

JANUARY 8. Went to Gide this morning around ten-thirty. I ask him if he has read Wilde's *De Profundis*, which has recently appeared *in extenso*, and he says he has, and what disturbed him most in the book was the way Wilde composed an attitude for posterity (even more than the accounts he gives of large sums spent to satisfy

Douglas' whims). . . . He looks for a file and opens it before me
to take out a letter from Lord Alfred Douglas, dated 1929, and
asks me to read it aloud. It is violent, extremely coarse. Douglas
had just read *Si le grain ne meurt*. . . . I recall this sentence:
"You would never have written such a book if you had been a
gentleman. It shows what an awful cad you really are. . . ." He
denies that there had ever been any physical intercourse between
himself and Wilde. All things said, he forgives Gide "because I
am now a Catholic" but nevertheless shows overwhelming contempt for him. The letter is an extraordinary piece of hypocrisy.
It is not so much a letter as a scene, one of the scenes that were so
frequent in Douglas' life. Gide tells me that he was not handsome,
but pretty, "yes, pretty is the word." He relates the scene between
Douglas and Wilde (see *Si le grain ne meurt*), Wilde trembling
with anger but remaining silent and saying to Gide, after Douglas
had left: "It's like that every day. . . ." We then talk about English poetry. Gide fetches his copy of Milton in the Tauchnitz edition (he noted on the flyleaf that he had bought it in Florence,
in 1912, but had had it bound later and that he had been particularly struck by the beauty of a passage in *Paradise Lost*, Book V,
lines 25–75; it is Eve's speech to Adam: "O sole in whom my
thoughts find all repose . . ."—a beauty that seemed to him un-
surpassed in any tongue). He shows me a number of passages
underscored in pencil and says that he had lately reread Milton's
two great poems "with rapture." Also talked about Marlowe;
Gide is particularly fond of *Hero and Leander*, and I quote a few
lines from the poem that make him smile. John Donne is also a
favorite with him, but when he speaks of the two portraits of the
poet, one when he was young and very handsome, the other when
he was dead and in his winding sheet, I call his attention to the
fact that the second likeness was made during Donne's lifetime,
when, no doubt to satisfy his strange obsession with death, he had
himself painted with his eyes shut and his face enclosed in a winding sheet tied in a knot at the top of the head, according to the
fashion then prevailing. In discussing Marlowe, we agree that if
one compared him with Shakespeare, Marlowe would probably
have been the greater of the two if he had not died so young. Gide
is the only Frenchman with whom I have ever had the opportunity of talking at such a length about English poetry, with which
he is very familiar. However, he did not ask me to come to see
him in order to discuss literature. A priest is to call on him. . . .

* * *

JANUARY 27.   At Gide's . . . One of us talked about chastity,
saying that at first it was easy to remain chaste, it even gave one
a feeling of unutterable freedom, but that after a year or fifteen
months, obsession appeared to play havoc, the whole energy of
body and soul seemingly employed to beat off assaults of the sexual
instinct. . . . In connection with Denmark, where I expect to go
soon, Gide talks about Andersen, of whom he is extremely fond:
"People do not fully realize that he is one of the only men who
ever created myths. The story of the little mermaid is a marvel."
"And the Emperor's new clothes." "The grand duke's new
clothes, Green, the grand duke's, but no matter, it's wonderful."

FEBRUARY 23.   Came back to Paris feeling very ill. Influenza.
Continued *The Red Badge of Courage*, a book that I had till now
found consistently admirable. The soldier is seized with panic
during his first battle, runs away, wanders here and there, is
caught in the turmoil of the fray and carried from one side to
another by the ebb and flow of armies. Enormous confusion. The
men's disarray, their sufferings, all this is shown with extraordinary vigor. It reminds one of the greatest writers, of Tolstoy. I
wonder if anything more eloquent has ever been written against
the crass stupidity of war. Yet the author composed his book
with accounts he had had from Civil War veterans. What genius
it took to bring to life the big monster called battle!

MARCH 6.   Yesterday, talked to Anne about *The Red Badge of
Courage*, which she admires, just as my mother admired it, and
which I too admired extravagantly at the beginning. But look!
The coward of the first two-thirds of the book turns into a hero
at the end. The young man whose panic fright was so wonderfully
described is seen, as the book finishes, proudly bearing the Union
flag into the thick of the battle. He has unwittingly become a
hero, like a character in one of Erckmann-Chatrian's novels. What
puts a finishing touch to disgust is that the author is a writer of
quality, but he is the one who had "cold feet," he sacrificed to the
public's taste. A true civilian book. A soldier would never have
flinched.

MARCH 7.   We are constantly told that the world is coming to
an end. I can't say that this makes much of an impression on me,
first because I am getting used to it and then because death is for

each of us a little end of the world. Yet, this idea of a possible and general annihilation finally creates a peculiar state of mind. There isn't an author nowadays who can any longer think: *non omnis moriar*. A concern for fame has been given such a blow that it is no longer possible to pose for posterity.

MARCH 17. Looked at photographs of the War between the States. I remembered Mr. Brooks, an old Virginian colored man, my grandfather's last slave whom he freed long before the war and gave a field and a small house by the roadside. We used to go to see him in a carriage or on horseback. My pretty cousin would wave her hand and cry: "Hello, Mr. Brooks!" And he would appear in his doorway, his charming old tobacco-colored face framed in a white beard. On being told that I was his master's grandson, he took both my hands in his and smiled. This doesn't sound in the least like *Uncle Tom's Cabin*! All the misunderstandings in history arise from the fact that the winning side's theory always prevails. If Germany had won the 1940 war, France and above all England, not to mention the others, would have appeared to be the great culprits.

MARCH 24. A long conversation about the devil. Lots of things that I will never repeat, but Father Couturier told me this, which is something to be remembered: the devil cannot perform miracles. Yet he can bring about circumstances that assume a supernatural appearance. No pacts, such as we hear of in time-honored stories, but a gradual paralysis of the will. I know that, just as Bernanos knew it. A man who gives in to the temptations of the unmentionable one, ends by no longer wishing for God, and there lies the real danger. Physical temptations count for nothing in comparison with spiritual ones.

Enraptured last night as I listened to Monteverdi's *Orfeo*, relayed by Berlin. Orfeo's voice had the beauty of a beautiful body, it turned into something physical, something tangible. Jacques Février, the pianist, asked me the other day if music was important to me, but I don't think I would write if I could never hear music. I have always come up against words, as one runs into a wall. Music alone says what I want to say. There are writers for whom words are accomplices, but this is not the case with me.

MARCH 29. Heredity. Between my great-grandparents and myself, during the whole of my childhood, a sort of barrage was set up by my father and mother, who led admirable lives. In their way, they were saints. They protected, concealed me from myself. When they died, I was delivered to the being that I have become, and this is not the finish, because one never gets to the end of discovering oneself. At one period, a sort of massive irruption of heredity invaded my being. Religious mania and the rest. I am the outcome of all these instincts. On certain days I have a feeling of being crushed. God knows all that, has allowed all that. . . .

MARCH 31.   Sometimes one must walk about in the depths of the abyss. Even if I go down as far as Hell, God's arm is long enough to bring me up again. Those are His very words in the Scriptures. He is there. Not only do I know it, but I *believe it.*

The human body in all its glory, the human body clad in its nakedness, like a royal vestment, the soul clad in the royal vestment made for it by God, the vestment that is flesh. Ah, how silly we are, we and our morbid ideas about modesty!

PALM SUNDAY.   "They know not what they do" would be the definitive words that would end all our problems, if we understood those words rightly; they would induce us to forgive our own selves. I have been reading Havelock Ellis, now very much outdated by more recent works. Yet, what pleasure Montaigne would have taken in reading him! Heredity. If the individual has the whole of the human species back of him when he seduces a woman, where is his sin? What resistance can he offer to a countless multitude that takes him by the shoulder and pushes him forward? Is instinct then allowed complete license? No, the individual remains free, in spite of everything, because grace is present and will act, unless he refuses it, but if he stumbles, I cannot help thinking that he will be shown boundless clemency, God's clemency. Heaven is paved with good intentions, not Hell, as is somewhat foolishly said. If the exhibitionist gives in to a deeply mysterious instinct that he inherits from a very ancient past, where the most obscene forms of worship were favored (that explains, according to Havelock Ellis, the solemnness with which he carries out an act that he himself cannot understand), how can one judge him? Will it be necessary to go back to Adam? One might cite as an example a very well-known English statesman who could not resist the desire to expose himself to women, if ever he was alone with one of them for a moment. This might raise a laugh; I think it tragic, considering the merits of the man.

APRIL 3. Last night I read a little book by D. H. Lawrence: *Obscenity and Pornography*. With his usual violence and intemperance of adjectives, the author dashes off at top speed along a road that can only lead him to absurdity, but as he can't help being the man he is, he says brilliantly things that invite thought, even when they seem questionable. Came across this: "For every man has a mob-self and an individual self, in varying proportions. Some men are almost all mob-self. . . ." "The worst specimens of mob-self are usually to be found in the professions, lawyers, professors, clergymen, and so on. . . ." "The public, which is feeble-minded like an idiot . . . is always exploited." He inveighs against puritans who reprove the sex-appeal of certain books. According to him, half the beauty that the world has produced is beautiful because of sex-appeal. "Even Michelangelo, who rather hated sex, can't help filling the Cornucopia with phallic acorns. So we can dismiss the idea that sex-appeal in art is pornography." Very well, but he can't prevent himself from going too far and says this, which raises a smile: "Boccaccio at his hottest seems to me less pornographical than *Pamela* or *Clarissa Harlowe* or even *Jane Eyre*. . . ." He calls puritanism the gray disease. "Without secrecy there would be no pornography," and he adds this which is extremely curious, for by dint of running away from puritanism he ends by rejoining it and himself talks like a puritan: "And the mass of our popular literature, the bulk of our popular amusements just exists to provoke bad habits." (It is I at present who play the puritan, for Lawrence expresses himself more crudely.) He censures these habits on account of the shame, the anger, the humiliation they cause. He talks at great length on the subject. Very deep truths mingle with enormous naïvetés.

APRIL 5. Last night, listening to Flagstad sing in the *Götterdämmerung* (relayed by the Scala in Milan), I realized that I was no longer in the least the enthusiastic Wagnerite of twenty years ago. No more today than in the past can I recognize any of the sensations described by the composer. In this respect, to mention completely different musicians, I feel in perfect agreement with Bach, with Gluck, with Brahms. Wagner still stuns and dazzles me, of course. One can still enjoy watching what Verlaine called "the great white barbarians" thunder by, but what does this music appeal to? The heart? Certainly not. The brain? No indeed. It is the strangest case I know of in music. One is moved, but why? I dare not write that one is moved through the senses, but am inclined to think so. Beauty of form always ends by acting on the nervous system. Although this immense show of strength produces its effect, I don't believe that a more inhuman music can be heard.

UNDATED. If I were to die tonight and were asked what moves me most in this world, I would perhaps reply: It is the way God passes through men's hearts. Everything is swallowed up by love, and although it is true that we shall be judged according to the degree of love we possess, it is also beyond all question that we shall be judged by love itself, which is none other than God. I believe that if lack of charity were called Evil, instead of weighing down the wretched human body under this curse, the whole of false Christianity would be turned upside down and at the same time the kingdom of God be opened to millions of souls.

MAY 24 OR 25. SALZBURG. Hotel Traube, in the Linzergasse, just where the Kapuzinergasse runs into it. Here for the last four or five days. Too many happy memories cling to us to prevent a shade of melancholy from overshadowing our walks through a town that has always been dear to me. It has changed, the world has changed. Salzburg is not quite the same person it was in 1930. I read Faulkner's *Sanctuary* in the Schloss Mirabell gardens. A book of extraordinary intensity. Not a trace of rhetoric, not a sentence that does not carry; I devoured it in two days, reading over certain passages to make sure of extracting all their pungency. One can't skip a word. What is admirable above all is the choice of details, the quality of the dialogue, the command of the narrative, which so skillfully wanders from the point.

MAY 27. *Crime and Punishment*. What can I say that hasn't already been said? For thirty years, I have hesitated to read Dostoevsky. I distrusted him, and rightly so. Had I read him earlier, a whole portion of my work would have been different. We sat down to read by the Wolfgangsee. Robert laughed aloud as he read Shaw's *Doctor's Dilemma* and I read *Crime and Punishment*. When Raskolnikov kills the old woman, I could not help giving a scream. When he killed Elizabeth, I put the book down on the bench and walked about to recover. What modern author is capable of writing such things? Not one. I was bowled over and still am. I see very well why Conrad would never read Dostoevsky. An instinctive and perfectly legitimate jealousy.

Most important conversations with Robert. The yearning to leave the world is so strong at times that I don't know how to resist it, but am nearly sure that this is the great temptation that must at all costs be warded off.

JULY 21. PARIS.   Just as some people continually wish to go south to sunny countries, I unceasingly hear the call of the north. It is more than a wish, it is the German *Sehnsucht*, a sort of perpetual languor deep in my heart. That is why the sight of a sea's milky waters, or a birch wood, affects me so powerfully. Hedwige, a character in *The Transgressor*, sprang from this. "Your name is like wind over the snow," someone says to her in an unpublished part of the book. Beauty, for me, is above all a thing of the north. I wonder what can be the cause of this.

. . . I found this, too, among my old papers, a prayer that I transcribe without comments. A trace of it can be found in *Moïra*. I had forgotten all about it. The awkward little text is dated May 8, 1924: "Lord, give me peace, silence, a quiet heart, a quiet mind. I did not ask this world for joy. The world came to me and offered me its joy. Its joy is bitter, Lord, and I do not want it or do not want to want it. Yours is the power to destroy my flesh, but I know that You will not before my hour has come, and my hour is a long way off, for great is my imperfection. Look, however, on the wretchedness of my flesh. Longings at dawn, longings at noon, longings at dusk. Did You ever suffer such wretchedness, Lord? You never mentioned it. No one ever mentions it. Can it be that it is shameful? Does everything great and noble belong to the soul, can it be that the body is nothing?"

JULY 26.   Father Couturier came to see me the other day. Regarding Michelangelo, no doubt "a godly man," according to the Father (who sends everyone to Heaven), he considers the Last Judgment in the Sistine Chapel to be "an entirely and absolutely religious painting. Of course, there are the naked men and women, but this does not alter the fact. The ceiling is another matter." "The ceiling," say I, "is the dream, no, the ravings of a man repressed." "Yes," answers the Father, "without any doubt, but one can suppose that Michelangelo hadn't the least idea of it." This is possible, everything is possible where a man as religious as Michelangelo is concerned. I would willingly believe him to have been very chaste. Otherwise, he would not have thrown over the ceiling those great muscular, disdainful *ignudi* who represent an extraordinary compensation for a devouring hunger. He possessed, in his mind, the most beautiful human beings that a painter's brain has ever conceived.

JULY 27. Robert was talking to me a moment ago about this diary, of which he has read large extracts in the complete text. He regards it as a book that, to his knowledge, has no equivalent, because it shows the whole of a man passing from one extreme to the other. I would very much like these pages to be published. I think it will be possible someday, because people will then be able to stand the truth better than we do in 1950, but I may be mistaken; one should always credit human beings with great stupidity. In the world's present state, this diary would dismay the very people it is made for. It is nevertheless my best book. (I am talking, of course, about the unexpurgated text.) That is why I want to save it. The one person I fear is myself and that mania I have for burning papers, every ten or twelve years.

AUGUST 27. SALZBURG. Read *The Brothers Karamazov*. Very deeply touched by Alyosha. He thinks that nothing evil can ever happen to him. Very beautiful. But what would Alyosha produce, if he were a writer? I might be told: "Alyosha could not be a writer." Writing is already evil, but evil is also action and act we must, because good almost always mingles in some way with evil. Does pure white exist among us? White is no more of a color than black.

SEPTEMBER 14. Visit from a young American Quaker. I look with enormous curiosity at a man who cannot lie. American law dispenses him from taking the oath because he is a Quaker. As in St. James' epistle, his yea is yea and his nay is nay. I find myself full of respect for this youth of twenty-five! He has a narrow face and intensely black eyes, almost too bright at times, I mean that when we get on a subject that moves him for some reason, his eyes begin to flash, like Joseph's in *Moïra*, and as it happens, he wants to know if religious feeling can reveal itself with the violence it has done in my book. At that moment, he looks so much like the character I have just described that I have to struggle with myself not to tell him so. A little later, he asks if French Catholic publishers, and mine in particular, exert pressure over their authors to obtain books that will serve the Church's cause. I thought for a moment before replying that my publisher is not what is called a Catholic publisher, seeing that he has printed numbers of works by unbelievers or non-Catholics, by Gide, for instance, and that, to my knowledge, no publisher exercising pressure over writers exists on this side of the Iron Curtain. The question was put without malicious intent, but it affected me queerly and I had to make an effort to answer calmly. The ideas we form of one another from continent to continent are so discouraging at times, and so strange, that one wonders whether they are worth refuting. Yet, one should.

SEPTEMBER 20.   Father Couturier came to see me yesterday. He was white as a sheet and looked very ill. He suffers from asthma. It took him almost ten minutes to climb my stairs. He spoke openly of the Church, seen from an administrative angle. "It is," he says, "a continuation of the hateful Roman Empire." He had refused to say the Mass of the Chair of St. Peter. "After all," he goes on grumpily, "the Pope is only the Bishop of Rome. The Reformation was necessary (not in the way Luther understood it, however . . .). There is no trace in the Gospel of this ecclesiastical government. The Gospel is, on the contrary, an anarchical book, almost tending to destroy family life ('If any man come to me and hate not his father and mother . . . ,' 'I am come to set a man at variance against his father . . .'), most marriages are a failure, children who live too long with their parents are good for nothing. . . ." By separating these sentences, I risk giving them a sound they did not have, but I am quoting his very words, and he spoke with a vehemence that struck me. As regards our latter ends, he is inclined to think that not *all* Hell is necessarily the place of suffering that people take pleasure in describing, and that Christ may perhaps return there once more to save what has been lost. Finally, on the subject of the wrong done to God by the wicked, a wrong that demands infinite punishment since it offends an infinite being, I tell him that such words are meaningless to me and he says I am right: according to him, that is the reasoning of theologians and he has a horror of theologians' reasoning, as I have. That is the very reason why I can talk to him. He brings peace, he gives it on behalf of God, without always being aware of it.

SEPTEMBER 23. Went to the movies yesterday to see a sort of documentary of our times. Gide, Jean Rostand, and several others speak. Picasso appears for a moment. It is explained to us that the world we live in would be a paradise if mankind applied its recent discoveries to the progress of peace instead of trying to use them for wars to come. Who doubts that? None of the atrocities of atomic warfare are spared us. St. Peter said that "the elements shall melt with fervent heat" and that "the heavens shall pass away with a great noise." This is something like what scientists prophesy, and they haven't read St. Peter. Sartre puts in a brief appearance, giving vent to a few truths regarding the responsibility each of us has toward the others. One of these days, if he isn't careful, he'll discover the Gospel.

SEPTEMBER 25. Last night I looked through Dante's *Inferno*, illustrated by Doré, an old tome that belonged to my grandfather and that has had such enormous influence on me. These pictures acted on my senses with a delay of ten or fifteen years, and the poet's atrocious theology left its mark on me. I used to take those frightful tortures literally. Curious to see that all this finds an echo in me, even at present. A voice whispers in my ear: "And supposing it were true?" I can't manage to silence it!

SEPTEMBER 26. Ever since I was fifteen, I have lived with a feeling of danger that has scarcely even ceased. I say scarcely. For I have had moments of complete security, but God alone gives them. Hence the delirious joy of converts. They think themselves safe, at last, they are saved. Unbelievers cannot have the least idea of what happiness this means.

SEPTEMBER 30. A moment ago I was in my room, looking at a big spot of sunlight on a door, when suddenly I was seized by that something I don't know how to name that I call happiness. It lasted at least five minutes. I fell asleep and, on waking up, once more felt that extraordinary emotion compared with which nothing in the world seems real. I don't know how to express it.

I believe that if all men lived according to the Gospel, they would experience what I am trying to describe. Deep, complete security: death no longer exists, nothing remains but love. All this in un-utterable sweetness. Strange that it should not depend on a state of grace, as everything in me shrieks that I am not in it. It is none the less a grace sent by God. Spiritual authors would talk, I suppose, of natural mysticism, but I am convinced that the happiness of Paradise is not made of any other stuff . . . in an infinitely higher degree!

OCTOBER 2.   This vague feeling of danger that I have always had from the mere fact of living in the world . . . Is it that the world is dangerous? Perhaps this is why monastic life used to attract me so powerfully. Returning from Saint-Jean-de-Beauregard, the same feeling of danger as we neared Paris. I have always had it, without knowing why. Once safe in my own quarter, the feeling abates without quite disappearing. A great confused threat.

OCTOBER 4.   Yesterday, a visit from a young Dutchman who talked to me about my books in such a way that I wonder if he doesn't know them better than I do. He prefers *Moïra* to the others and has something curious to say about each episode, rec-ognizes the white apron worn by Joseph as the one I had given Serge in *Midnight*! He sees a certain likeness between Claude in *L'Autre sommeil* and Praileau in *Moïra*, and I tell him that he is perfectly right, the two characters were drawn after the same model, with a few modifying details. And feeling I could trust him, I tell him the whole story of B., which has had such a deep effect on me. We were walking along the Seine, one morning in 1923. I had said to myself: "I'll tell him what is in my heart be-fore we cross the Pont-Royal." Taking his arm, violently moved, I said to him: "I have something to tell you, something most im-portant." He often laughed at my serious expression: "All right, go ahead, I'm listening." We reach the bridge, I thought I would drop to the ground. I then see clearly enough that if I speak, I will immediately lose B.'s friendship, and for ever. I said: "I've thought it over. I mustn't." It was one of the painful moments of my youth. B. never knew anything about it. He is still as gay, as good as ever, always pokes a little fun at me when we meet, which is seldom, for he lives a long way off. He once gave me a terrible talking to, on seeing me with a volume of Baudelaire in my hands.

He was puritanical to the backbone. We were twenty. I looked at him in despair. How could such a gulf be crossed?

OCTOBER 24. Yesterday afternoon, went to see Jouvet at the Athénée Theater. You climb two flights of very narrow stairs, then you enter a low-ceilinged room, so dark that the lamp on the long table is lit at three in the afternoon. On the end wall, a painting representing, I think, the actors of the Commedia dell' Arte. On the desk, a photograph of Giraudoux smiling, with a slightly mocking expression behind his tortoise-shell-rimmed spectacles. Jouvet has scarcely changed since I saw him in 1932. A little heavier. Black hair brushed away from the brow. Dressed with rather British elegance in dark blue. He tells me that I have not changed and I return the compliment. "Oh," he says, "it's my business not to change." His voice is smooth, even, a trifle low, the sentences cut short, as though with a knife. We talk about his Tartuffe. He makes several bitter remarks about the obtuseness of critics, wails over the poor quality of the modern stage. *Le Maître de Santiago* finds favor in his eyes, and he is sure that *Port-Royal* will be a fine play, but he is ill disposed toward F.M. "He doesn't like the theater or actors, he doesn't like Molière, he only grants that, having paid his actors to the end, the gesture will be put to his account. But he thinks that Molière is damned, in spite of this. . . ." I can't help laughing: "Does he share God's secrets?" Jouvet looks at me with shining eyes: "God? He has put Him in his pocket." I change the subject at once, feeling he is moved. He asks questions about *Moïra*. "Why did Simon kill himself?" he says abruptly. "On account of Joseph." I explain that Simon walked into my book of himself and almost forcibly. He listens attentively (he listens wonderfully, like Gide, like Simone; he listens like Robert). Then he says: "You are a born playwright. This is your opportunity. So everything is settled. We rehearse in February and I put the play on in March." I laugh once more and tell him that not a single scene has been written yet, that my mind is still very vague about the play he asks for. He looks at me severely and says in his strange, colorless voice: "It's time you gave us a play." I leave shortly after.

OCTOBER 29. Having read half of *Armance*, I closed the book to avoid dying of boredom. For at that point, sparkling conversations and ultra-subtle complications begin. . . . What I don't care for is Stendhal's personality, his affectations, his terror of being taken for a bourgeois, his passion for getting on in society. On the other hand, what is captivating and genuine in this great creator is his admiration for youth and his rather pathetic efforts, in each of his books, to disguise himself as a good-looking young fellow and to imagine himself as fascinating, agreeable, a lady-killer. That he should play a losing game in *Armance* is very significant, for he comes to grief but, in spite of all, retains the qualities of physical beauty and intellectual superiority.

NOVEMBER 6. At Antwerp, a walk through the zoo. Profoundly sad to see all those caged animals. It is perhaps one of our greatest sins to put an antelope or an eagle behind bars, but we are all of us such barbarians that we are not even aware of it. A couple of crows from the Congo, sleek and fat, shiny as freshly polished boots. Brown zebras striped in black; their rumps look like magnificent agates. An immense condor, its head hooded in a sort of white woolen bonnet and with black, spreading wings, motionless except for the tips of the wings, which stir imperceptibly, wings of a terrifying size, made to thrash the air at dizzy heights. It stands like a man being measured for a suit. The polar bear and its sinister waddle, its head shaking ceaselessly and, without ever interrupting this motion, opening its jaws at times to show, in a huge yawn, a dingy mauve tongue. I left after a few moments. I loathe zoos almost as much as I do concentration camps, which they very much resemble, anyway.

NOVEMBER 9. PARIS. If one only thought it over for a second, who is not ashamed of his life? I am ashamed of mine very often, but I do work. Very much struck by a visit from poor G. The suffering written over his wretched face. A strict moralist would tell me that his is a wicked suffering, that of ungratified desire, but I don't think there is such a thing as wicked suffering or one kind of suffering for the devil and one for God, there is simply one suffering, the one that life is made of, the stuff that life is made of. I used not to think so, I think so today.

An astounding article in *Life* about the present state of our astronomical knowledge. A subject I know nothing about, but that always enchants me, because it puts everything in its proper place with staggering authority. According to Einstein, if I understand aright, which is not sure, we are inside a virtually immeasurable sphere, the universe; and outside this sphere there is nothing, an unimaginable nothing. The stars, in vast groups, rush through space, moving away from each other with incalculable speed. Reading such things, you wonder what meaning our little worries can have. What does all this signify? The earth is so small, so lost in these abysses, that it would be quite as reasonable to say that it does not exist. And yet, at this very moment, poor Georges Poupet is suffering in his rue Garancière bedroom and telephoning his friends in that woebegone voice of his. This is only one instance in a hundred thousand. If the earth exists, it is because it is peopled with souls, and if God sent his only son to mankind, in this infinitesimal spot, it is perhaps because there are no souls anywhere but here. This bears out my idea that we are far more of souls than of bodies and that what we do is most important, in spite of everything, because we are souls. What overwhelms is the notion of space, because no matter how much we enclose the universe on all sides, it is impossible that space should not continue farther on. Be it as it may, I wonder what becomes, in all this, of literary ambition, fame, and the world's gimcracks.

1951

JANUARY 20.   Went to the theater last night. *Les Mouches,* by Sartre, an astonishing, very powerful play and not without beauty. Electra's speech to Jupiter's statue: "Heaps of filth! etc." The author's atheism is given a free hand, and I don't doubt it might perturb many in the audience, but the god shown us by Sartre is so mediocre and so limited that one can easily imagine the playwright's atheism in regard to a god of such paltry dimensions. If God were Sartre's God, God as Sartre sees Him, I would be an atheist twenty times over, I would be the atheist of such a god and a fanatical one too, but this is a case of mistaken identity.

JANUARY 28.   I called up Gide this morning and went to see him. Another visitor was there before me, Jean D. Gide says he is very tired, thanks to a *good night* obtained with the help of a sleeping pill; he explains that a sleepless night leaves him rather

alert sometimes, but that after a long sleep, he is occasionally
"stranded," as Valéry used to say. A little later he turns to Jean D.,
who is a Catholic, and says: "We must ask Green where to find
the sentence we were talking about just now." And staring me
full in the face, looking rather severe, he asks: "Where is this
taken from: 'You would not seek me if you had not already
found me'?" I can't help murmuring: " '. . . if you had not
found me.' " And I add aloud: "The sentence is in Pascal's *Mystery of Jesus*." (I concealed my amazement as best I could. Can
it really be Gide asking me such a question?) "Ah!" he cries. "So
it isn't in the Gospel!" Then I tell the story of Father B., one of
the most learned men I know, who said that as a student he had
looked high and low in the Gospel for "These particular drops
of blood were shed for you." All honor to Pascal for being able
to cause such mistakes! But Gide tells me that he prefers reading
Bossuet to Pascal. And he adds this, which shocks me: "In Pascal,
there are only ten cries from the heart. One could quote them.
The rest does not attract me, except the letters to Mlle de Roan-
nez." I then mention Bossuet's letters to Sister Cornuau, but Gide
has not read them. Is this possible? Perhaps he has forgotten them.
What he says next is what people almost always say when Bossuet's name comes up: "I read Bossuet for the style." He passes
very quickly from one subject to another, picks up from the
table a small, very badly printed book: "Here is a book I used to
be fond of that I now find disappointing." It is a copy of La
Bruyère. However, he likes La Bruyère's *Dialogues on Quietism*,
which has just been reprinted, although he doubts the work's
authenticity. He suddenly exclaims: "A writer I don't at all care
for is Chateaubriand." "Not even *Les Mémoires d'Outre-Tombe*?"
I asked. "No, I don't like that either." "But the parts about his
childhood?" "Ah, people always mention those! But all the rest
bores me." I remember the day in 1937 when, as we walked down
the boulevard des Invalides, we talked about Chateaubriand. Gide
had noticed the word *chauvir* (to prick up one's ears) in one of
my books, and I quoted a sentence from *Les Mémoires d'Outre-
Tombe*: "My luck sometimes pricks up its ears." He told me then
that he had never read the *Mémoires*, which greatly surprised
me. . . . Today, I feel that he is trying to talk as he used to. He
does not want to disappoint us, but in 1930 he would never have
spoken as he does now. Sadly, I am obliged to note that what he
says is poor and cold and that he has had to cudgel his brains to

say it. He is very old and knows it perfectly well. "Old age is a horrible thing," he says. "Aren't there a few compensations at least?" I ask. He collects his wits and, as though to contradict what I have just been thinking, finally murmurs what I consider a very fine thing. "It is harder to carry one's glass to one's lips, but one feels less thirsty." "And what about serenity?" (I ask this.) He turns to Jean D. and then says: "There is no serenity except in cloisters, the one that faith brings." (But what a contempt he probably has for that kind of serenity!) Jean D. gives a very good account of a taking of the veil that he had witnessed. Gide smiles and tells a story about a child who, on seeing a nun behind a convent grille, after a similar ceremony, asks: "What would happen if they let her loose?" He goes off into gales of laughter, tells us that as far as he can learn, the Church is not at all the same as she was at the time when she was attacked and that she has become more tolerant. "Father Valensin once said to me: 'You have a sense of mystery. That is sufficient.' " Gide adds: "Everything was going smoothly, and then came the Encyclicals!" (He says the last words with such emphasis that one feels tempted to write them in capitals. He sounds as though he were saying: "We were peacefully picnicking on the grass and out came the rhinoceros!") Neither Jean D. nor I say a word. I ask him if he is planning a journey and he tells me he is going to Morocco. "A rather long trip," I then remark. "Yes, but such long journeys tire me less than walking from here to the dining room. It's my heart that is weak." He spoke affectionately to us both.

JANUARY 30. The other day, at the mention of Pascal, Gide exclaimed: "Ah, that makes me feel wide-awake! Yes, Pascal . . ." He needs literature as a stimulant. I noticed this once before in 1949, when we talked about Montaigne.

FEBRUARY 23. Went to Gide's for the last time. A silent crowd in the dark entrance. I recognize Roger Martin du Gard, Gallimard, Jean Lambert, Marc Allégret. All of a sudden, I see Gide in a room adjoining the drawing room. He lies on a small iron bed, the tips of his fingers joined. Not quite a prayerful gesture, although it reminds one of it. His head is thrown back and looks very majestic. He seems to be thinking rather than sleeping. As I went downstairs, I met Jouhandeau, all keyed up at the idea of seeing a corpse. . . . "I can see that you feel very badly," he said

to me, "for he was so fond of you." Did not answer. In the street,
to my great shame, I cried. Strange. It has always surprised me
to find how much attached I was to him. Mauriac writes, in the
Figaro, that Gide chose evil. What does he know about it? What
do any of them know about it? God alone knows.

FEBRUARY 28.   Great hilarity in Paris over a telegram received by
Mauriac a few days after Gide's death, which read: "There is no
hell. You can go on a spree. Inform Claudel. *André Gide.*"
    Noted this in St. Jerome: "Our sins are what makes the bar-
barians strong. . . . Our vices are what bring about the defeat
of Roman armies. . . ." This reminds me of Calvin's sentence:
"God will speak to us with great blows from halberds, with great
blows from pikes and harquebuses: we will not understand a word,
the language will be most strange." Thought a great deal about
the carnal problem. If an unreasoned phobia for the body existed
formerly, we are certainly in danger of swinging in the opposite
direction at present, and not only us laymen, but some part of
the clergy (I am thinking of the priest who went to see Gide and
so wholeheartedly threw St. Paul overboard). "I have not lost
faith," says someone in Bernanos's *Diary of a Country Priest,*
"because God has been pleased to preserve me from impurity."
Now chastity is simply too heavy a burden for present-day humanity, because faith has weakened. Less and less are we Christians. We rebel against the New Testament when it irks us (particularly St. Paul). It is a sort of heresy that is gradually taking
shape. Is my case different from that of millions of Catholics?
But I don't want to be a heretic. As time goes by, I realize the
importance of every hour that falls into everlasting nothingness.

MARCH 3.   Long conversation with Robert about music. I was
telling him again that the least song by Schumann wrings my
heart and that Bach's music is like an invasion of the soul by faith,
whereas Wagner remains mysteriously *exterior,* no matter how
much admiration, how much surprise he provokes.

MARCH 7.   Reading Emerson again. "The Oversoul." Some sentences are so beautiful that they should be able to change our life.
That, at least, is the impression one has for a few minutes. After
which, they return to the general current of ideas. He says that
man is a river, the source of which is hidden. Magnificent. A
source that escapes psychoanalysis.

* * *

MARCH 16. A letter from Allen Tate telling me that he has read *Moïra* and sees it as "a parable of the great Protestant neurosis of our world." But I wanted to go beyond denominational borders and get at puritanism under any religious form, Catholic as well as any other. In connection with this, I note a statement made by a group of American bishops: "Sex is one of God's endowments. It should not be ignored or treated as something bad."

Quennell's *Byron.* The constant suffering inflicted on his pride by a misshapen foot, the gliding walk he invented to conceal this defect, what a cross it must have been to a nature like his! This delicate, sensitive man none the less rented a window to see a man hanged (in front of Newgate jail). I have always thought him to have been misunderstood. The disappearance of his diary is an irreparable loss. There was in him a religious man. All that one sees is the lady-killer.

MARCH 21. Still reading Quennell's *Byron.* Impossible to pass judgment on Byron, because the outer man had taken on inordinate importance, concealing an unknown one, probably terrorized by his nurse's Calvinism. His bad taste, his ignorance, the legend that has established itself in lieu of the truth, as sometimes happens.

MARCH 24. Finished Quennell's *Byron.* That great rustling of skirts leaving the drawing room when the poet took up his stand there, an elbow on the mantelpiece . . . England had had wind of his sexual eccentricities (his sister, his wife). The unfortunate Annabelle Milbanke had confided the most amazing things to Dr. Lushington. One woman remained in the drawing room, a carrot-head who said to Byron: "You should have married me. I would have known how to manage you." Life is a novel of most unequal talent, but this scene is admirable. The account of Byron's flight to Dover, a prey to the creditors who came to seize him. Nothing remains to him but his carriage, which the bailiffs, much to their regret, were not able to seize, having arrived too late that morning. His despair when a few gray hairs stray into his lovely curls. And he is getting fat. All this is strangely melancholy. Nothing so much resembles a life that fails as certain successful ones.

Read an essay on my works. It has sometimes been said that the two great literary influences in my life were Poe and Hawthorne. That would be counting for nothing the first eighteen years I spent in France, which molded me. One would think that

I was born at nineteen, at the University. In this same essay, the Bible is not even mentioned.

Placed end to end, my conversations with André Gide might lead people to think that we saw each other frequently, but a more attentive look at the dates will dissipate this illusion. To tell the truth, I have never been able, so far, to give the public anything but small fragments of a long conversation that never took place, because circumstances were never propitious. The necessary element would have been, for instance, the opportunities afforded by a long journey, and this journey, which we both wished for, was put off from year to year until it was too late. I always had the impression of seeing Gide by fits and starts, and he probably felt the same, as he often told me that we had a great deal to say to each other but lacked time; now it has gone for ever. However, I think that the essential was said.

True, I might have seen more of Gide, but I made it a principle never to ask for an invitation, but to go to see him the moment he asked me to. In this way, I was sure that if he saw me, it was because he wanted to see me. For I knew him to be badgered by visitors and dreaded not so much to be importunate as inopportune. I have suffered too much myself from what Montherlant calls *biophages* (or people who devour the lives of others); nothing would have induced me to be the caller for whom a clock is placed well in sight.

No matter how incomplete the notes I took on Gide, they will, I hope, give as fair an impression of him as possible. I have described him as he appeared to me, but the Gide we saw on his deathbed carried away the secret of one of the most complex personalities of all times. What attached me to him even more than his talents was an all but fanatical fidelity to the truth as he saw it. Even the ancient world never produced a man who stuck more firmly to his opinion when he believed himself right, and at times he reminded me of an old Roman.

My return to the Church was, in his eyes, a sort of scandal to which he was never reconciled. Our friendship was obliged to round a Cape Tempest on several occasions, but now all that is in the far past. I can't help thinking that if I had given in to his arguments I would perhaps have lost some of his regard for me, and that it interested him to see if I would hold fast. Summed up in this manner, the question appears simple. With him, however, nothing could be entirely simple. How I hesitate to write the

following sentence, convinced as I am of the misunderstandings
it will give rise to! Since my return to France in 1945, I never
had an opportunity of seeing Gide without his attempting, one
way or the other, to aim a blow at my faith. In my case, conversion for him meant yielding to the force of heredity, and Gide
would not admit that anyone could yield. It would be understanding him very badly to say that he played the part of Satan.
Quite the contrary, his purpose was to *save* me. He wanted to
win me over to unbelief and exerted all the zeal of a Christian
trying to convince an infidel. That is what perturbed me. Any
means seemed good to him in order to make me doubt, because
that was the price of salvation. And what was religious in him
lent a particular form to his atheism, and to his nonbelief the
aspect of a religion. On the other hand, his extraordinary intuition
of human beings allowed him to sense how much I was upset by
our talks on Catholicism, no matter what pains I took to hide my
state of mind. I sometimes eluded this trying subject; he brought
me back to it gently, firmly, with the obstinacy of a missionary.
Finally, he realized that he was wasting his time (I could no more
fall back than a man with a wall behind him), but he never quite
gave up trying to *convert* me, and did so visibly for conscience'
sake and sometimes against his will. The last time I saw him, he
asked me a question, from which I am wary of drawing any conclusion, but that in my mind assumes the particular character of
ultima verba. In that serious voice of his that agreed so perfectly
with his expression, he asked if I read my Bible every day. At
another time, I would have smiled at words that reminded me
of my Protestant childhood, but I did not feel like smiling that
morning. I answered yes, that I always read it, and he fell silent
for a moment. Did my reply please him or not? I don't know. I
record this incident to show to what an extent it would be difficult for me to judge him, if ever I felt like it. But judging does
not interest me. . . .

MAY 16. One of the most complicated problems of my literary
life has always been that of letter writing. I think that a writer
should keep up a constant fight against people who prevent him
from doing his work and, I say it sadly, against those who write
to him and expect an answer, an answer that will never come.
What they don't know is that the time and sometimes the energy
devoted to answering them would be more profitably used for a

book; now, what they want, in fine, is a book. Be it as it may, I remember a friend's indignation on seeing a file on my table thus inscribed: "Letters demanding an immediate answer." For he knew very well that no matter how demanding those letters were, they would obtain nothing but a deep silence, and perhaps he thought there was a touch of cynicism about that superinscription, but I am not at all cynical and, on the contrary, these words meant something like this: "Aren't you ashamed?" I no longer feel the least shame nowadays; I am resigned to a state of things that I cannot help. After writing for a couple of hours, I am no longer fit for anything but a walk or for jotting down a few notes in this diary. The very few letters I have written, except the five or six that have really counted in my life, are of no interest to me. Yet how eagerly I throw myself on the morning mail! I believe I would be sorry if no one wrote to me any more.

MAY 17. A formal lunch at the Ritz. I am seated next to Pierre Brisson. Facing us, Claudel, Guéhenno, David Rousset. Claudel talked admirably about the earthquake at Tokyo, in 1923. A horse finds itself on the second floor of a bank. A lady, stark-naked in her tub, on top of a wall and around her, nothing. In the dirty water of a sewer, on a roadside, the Italian consul. A policeman paces calmly up and down (no sign of panic anywhere). He throws a contemptuous glance at the Italian and says: "Well, you have earthquakes in Italy, don't you?" The first quake was felt at five minutes before noon. At noon, in an appalling din, the sound of a cannon shot announcing noon, as usual, could be distinguished. Someone asked Claudel: "What impression does an earthquake make?" Answer: "It's like seeing a most respectable lady suddenly raise her skirts and dance like a lunatic." He next talks about Vergil and calls him "the greatest among all poets." Quotes from memory rather long passages but recites them without scanning, as though they were prose. . . . Guéhenno speaks passionately about Greek and Latin and the poverty of classical education, as it is now understood.

JUNE 8. The day is drawing in. This is the hour when, some twenty years ago, I simply could not stay indoors. I left my room as soon as the city lamps were turned on in my street. Those interminable walks, the source of so many of my books . . .

* * *

JUNE 12. Last night, saw Sartre's play *Le Diable et le bon Dieu*. The author talks to us about God for almost three hours and tells us why he does not care for Him. This is a most questionable form of atheism. The play is somewhat sharply criticized by a number of spectators who declare themselves unable to stand such an avalanche of blasphemies, but I prefer blasphemy to luke-warmness, and certain scenes are admirable, particularly that of the wager. There is enormous strength in the play, together with great incoherence. I think the group of scenes in the second part are badly connected. Here is a very Sartrian line: Götz says in the presence of a priest (this should be checked as I am quoting from memory): "If God exists, man does not exist" (incidentally, what mystic has not felt this: "What am I in Your presence, Lord? A nothing"), "but if man exists"—and here we have a consider-able piece of roguishness—"then God does not." The priest rushes away shrieking before hearing the end of the sentence. I stayed till midnight, leaning out of my stage box, listening to every word of this strange drama that touches on the only interesting ques-tions in this world.

JUNE 14. Had lunch yesterday in what is called society. After lunch, a young pianist sat down at his instrument and played a few measures of different pieces. "Whom is this by?" he asks. Silence. I am amazed. Not to recognize Schumann's "Nussbaum" and to mistake one of Mozart's concertos for Chopin, as some-one did . . . After hesitating slightly, I answered and answered right, for a musical memory is, together with a visual memory, the only one I possess to a rather unusual degree. No memory for words, alas, or a weak one acquired only at the price of great efforts. I learn languages easily, but can't remember ten lines of verse for more than a month or two.

JUNE 24. There is a certain benefit in looking long and very at-tentively at objects that we see every day and no longer notice. My eyes suddenly light on a wastepaper basket and there it is, called to life. I had never observed the delicacy of its wicker sticks, some of which are honey color when the light strikes them, and the three rings that hold them together shine like ivory. Soon, nothing in the room exists but the basket, and this lends it con-siderable importance. Caravaggio or Zurbarán or Dali would have faithfully reproduced its beauty, would have known how to give it a place to itself, to make it stand out clearly in the material universe. For more than twenty years, it had waited humbly for the moment when my eye would unexpectedly light on it. And so it is with everything.

JUNE 26. Had lunch with a religious to whom I said: "In each of us is a sinner and a saint. One and the other develop, each on his own plane. The one and the other, and not the one or the other. Both at the same time. While the saint develops—if the man is a saint—the sinner in him develops on the imaginative plane (the temptations vary from year to year, following a curve peculiar to each individual's temperament), and meantime the saint develops on the spiritual plane. If the man is a sinner—that is, if the sinner gets the upper hand of the saint—the saint develops as best he can on the imaginative plane (a yearning for holiness). That is why a converted sinner never starts from scratch. He has progressed during his life of sin. The saint that he was to become has progressed. In the same manner, a fallen mystic becomes an out-and-out sinner, because the carnal man had continued to develop all along, in spite of the saint's efforts." The religious listened attentively. He too had gone through moments of great suffering. Now, why is it needful to suffer? We too often forget that the symbol of Christianity is an instrument of torture, we forget it because crucifixion is no longer in practice. To realize this, we would have to imagine a religion whose symbol would be a guillotine or a gallows. That would frighten us. We would run away from it. No one runs away from the cross. We buy pretty ones that are worn as jewelry. Some are made of diamonds. Let us think this over a little. This superannuated instrument of torture no longer makes anyone shudder. There must have been a time when it made the bravest quake.

JULY 1. The minutes of Wilde's trial make very strange reading, for they show that his biographers have not turned all the facts of this business to the best account. From a psychological point of view, some of the evidence is extremely picturesque. Witness what William Parker relates about the supper to which he and his brother Charles were invited by the author, the latter feeding Charles with his own spoon and fork and this, which is even more unpleasant when you think of the man's age and physique and particularly his bad teeth: he held a cherry between his lips and young Charles was supposed to take it with his own and swallow it. All this is painful reading. Didn't Wilde see himself as he was? Pages and pages of questioning. His sheets are constantly examined and hotel maids report on them. . . . And also, those slips of paper that were handed to the judge, slips on which names were written, names that should not be pronounced, names of important people, too important to be troubled by the police. The trickery, the hypocrisy of the whole business; the unfortunate carouser hedged in by judges and lawyers who talk as though they were as white as the driven snow. This trial is what has given me the most serious doubts of present-day justice since my university days. "If that's their idea of justice . . ." I used to think.

JULY 3. A visit from André Parinaud, a newspaperman, who questions me about the sources of my novels. As I listened to my replies, I thought: "Why don't I write all this?" But I have, in my notebooks, and the whole thing is scattered through my diary. The War between the States, in which my childhood found an inexhaustible source of melancholy. Why teach children history? My twelfth, my thirteenth year were tinged with gloom by the accounts my mother gave me of the South's crushing defeat. My country no longer existed as a nation, it had been suppressed by history. This was the cause of a first and powerful feeling of isolation, of a circle traced around me. At the lycée, little Roger Laubeuf said to me: "You belong to a nation that no longer exists and to a religion that no one ever heard of." For I had tried to explain to him that although my religion was Protestant, it was neither Lutheran nor Calvinist. Even at that age, I could not talk like other people. No more than I can now. As a child, I wanted to be like the others and never succeeded. In short, I acted like a simpleton. I was alone, among all those clever little French boys. Something of this remains in me. Almost all my characters are solitary and cannot climb over the wall that separates them from their neighbor. "*Der Menschen Worte verstand ich nie.*" This line of Hölderlin found an extraordinary echo in me when I read it for the first time.

JULY 6. Ran into Malraux in an art photographer's shop, rue Bonaparte. He is very pale, asks me at once what I am looking for, and the question strikes me, for to tell the truth I am not looking for anything in particular. I walked into the shop much as one opens a picture book. Malraux launches almost immediately into what I can only call a magnificent speech on the pages I wrote about Gide in *La Table Ronde* ("It is," he says, "the only accurate portrait that anyone has ever made of him"), but I find it impossible even to give an idea of the brilliant way in which he lengthily enlarged on the subject. A summing up would only impoverish and denature it. How often have I felt this in talking to Malraux! His thought is so swift, so numerous are the ideas he suggests, that an attempt to fix it all in one's memory overcomes one with despair. A little depressed to think of everything that is lost, of everything that Malraux deprives us of by not writing what runs through his mind instead of just saying it. I had the feeling several times of standing face to face with Thomas De Quincey.

JULY 9.   As I get on in years, I believe more and more that I am going to die, and, at the same time, I believe more and more that I am not going to die. Death to me seems both inevitable and impossible. This is no doubt because the body's machinery has been working too long for me to be able to conceive of its stopping. At twenty, one is not really used to existing. One continues to be surprised by it. At my age, one is so accustomed to it that a state of nonbeing becomes almost impossible to imagine (naturally, I am speaking of the body's nonbeing).

OCTOBER 25.   Give me pen, ink, and paper and I will always find a way of entertaining myself, if it is only a question of entertainment. For I can create for myself an enchanted country in which I wander about at ease.

NOVEMBER 4.   I was talking to a priest about all that is inexpressible in us. He quoted a saying of St. Thomas' that I thought very fine: *Omne individuum ineffabile.* I was reminded of what Fénelon wrote: "I have never said anything that did not seem to me untrue a moment later."

DECEMBER 4 OR 5.   A visit to Colette in her little red drawing room at the Palais-Royal. She had written me: "If I were Julian Green, I would go to see Colette." Her face has not changed since I last saw her at Mme de Polignac's, before the war, and no one could look at her without loving her. Her large eyes are the most beautiful ones I have ever seen in a woman, eyes as beautiful as an animal's, brimming over with soul and sadness. She scolds me for not having been to see her sooner, when, she says, she was in better condition. On the long table that bridges her bed is a great jumble of letters that will never be answered, she tells me. She picks one up at random and murmurs: "What dirty dog is this who talks about my 'long experience of life'?" Picture books make her scream with admiration, like a child: "Oh, what lovely birds! Just look . . ." She hugs the copy of my diary that I have brought her and says: "I'll save it for tonight. . . ." No, dear Colette, neither for tonight nor for any other time, but this little fib touches me as much as a great compliment. She tells me the story of two swallows that she used to take to school with her, as a child, and that have to have . . . "Worms?" I ask. "Worms! Of course not, my boy! Live flies. You don't know swallows. Their contempt is superb, superb. . . ." At that moment, in comes an old gentleman who talks to us about pornographic books. He leaves and Colette says pensively to me: "How young you look! You're right. Old men are lousy."

DECEMBER 22. Jean Duché was talking to me about culture. I told him that in my opinion culture was not so much a question of knowing and remembering as an aptitude for receiving, for being able to recognize beauty and to enjoy any great book. I told him what an enormous influence the literature of the Far East had had on me: the choice of details in narratives, the omission of everything that should not be said. When we say everything, we write like barbarians.

1952

FEBRUARY 2. An evening reception. I have a horror of this kind of party. Several times I lost all sense of what is called reality and lapsed into silence. Toward the end of the evening, a nightmarish scene. All those old men, all those old women, came up to the sofa where I was sitting with two ladies. They approached like babies, clinging to their armchairs. We all of us stayed for three hours, and nothing curious, or amusing, or important was said. What good is this idiotic worldly life?

FEBRUARY 15.   Spent the evening with a religious. He told me several things that struck me, as much for the meaning they assumed in my eyes as for the answers I heard myself make. It happens that we ourselves say things that surprise and inform us. I don't know how that can be, but I noticed the fact years ago. This religious was talking about a priest who killed himself because of an uncontrollable passion. "He had," I said, "a very poor idea of God's mercy." "But he was insane." My guest's own face had a sorrowful, noble expression as he talked about all this. . . . I think that God does not want the paltry little order we sometimes build up so carefully, with Bible readings and prudent little prayers; He saves us in a disorder which is His order and whose laws we don't quite understand. "We go to Him in the midst of all this verbiage," says Father L. Everything is jumbled up in an inextricable confusion. How can this be made clear to anyone at all? One always seems to be saying the opposite of what one thinks, or to be trying to justify evil, or to floor sinners. It is best to keep silence, although there are times when one suffocates. I could not sleep last night.

FEBRUARY 16.   Vice can be depicted, but love can no more be described than light itself. The idea we give of ourselves is always simplified and contradictory.

FEBRUARY 28.   "The terror of loving what one loves . . ." This sentence of Valéry's (essay on Stendhal) is a good summing up of my play (*South*). A play written in a strange way. I am discovering the real subject as I am about to reach the end, as has so often been the case with my other works. I must go on with it to the finish in order to explore its whole meaning. Knowing about it from the start would bore me so that I could not write another sentence. When I wrote the first act, I had no inkling of what it was all about. I am always outdistanced by my characters. They are so crafty. . . .

MARCH 12.   Have begun reading Lancelot's [1] *Memoirs*, which

[1] Dom Claude Lancelot, a seventeenth-century writer of the Port-Royal community.

plunge me deep in thought. There is an almost irresistible force in our lives that drives us forward, but where does it come from? I have had the vague idea, at times, that perhaps it does not come from God but at this point we wander in darkness! For it may be that God wishes us to give in to a force whose effects will be useful to some people. Our books originate from this force, and I think that God wishes us to write our books, but if we continue to do so, will we be saved? Can God wish anything for us but salvation? This would be inconceivable. Strange to have to write that, with years, personal salvation seems to me less important than universal salvation, and I don't know whether this is right or wrong.

MARCH 17. Yesterday, a visit from one of Gide's friends. He talks about what he calls this writer's coldness of heart. I remember that Gide once said to me: "Love has never made me suffer." This seemed to me so strange that I finally believed that I had heard wrong, but my visitor confirmed the statement. "Your feelings will be your undoing," Gide often said to him.

MARCH 20. A great longing to write a book. I was talking to an English poet the other day and, as Eliot's name was mentioned, I said that I was very fond of the poet, without being very sensitive to the music of his verse, even in *Four Quartets*, and doubted if there were any. "Yes, there is," he replied gently, "but it is everyday music." This struck me. It was aptly said and in a most precise manner.

APRIL 2. MONTE CARLO. Called on Somerset Maugham in his villa at Cap Ferrat. Renoirs and Toulouse-Lautrecs on the walls. I greatly appreciate his courtesy. He is broad-minded, simple-mannered, attentive to what is said to him. He talks a little about Gide, thinks *La Porte étroite* is not a good novel because the actions of his characters are not "sufficiently motivated." He is very keen on motives. They are one of the strong points of his stories. In his opinion the best style is "an easy conversational style," and he cannot understand the agonies of style, such as Flaubert describes them to us. . . . I think I could have confided in him, a thing I could never have done with Gide. There is something indomitable and honest about him.

* * *

Bapler

APRIL 4. PARIS. Unquestionably, I buy too many books. I buy them every day, new and second-hand, French and English. What a pity one can't, at the same go, buy the time to read them, says Robert. At this very moment, I am almost certain of not being able to take all this in before dying, but I cull a few pages here, twenty there. I reread. When I travel, I take five or six books along, even when it only means going away for two days, as happened quite recently. At Monte Carlo, I had my Bible, a Baudelaire, a Verlaine, and a volume of Plutarch's *Lives* translated by Amyot. I don't want to be reduced to reading one book only, for I might not be in the mood to read it that day. I must be free to choose. This sometimes makes my suitcases rather heavy to carry. "There can't be anything in this but a corpse, alcohol, or books," an American porter once said to me as he lifted my big suitcase.

I had a vision of Hell at Monte Carlo. In the main street, standing at a newspaper stall, was a poorly dressed old man, his white locks straying from under his cap. Inside the stall, a perfectly motionless saleswoman. With trembling fingers, the old man turned the pages of a magazine that he was allowed to look at without charge: an album of naked women.

HOLY SATURDAY. I have never known a Good Friday when I was completely free from all anguish. As early as two-thirty, unutterable sadness wells up in me. Yet an incident took place at Saint-Thomas d'Aquin that would have seemed funny at any other time. I was standing by a *prie-dieu*. The church was packed with people. A beadle came up to me and touched my *prie-dieu*. I understood, wanted to argue, felt myself choke with anger. The man said: "It is for M. le Curé," and that leaves me speechless. I let him remove my *prie-dieu*, thinking that M. le Curé really needed it, which is ridiculous, for M. le Curé is naturally in the choir, with the clergy. I moved away, genuflected before the high altar, and went to the chapel at the back of the church to attempt to calm down. For I had seen the beadle give my *prie-dieu* to a very old gentleman. He had lied to me. How joyfully would I have broken that piece of furniture on his head! I tried to pray but was upset by this silly business and also by the words that fell from the pulpit, for they were remarkably feeble. After quite an effort to recover, I walked out of Saint-Thomas and went to the little Ukrainian church on the rue des Saints-Pères. It was empty.

I stayed there for a moment. What an army of *prie-dieus*! I had only too many to choose from. I quieted down, pulled myself together, and went out. How often have I not thus choked back my anger! Yet people think me gentle. My only reason for noting an absurdity of which I am ashamed is that it amuses me now.

MAY 12. One of the greatest encouragements that I ever received came from Rilke, but I was only told of it many years after his death. After reading *Avarice House*, he said this to Mme de W., who noted it: "You'll see, he will be a poet." I never wished to be anything else. I think I am a poet who has strayed into prose.

MAY 28. I met Auden, a poet I have long admired, at Mme Gillet's. Also present was Professor Delay, to whom Gide had once sent me with the idea, I suppose, that he would cure me. Cure me of what? Of faith? I had a perfectly frank talk with him at the time, one that I recall with pleasure, for Professor Delay's delicacy and intelligence led me to tell him things that I would certainly not have confided to just anyone. Later, much later, Gide talked to me about this conversation, of which he knew nothing but the broad outlines. He had asked Professor Delay if he thought I would be cured. "But suppose the patient does not *wish* to be cured?" answered the professor.

MAY 29. A visit from an American writer whom I knew when I was young. He is the same as he used to be, but his hair is quite gray. Says he had a very serious disease of the mouth and that it was the way God had punished him for having talked too much and been too fond of physical love. He has given Kinsey his private diary and advises me to do the same, thinks one should never burn anything. He had a terrible shock when he was told that he was ill and might die, and stamped with despair, alone in a field, at the idea that, for instance, he would never again hear Bach's cantatas. Talks about Melville's intimate papers, which have been made away with. He himself has written things of the same type, but, he insists once more, nothing should be burned. I have the impression that he has a great deal to say, is conscious of great interior wealth and wishes to give it all away before leaving this world.

* * *

JULY 16. Why do you make gestures that are not your gestures? Why do you say things that do not come from the truest part of you? Why this make-believe? There is a certain kind of make-believe which one acts to deceive other people. This one is of no interest to me. There is another which one acts almost automatically because it has become a habit—whether it is a question of passions or courtesy. This one is more serious, it means playing the world's game, to all intents and purposes the devil's game. I cannot accept it.

JULY 19. A moment ago I saw Praileau, the Praileau in *Moïra*, a novel he will never read. He is in Paris with his wife and two small daughters. He makes gentle fun of me, as he used to. If he knew me as I know myself, what would he say? Nothing unkind, but he belongs to the race of the righteous. When I look at him, I have no difficulty in seeing him exactly as he was when I knew him in 1920. I asked how he had obtained my address, as we have not corresponded for years. He said that he had entered a bookshop and had asked to see some of my books. He was handed a copy of *Moïra*. He noted the publisher's name and the latter told him where I lived. What irony lies in all this. . . .

JULY 21. Yesterday, on the sidewalk outside a café, I caught sight of S. A tragic, resolute face. What a hell he makes of his life! But he knows what he wants, he really wants it, whereas I don't in the least want what I want. There is always someone in me who says no. Looking at S.'s face, I wonder if the pitiless obsession that hounds him from one place to another at all hours is not a sort of madness, but his features have a dignity that is very foreign to the idea that people form of vice, there is an accepted suffering; for him, the game is worth the candle. He is unaware of the sympathy I feel for him, and this sympathy can be explained only by the fact that, in his way, he has a sense of the absolute.

AUGUST 18. MUNICH. Munich's ruins are dreadful. Cocteau used to say that Paris would make beautiful ruins, but ruins cannot be improvised. It takes centuries to give them the loveliness we admire in Hadrian's Villa, for instance, or at the Forum. Towns suddenly transformed into ruins are simply hideous: Hamburg, Bremen, Le Havre. Stones should crumble down one by one, under the onslaught of time, and grasses flourish in crannies, with the sun to gild the whole thing. I cannot see any beauty in the great blackened debris that now strews part of Europe.

AUGUST 31. CORTINA D'AMPEZZO, IN THE DOLOMITES. Read an article against capital punishment. There are things that we should know. Descriptions of executions. A man being electrocuted: his horrible leaps within the leather thongs, the dreadful sound of the air escaping from his lungs, the smell of roasting flesh, the oil that streams down his charred face. A man who has been hanged and whose head is sometimes torn away, because of the weakness of his neck. I was almost sick, but forced myself to continue reading. We are not civilized, that's all there is about it. That slim little book, the Gospel, beams over our barbarity, but scarcely anyone takes it to heart. . . . I would like to be free, not free like people who are surfeited and no longer hungry, but free as the children of God are free. When one writes such a sentence and then lays down the pen to think it over, can it be possible that one is lost? ✓ I want to believe in certain signs. I sometimes try to reassure myself by interpreting them favorably. I wonder if the sensuality that lies in each of us is not a kind of accident and if something is not concealed in our heart of hearts that will get us out of trouble.

DECEMBER 14. PARIS. Sometimes, when I think of my life and see in it all the contradictions that sadden me, it seems as though a voice I know so well says to me: "After all, haven't you got what you wanted? What could you complain of?" But that is precisely what worries me. Is that violent desire to quarrel with the world ever followed by a result? Can one go on living like this until death, in a constant state of rebellion against one's self?

DECEMBER 23. First auditions of actors on the stage for *South*. Slept badly because one of the actors I counted on most for the part of Ian did not live up to my hopes, and I will have to make him understand this. On the other hand, a peculiar thing happened that I will not forget for a long time. We had listened to six or eight actors, when a skinny, sickly boy appeared on the stage, holding in a shaky hand his role, of which he had not read a word. I think that I shall always remember that gaunt face, those sunken eyes, those white cheeks. What's the use of hearing him? But the

stage director, Mercure, comes and tells me that the young man
is in great difficulties, that his child died the night before. He is
only twenty-one. He stammers appallingly, and all of a sudden, a
kind of miracle takes place: his admirably well-pitched voice
begins to give sentences a meaning and a depth that make us all
prick up our ears. He was merely given this direction: "You are
acting the part of a very simple, very pure character" (for the
role was that of MacClure). Quite soon, I felt very much moved.
It is impossible to understand how a boy who hasn't the least idea
of what all this is about, and who, I am assured, has never been on
the stage, can manage to put so much soul and intelligence into
a rather difficult part. Before five minutes have gone by, he has
complete mastery over himself. He says and does what he wishes
with supreme self-assurance. Mercure then asks him to read a
passage in Ian's role and he does so with wonderful ease and authority. We will certainly take him. He is, I believe, of Flemish
origin and is called Vaneck.[1]

1953

MARCH 23. I have not kept this diary for almost a month, when
it would have been interesting to note certain things that will
gradually escape me. It is still too early to know whether or not
my play will succeed in finding its public. So far, we have had
almost full houses, in spite of a partly hostile press, or so I am told,
for I have scarcely read anything that has been written about
South. After the dress rehearsal, I locked myself into an office at
the Athénée and within an hour made cuts that Mercure approved
of. During the dress rehearsal, I was in a sort of waking dream. I
saw lots of anxious faces, but the fact did not worry me at all.
There was a single moment of anguish—but a horrible one—when
I felt the audience waver. A few days later, however, I admit to
having been frightened for a minute—it was quite paralyzing—but
no one ever knew of it. I go to the theater every night and stand
behind a bit of the scenery. Vaneck is excellent. All this has

[1] 1963. Vaneck is now a very well-known actor.

stirred me deeply. So many childhood memories suddenly coming
up to the surface, as though they rose from the bottom of the
sea, and the South there, on the stage, under my very eyes.

MAY 14.   I have gone back to reading Montaigne with delight.
At twenty, I couldn't. Such continual vacillations between yea
and nay irritated me. I detested fine shadings of thought, I was
passionately fond of downright statements that fell like blows
of an ax.

MAY 26.   Listening to Bach's Cantata No. 32, I realized how very
near the invisible world is to us, if we do not drive it away. When
I heard his cantata for the first time, around 1926, it stirred me
so deeply that I foresaw it would be necessary for me to change
my whole life, but that I should remain in the world. Impossible
to express how great a part Bach has played in my life; it is he,
more than any other, who has reconciled me to the idea of dying.

NOVEMBER 10.   Thought a great deal about death, about my own
death since it is waiting for me at the hour appointed by God.
For several months I have had a pain, slight, to be truthful, but
persistent. This morning, as almost every day, I had taken a volume from my bookcase, thinking it to be the Vulgate (I wanted
a little change from the English translation of the Bible), and by
mistake pulled out the Book of Isaiah, translated and annotated
by Father Condamin. As I was about to replace it, I thought: "No.
If you took it out, this must have a meaning." I opened the book
at random and chanced on the following verses, which struck
me: "I shall go softly all the years of my life in the bitterness of
my soul. O Lord, by these things men live and in all things is the
life of my spirit: *so wilt thou recover me and make me to live.*"
From that moment, I did not give my pain a thought.

UNDATED.   A long talk with Robert about music. I had been very
much impressed by Monteverdi's *Beatus vir.* He speaks a tongue
that has disappeared, a divinely serene tongue and so sweet that,
after him, there is something rude and harsh in the greatest composers, who seem to create havoc and to throw furniture out of
the window. Sunday morning, I listened to Bach's wonderful
cantata: *Ach wie flüchtig, ach wie nichtig* . . . A marvelous
prelude showing the world's agitation, a music of extreme violence

that filled all three of us with admiration and gave me a great longing to change my life. But what does changing one's life mean? To leave the world? And what if one shouldn't?

NOVEMBER 17. It is sometimes in watching the fire that I find what I have to say. All my books have sprung from my dreams. They are not for the many, but I think there will always be a few readers to be fond of them, and these are the ones for whom I write.

Too many books in my flat. I was obliged to sell some, those of no interest to me and whose pages I hadn't even cut (if people only knew all the books I haven't read). . . . In the case of Gide, I was interested only in his personality, with the exception of *Thésée*, the *Journal*, and *Si le grain ne meurt* (also the *Retour du Tchad*, but that he called a *Nebenwerk*). My bookseller tells me that all writers sell the autographed copies that are sent them, and he mentions a poet who even adds a few words of his own to the inscription, to increase the value of the book. Léautaud makes no bones about lighting his fire with the books he is sent. It seems that Valéry did the same during the Occupation, saying that the blaze gave him at least fifteen minutes of welcome heat.

NOVEMBER 26. Virginia Woolf's diary is beyond doubt an event (in England, at least). At first, one is dazzled, then defects begin to be apparent. "I, the greatest woman writer in England," is what she more or less says. A stupid conversation with Lytton Strachey that is supposed to be brilliant. Somewhere else she talks very well about the "pinch of essential dust that the French put into their books." She speaks a little foolishly and, if I may say so, Britishly, about Americans. Her opinion of them in no way differs from the usual commonplaces. And with it all, she has gifts that the greatest writers might envy her. I saw her only once, in 1929, at a literary gathering that took place in a London drawing room. She and I were being awarded a prize. May Sinclair presided, poor terrified old lady, who knew neither what to do nor what to say, pausing after the first sentence of her little speech to murmur: "Oh, I'm so frightened!" I then asked Virginia Woolf if she wanted to speak before I did. She was very nervous, her hands in constant motion and beating like wings. She threw me the glance of a hunted animal and said: "No. You go first." And I went, a little as though I were going to my death. I remember talking about my English grandfather. Virginia spoke next and said insignificant things, but she created a great impression. There was a mixture of disdain and fright in her long face.

DECEMBER 3. Sad to think that a very distant threat of death, a very light roll on the drum, as the Chinese poet says, is necessary to show us the true face of those around us, for we do not quite see beings as they are; what is luminous and good in them is too often concealed by daily life.

1954

JANUARY 5. Went to the rue des Plantes yesterday to see Father Couturier in a hospital. He is very thin, sits up straight in bed, tells me that he has been ill for a year and will be for another, if he recovers. An American specialist sent him word that the first stages of his sickness were the most dangerous and that, once he had weathered the first year, he stood a good chance of getting well. He is serious, smiles seldom, but is very calm. We talk about the world of the senses, and I ask him if it has ever occurred to him that the world as we see it does not exist. "No," he says firmly, "it is too beautiful as it is not to exist as we see it." That is the way a painter would speak, as he himself agrees. I then remark that the world is still more beautiful than we suppose and go on to describe the pebbles I once saw in a glass cabinet, in America, ordinary pebbles picked up on a road, but under a fluorescent light each pebble became a precious stone, a big sapphire, a ruby, a huge diamond. The whole of creation may have been thus before original sin. Traces of this splendor can be seen here and there, in the human face, which will always be the marvel of marvels. A little later, I tell Father Couturier that it grieves me not to be able to write at present, that this has always been the case since I was twenty-five, and that the interval between two books was always very painful to me. At such times, I have a feeling of having lost my gift. On the other hand, it is useless to urge myself on, it does me no good. I have to remain idle, because this idleness later becomes fruitful. The Father told me that all artists go through such phases. Just before leaving I asked him if he thought it unreasonable to believe that I could work out my salvation in writing books, and he answered that it seemed natural to believe this.

Read the Bible. If the story of David and Jonathan were told in transposed form, how many people among Catholics would cry shame!

FEBRUARY 11.   Stopped keeping this diary because I felt sick at heart. Father Couturier's death was a great blow and I don't know what to say about it. The world seems to me poorer now. The poor Father had a difficult end, struggled for breath for ten hours, finally offered up his life immediately after receiving Extreme Unction. What life has ever had a happy ending? Always the same dreadful tragedy. Thought of him, of his charming smile, his extreme simplicity of heart. Having written this, how is it possible to talk of anything else?

FEBRUARY 13.   Went to the Faubourg Saint-Honoré chapel for Father Couturier's funeral. A great many people. I have rarely seen such distress in the faces of so many men and women. The Brothers in black and white robes going to fetch their dead brother, the coffin covered with a stole, six tapers around the bier, the *Dies Irae* sung very softly as though to tone down its terrible threats—there was so much grief and affection in all this that I was very much upset.

MARCH 15.   Listened with Anne and Robert to two cantatas by Bach, *Ich bin vergnügt* and *Gottes Zeit ist die allerbeste Zeit*, marvelously sung. With Bach, feeling is seldom on the human plane, but a few notes are enough for him to carry us to the world of the absolute, which is his world. I wonder how it is possible to listen to him and not believe. Yesterday, someone told me that I was too serious. But serious does not mean sad. I am not sad, on the contrary, I feel a supreme joy rise within me that makes me deny death, old age, and nothingness.

MAY 3.   I wonder if I dare write what I think. Yes, I do. I believe that in the very depth of sin, God watches over us with extraordinary attentiveness, as though over a prey, but not as devotional books usually say. Drag a writer away from his sin and he no

*assertion – exist
for her
now*

longer writes. This, I admit, is a horrible statement to put into words. Is sin necessary to his works? Who would dare say such a thing? But remove sin and you remove the works. Are the works necessary? You might as well ask if a writer is necessary. He is inasmuch as God wishes him to exist. Purify the sources? But it does not seem evident that writers who have tried to do this were successful and that their works were improved by it. One must be pure from the start and remain so. That was the case with Bernanos. I don't know if present-day Catholic writers are pure. There are moments when I doubt it, but I know that I am not, hence all my difficulties. I can withdraw from the world, as I have so often been tempted to do, but then, no more works. Now, I believe that I came into this world to write books and to reach a few people.

MAY 9.   I was telling someone here who asked me certain questions that I had suddenly stopped smoking in 1944. And why? Because I smoked too much and, above all, too fast. I had fits of giddiness that were rather unpleasant, but not always. Once, sitting in an armchair, I had a very distinct impression of being at the far end of the room. My body was seated, but I (if such words have a meaning) was some distance away. That was the day when I gave up tobacco. I sometimes dream that I am smoking. The man I was talking to said that thus to resist a habit corresponds perhaps to the wish we sometimes have to punish ourselves, and that this wish finds expression in various ways. Montaigne says very sensibly that sexual moderation is more difficult to practice than total abstinence.

MAY 22.   This morning, the Ascension cantata by Bach. When the "great" are right, they are right in a way that verges on the miraculous, I mean that when they assert something, as Bach does, the rest of the world, everything outside that assertion, ceases to exist for the time being. These are the "tremendous statements" spoken of by Auden, in connection with a city orchestra, it is true, but the term holds good for those I call the great, the elders of our race. Thought today that I would die at the exact minute that God has chosen for me, and that He has chosen lovingly, for He does all things lovingly, otherwise would He be God? And He knows that the minute of my death will be the one when I will be with Him, at last.

*   *   *

handwritten margin note: God, in his wrath

JUNE 26. Had lunch with Béguin, who tells me several important things, for he is among those—how many are they? Four? Five?—who talk to say something that one remembers. We were speaking about prayers, which are all granted, sooner or later, but one has to reach the age of fifty to discover this, with the necessary perspective. Youth does not know it. One ends by getting everything one wanted, which is not always a good thing. Béguin tells me that all the longings of youth are so many prayers, unconscious prayers, and prayers that are granted. In connection with this, I quote a sentence from Racine about God, who, in His wrath, sometimes gives us what we ask. Real Jansenism. A little later, I say to Béguin: "What makes my strength as well as my weakness is that I am both younger and older than the men I have to deal with. I have kept my childhood and have intuitions that they do not possess, because they have lost theirs. I am clumsy in a struggle. I lack weapons."

JULY 2. Listened to Couperin's *Tenebrae*. The title is sung at full pitch by the contralto. Magnificent. The extremely severe, lovely modulations go to the soul, brush aside the sensuous world, give you back to God for a few minutes.

JULY 23. Very much impressed by Father Bouyer's book, *Du Protestantisme à l'Église*. One must search one's own heart, seek God at any price; it is the only thing that counts. I felt deeply anxious as I turned the pages of this book. In this study, where waves of silence seem to break one after the other, I think that God has spoken to me more often than anywhere else. I have followed the carnal instinct against my heart and often with such horror that no man could have an idea of it unless he had experienced the same dread. I do what I don't want to do. Copied my diary for 1953. That will keep me busy and prevent me from falling into discouragement. I realize better that God holds me firmly by the hand, and will not desert me in the darkness.

JULY 25. Asked to be given a horror of sin. It is a great gift, and I don't see how else to keep out of trouble. Passions darken the soul. We live like madmen.

JULY 27. Yesterday, a visit from a young Englishman who is choirmaster in an Oxford college. He speaks disdainfully of John

Blow and contemptuously of Handel. "He reminds me of a country squire. And then, he is so facile. . . ." *Facile* pronounced with a shade of disgust. After he left, I listened to a few of the "English Anthems" by the incriminated composer, as well as *Acis and Galatea,* which I like so much, and, true enough, facility can be found there and, what is more serious still, Handel is never satisfied, once he has said something, until he has said it again, in the same terms, and that is not enough for him: he has to say it again. There are repetitions in Bach, but you always feel that they differ a little one from the other, even when he changes nothing in his phrase. A phrase by Bach repeated twenty times becomes more and more profound. Handel usually remains on the surface; but I still remember the extraordinary effect produced on me by the *Messiah,* at Salzburg, two years ago, and I will always admire this very great man.

AUGUST 7. GENEVA. Colette is dead. Last night, wishing to be with her a little, for I am very fond of her, I picked up *Sido* and, opening it at random, found this. She has just described in a masterly way—for no one has her gift for taking you where she wants, with the help of a few sentences—two lost springs of water that she remembers with the deepest enjoyment, and she says: "Just by talking of them, I hope and wish that their taste will fill my mouth when all is ending, and that I may carry away with me that imaginary swallow. . . ." How can one not believe that Colette is at this moment drinking the waters offered to the Samaritan woman?

AUGUST 16. Today, for the first time in my life, I regretted not being fifteen. I was lying on my bed after lunch, reading Montaigne, when this unreasonable regret seized me. I thought about the sweetness of those distant years, of all the time that lay ahead of me then, and that I was inwardly certain of having ahead of me, for contrary to what one so willingly imagines at an age when one is so romantically inclined, I did not believe in the least that I would die young, I even thought that I would live quite a number of years and felt rich because of all this future time, whereas now, each day as it ends leaves me a little sad, for I know very well that it counts.

AUGUST 26. Copied a number of passages from Calvin's *Institu-*

tion Chrétienne, for I have to return the book. There are things in it that could not be believed unless one saw them in print, for they might have been invented by spiteful Catholics. . . . Every sentence tells. At times, one is reminded of a ruler hitting the edge of a desk, at others, of a sword stroke falling on a rebel neck, but the marks of literary greatness are there. The passionately interesting thing about Calvin is that he almost always goes too far. Where others would not dare to venture, he charges at a gallop. And with it all, through the sheer force of reasoning, he is monstrous. He is reason gone mad. This said, he has a feeling for the divine to an extremely rare degree. One can imagine the saint he might have been. On the other hand, one can easily see what a choice place Dante would have reserved for him in his Inferno, but it is far simpler to condemn the reformer than to appreciate the exceptional majesty of certain pages where he speaks of God as a doctor of the Church might have done. Why should he have become the doctor of despair? He has done a great deal of good and a great deal of evil in quickening a sense of sin in certain souls and in giving others a panic terror of damnation. One could not assert that God did not wish Calvin to be Calvin. And anyway, what can one assert?

Around the middle of the last century, there were cases of acute melancholia (I might simply call it insanity) in my family; a melancholia caused by the idea of predestination as conceived by Presbyterians (to all intents and purposes Calvinists).

Yesterday, in a small street that leads up to the cathedral, I bought another very nice copy of the Book of Common Prayer, in a second-hand bookstore. It was the book my mother used and through it, I must say, she left quite a strong mark on me. The young American Quaker who wrote a thesis on me would take this for a sure sign of what he calls my Protestantism, but I am nothing of a Protestant and what I seek in the Book of Common Prayer is the best that Catholicism has left in it.

AUGUST 27.   Dined at Mies, yesterday. We were a large party, and that invariably makes my head swim. I say what I feel I shouldn't say and, once at home, am angry with myself—but enough of that. One of the guests, a French psychiatrist, talked to me in an interesting manner about the dreams of the insane. He has studied them for years, has often heard words pronounced by lunatics in their sleep, and, as far as such things can be known, it appears that they have *reasonable dreams*. It would seem that a madman who dreams, dreams only of normal life. Our own dreams are our form of madness, and if we did not dream we might possibly become insane. As the psychiatrist asked me certain questions, I said this to him: "My books are my dreams. They are what have allowed me to keep my balance." Their symbolism, if they are symbolical—it seems that Stekel said they were—all these strange themes provided by the subconscious act in accordance with secret laws of which I am ignorant and wish to continue to ignore. The man I was talking with said that a psychiatrist could easily cure me of the anguish that is so apparent in my books, but, I replied, if you remove the anguish, you remove the books, and if there are no more books, who knows if the former anguish will not be replaced by another? There was no answer. I talked very indiscreetly about myself, a thing I scarcely ever do. As a rule, I listen and the others are the ones to give themselves away.

Thought about predestination. God has honored us with the freedom to choose between good and evil. Hell is the risk we run, although it seems to me difficult to lose your soul if you don't want to, and who, with a full knowledge of the case, would want to? If the risk is removed, man's salvation is assured, but he can no longer be said to be free, as God is free, and this diminished creature would no longer be in the least equal to its fate, which is an admirable one.

Thought about the idea I had of Christ when I was a child, then the one I had later, at twenty, and so on to the present time. It was the same Christ, but I always saw Him differently, for as a child I saw Him as my elder; and once I had lived beyond His years, I saw Him in a certain fashion as my junior. I changed but He did not, and yet He did. He changed in an astonishing way. This should be developed, but of course avoiding the pietistic tone that is the devil's most ingenious invention, since nothing pulls one away more violently from religion. One should have outlived youth, I think, to begin to understand Christ a little.

Who could help being attached to this house, with its big, low roof, its bright rooms, its air of happiness? From my window, I see a large square lawn sloping down to the lake, bordered with clumps of shrubs. One can catch a glimpse of water through the trees and, in the distance, of Geneva crowned by the cathedral. At nightfall, the garden is extremely beautiful, moving, lovely as something about to die; the greens are deep, the air seems motionless. I must own that it makes my heart ache to think that this holiday is ending. That everything must end used to make me despair as a child, and thanks to an intuition so frequent at that age, I have distrusted all that passes away and unceasingly sought for the invisible that never ends. We sometimes see traces of it in the eyes of those we love.

AUGUST 29. Today's walk, the last one, was the most beautiful of all, but it would require other gifts than mine to talk about it. I am as fond of trees as it bores me to describe them, because I feel that others could do it as well as I, if not better. A subject at which one excels should be found and stuck to, otherwise one resembles too many novelists.

I happened on a passage in Gide's diary that concerns me. He imagines that when I told him that my characters led me at their will, I said this to please him, but I had already said it long before knowing him, to Frédéric Lefèvre and others. What should be known is that Gide had just presented me with a fine copy of his *Journal des faux-monnayeurs*, in which he wrote that he followed his characters' lead, but what he was ignorant of is that I didn't read his books often and that I had not read that very one, because I had not read (and still have not done so) *Les Faux-monnayeurs*. I am sure this must seem scandalous to certain people, but I can say it now that Gide has gone. I admired what he had to say to me, but far less admired what he wrote, although I kept this to myself. I liked *Si le grain* (as he called it) and also, much later, his *Theseus* and many parts of his diary, but his novels disconcerted me; I had tried to read them and as quickly dropped them. A whole portion of his work was inaccessible to me. I could never talk to Gide about what he wrote, and for a good reason. His book on the Congo held my attention, not because of the Congo, but because of what he told us about himself. He was passionately interesting when he talked about what he thought, about what he was, but he did not correspond to the idea I have of a novelist and certainly not of a poet. I was writing my fourth book when I met Gide and opened one of his works for the first time. He never talked so well as when he talked about himself, but there, he excelled. He once read me a speech from his *Oedipus* which I found terribly labored. I kept silent and think that this annoyed him a little.

*   *   *

SEPTEMBER 6. PARIS. This is my birthday and it is also St. Julien de Brioude's day, or was, I think, when I was born, although my mother had no idea of it. I can't really believe that I have reached the age I am, for it seems to me that I have been the same person since I was twenty. No matter how much my mirror gives me the lie, I look in it and believe what it tells me, but immediately after, forget what I saw, like the man in St. James' epistle.

OCTOBER 30. "The waters of Babylon flow, fall, and sweep on." This sentence from Pascal delights me. Apart from the meaning, its softly muffled music, its movement, its pace, all seem to me to possess the magic quality of certain chords that haunt the mind, without one's quite knowing why.

The truth should be acknowledged: if we read the Bible today in the vernacular, it is because the Church allows it, but it is also because certain courageous Protestants desired it and went to the stake on that account. Without the great Reformation movement, when would the Church have permitted the translation of the Bible into common speech? We are free to believe that we would have waited a long time. At the present day, many Catholics still think that the Church forbids reading the Bible. Those Catholics hold to the times when the Church forbade a layman to own a copy of the Bible in the vernacular. Why this interdict? Did the Church foresee the heresies that might spring from a close scrutiny of this book? The reformers forced her hand. Nowadays, she multiplies the number of translations to be used by the faithful, but isn't it very late? Modern France bypasses the Bible. You can't spend an hour with an Englishman without some allusion to the Bible slipping into his conversation, at times unconsciously: he will quote it, without always being aware of what he is quoting.

NOVEMBER 4. A few days ago, as I was filing letters, I came across one from Father Couturier written a short time before his death. He had insisted on reading *South*, and I had taken him a copy. The answer came quickly. These lines are an extract: ". . . You have dealt with this delicate subject without one's being able for a single instant to forget and disregard the seriousness and grandeur of such a tragedy: no one has ever done this before. Please God that it may contribute to increase charity among us and a greater respect for grieving hearts."

Yesterday morning, went to the place du Parvis Notre-Dame to say good-by to the actors who are going on tour with *South* (in the provinces, then in Switzerland, Belgium, and finally North Africa). The cathedral is a very great personage who prays, her head lost in the sky. I wandered under the lofty vaultings. Very few people, except around the statue of the Blessed Virgin, where I paused for a moment. Also went to Saint-Julien-le-Pauvre, where I asked for the theological virtues, no more no less. The silence of this marvelous little church where Dante perhaps prayed. Outside, the cries of children.

NOVEMBER 15. A few sentences about me in a recently published book. It is said that my childhood was not spent in France, that I am a Virginian. This is most interesting, for ever since 1924 I have said and never ceased saying that I was born in Paris, in the Ternes quarter, that I pursued all my studies at the Lycée Janson up to the *baccalauréat* (the school-leaving certificate), that I had great difficulty in learning English, that my nurse, Jeanne Lepêcheur, taught me the first words that ever left my lips, that I had gone to America for the first time at nineteen, etc. I have written all this in my diary, in articles, and in a somewhat detailed account of my childhood called "*Quand nous habitions tous ensemble*," which appeared a few years ago in a Paris weekly. Nothing can be done about it. Gide died with the idea that I was born in New Orleans. I had rid him of the notion that I was born in Canada. And then, what importance can it have? But it amuses me to watch a completely false legend being trumped up under my very eyes. If people are mistaken about me, how many errors are made about other men, dead or living? It is apparently hard to imagine that an American can be born elsewhere than in America, can be born and brought up in Paris.

NOVEMBER 25. I had a bad night after a long conversation with Béguin, because he is one of the very rare men with whom one can go to the bottom of things and reach the essential. My heart beat violently several times during our talk, which lasted almost two hours, I think. As I was speaking to him about the apparent futility of what is called a self-examination, as all one sees lies on the surface, while all that is most important remains hidden, Béguin told me that it is perhaps better so, that if we could know how God works within us, we would not be able to bear it. I believe that most men live in deep ignorance of themselves, of the riches

Each human life is a path that leads to God

that they turn to no account, of an unutterable happiness that they pass by wailing over the sorrows of this life. . . . Only in prayer does one have a feeling of the deep reality of all this. The world's futility is overwhelming at certain times, but one has to pretend that everything is real; indeed, it is even a duty to act this sort of comedy, but one should never lose sight of the fact that it is a comedy.

UNDATED. There is someone within us who *knows*, whereas the person who speaks and whom we take for ourselves does not know. I could give numerous instances of this. I can remember two that made a strong impression on me. The last time that I saw André Gide, he was certainly not in good health, but he moved about much as usual, it seemed to me, and I think he would have been surprised to be told that he did not have three weeks left to live. When I was about to go, he looked at me gravely and asked me a question that I could not help finding singular: "Haven't you anything else to say to me?" I answered no, and we parted. Only after his death did the question assume its full meaning. I certainly would have had something else to say to him, had I known, and I am convinced that in Gide's mind the little, apparently insignificant question had nothing of a foreboding: he did not *know*, any more than I did. Something of the kind, although more moving, happened when I saw Father Couturier for the last time. (Incidentally, he admired André Gide and would never allow him to be attacked in his presence.) I had gone to see him in his hospital room. As a rule, I stayed only half an hour, knowing that visits tired him, and he never pressed me to remain. This time, as I rose to go, he asked me to stay, and I sat down again. Fifteen minutes went by and once more I got up. "No!" he cried, and asked me so insistently to stay that I neither dared nor wished to refuse. I resumed my seat and he smiled at me with that almost divinely kind expression that lit up his face and endeared him to me so much. My hand lay on the bed and he touched it with his. I can't remember what we said to each other, but in actual fact and without having the least idea of it (for he hoped to recover and I wanted to believe that he would get well) we were saying farewell.

"Each human life is a path that leads to God." This was said by Husserl, unless I am mistaken. Blessed be the men who say such things, for they help us to live and to stave off despair.

* * *

NOVEMBER 29. Since I was fifteen, I think that I have never felt closer to the Church nor more deeply in agreement with her. I particularly wish to say this so clearly and in such a manner that no doubt can remain in the mind of whoever reads these lines—if this diary is published. Generally speaking, I am rather indifferent to everything that can be said about me, but this does not hold good for the faith that I have received and wish to keep until the end. For I am extremely sensitive on this point. . . .

DECEMBER 15. Sometimes, when I blow on my fire, which won't catch, I hear street noises that come to me through the chimney, and it wrings my heart a little because I remember my childhood. We weren't well off, but how happy we were! Then, from my mother's room, I heard distant street noises, as I hear them now, stretched out on the carpet and blowing on the embers. I wonder how one can possibly live believing that we will never again see those we have loved. It is enough to drive one crazy. But we who have faith know very well that they are waiting for us.

DECEMBER 17. Had lunch with Béguin and his wife the other day. She says this, which I think very fine: "Human love changes, sometimes ends. With God, you can always begin again, nothing is ever ended, no break is ever final. . . ." God is very vulnerable, as Jacques Maritain so admirably says. But He is always there, asking us to come back to Him. Come back, a term that runs through the Bible like a long-drawn-out cry of love. Come back to Me who love you. That is what God never ceases to say to the soul.

One of my very first childhood memories is, I think, rather curious, because it gives one of the keys to my whole life. I am alone in the garden of the cours Sainte-Cécile. It must be eight in the morning. I don't know why I am alone in the garden, which seems to me immense and which I have attempted to describe in *The Dreamer*. The air is fresh. I hear someone playing the piano in a neighboring house. A tune I know, because my sister Mary plays it at home: Mozart's "Turkish March," and it occurs to me that all this is queer, queer to be alone in this place. I am happy—I always was at that age—but wonder what I am doing in this garden. Now this garden is the world, the earth, and the feeling I had then has never completely left me. I will always feel a stranger in this world and it will always be impossible for me to understand why, but I am sure that others must feel as I do.

* * *

DECEMBER 22. This evening, irritated beyond measure by a number of things that I don't even wish to mention, I opened the *Divine Comedy* at the beginning of "Purgatory." A delicious breath rises from these pages, great happiness possesses the soul and hope returns, that hope of salvation that will carry us to the bright shores. Dante and Vergil have come up from Hell and stand by the waterside. A great skiff advances toward them, moved by an angel who stands at the helm with lightly beating wings, and in the skiff, a hundred souls who come from Earth singing *In exitu Israel.* They land, and as they go closer to the two poets the first soul to recognize Dante is the musician Casella. They are about to suffer, the mount of purification must be climbed, but they are saved, they are blessed. How much truer all this is than theological treatises and their somber reasonings! It grew late, but I could not tear myself away from a book that restored peace in me. I went as far as the three steps at the top of which stands an angel holding two keys that open the great door shown us by the poet. The first step is white and like a mirror; one looks in it and sees oneself: this is the sincerity of the soul. The second is made of a black and very hard stone; it is broken: this is the contrite heart. The third is flaming red: this is love. The angel has been given the keys by Peter, who says that it is better to open the door by mistake than to leave it shut. Now, it opens more noisily than the Tarpeian Gate, for it is the penitential door, and rare are the times when it turns on its hinges. At this point, I closed the book, filled with a new happiness.

1955

JANUARY 3. If the devil wrote music, it would be Tchaikovsky, seductive, skillful, and vulgar. Its languishings would excite the coldest listeners for a moment. Suddenly, it goes crazy with pleasure, for no known reason, and who would not follow it, who would not let himself be carried away by this whirlwind? It ignobly titillates. All at once, it puts on the grand airs of an exiled queen and goes its way, sad and contemptuous. Then, with a dirty wink, it begins jiggling again. Yet one listens. It has extraordinary charm.

* * *

pleasure-loving

JANUARY 17. The autobiography of St. Theresa of Lisieux has been in the house for the last three days. I mean the *very copy-book* [1] in which the saint wrote the story of her life. I examined it one evening when I was alone. It was there on the table where I am writing these words. A buff cardboard cover; nice neat lines allowing no space for margins. Some sentences have been crossed out, others erased. Strange to think that this precious manuscript should have found its way to my study.

JANUARY 31. The faces of people who have something to hide are like a wall. Better still, they are like a bricked-up door whose outline can nevertheless be vaguely distinguished. I thought this as I observed a very proper and aggressively respectable old gentleman. And yet, everybody knew only too well . . . He imagines that this cannot be seen, because he has taken pains not to let anything appear, but his poor face shrieks the truth. Nothing, to my mind, is sadder than such a farce that takes in no one except the man who acts it.

MARCH 3. What I have against a life of pleasure is that it kills in a man all aptitude for love. It gives him the heart of a eunuch. I said this to someone who was piqued by my remark, but I feel strongly that I am right. Nothing is colder than a pleasure-loving man. This is perceptible only in the long run, because during youth there exists the eternal misunderstanding about desire and love, which are taken one for the other. Love is not necessarily linked to desire; it surpasses it continually, but love is not to be met every day, it does not run about the streets: in fact, that is precisely what it never does.

APRIL 2. I keep this diary far less regularly than in my youth, when everything was new to me and it seemed a duty to describe even the shape of a flame in the hearth. Not that the beauty of a fire no longer touches me, far from it. The older I grow, the more sensitive I am to the splendor of the visible world, of all that God shows us, and that we scarcely glance at, but my time is running short. I use my days sparingly, which is foolish as duration is an illusion among others. We are going to die in a couple of hours, said St. Teresa of Ávila.

[1] This copybook had been entrusted to my sister, who, under the direction of a Carmelite Father, was doing some collating.

Yesterday, a party in what is called society. I could not avoid going without hurting some people's feelings, and, I don't know how, rather late in the evening a discussion arose about religion and more particularly Purgatory. A man I like very much and see very little talked of his horror of death: "Never leave a dying man unattended. . . . The loneliness of the dying is horrible." Although he is not a Catholic, he spoke in a touching manner of the dying who leave this world supported by the Church's solicitude and love: "The Church prays for them, comforts them with the last sacraments." I said to him: "A Protestant dies with a certainty of salvation, as this forms part of his faith." (I thought of my grandfather, who, just as he was about to give up the ghost, said: "Give me my stick; I am going to Heaven.") He smiled sadly: "For two pins," he replied, "some people would say to God: 'Lord, here is a very choice soul. You must take great care of it.'"

APRIL 7. Someone asked me if he should answer a rather low attack from a weekly magazine; I advised him to keep silent. Silence is a wonderful weapon, but it has to be handled with great care. One must know whom it is being used against, and what meaning it will assume in the mind of whoever is answered in this way. There is an indignant silence, or a wounded, disdainful, contemptuous, amused, sarcastic one, one that is full of sorrowful reproach, or one that is pathetic, jeering, jovial, teasing, furious, vengeful, etc., etc. But it always ends by being rightly interpreted, unless it is the mysterious silence that leaves the opponent in doubt, and this last is exasperating. Bossuet used it against the Protestant minister Jurieu, who accused him of being father to several children, or it may perhaps have been the silence of baffled rage, or that which we have all used and misused: the silence of indifference. To complete the list, let us finally mention the silence that says yes and the silence that says no, and the silence that would almost justify murder, because it says neither yes nor no.

APRIL 9. Faith means walking on the waters. Peter himself had begun to sink when Jesus stretched out His hand, reproaching him for doubting. Now, we must believe. In an atheistic world, we have received this exceptional gift. In wind and in darkness, if the ground gives way under our feet like water—and who has not felt this at some time or other?—we must go straight ahead, in spite of all, and grasp the hand that is stretched out to us.

APRIL 10.   What is love? There is a letter from Keats to his sister Fanny in which he, the unbeliever, the pagan (dear pagan, may you be in Heaven!) explains to the youthful Protestant what she will have to say and do at her Confirmation, and he explains at length, he tells everything he knows, everything he remembers of a faith that is his no longer. He refers her to passages in the Scriptures. He thinks that the Extreme Unction of the Church of Rome is called thus because of "anointing the extremities of dying persons with holy water" (letter of March 31, 1819). He cannot help writing God with a small "g" through a sort of upside-down bigotry, but there is more love in this letter than in many a pious speech that one reads with disgust.

How is one to pray? I have read quite a large number of works on methods of prayer and was never able to derive any benefit from them. It seems to me that to place oneself in the presence of God and to know that He is there would be enough in most cases, but is that praying? I think a great many people would say no, and yet it does one good to remain before God in silence, to keep silence before Him. Talk to Him? Why, I believe that when one has said the *Pater* and the *Ave,* nothing else is worth while, except silence.

APRIL 12.   Yesterday, a visit from a journalist who asks me lots of questions about myself, my works, my views of Christianity. This continues for a couple of hours, and I feel weary. I think that what men say, no matter how well or how fully, does not ring like the Gospel. They wish to prove to you that the sins of the flesh are not sins, and they do so brilliantly. No sooner have they left than you pick up the Bible and it speaks a very different language. One is free not to read it, but one cannot prevent it from existing in our world and continually saying no when the modern world says yes. Because of this, I feel a little lonely at times and a little sad.

Later, a visit from a Pole whom I like very much although we rarely meet. He talks extensively of my diary and thinks it rash of me to have revealed graces that were granted me. Why? Because God might not grant me any others? But there is no such keeping of accounts with Heaven that I know of, and also I have only hinted at what is very vague and very usual. The question would be, rather, to know if it is not a duty to bear witness and if it is not a sort of injustice to keep to oneself what has been received. I told my visitor that I was happy to be alive and, above all, indescribably happy that God existed. This feeling is very powerful and also obscure, and words do not express it properly. I admire, yes, I admire the strength of character of atheists who can live and bear the burden and heat of each day without the Almighty on whom to lean. It has never appeared to me possible to live without believing.

UNDATED. The conversion of a little quite ordinary soul seems to me as miraculous as the conversion of a great soul, and a slow, almost imperceptible conversion just as admirable as a sudden conversion that fires the imagination. I even wonder if a man very gradually attracted to God does not offer a better example of the power of love. A man prostrated by Grace who then and there breaks all ties with the world, that is indeed an extraordinary sight, but a man fettered and bound by the world's pleasures, to such an extent as to seem impossible that he could ever be able to leave them, and who manages, in spite of all, through the infinite patience of Grace, to destroy the snare, thread by thread, and suddenly free himself from all these deadly complications—what is more astonishing, if one thinks this over?

MAY 26. I scarcely fear death any longer. (And supposing it were there, all of a sudden, what would you say? Would you talk in the same way? I wonder.) The earth is the womb of our mother who bore us and which we leave to be born. This should only terrify people who refuse the word of God. Yet, I was thinking the other day of what I had written about the Church sorrowing over her departed children, a sorrow I can't understand, because it means they have gone to God and that the earth is shown us as a land of exile (nightmarish funerals, black draperies, doleful hymns, etc.), and remembered that when Jesus heard that Lazarus was dead, He wept, just the same.

Read with dreadful sadness the accounts of tortures inflicted during the sixteenth century upon Protestants by Catholics, or upon Catholics by Protestants, for none were more cruel than Protestants (they sawed Catholics in two by sliding them naked over tautly stretched ropes; and who can forget the martyrs of Gorcum and their long-drawn-out agony on the gallows?). Human cruelty is practically limitless, because it would seem that our imagination tends more strongly in that direction when the devil allows it full play. Beyond eroticism, but in the same direction, lies the hell of cruelty, and the further one goes in eroticism, the closer one gets to this hell. That is why excesses in the sexual sphere end by creating terror, crime being the natural result of eroticism.

MAY 29. One must make up one's mind to be badgered by the devil until one dies. I sometimes hear it said: "He has faith, he has found peace once more." But Christ came to bring a sword, not peace. I had a letter from Jacques Maritain this morning and it contains an idea that I think very fine: having so often wished to be removed from the world, I should consider that I have left it, because faith isolates us. I too believe that faith isolates us, not from the humanity for which Christ died, but from the world for which Christ did not pray.

WHITMONDAY. A desire for literary fame was very keen in me until I was about twenty-five. It lessened at the time when I discovered that the world did not exist at all in the way that we imagine it, but that desire of mine for fame did not die without a struggle. I can say today that practically nothing of it remains in me. In 1955, I can write with assurance that I no longer have any worldly ambition. The desire that my books should live on would seem to me ridiculous, if I fostered such vain imaginings—for in me, one part of my being always judges the other. A writer's fame—I have already said this elsewhere—has become a paper glory . . . and our paper is worthless. That of the seventeenth century, the fine, laid paper on which I read so many books that I love, this fresh, white paper has kept all its pliancy, whereas our paper turns quite yellow within thirty years' time, and in reading a book printed around 1925, one runs the risk of actually breaking its brittle pages, just by turning them.

JUNE 1. Last night, I was telling Anne: "Since 1938, I have never had the shadow of a doubt concerning faith. The Catholic faith with all its mysteries and obscurities seems to me evidence itself, but evidence viewed from a world of darkness." Such a complete absence of doubt sometimes makes me pause, for the greatest of us have had doubts, and terrible, harassing ones (St. Paul of the Cross is one example among many). Our responsibility is all the greater for our having a vigorous faith. Thought a great deal about these things because of a letter I received this morning. It came from a man for whom I have a great regard, and I wish with all my heart that I could answer him, but when confronted with atheism I am as mute as I would be facing a phenomenon that is impossible to understand or to believe real. My correspondent cannot imagine that a believer might be anxious about his salvation, but the uncertainty in which we live justifies such apprehensions to a large degree. Protestants are the only ones who are certain, according to their views. We Catholics can only hope, but to hope is a duty. This said, I wonder if, in reading this diary as one would read a novel, with the author as its hero (?), a believing reader might not be led to ask: "How will this end? Will the hero be lost or saved at the end?" The question would seem to me quite an apt one. I wish it were for me the most actual of questions, one that would disturb me a thousand times more than it does. Of course I have not the least certainty of being saved, but then I do not feel the terror of people who think themselves lost. I could be told that this is meaningless, that you can agreeably put your eyes out, as Pascal says. I know that perfectly well. I even add that my qualms are not great enough concerning all this and the few I do feel have been obtained only by cudgeling my brains and searching the Scriptures for passages best fitted to make me quake, and that's the truth.

JUNE 16. Sometimes I am seized with such a deep and perfectly inexplicable sadness that the whole world suddenly appears void of any meaning. Void the present moment, void the words we utter, void all our motions and all our efforts to accomplish anything whatever. Those are the hours that I dread most, those where nothingness asserts itself. I felt this powerfully once in Naples and once again in Stockholm. It is the wind of despair rising to lay everything flat. The devil, the face of the devil.

JUNE 18. Abbé Pierre said this, the other evening, on the air: "Love must precede love. To go to the poor with pockets full of dollars is nothing. They must be loved. I refused money offered me by Americans and asked them to spend it on their own poor; they have plenty. What I ask them for is love, before anything else. I don't want France to look like a beggar in American eyes." I think I have noted his words accurately.

Anne and I went to see the Maritains yesterday. We found them just as we had always known and loved them, and when I say the Maritains, that includes Véra, Raïssa's sister. No one will ever quite know what their affection has meant to me. One of the greatest favors ever granted to me by God was to place Jacques on my path in 1924. I particularly want to say this.

JULY 3. Long conversation with Robert on the subject of music and in particular of Beethoven, whom I no longer care for as much as I did, except his chamber music, which is quite obviously the peak of genius. His symphonies (all but certain parts of the Ninth, which I avoid hearing because I like them too much and don't want to tire of them), his symphonies I simply cannot listen to, and this holds good for his overtures. Why? Alas, something in me no longer echoes these heroic aspirations. This juvenile enthusiasm wearies me, these cavalry charges, this continual cry of "Forward!" Stimulating music, yes indeed, but not to me. On thinking it over, what I have just written seems to me perfectly ridiculous. I can't hear *Egmont* without a pounding heart. And *Fidelio*, in spite of the opera's being inacceptably conventional to my mind . . . What bothers me, in all opera, is an effort toward realism that can only be ludicrous. Opera singers are almost always wretched actors. Monteverdi's *Combatimento di Tancredi e di Clorinda* seems to me far less false: here the characters declaim without budging and are so conventional that they finally escape conventionality.

I was telling Robert that so-called gay music can be heart-rending, and that, for this reason, I find it difficult to listen to some of Schubert's allegros (and those ghostly scherzos where death has already joined the dance), whereas, when Bach says "Remember that you must die," it is stimulating, but Bach has never saddened me. An agreement should be reached about the words *sad* and *gay*. I can't listen to Schubert when everything is going wrong. His tenderness demoralizes me.

JULY 7. At twenty, I believed in my elders' answers, I thought they knew. Now that I myself am an elder, when people come to me full of questions, I don't know what to answer. The more I go, the less clearly I see; but the thicker the night, the greater faith must grow, otherwise how can one live in this darkness?

OCTOBER 17. There are days when one avoids writing because

nothing good could come of it and the words shaped by the pen are simply too carnal. It is odious to be the threshold of sin for others. . . . I think that if I had been twenty in a period of such extreme facility as this one, where morals are concerned, nothing much of what is solid would have remained in me. I would perhaps have been incapable of loving, and who knows if faith would not have been shipwrecked along with the rest? I must say that I used to live in amazing ignorance of what went on around me. This kept me in a state that ranged from enthusiasm to melancholy and allowed many feelings to develop in me, feelings unknown to present-day youth. They lack a certain ingenuousness without which no real love exists. What they call love, as far as I can see, are affairs that last a few weeks or a few hours. They believe in nothing.

OCTOBER 19. More and more attracted to chamber music, that of Mozart, of Beethoven, of Brahms. Everything interior that can be said—two violins, a cello, and a piano can say it; the rest, the great orchestral ensembles, are often only there for decorative purposes. Bach needs only a voice and a flute to open Heaven to us.

OCTOBER 28. That sensation of danger, so strange because it is both so vague and so powerful, that fear lessens and calms down in the presence of certain people one is fond of. My father reassured me completely. I have often wondered if his goodness and innocence did not verge on a sort of holiness of which he had no suspicion. We seldom talked together, but there was a drawer in my room where I kept confessions that it never occurred to me to lock. One day, returning from a journey, I discovered that the drawer was empty. I was so casual and carefree that I had forgotten all about it the next day. I was twenty-three. The idea simply crossed my mind that someone had read and destroyed these papers, but I never opened my lips about it and no one ever mentioned the subject to me.

NOVEMBER 4. *The Transgressor* has had a good press, contrary to my expectations. Five or six times in my life, not more, not many times more, I have wondered what would remain of all my works; I would like this not to be indifferent to me, but then so many things are indifferent to me since 1940 and more particularly since Hiroshima, which has separated us all, every one of us, from a great part of ourselves. . . .

Yesterday a visitor asked me the name of the stove that heats this room where I am writing (it has a long pipe that comes out into the room and is called, I think, a *cheminée à la prussienne*). He had never seen anything like it, and I believe that in another twenty years, all such heating appliances, wood or coal fires, will have disappeared. We will have rooms without mantelpieces, commonplace and decentered, for in a sense the hearth is somewhat like the soul of a room, toward which one goes and sits. A blazing fire is wonderful company. It helps one to think, it flickers, it blazes, it is there. I look at it whenever I raise my eyes. There is an affinity between us.

NOVEMBER 5. Yesterday, a visit from an Italian professor. He talks to me about his country's spirituality, such a curiously moving one. An unlimited trust in God that fits in with the *mala vita*, prostitution, etc. An unmarried, pregnant woman throws herself out of a window, grasping a crucifix. He tells me that he once rented a room in a southern Italian town, in which to work during the day; he discovered that it was rented to lovers at night and, complaining of this to the lodginghouse-keeper, who was very poor, she said: "Yes, they live without benefit of clergy, but they love each other." We next talk about charity, and I remark that rich men's charity is often a mere form of condescension and that they rid themselves of the poor by giving them money. "Yes," he replies, "in Italy the poor give alms to the poor, and they do it lovingly."

NOVEMBER 13. One should try to remain alone. To be able to do this, one must refuse success, I mean easy success, for in going from one easy success to another, one ends by being lost. Come honors and all is over. . . . I am a Catholic, but a suspicious one in the eyes of certain Catholics because I read the Bible. All this apropos of a doctor who said to me yesterday: "You are no longer free because you are in the public eye." But one has to remain free, even at the price of solitude.

NOVEMBER 16. So few men are in their proper place in this world. . . . This strikes me more and more. Am I in my proper place? It doesn't much matter now that the game has been played.

(How I love the sound of bells brought to me on the November air, through the drawn curtains of this room, so far away from the world! The presence of such a quiet and beautiful hour is worth noting.) If I gave up painting long ago, it was no doubt because I was afraid of not excelling in it. I was unconsciously ambitious. This seems strange to me now. The first time that I saw my name printed in a newspaper, in a stationer's window, I ran away. Yet, I think that I was born to write books. What books? This one, perhaps.

NOVEMBER 19. . . . This morning, I had a letter from a priest who writes: "You are alone." And he adds: "You are saved." Saved—how does he know? But alone, yes. To be truthful, and strange as it may seem, I do not know a priest to whom I dare tell, in this very room where I am writing, even a quarter of my difficulties. We talk about books, of course, but for goodness' sake, what is a book and what reality can it have? Now, the soul is real, is cruelly, sorrowfully real. My correspondent also says: "One obtains from God as much as one hopes to get." Yes, and in that case, I want everything. This is what constitutes the deepest part of certain lives that are so disconcerting on the spiritual plane. Perhaps, then says a voice I know so well, but what about that black notebook? There is always a black notebook in every man's life. Ought I to say all this? Beyond any doubt, there are days when one ought to say what one doesn't want to say. It was not without uneasiness—why not write "not without dread"? —that I reread the last chapters of Isaiah yesterday. Such anger directed against me, against any man who receives the word, since no man is pure before God, but also those marvelous promises of a universal conversion . . .

NOVEMBER 21. I wanted once more to hear *Schlage doch, gewünschte Stunde* with Robert. Only very great men can reach this divine simplicity, divine because it comes from God. Compared with this, the enormous and magnificent intricacies of a composer like Wagner . . . Yet I don't think I will ever tire of listening to the *Meistersinger,* even the overture, too well known, but as beautiful as the sun breaking through the clouds and beaming light in all directions. This is genius in all its wonderful self-assurance, I was going to say: insolence.

* * *

NOVEMBER 26. A priest was telling me of his indifference to graves, for those of his own dead. "I go to visit them out of politeness," he says. This devotion to the dead, according to him, corresponds to a very ancient idea that the neglected dead wreak vengeance on the living. But then, to appease them once a year with a bunch of chrysanthemums . . . My own particular cemetery lies in morning and evening prayer. That is what counts. And also, there is no cemetery because there are no dead. The departed live in God, and God said that He was not the God of the dead but of the living.

DECEMBER 2. Talked about Gide with someone who knew him very well. I told him that he would not perhaps have had that very bitter and very stubborn hostility to the Church if it had not shown itself to him under the features of So-and-So, if we Catholics had been different and above all better, I mean better Christians. We have our responsibility in this matter. And also, in regard to believers, there was something in him akin to the resentment that old men harbor for young ones who still have a heart to love with, whereas old men no longer have one. I have felt more than once that he was vexed, and very much vexed, not to be able to believe. Hence that acrimony and the constant malicious teasing to which he subjected my visitor and myself.

DECEMBER 9. Satan's power is enormous, his subtleness extraordinary, but God with one breath knocks all that down. Then what is the power that works on us unceasingly and that patiently leads us toward our end, even through evil? We recognize God in the darkness, His voice which is not a voice like ours, His voice which has the same quality as silence and which makes the heart beat. . . .

DECEMBER 20. My sister Eleanor writes us from London that everyone is getting ready for "the great Christmas bacchanalia." Indeed, what other name could be given this feast? It no longer has any really Christian meaning for the immense majority of gluttons and spreers who celebrate Christmas Eve with parties. The birth of the little Jewish child who saved us has become the pretext for extra debauchery.

DECEMBER 23. "Back of nature lies a dreadful power," said

Father Pouget. Whoever has not felt this intuitively, at least occasionally, at least once before dying, does not know the meaning of life. That power is God, and it may indeed appear dreadful, because of the enormous force it implies. It is legitimate to be frightened. The Scriptures even think this to be a very wise thing, but that dreadful power is love. O You whom we do not see, but whom we feel around us and whom we constantly offend, how could the man who knows You are there manage to resist You? Words are suddenly dumb when such things are to be expressed. In such a case music alone speaks, and great writers are great only in so far as their thoughts blend with music and they speak its tongue. Away with a man who has no music in himself!

DECEMBER 27. A sermon by John Donne on death. He turns sleep into a daily death and declares that we deliver ourselves to our enemy when we lie down to sleep. What a good time those puritans unconsciously had! For this is nothing but a sinister play of images, the fancy of a great poet who was both fastidious and obsessed. Death wreaks vengeance on Donne's own self. This is the favor that Donne asks of it. Donne the preacher kills, and kills over and over again, the young profligate he was at twenty, he slits his throat with ferocious joy, he tramples him, he delivers him to the worms, he damns him.

1956

JANUARY 4. This, in a letter from Keats: "I carry all matters to an extreme—so that when I have any little vexation it grows in five minutes into a theme for Sophocles." Suffered a little from this all my life, with the difference that my imagination, without enlarging facts, tends to distort or denature them. Maybe this is the novelist working in me! Now, the novelist in me is none other than the madman I would perhaps have been if I had not written novels. I am probably exaggerating a little, but I owe my equilibrium to ink and paper.

Bremond. Oh, Abbé Bremond, how you annoy your reader when you give him to understand that you think him well informed about all sorts of things, when you know perfectly well that he knows nothing at all! That allows you *modestly* to show off your knowledge.

JANUARY 21. I burned quite a number of papers last night. I hated to do it, I admit. As I stood before the fire, poking at these pages, I thought that behind me, helping me to make this difficult gesture, were generations of believers, all the members of my family who firmly believed, those whom we rather lightly call fanatics, and they whispered to me: "Far better to burn all this than to burn yourself."

JANUARY 22. To slip a few papers under blazing logs—such a simple gesture. An impossible gesture to make, seemingly, but once it is over you realize it was nothing. . . . Many of these pages would have been considered harmless by most people, but I am so constituted that at certain moments everything is poison to me.

JANUARY 24. It is useless to attempt to get ahead of divine action. Our soul is an abyss into which we vainly peer. We scarcely see anything, but something is happening there—a great drama, surely; the drama of Adam's salvation. The Church puts these things to us as best it can, but in a necessarily imperfect tongue, that is, the human tongue. It makes us familiar with extraordinary ideas that lose much of their strength with time. Happy the man who, in growing older, can feel the mystery increasing beyond all expression. . . . In the Second Epistle to the Corinthians, chapter 4, it is said that the Gospel is hidden to those who lose their souls. It is also said that visible things are temporal and the invisible ones alone are eternal. This chapter, together with the Gospels, Psalm 23, Psalm 50, the whole of Psalm 68, the last chapters of Isaiah, and some in Ezekiel (notably the thirty-third) are the great lights that shine in my darkness.

FEBRUARY 6. It is childish to cling to what we have learned, for what we know is of little weight, but I admire people who know what they know thoroughly, who don't know it in a slipshod way. With time, I must admit to having lost the taste for learning just to acquire something that I will not retain. What becomes passionately interesting is to exist. I don't mean hanging on to life, but to break away from all things transient. Let things drop, Fénelon often said.

An article by Cartier about the most recent astronomical theories. The universe breathes. After a period of expansion (which is ours at present) will come a period of contraction to annihilate us in fifteen billion years. Creation incessantly renewed, galaxies wandering off into space beyond frontiers that our curiosity cannot cross. . . . In disappearing they are replaced by others—and that endlessly. We were brought up in a universe where everything was still in its place, the earth, the stars, and instinctively we put ourselves in the center of all this, we had the illusion of a certain peace amidst infinite spaces. . . . We would look at the sky before going to bed. Orion is there. Way up high, the Great Bear. And now we have figures and a rumpus that make our heads swim. The truth is that the Middle Ages continue within us, although we are not aware of it. We are gradually struggling out of it, but we drag after us great fragments of the story of humanity and it is not easy to get free of them. This article is worth many a so-called religious book.

MARCH 8. We are growing old and our decaying civilizations are going, one after the other, but God is always new, He is always there like a beautiful, fresh, clear morning, and that is how we will meet Him again after the night and storm of sin. His wealth of forgiveness is without limits. He is youth eternal.

MARCH 9. Reading is a form of laziness in so far as one allows the book to think for the reader. The reader reads and imagines that he thinks; hence a pleasure that flatters vanity with a delicate illusion.

Nothing seems to me more demoralizing than certain works on sexuality. I am thinking of the confessions that are sent to specialists who publish them. All these things said in cold blood, couched naked on paper, these horribly precise words, the clinical sentences bereft of frenzy, for nothing but sensual frenzy could make them pass. On reading these pages, how could one help from longing for the absolute?

Music lends beauty to the places where it is heard. Wicked words make ugly and sadden the places where they are uttered. Blasphemy makes the walls totter, coarseness sullies them; everything turns poor and shabby, through some unknown and strange magic, in a room where people express themselves badly and boredom creeps into a man's heart.

. . . There are moments in our lives when madness bursts in and triumphs, be it only for a few seconds: first, in sleep, through the gate of horn of dreams; second, in sexual intercourse.

UNDATED. Late this afternoon and much against my will, I went to a reception held in gloomy drawing rooms where despair walks sumptuously to and fro, the despair that follows wealth like its shadow. Men in uniforms. A member of the French Academy, whom I used to know, passes by me, glides by me like some gigantic fish in his green uniform. Princes of the Church. I remained almost dumb in this strange place and left after a short time, wondering what it could all be about. We are told that our dreams are absurd, but I have had many that seemed to me more reasonable than these queer fifteen minutes.

GOOD FRIDAY. Thought of a sentence that I once read in an English book. It seems to have no meaning and yet has a very great one: "How close I was to God when I was far from Him!" An illusion, no doubt, but nothing gives me a keener longing for God than sin.

APRIL 9. The act of photographing a face is a sort of magical operation. The reason why so few photographers faithfully reproduce the face that I see every morning in the mirror is that they do not know it. An unknown man comes to my house and photographs an unknown man (unknown to the photographer). The result is null. The camera has seen me but has understood nothing, guessed nothing. The photographs taken of me by people who know me well are quite different, for they show what these people think of me, and the camera sees what the photographer sees. An American came here and took some rather poor likenesses of me, for he had at his disposal a highly—too highly—perfected camera that spared him the trouble of looking, not with the eye, but with what should think and understand within us. I say this because what happens to me in this respect happens to everybody else. A photographer cannot dispense with also being a painter.

MAY 5. The only books that count for me are those of which

one can say that the author would have choked to death if he had ✓
not written them. Namely, those by Dostoevsky. The rest is
scarcely more than brilliant stuff and nonsense such as we are
offered nowadays. In talking about all this to a young writer, I
thought of what the Flemish drapers said in the fifteenth century
when a war with England deprived them of the wool they needed:
"You can't make cloth without wool." Where is the wool in all
these novels, and of what stuff, of what imitation cloth are they
made?

MAY 20. In growing older, we become our parents. Their prin-
ciples end by getting the better of the ones we had in our youth,
which were perhaps those they had in their own. When one has
had parents like ours, there is room for hope, but we should choose
our parents carefully!

MAY 26. I have been asked questions about *The Transgressor*.
To my mind, Jean, like Hedwige, is a victim, without her innocence, but nevertheless a victim. He is a transgressor in the eyes
of those who dare to judge him. So I might be told that the title is
ironical. Yes, of course, but bitterly ironical. What I condemn in
this character is what I also condemn in all the men and women
who cast a stone at him. One's hands should be clean indeed to
cast a stone, but what is remarkable about clean hands is that they
don't cast stones.

MAY 28. In a corner of one's room when the day is closing,
when the sounds of the city and of life die down a little, when in
us lies the silence of twilight where God is perhaps more perceptible than at other moments—that is the time to open the
Bible and listen to what it is going to say to us. To talk to God
with a heart still warm with happiness. How He must love to be
told that He is loved! And the more we tell Him so, the more He
loves us.

I think that nothing in the Old Testament surpasses the beauty
of the third chapter of Jeremiah, no matter how terrible, how
disquieting it may seem. The Bible is a book that stays open for
ever, since it speaks only of the eternal present.

MAY 30. A young man who almost took orders said the other
day: "I prefer pleasure to God." And I prefer this alarming sen-

tence—alarming for him—to lukewarmness. That is the way violent, headstrong men speak. The lukewarm rarely return to God. The violent suddenly return to God, and for ever.

JUNE 14. A letter from Germany blames me for Jean's suicide in *The Transgressor*, even more than for Hedwige's, because Jean believed in God. "God's purposes should be obeyed and life should not be cut short," writes my correspondent. This is undoubtedly true, but a novel is not a handbook on morals, it is a mirror in which we see life, and if what I see is tragic, isn't the story of humanity tragic on every page, and daily newspapers as well? Give us newspapers that contain good news only and I will write optimistic novels (as a religious asked me to do). Let the condition of man be changed, let life be changed. "Life is not so black," old Mme Alphonse Daudet said to me. How often have I heard this remark, and heard it from people whose families could vie with the Atridae.

JUNE 15. Not to forgive oneself anything is a kind of sin. There is a great deal of pride in being, or wishing to be, more severe than God. That man within us is the one we ought to kill.

I was told the following story. It concerns a man who was very close to me, one of the best Christians I have ever known. Long before the 1914 war, he had an exporting business in Savannah. One of the men who worked for him proved most unsatisfactory, in spite of all admonishments. He was a slightly unbalanced Spaniard. The manager finally decided to discharge the man, who refused to go. Things dragged on from bad to worse. One day there was a row. The Spaniard, on being told once more that he was dismissed, declared that go he would not and clung to his desk. This article of furniture was carried out of the house and set down in front of it, on the wharf. There stood the Spaniard, behind his desk, in the open air, haranguing the passers-by. He shrieked, he cursed his former boss, he prophesied that not a cent of the money inherited by the latter from his father would be left. And this came true literally. God took away all the money this man had been left by his father. Perhaps this is the way God saved him. I knew someone who had witnessed this strange scene in the port of Savannah. I think it rather fine. The novelist called life is sometimes well inspired.

* * *

JUNE 21. Among Mozart's works, *The Marriage of Figaro* is the one I like least, and I wish I knew why. It is a shadowless opera, and this no doubt is why it does not charm me like the rest, where, at some time or other, you always find the exquisite melancholy that makes me so fond of Mozart and that distinguishes him in my eyes from composers with unalloyed high spirits. I except the Countess' aria, through which runs a regret for childhood and lost innocence. The *Marriage* is in broad daylight, a blinding Italian light, *deafening* at times. Such aggressive gaiety makes me feel like running away, no matter how much admiration the music's formal beauty arouses in me.

JULY 5. At Mareil, near Paris, which we reached a moment ago in the finest possible weather. The house is rather old. The staircase must have been built at least two centuries ago. The large, fine semi-Romanesque, semi-Gothic church is separated from us by a path on the other side of the garden wall. The garden is a stretch of lawn hedged in by clumps of flowers, and at the far end is a sort of terrace buried in trees. All this is quiet, secret, a trifle dark no doubt at certain times of the day, but how much I enjoy being within these walls! I have a beautiful room with two windows facing each other. The sun passes through the muslin curtains as through a mist. Here, life pauses for a moment in its hectic race. You can breathe, look around you. Anne will be with us in a few days. Yesterday, as she was putting sheets in a suitcase, happy at the idea of going away, she said to me: "This is like old times, when we went to Andrésy, in July." And she carries the sheets as my mother used to carry them, but it is no longer quite like old times, alas, too many of us are missing. Mother packed the sheets in a big wicker hamper, and the creaks of the lid as it closed were like shrieks of pain. All that is far away. And the children, the others, where are they?

JULY 6. It would bore me to have to describe this house, except in a novel, I mean that it would take too much time. Its façade is covered with red roses. The house is so old that you feel it would be impossible to make a gesture that it has not seen made thousands of times. In the room where I am writing, the sun stretches over the floor the same golden rectangle that it laid there in 1700 or earlier. What strange thoughts have moved to and fro within these walls, how many prayers too, perhaps, how many unacknowledged ambitions have ripened under its long black rafters, only to be disappointed later. . . .

I am plunged resolutely in Jane Austen's *Emma* for a change of atmosphere and to prevent my being bewitched by Port-Royal. Miss Austen's world is a very quiet one. The heart's beat is steady, there is no screaming, but hidden emotion lies under these appearances of calm and uniform good breeding. The author's subtlety of observation might easily go unnoticed these days. Everything is said with bated breath. Compared with this novel ours seem very ill bred, very vulgar, and very heavy.

JULY 8. Just now, I was talking to Robert about Proust and trying to make myself understand why I admire this writer so much, although I like him so little. What I have against him are his characters, his innumerable models, several of whom I know and who have attempted to make me love Proust as much as they did and who irritated me on account of their pretensions to intellectual refinement, which was an imitation intellectual refinement, and their fashionable jargon, their sham simplicity, their spurious enthusiasms, their search for psychological complications, the crashing boredom they exuded because it was all intensely false. I except the most Proustian of Proustians: Lucien Daudet (son of Alphonse Daudet).

JULY 9. Alone in the house, I continued reading Jane Austen in the charming and tiny ground-floor library. She overrefines feelings, but with such a firm, light hand that she makes us seem gross and bearish. How pleasant it is to be plunged into a world so peaceful that the arrival of a letter is a sort of event!

JULY 14. How can one think oneself pure when the ancient corruption of the human race is felt to the core of one's being? Who has not experienced the horror of knowing himself deeply enslaved by human beauty, even if only for a second, a flash? What's the good of deceiving oneself? Could one possibly imagine that, by imitating the actions of saints, one becomes saintly? This is false. Everything is different inwardly. Holiness that is only an outward show is perfectly ridiculous, and if we believe in it we are silly. I have the feeling of never having gone beyond outward appearances, that I have been satisfied with fine semblances. What's the result of these idiotic efforts? I secretly rebel, not against faith (God forbid), but against myself who understand nothing about matters of faith, who do not even know what faith is—and in that I am not alone; I have hosts of Catholics with me, and particularly, theologians.

JULY 15. The secret is to write just anything, to dare to write just anything, because when you write just anything, you begin to say what is most important. You must let your hand run along the sheet of paper for a while. Then someone guides it, someone you don't know and who bears your name. How old can he be? A thousand years, I think.

An expression that I like in *Emma*: "To be in charity with oneself," to be at peace with oneself and, better still, to love oneself, to forgive oneself. Why not? ". . . I love my neighbor *as myself* for love of You," says the act of charity. Then may this terrible, homicidal, and constant struggle against oneself cease!

JULY 26. Read Jane Austen. I am glad to have undertaken to read *Emma* but am impatient to get through with it. The guiding thread is a little tenuous and it requires very great attention to prevent its slipping out of one's fingers. The dialogues are often admirable, but the action boils down to very little. At one point, a young man asks a girl to play on the piano a waltz that he has just heard. "She played," says the author. And that is all. Not another word. This is not dryness but an exquisite restraint that might wrongly pass for poverty in 1956.

JULY 30. Robert was telling me that it was probably owing to reading the Bible that I had become, as he says, nontemporal (with the serious inconveniences that can result from it in everyday life), and it is true that the Bible has freed me from some of the fascinations of this world. I know the devil's old spells only too well. I can no longer believe, if I ever did, in the reality of honors, of reputations, of pleasures. But I feel lonely. This crumbling world has never been more convinced of its own existence.

AUGUST 1. I was struck by a book about Gide and his wife. If Mme Gide was as intelligent as her husband believed her to be, she could not have ignored how much she would hurt him by burning his letters to her. On the other hand, if she thought it her duty to punish him, taking the place of God, I cease to understand her, no matter how admirable she was in other ways. Who knows if she didn't kill in Gide a better man than the one we knew? Didn't he say himself, and most explicitly, that if this correspondence disappeared, nothing would remain of him but an incomplete, inaccurate, caricatural, grimacing picture and that what had been his true representation would be wiped out for ever?

AUGUST 3.   A walk in the forest of Saint-Nom-la-Bretèche; the earth is black and the light is such as is found in a cellar. I remembered what St. Bernard said: "In woods, you will find something more than in books." But what do books give us? We gradually forget them. Most serious of all, if we aren't careful, they end by thinking for us. They ask nothing better. Yet what they have to offer us is immense, they teach us to find within us the truth that God has put there and that is God Himself. Nothing else on this earth is of any interest but the discovery of God within us. Now, He is there, whether we know it or not, whether we feel it or not.

An excellent chapter in *Emma* where the heroine publicly insults a poor old lady whose intemperate chatter exasperates everyone. Once at home, she is filled with shame and remorse and weeps secretly. Mysterious Jane Austen! How I would have dreaded living with her! Not one of my weaknesses would have escaped her, for she saw everything with a pitiless eye. Emotion, with her, is always delicate, but then everything is delicate in this woman, cruelty like the rest. One can say that she is almost unknown in France because translations only thicken and coarsen such a very light and very subtle prose.

Why do you want to be a better man? (This question could be asked of every man.) Because you would love yourself more if you were better, you, always you, black or white. You will be a better man only when you have completely lost sight of yourself and will then think of your Creator. No more diary, no more mirror, no more self-complacency. A fly, after long wanderings over a windowpane in search of the sun it sees but cannot reach, being separated from it by this sheet of glass, will fly out of the window when death opens it.

AUGUST 11.   We are returning to Paris day after tomorrow. What a number of walks, of villages lighted on, with their little Romanesque churches that, in solitude and silence, pursue the great

Catholic dream! Houdan, Nonancourt, Herbeville, Orgival and so many others. Immense fields framed by woods, hills as far as the eye can reach, the most beautiful landscapes in the world, those of my childhood, those of happiness.

AUGUST 17.   To many men, the horror of going to confession is an insuperable trial. To be thrown like a criminal at the feet of a judge before whom one shakes with fear, that's what it is. Afterwards only do you realize that the judge loves you so much that He died for you and died for you on the cross and that, of course, He forgives everything.

AUGUST 24.   A certain man I know is devoid of real humility, but he has a showy modesty, an ostentatious modesty that is worse than anything and fills me with the most violent disgust. I prefer bare-faced pride, pride in all its foolishness and vulgarity. How difficult it is to save a man of letters! But nothing is impossible to God, since He manages to save even the rich.

AUGUST 29.   Thought last night of the sight presented by humanity. It is wounded, crippled. This escapes our notice, but an angel ignorant of earthly matters and of the state of mankind would be horrified. What a sorry sight we are! One need only observe passers-by in any street. They all bear the stamp of a frightful and most ancient catastrophe. We are told of the havoc an atomic bomb would wreak, but there has already been an atomic bomb: the punishment of original sin that has left us in a state of woeful inferiority in comparison to what we should have been. Yet there are human beings who resemble the idea we can form of humanity before the Fall. One sees faces and bodies so beautiful that they surpass what words can say of them, but this does not last and no sooner do they reach the age of twenty or thereabouts than something fades. In the reckless admiration inspired by a beauty that is both frail and marvelous and is the cause of such great tragedies, one cannot help but see what is pathetic and pitiful in all this. The expression and the whole person of those whom life has not yet touched, has not yet disfigured, hold a reflection of vanished glory.

SEPTEMBER 28.   Pascal said almost all there was to say about one side of Montaigne when he wrote: "He inspires a certain unconcern for salvation." Of all the things with which a man I like so much could be reproached, this one is to my mind the most serious. It is nevertheless true that St. Francis de Sales delighted in him and read him with other eyes than ours. The Bishop of Geneva would have been astonished to hear that the time would come when one of his favorite authors would be placed in the Expurgatory Index. Be it as it may, it is characteristic of a huge part of modern literature to inspire this unconcern for salvation. The Gospel's urgent, burning message is passed over in silence. People write as though there had never been a Gospel. The Gospel's voice is not heard in the books we are given to read, love is dumb. In literature, everything that does not lead you to God imperceptibly detaches you from Him. The great scandal is that pietistic literature turns you away from God more forcibly than does the unbelieving kind.

OCTOBER 5.   Read some of the Psalms in Monsignor Knox's translation. I don't hesitate to call it simply scandalous. Scandalous because of its ugliness. Psalm 23, *Dominus pastor*, is horribly badly rendered. His prose has neither the rhythm, nor the metrical number, nor the music that such a text demands, and moreover it is *unsingable*, whereas the Protestant version (in the Book of Common Prayer) possesses this quality to an eminent degree.

OCTOBER 13.   The devil is a great moralist and a great puritan. He suggests great austerities which he very well knows will bring about spiritual disasters. He never suggests small sacrifices, he aims at what is grand, sensational, at everything striking, at everything that stirs the imagination. And with it all, he is the most skillful, the most crafty of artists. Music is a great help to him. A beautiful voice serves him wonderfully well, for he manages to turn it into a beautiful body, no less. He is very sentimental, very tender, and speaks with exquisite gentleness. And every one of us is taken in by this. We spend a good part of our lives in letting God rescue us. Sad to have to say that every day, perhaps, we pass by our own self, by the self that we might have been.

God alone can understand you perfectly, you who read this. The words we use in attempting to explain ourselves serve only to confuse things. The French imagine that everything can be understood, can be clearly explained ("What is not clear is not French"). They make an exception for the Creator, faith obliges them to, but if the Church were not there to keep a watch on them, they would define Him.

OCTOBER 14. The West has never produced the founder of a religion. It has received its religion from the East, and we Christians as well as the others. This is a fact that we should not forget. We are Occidentals faced with an Oriental conception. Hence the bewilderment of certain among us.

OCTOBER 17. I can no longer speak except in a whisper, and there is too much noise for me to make myself heard by a great number of people. I don't complain of this.

OCTOBER 19. Yesterday, I had an appointment with my publisher. As usual, I was a little early and waited in the entrance hall, seated at one end of a long table strewn with books. At the other end, a woman, youngish, well dressed, with a modest air, her hands clasped over her handbag. A door opened. The publisher's secretary went up to the lady, gave her a manuscript in a folder, saying: "We're sorry. It's a little too pornographic." The lady took the manuscript, smiled, and left. What struck me was that these few words were spoken in a quiet, commonplace tone, as one might have said: "We're sorry. It's a little long. Too long by fifty pages." A whole aspect of our times was shown up in this short scene. Even *porno,* as it is called, has lost its prestige. Maybe, in a not too distant future, we shall once more have novels where all the characters will always keep their clothes on.

OCTOBER 21. . . . Which of us is really represented by what he writes? Which of us does not surpass his letters, his works? Is there a writer who does not live and breathe between the lines of his books? Yet you can't shut up a man inside his sentences. He will always escape, and only a close examination of texts can give you an intuition of what has not been written and what is often the essential part of what you want to know. I know only too well to what an extent this is true of me and all the more so of the greatest writers. . . .

OCTOBER 24. We don't give much to God. We even give Him so little that I wonder what name this little can have. It is nothing, and even less than that. We are ourselves. The saints are a different matter. As regards us, we would willingly accept a halo, but energetically (or slyly, or subtly) refuse the cross that is offered us, the hard, dry, cold, bitter, bloodstained cross. Yesterday, a Carmelite Father was telling me that the eccentricities of saints can be explained by the fact that they feel they are saved and that nothing in this world matters to them, except the love of God and the love of one's neighbor; so they give themselves up to their whims. They are not great conformists.

DECEMBER 14. That the body can suffer and the soul be happy, and very happy, is an aspect of life that unbelievers cannot even imagine.

DECEMBER 15. Kant said that the sight of a starry sky annihilates us as physical beings. It annihilates us, tears us away from the earth, and throws us into the infinite. I have often wondered if it were possible not to feel the tremendous attractive energy of the firmament. How I loved the word firmament when I was still a child! To me, it seemed filled with light. My first purely religious emotion, so far as I can remember, goes back to my fifth or sixth year. I think I have mentioned it elsewhere. I was in my parents' room, rue de Passy. The room was dark, but through a windowpane I saw thousands of stars shining in the sky. This was the first time, to my knowledge, that God spoke directly to me, in that vast, confused tongue which words have never been able to render.

DECEMBER 17. Someone I am very fond of told me that he had great difficulty in going to sleep, because anguish grips him the moment he turns out the light. It is the anguish of solitude, the fear of dying in the night. A short time before, he spoke to me about the extraordinary effect produced on him by the cantata *Schlage doch, gewünschte Stunde*, which immediately carried him away to another world filled with unclouded serenity. I told him that this was the real world, and the one that frightens and makes us suffer is a world of terrible delusions; it must be quitted at all costs, but what keeps us there are covetous desires of all kinds, which are our tyrants. Our real master is Jesus. He alone will free us from the terrors of this life. The first step is to leave pleasure behind; the rest follows of itself.

1957

JANUARY 4. Do I really know the Bible well? The truth is that I wander through it like a blind man in a palace where he has lived since childhood. I feel along the walls, I find my way. Yes, that is it, but a ready memory of the texts fails me. I locate and rediscover them pretty well, if I am given time enough.

A young foreign student told me that he can find no pleasure in reading a book that does not belong to him. It may be shameful, but I have the same feeling without being quite able to explain it. I get no benefit from reading a borrowed book, which I ✓ am afraid of losing or spoiling. Similarly, it is as painful for me to lend a book as it is agreeable to give one away, and I have given many a one in my life, but it is enough for a book to disappear from my shelves to feel an urgent, cruel need of it.

JANUARY 15. Yesterday evening, in the chapel of Foreign Missions, rue du Bac. There were present a very old white-bearded priest, four nuns in black, and two or three laymen, all absorbed in such deep meditation that for twenty minutes I did not hear the least sound, and had I closed my eyes, I might have believed myself completely alone. There was something magnificent in this silence. Father Surin says that God visits souls only when they are *still and empty*.

JANUARY 23. AT GSTAAD. Everything in our lives being, it seems, of a sexual nature, our gestures, our way of sitting down, the most innocent of our little manias, the good and bad books we read, the manner in which we soap our bodies, everything, in fact, how can we not see that when a man gives up physical pleasure, he replaces it instantly and unconsciously by thousands of small things that are a sort of compensation to him for what he misses? Am I wrong? I don't think so. I believe that taking a nap, or eating a cake, or settling into a comfortable armchair simply means cheating one's hunger. A hunger that one doesn't even wish to name. Mortal sin is sent packing, escorted to the city gate with a great beating of drums (the devil does the drumming), but sensuality tiptoes back, creeps in at the back door, duly disguised. Saints who sleep on the floor and fast so severely have understood this. You don't win the game by confiscating the body's sexual organs, to speak plainly. Sexuality looks elsewhere for shelter, it can even conceal itself in mortifications.

. . . A religious said to me: "You can't talk to a dying man of Extreme Unction. You run the risk of hastening his end. You must show mercy. . . ." Is it really being merciful if the man is truly at death's door to let him leave for the next world without a sacrament that would be of such immense help to him? For my part, I beg that the truth will not be withheld from me when the time comes. I don't want to be shown that kind of mercy.

JANUARY 26. In Milton Waldman's *Elizabeth and Leicester* there are interesting remarks about the art of the theater, which is so often impersonal, whereas a novel delivers up the author, body and soul. Thirty-seven plays and two long poems have been attributed to Shakespeare, but what do we know about the man he was? Nothing, except that he was a great genius and that he worked a lot and quickly. He was so much the lover and the loved one, so much the traitor, so much the king, the faithful knight, the clown and the gravedigger, the drunk and the scholar, the dotard and the nurse, that one no longer knows where to find him, or what his beliefs and thoughts could have been. What stands out most plainly, I think, apart from a certain conventionality that I cannot admire, is a frantic love for beauty and youth.

FEBRUARY 11. PARIS. Saturday, an anniversary Mass for Father Couturier. About forty persons were present. I was glad to see Mauriac as well as Jouhandeau and Cassou, but was unable to talk to them as I wished. A religious read fragments of Father Couturier's letters between the Gospel and the Creed, at the altar. *"Faites ce qui vous chante et cela chantera en vous."* (This sentence remembered among several others.) Father Couturier writes that he has called on Matisse and on Colette and "that both are going to Heaven without the shadow of a doubt." This would seem to exempt us from praying for them, a drawback to the rapid canonizations habitually decreed by the Father in the goodness and pureness of his heart. He sent everyone to Heaven. Thought of him affectionately. How I wish he were here.

FEBRUARY 13. Another morning spent in useless efforts. That is exactly the way it was when I wrote *The Dark Journey* or later when I wrote *Midnight.* Experience does nothing, brings nothing, gives no facility. Finally there will be a book, but at what a price! To want to work and to be unable to, as this morning, is a sort of tragedy for me. The power is there, but not released, for some unknown reason. If I force myself to form words on a sheet of paper, I fall into abstraction, and when I fall into abstraction, it means that I *see* nothing; now, if I see nothing, it is better not to write. Today, I feel that words resist me. This is such a frequent experience that, having noted it, I won't refer to it again.

This, in Montaigne: "Some make the world believe that they believe things they never do. Others, and they are the greater number, persuade themselves they do so, being unable to conceive what it is to believe." Unable to conceive what it is to believe. Can this be better expressed? The quotation is from Book II, Chapter 12. Nowadays, many are atheists without knowing it and would be dumfounded if told so, but what effect has their so-called faith on their daily life? Does it make them give up a single pleasure, a single meanness? Does it disturb anything? Montaigne is right when he says a little further in the same chapter that we are only lip Christians.

MARCH 5. . . . I have the ever-increasing conviction that in each of us lies someone unknown to us on whom God keeps His eyes fixed from our birth to our death. That someone is ourself, it is you who read this. When you do right you think yourself good, and when you do wrong you think yourself wicked, but the one you really are is quite different and you do not see him. When death comes, there will no doubt be happy surprises; there will also be terrible ones, the happy surprises being for the sinners, I hope. The other surprises . . . I won't dwell on this.

MARCH 15. It is an illusion to believe oneself to be alone. One can't be a Catholic all by oneself. One is a Catholic in the mystic body of the Church, or not at all.

If anyone ever had the idea of writing my biography, which will not happen during my lifetime, what should be pointed out is the enormous influence that Byron had over the first years of my youth, not the Byron of the poems and the attitudinizing, whom I don't care for, but the Byron at whom I guessed and who was revealed to me by Peter Quennell's books around 1950. I thought about him so much that I almost imagined having known him. To-day this seems peculiar to me and yet it is true. Until the age of twenty-four, I was under this strange spell.

MARCH 29. To begin a novel, the adventure that a fresh exploration of the outside world represents, is also a long journey inside oneself. There is, I know, the problem of the evil one is led to describe, but what is a novel made of, if not of evil? Remove evil and what remains? Good—that is, white. Black also is necessary. It might be said that this is where one runs a risk. I take that risk. It forms part of my vocation.

APRIL 9. Yesterday, I laughed when someone said in my presence that saints have no physical desires. Perhaps they have more of them than we do, we who are nothing but sin from head to foot. I remember the expression of a priest as he once said to me: "Deprivation of pleasure is a cross one never gets used to."

APRIL 13. One loses all in losing grace. Many a time have I heard this said, but it is curious to observe that a single sin *disenchants* the whole of the spiritual world and restores all its power to the carnal world. The atrocious chaos immediately *reorganizes* itself. How does this happen? I don't know, but it becomes impossible to understand the book one enjoyed the day before; I don't mean impossible with one's head, with one's reason, but with the heart, with the soul if you like, it is no longer possible. A veil stretches over the page. The book is the same, the reader's soul has grown dark. Suddenly, the sensuous world becomes unquestionably right. One must give in to every desire, have a good time, the best possible, possess all sorts of things. This is the dreaded breach through which the devil enters, but a single act of contrition is enough for this wretched phantasmagoria to vanish and for the marvelous presence of the invisible to return. A man who has not felt such things does not know one of the greatest happinesses to be had on earth.

MAY 2. Have taken up Fénelon's letters again. His great letter to Louis XIV will never cease to astonish me. If it is true, as Saint-Simon says, that Fénelon reminded him of a water tap, one must admit that the day when he wrote that letter, the tap let out scalding water. If anyone ever foresaw the 1789 earthquake, it was Fénelon, Archbishop of Cambrai.

* * *

MAY 5.   In all books, in all painting, in all music, I can't help seeing two kingdoms, one constantly invading the other. It has to be
so, it has to be that light rushes upon shade and that shade throws
itself on light to blot it out, but this takes place within us. Outside, nothing moves, nothing changes. This might even lead us
astray.

MAY 6.   Yesterday evening, someone I am very fond of made me
listen to Brahms' *Requiem,* and I don't know which I found more
beautiful, the very grave, very luminous music, or the face of
the one who listened to it. In eyes that have looked at me for
more than half my life, I read deep attentiveness to all that is invisible. That is religion. I don't know why it is sought for elsewhere.

MAY 12.   A young Catholic tells me that he is disturbed by
the thought of the harm he may do by writing the novel he has
in mind. That is thinking up trouble! I am not the one who should
be consulted on this point. Racine endangered many a soul. Should
he not have written *Phèdre?* (Whom would he perturb nowadays? Some poisons evaporate.) Baudelaire is infinitely more dangerous. Should he not have written *Les Fleurs du mal?* That seems
absurd. Yet words wreak terrible havoc. They have a shape, a per-
fume, a contour, a warmth, a sweetness, they take the place of what
they describe and create in the reader a sort of hallucination, because they are produced by a poet's hallucination, if he has genius.
   Reread some pages in Dante. He meets Latini in Hell (this is
a little harsh, but we'll let it go at that) and the latter looks at
him "like an old tailor as he threads a needle." Ah, to be able to
write like that! One of the elements of Dante's genius is a scrupulous truth of observation and an inimitable gift for everyday
imagery.

MAY 15.   Someone told me with wonderful humility: "Unfortunately, I am an erotomaniac." But there is nothing surprising in
this. Almost all men are erotomaniacs, from the most dissolute to
the holiest. A seventeenth-century writer informs us that St.
Jerome and St. Bernard (I wouldn't have believed it of St. Bernard) were continually harried by "dirty thoughts." I don't know
what an idea we form of saints. Yet, they aren't born with wings.
St. Alfonso Liguori was a martyr to certain carnal obsessions.

I listened to Mozart's music. His very lightness is not free from sadness, his joy is shrouded, but human joy is always shrouded, because death exists. It is impossible to have any lasting happiness in a world where death exists.

MAY 21. This morning, I went back to my novel, which takes place in America (I hesitated a long time as to where the action should be situated). Not without melancholy do I remember America in 1920. I suffered a great deal there but finally became deeply attached to it. My holidays in Savannah came back to me. Those wide avenues were where the devil lay in wait for me with the poetry of night, the scent of night, and a setting of white columns and black shadows on the silvery streets, the mystery of squares filled with the odor of shrubs. I knew nothing, suspected nothing, but poison was already stealing into my heart—how, I don't know. At times, I thought of what one of the rue Cortambert nuns had said to me, all in white behind the grille of the little parlor that smelled of wax: "Beware of the world . . . The world . . . The world's poison . . ." All that is far away. From the armchair where I am writing, through the white curtains, I can see the big tree, each of whose leaves flutters in the sun, each one living, palpitating, and the tree bends forward and straightens, like a pitching ship. What a silence in these rooms, in the heart of a city haunted by noise! By straining the ear, all you can hear is a long murmuring, like a very distant storm. That is all.

JUNE 6. A long walk along the quays, but in the Paris of 1957 continuous noise spoils what used to be delightful strolls. Only five years ago, you could enjoy sauntering through the streets; this is no longer possible. I examined with interest the celebrities of yesterday in the boxes of the second-hand booksellers that line the quays: the charnel house of literature. That is where we shall all be thrown. What an atrocious little farce is literary glory! The most disappointing of all. "What makes you write?" was the question asked before the war. In my case, I don't know. Something drives me to, and it is certainly not a desire to be known and praised. I want at all costs to express myself, that's all.

JUNE 11. Yesterday afternoon, around five-thirty, I put down a volume of poetry and thought that never, in the future, must I remember the minute when God's grace was so clearly offered me, a grace which I did not make use of—that the memory of that minute should never find its place in an eternity of despair. One should not remember the moment when, in a room in Paris, on a fine summer afternoon, one heard the call of God, the repeated call of Christ, and never should this instant return to one's memory . . . at what place, Lord? Parted from You for ever.

JUNE 18. An American poet sent me the account of a crime committed in New Jersey by a most pious young Protestant, a great hymn singer, a great reader of the Bible, one of Billy Graham's most ardent listeners, scrupulously clean, handsome, who raped little girls (eight to ten years old) and who recently murdered a girl of twenty by strangling her with her belt after having raped her. When he went home, *hearing* of the murder, he knelt with his parents and prayed for the murderer to be discovered. He is to die in a few weeks and, it seems, prays most fervently. What takes place in this unfortunate soul? (How can I help being reminded of *Moïra*?) To kill him is useless and barbarous and will not frighten future murderers, because a man who commits a sexual crime is incapable of reasoning at the moment when he perpetrates it. He is a lunatic who should be cared for.

JULY 10. A visit from a young Catholic who talks to me about physical passions. He believes that they calm down with age. I said: "If this were so, we would all have heard of it." The truth is that if one could enter a seminary only at forty instead of at twenty, there would be only half the number of applicants. No matter how strong passions can be in a boy of twenty, they are not yet too deeply rooted, they are not yet too cumbersome and leave him free. It is only with time that they take root and everything feeds them, good as well as evil, a taste for beauty, a love of music, of books, even the satiety that creates a craving for novelty. A young man can control, transcend himself, a mature man slowly becomes obsessed.

JULY 22. "Whore!" cried Savonarola on seeing a provocative and handsome boy. I have always imagined the boy with the looks of the young man painted by Botticelli (some say by Ghirlandaio) that hangs in the Washington museum of art. He has the insolence of his years. You can't hold that against him, but his cold, cruel, calculating, and appraising eye is that of a woman of fifty who knows how to size a man up. He has perhaps sent many a soul to the fire that is never quenched and no doubt continues to act on souls through the fearful magic of art. You can understand perfectly and of course be glad that the painter did not throw the picture into the bonfire of vanities, although that is none the less its proper place. Shelley could not see Michelangelo's Bacchus without uneasiness and thought it the image of vice. Hawthorne found something diabolical in Praxiteles' Faun (but the blood of witch burners ran in the great American's veins). What would one and the other have said about the young unknown in Washington? There is fearful power in him and he defies what is best in man. Savonarola's enemy was that boy.

JULY 31.   I have been asked to write the scenario of a film about *Dr. Jekyll and Mr. Hyde*. I accept in theory. The subject is almost too good, and I have thought about it so often since I first read the book at the University. . . . I read it again recently. It is very profound at times, but Hyde, who is the wicked side only of Jekyll, dies, and because of his death, Jekyll dies too. This seems neither convincing nor fair. If what is bad in us brings about the death of what is good, it would be too horrible. The truth is that good and evil are inextricably mingled and the one cannot cause the death of the other. One does not kill the other. One is not alternatively all the one or all the other. The story is very clumsily told. There are too many repetitions, too many returns to the past, too many letters, too many envelopes to be opened later, etc. But what a great book!

It sometimes takes an almost superhuman effort to absolve oneself, to plead not guilty in one's own eyes. Charity will give us the strength for that, charity for that neighbor of ours who is our own self.

AUGUST 5.   The reasons that make a book like *Romola* unreadable nowadays teach us something about novels in general. Handsome Tito and handsome Romola get married, but no matter how much they are enamored of each other's beauty, the author gives no indications of a carnal bond existing between them. They quarrel and part on account of some business of a bookcase being sold without the consent of one of the pair. Victorian puritanism will not allow any sensuality whatever to be expressed. No matter how much of a positivist the author was, she believes in the devil, and, for her, the devil was sex. It is fetishism in reverse. Since then, we have seen authors made idiotic by the fascination of sexuality. Both phenomena are to be distrusted.

AUGUST 10. Looked at my notes on *Romola*. One made me smile. Speaking of Tito, George Eliot says: "his loathsome beauty." This is indeed the sort of reproving gluttony I mentioned earlier. The characters stop at the waist. At about the time when George Eliot wrote her tiresome book, Dostoevsky was working on *A Raw Youth*.

AUGUST 12. Moral theology textbooks are often exasperatingly ingenuous. It is a mortal sin to look at certain parts of the bodies of men and women in the street, but this is not so of legs and faces. And supposing legs and faces are what disturb one most? How can such balderdash continue to be printed?

AUGUST 22. Yesterday, at Larchant, I saw a magnificent church, half demolished by Protestants in the sixteenth century. What remains is very beautiful. A spiritual force assembled these stones, threw these towers into the clouds. In our times, what is spiritual can be found only in books, and even so . . . In the old days, the smallest village church said its prayers with commanding majesty.

AUGUST 30. In a life of Pope by Edith Sitwell, I note the story of Wycherley, who lost his memory at thirty and died at seventy without having recovered it. He read Montaigne and Molière, and a little later imagined that such or such a sentence or scene was his, which explains the plagiarism of *L'École des femmes* in *The Country Wife*, a first-rate comedy, anyway. At bottom, the man who lost his memory had an astonishing one.

NOVEMBER 20. Listening to Chopin the other evening, with all the pleasure I usually feel, I wondered suddenly: What can be lacking in him? And the answer came at once: Heart. This sumptuous show of melancholy, these cries of despair, these sobs of sadness are not heart, but a counterfeit heart for the use of sensitive souls—who can be so very hard. This takes away from the admiration I have for the composer. He can be heartbreaking when he is simple.

* * *

NOVEMBER 27. A visit from an American friend of Kinsey. He talks to me at length about the latter, whose work is, and I don't doubt it, most important. Also talks about an author who can no longer write (this can happen: *homo unius libri*) and who keeps copies of all his letters, which he considers of great importance. How queer such literary preoccupations seem to me! Our world is ending and still we worry about our sentences, about the fate of our letters. This kind of madness allows us to live in surprising tranquillity.

DECEMBER 6. In one of his sermons, John Donne says that man is "a sick god." Nothing could better describe present humanity. It is a sublime cripple. It holds an immense power in its hands, such means of doing good and evil as perhaps it never had before.

DECEMBER 16. A priest told me that he was against wearing a cassock. He would like Catholic ecclesiastics to dress like Protestant clergymen. "The cassock," he says, "is conspicuous and prevents visits to people who dare not receive priests."

Regarding the novel I am now writing, I would like to say this, which is true of all my books: there comes a time when great breaches are made through which passes something that does not come from me, but from another who frightens me, as might another self more imperious, more commanding, and more assured than the self I know. What writer has not experienced this? Having said these things, I won't mention them again.

INDEX OF NAMES

PAPER MONEY

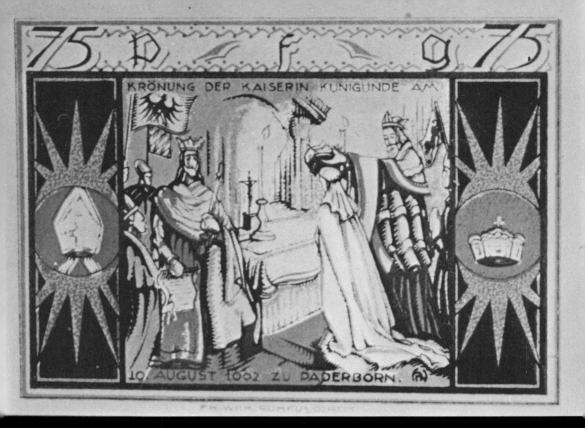

KRÖNUNG DER KAISERIN KUNIGUNDE AM

10 AUGUST 1002 ZU PADERBORN.

EMPFANG DES PAPSTES LEO III DURCH

KAISER KARL D. GR. IN PADERBORN 799

PAPER MONEY

Ian Angus

St. Martin's Press
New York

In the same series:
STAMPS, POSTS AND POSTMARKS—Ian Angus
COINS AND MONEY TOKENS—Ian Angus
MEDALS AND DECORATIONS—Ian Angus

ACKNOWLEDGEMENTS

The author and publishers would like to thank
the following for permission to use photographs
for this book.
The Bank of England, Barclays Bank, the British
Broadcasting Corporation, Roy Dotrice, Mary
Evans Picture Library, Government of India
Tourist Service, Imperial War Museum, Institute
of Bankers, National Army Museum, National
Portrait Gallery, Spink & Sons, United States
Information Service, Richard Wattis.

Series of notgeld from Paderborn, illustrating scenes from the history
of the town.

Library of Congress Cataloging in Publication Data

Angus, Ian.
    Paper Money.
    Includes index.
    1. Paper money.   I. Title.
HG348.A5   1975   769'.559   74–33903

Printed in Spain
First published in the United States of America in 1975.
Published in Great Britain by Ward Lock Ltd., London.

CONTENTS

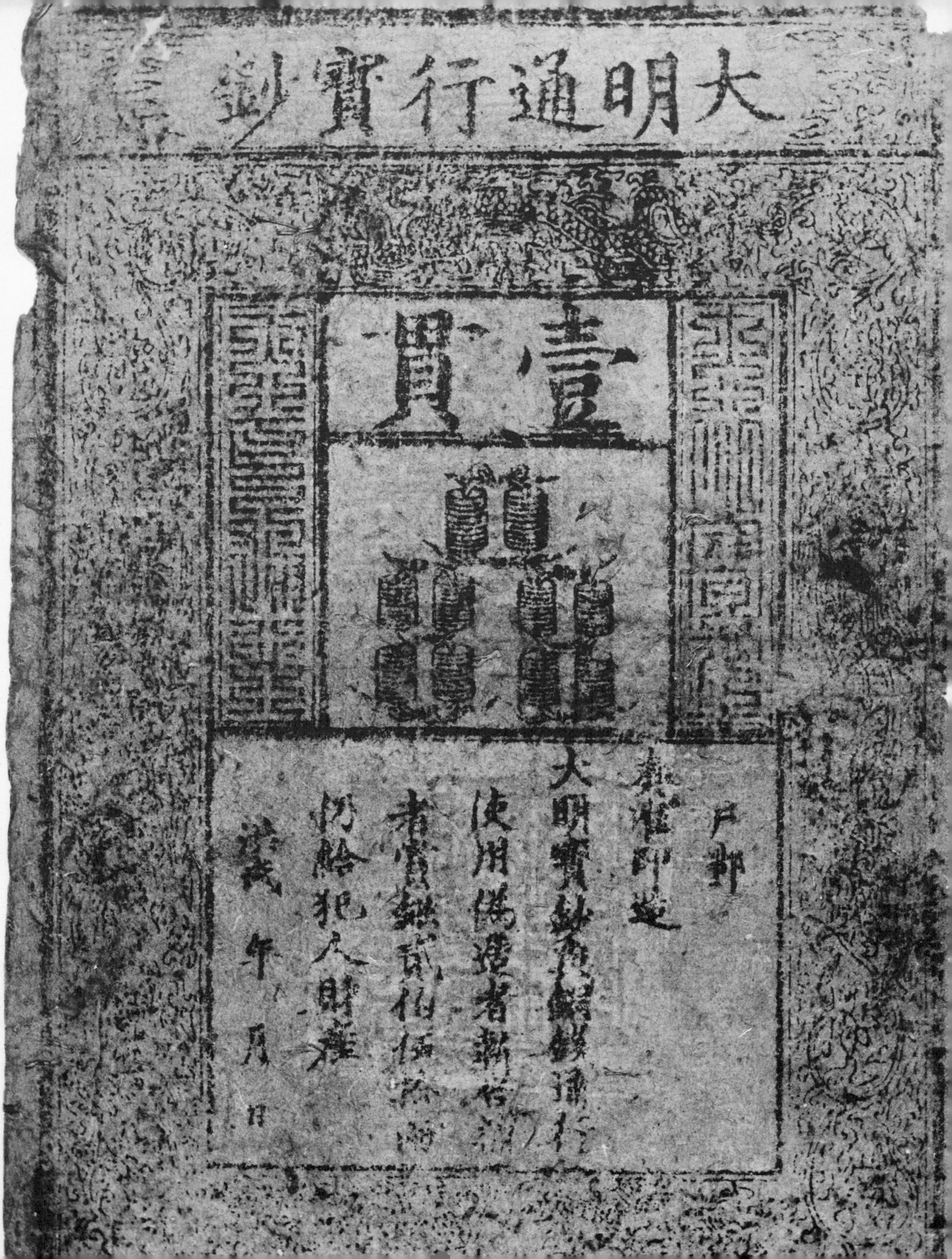

大明通行寶鈔

壹貫

戶部

奏准印造

大明寶鈔與銅錢通行

使用偽造者斬告

者賞銀貳佰伍拾兩

仍給犯人財產

洪武　　年　月　日

1
THE ORIGINS OF PAPER MONEY

Paper money has been scathingly referred to by Enoch Powell, the politician who is also a well-known coin collector, as something "which does duty for money in our degenerate age". From this it would be reasonable to suppose that paper money is a tawdry substitute for the real thing—gold and silver—in an age when money has ceased to have real value. With mounting inflation and continual rises in prices, many people would be inclined to agree but while it is true that paper money has been used to a very large extent in the twentieth century, it is by no means a modern phenomenon. In Britain, America and many European countries, paper money was in use three centuries ago. In Asia, however, paper was being used as money while Europe was still in the Dark Ages.

Appropriately enough, paper money began in China where paper itself was invented. The earliest form of paper money was produced during the T'ang Dynasty, somewhere between 650 and 800 A.D. At that time the coins used in China were made of bronze, and large quantities of bronze *cash* were needed for even the smallest business transaction. This was not only inconvenient because of its weight, but also rather insecure. The cumbersome wagons used to carry these coins from one part of the country to the other were likely to be ambushed by bandits and it was in an attempt to foil highway robbers that the Chinese merchants invented *fei-ch'ien*, literally "flying-money", consisting of

A rare Chinese Ming note, made from the bark of the mulberry tree. Note the picture in the centre, representing the piles of copper cash which the note was worth.

paper drafts negotiable in bronze currency. These drafts were not authorised paper money in the modern sense but they undoubtedly paved the way for the paper money introduced by the Sung Dynasty about 1000 A.D. These Sung notes were redeemable in coin and quickly gained acceptance.

Unfortunately the number of banks grew rapidly (there were no fewer than sixteen in the Sze-ch'uan Province alone) and they were all too readily tempted into issuing more and more notes without the funds or assets to back them. These notes, known as *chiao-tzu* (exchangeable money) soon lost the confidence of the people whereupon the government began issuing *kuan-tzu* (citadel money) which, in turn, was over-issued and led to an inflation which contributed to the downfall of the Sung Dynasty in 1278.

Their successors, the Yüan Dynasty (1270–1368), also issued far too much paper money. Before the end of the Mongol occupation of China this paper money had been reduced to utter worthlessness. A few examples of these very large and imposing notes have survived to this day, but rather more plentiful are the notes produced by the Ming Dynasty (1368–1644). They were made from the bark of the mulberry tree and printed from wooden blocks. Marco Polo describes in some detail the paper money of Cathay, as China was then known:

"All these pieces of paper money are issued with as much solemnity and authority as if they were of pure gold or silver; and on every piece a variety of officials, whose duty it is, have to write their names, and to put their seals. And when all is prepared duly, the chief officer deputed by the Khan smears the seal entrusted to him with vermilion, and impresses it on the paper, so that the form of the seal remains printed upon it in red; the money is then authentic. And the Khan causes every year to be made such a vast quantity of this money which costs him nothing, that it must equal

A cylinder seal showing King Darius of Persia. Each merchant had his own seal which was unique.

in amount all the treasure in the world. When any of those pieces of paper are spoilt—not that they are so very flimsy either—the owner carries them to the mint, and by paying three per cent on the value he gets new pieces in exchange.''

With the collapse of the Ming Dynasty in 1644 the use of paper money came to an end. Two centuries later, however, the economic crisis caused by the T'ai-ping Rebellion of 1853–64 led the Imperial government to resurrect paper money as an easy way out of its financial difficulties. From then onwards China became one of the world's most enthusiastic issuers of paper currency, with disastrous results on the economy and political stability of the country.

The designs of these early Chinese notes were often very elaborate, and usually had some religious significance. The *chops*, or seal marks added in vermilion ink to make the notes authentic, were inscribed in Chinese characters and took the form of such phrases as "to circulate as cash" or "to circulate under the Heavens". Some notes even depicted a number of coins, of the equivalent value, so that no one would be in any doubt as to the value of the note.

Banking in Europe

There are numerous references in the Bible and the literature of ancient times to money-lenders and others who, in effect, were the world's first bankers. The Babylonians, Egyptians, Greeks and Romans all had elaborate banking systems whereby rich merchants and goldsmiths lent money to businessmen or stored money from others. In Mesopotamia, the Igibi Bank is known to have been lending money and receiving deposits in the middle of the sixth century B.C., if not earlier. Banking transactions are referred to frequently in accounts of life in Roman times. In medieval Europe, the rich merchants of the Italian cities of Milan, Venice and Genoa, the Hanseatic ports of Hamburg and Lubeck and the international towns of Antwerp, Bruges and Geneva were acting as bankers; lending and receiving vast sums of money. Many of these transactions were done on paper or parchment and took the form of promissory notes. A merchant "A" would give a note to a banker "B" promising to pay him 100 marks when his ship returned with a cargo from the East. The banker "B" might then use the note to pay goldsmith "C" for a quantity of silver or gold. Goldsmith "C" might use the note to pay farmer "D" for a quantity of corn. Finally the farmer would present the note to the original merchant "A", when the date for payment fell due, and demand 100 marks in coin. In this way promissory notes came to be accepted in much the same way that we use paper money today. Sometimes these notes might pass from hand to hand for a considerable time before they were eventually presented to the original issuer for redemption.

The earliest promissory notes would have been made of vellum, parchment or some kind of animal skin. Paper was virtually unknown outside China

until the middle of the twelfth century and came to Europe via Arabia and North Africa. Herault, in France, claims to have had the first paper mill in Europe, established in 1189. For hundreds of years thereafter paper continued to be a scarce commodity in Europe.

In England the earliest kind of paper money consisted of notes issued by goldsmiths as receipts

William Paterson, 1658–1719, founder of the Banks of England and Scotland.

for valuables deposited by merchants in their vaults. These receipts could be used as securities to get a loan, and, like promissory notes, tended to circulate quite widely as a form of currency. These receipts and promissory notes were accepted as legal tender following an Exchequer Order made by the authority of King Charles II in 1665, but another thirty years elapsed before paper money, as we understand it today, was issued in Britain.

William III, during whose reign the Bank of England was founded.

Mary II who died in the year that the Bank of England was founded, 1694.

Swedish Paper Money

The first paper money to be issued in Europe made its appearance in 1661. The Stockholm Bank of Sweden issued credit notes (*kreditivsedlar*) in place of the copper currency which was rapidly losing its value. The idea of producing these notes originated with Johan Palmstruch, a Dutchman living in the Latvian city of Riga (which was then a dependency of Sweden). Palmstruch put forward this idea in 1652. His notes were the first bank notes in the modern sense and not like the previous receipts given by goldsmiths and merchant bankers for specific deposits. They were current in the hand of the bearer and did not earn interest, as the promissory notes often did.

None of the first issue of *kreditivsedlar* has survived and fewer than a dozen specimens of the issues of 1662 and 1663 are now in existence, all in various museum collections. The issue of 1666, however, is much more plentiful, though this was the last to appear. These notes seem to have been readily accepted by Swedish businessmen, being much more convenient to handle than the cumbersome copper-plate money, but the Stockholm Bank gave way to the temptation of over-issuing. As early

Charles Montagu, 1st Earl of Halifax, 1661–1715, who supported Paterson in starting the Bank of England.

as 1663 the Bank was unable to redeem its notes and two years later the Swedish government decided that they should be abolished. The last issue was redeemable in silver thalers, since copper went out of circulation in 1665–6.

Early Paper Money in England and France

Paper money became popular at the end of the seventeenth century in Britain and France, thanks to the efforts of two Scotsmen. William Paterson founded the Bank of England in 1694 and the Bank of Scotland the following year. His fellow-countryman, John Law, founded the first French bank, the *Banque Generale*, in 1716. Both men realised the convenience and advantages of paper money and were responsible for the first issues of bank notes on both sides of the English Channel.

The earliest notes of the Bank of England were issued in 1695 and were in denominations of £10, £20, £30, £40, £50 and £100. Altogether some 12,000 notes were issued in 1695–6. The notes were large in size and beautifully printed in black copper-plate on white paper made of a mixture of linen rags and cotton. The date, bearer's name and cashier's signature were entered in hand-writing,

while the rest was printed. In the top centre was a little picture of Britannia seated and holding a spear and an olive branch. At her side was a shield bearing the cross of St George and at her feet was a pile of coins. At first the value of the note was printed, but later issues showed the amount in handwriting. The same basic design was retained for the higher-value Bank of England notes until 1956. Many people will recall the old-style "white" fivers. Partly because of their high value and partly on account of fear of forgery, tradesmen and shop-keepers used to insist on their customers writing their names and addresses on these notes whenever they offered them in transactions.

After founding the *Banque Generale*, John Law formed the French Mississippi Company of Louisiana in 1718 and speculation in its shares was equalled only by the British South Sea Company. Like the latter, the bubble burst in 1720 and Law (who by this time had been appointed Comptroller General of France) had to flee the country. Under Law the *Banque Generale* also issued its own notes, but these were quite ordinary in appearance. Apart from their serial number, which was written in by hand, the notes were printed in black on white paper and promised the bearer on demand various sums in *livres Tournois* coined in silver. Examples of these notes, issued at Paris between 1716 and 1720, are now quite scarce. Law had several theories regarding economics and though he was discredited in 1720 his ideas survived him, to cause untold misery and financial chaos to his adopted country. He had proposed a land currency equal to the value of the land and to the value of actual coined money without being subject, as was coined money, to a fall in value. This system was adopted by the French government, when on the verge of bankruptcy, and this precipitated the Revolution of 1789–92.

Paper money known as *Assignats* were issued in 1789, their value backed by the land confiscated from the Church at the outset of the Revolution. Each note had a nominal value of 100 livres bearing interest at 5 per cent. A total of 4,000 million livres was put into circulation in the first issue alone. Within a year the interest had been reduced to 3 per cent and a subsequent issue of 800 million livres bore no interest at all. The output of paper money grew faster and faster; by the middle of 1794 a total of 8,000 millions had been issued, but within two years the amount in circulation had spiralled to 45,500 millions. The value of the *assignat* fell rapidly. Even the earlier issues were reckoned to be worth only 20 livres in coin for every 100 in

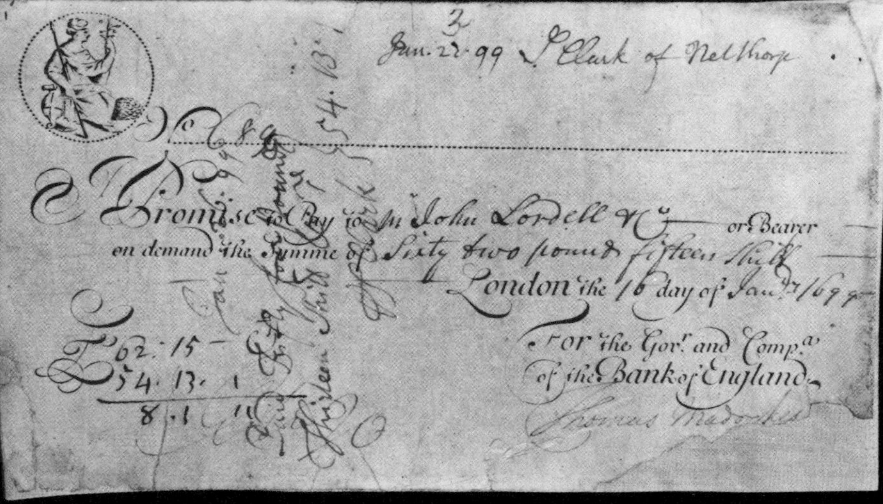

3

Jan. 22-99 J. Clark of Nelthrope

No 684

Promise to pay to Mr John Lordell & Co or Bearer
on demand the Summe of Sixty two pound fifteen Shill
London the 16 day of Jan.ry 1699

£62:15-
54:13:1
8:1:11

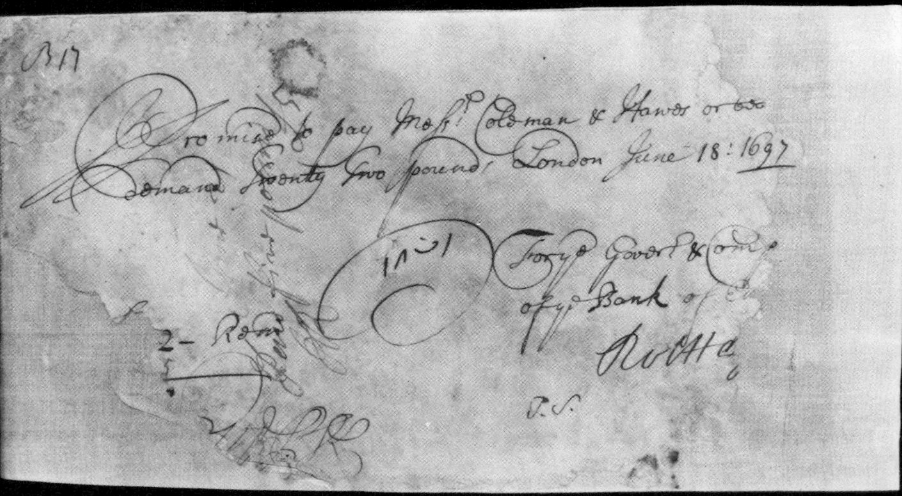

For the Gov.r and Comp.a
of the Bank of England

Thomas Madockes

B17

Promise to pay Messrs Coldman & Hawes or
demand Twenty two pounds London June 18: 1697

For ye Gov.r & Comp.a
of ye Bank of E.d

Robt Co

T.S.

ONE

BANK No. 9478   No. 9478

24 Feb.ry 1793

Promise to pay to Mr Ab. Newland, or bearer
on Demand the Sum of One Pound
London the 24 day of Feb.ry 179

For the Gov: and Comp.a of the
BANK OF ENGLAND

£ One

Ent.d W. Forist

PAID
4 JUN 1920

A totally hand-written Bank of England note of 1697 for the sum of £72.00. It is signed by Robert Hedges, the second cashier.

A Bank of England note of 1699 showing the earliest vignette, for the sum of £62.15s.

A Bank of England £1 note issued during the restriction period of 1797–1821.

The Bank of England.

The Storming of the Bastille, a contemporary print.

paper. By 1793 the depreciation had reached 97 per cent. The government body known as the *Directoire* fixed the value of the *assignats* at a thirtieth of their original value and then reduced it to a hundredth.

When the *assignats* sank to utter worthlessness the government had recourse to territorial money orders known as *mandats* which were put into circulation at the rate of one for 30 *assignats*. These notes were no more trusted than the *assignats* and actually depreciated more rapidly. In many cases the *mandats* were worthless before they could even get into circulation. The *Directoire* finally gave up its experiments in paper money in 1797 when *assignats* and *mandats* were called in and exchanged for coin in the ratio of one livre coin for every 3,000 livres paper money. Genuine examples of these interesting mementoes of the French Revolution are plentiful and can still be picked up for quite small sums, but there are numerous counterfeits and bogus items which were produced to deceive collectors.

2 BRITISH PAPER MONEY

By the close of the seventeenth century, London was becoming one of the most important trading and commercial centres of the world. Its rich merchants and goldsmiths, many of whom are remembered to this day in the names of the banks —Martin's, Lloyd's, Barclay's, Glyn Mills, Cox and King's—had been issuing promissory notes and receipts for valuables for many years and these pieces of paper were accepted as if they were actually money. By 1680 there were about fifty of these merchants whose promissory notes were readily acceptable. With the rapid development of England as a trading nation it became necessary to establish some sort of national bank. In 1694, during the reign of William III and Mary, the Bank of England was founded by William Paterson, a Scotsman whose proposals were readily endorsed by Charles Montagu, the Chancellor of the Exchequer at that time. In the year of its foundation, the Bank of England issued only a few notes, for £20 and £50, and these were entirely hand-written, like the merchants' notes.

The first printed notes were released on 5 June 1695 and measured 4·4 by 8·2 inches. These notes, already referred to, had a rather short life and are consequently now very scarce. They were withdrawn from circulation because a cunning forger had obtained a quantity of paper from the same supplier as the Bank, and then produced excellent

A bank-scare of 1888; depositors claiming their money from the National Penny Bank.

The Bank of England issued new £1 notes in 1917 the year of this battle at Messines.

imitations of the notes. The Bank got round this problem by using a different type of paper, with a marbled pattern of the sort which is often found in the end-papers of nineteenth century books. As a further precaution against fraud these marbled paper bank notes were cut in half and only one half given to the customer. When the note came back to the bank it could be checked against the other half to prove that it was genuine. None of these marbled notes has survived, but the practice of cutting notes in half continued for some time. Later notes may be found with curved cuts between the two halves as well as a printed design. A watermark was adopted as a security measure in 1697. Watermarks are caused by a slight thinning of the paper at a particular point, so that they show up when the paper is held up to the light. They result from the use of special wires or strips of metal fixed to the dandy roll which is rotated over the paper pulp during the manufacture of the paper. Specially watermarked paper has been used for Bank of England notes ever since then.

The bank notes from 1696 to 1725 had the amounts written in by hand and they could be issued for any odd amount from £10 upwards. Regular denominations were re-introduced in 1725 and notes were issued for £20, £30, £40, £50, £60, £70, £80, £90, £100, £200, £300, £400, £500 and £1,000. In 1759 notes for £10 and £15 were added, and six years later a £25 note was issued. The Bank of England did not issue notes of lower value, and it was left to the many private banks, which mushroomed in the eighteenth century, to remedy this deficiency. For much of the eighteenth century there was an acute shortage of coins, especially of copper farthings, halfpence and pennies. Tradesmen and innkeepers often issued copper tokens which served as low-denomination coins, while the numerous banks issued notes in denominations of one penny upwards.

At a time when many people were illiterate, a tenpence note of a private bank could be—and often was—mistaken for a Bank of England £10 note. Some of the less scrupulous banks produced notes which were not dissimilar to the Bank of England notes and though they were inscribed at a fraction of the amount, these were sometimes palmed off on simple country folk as though they were £10 notes. In addition to these confidence tricks, many of the country bank notes were easily forged despite the stern penalties (including hanging in some cases) for those convicted of forgery. In 1777, an Act of Parliament was passed forbidding the provincial banks from issuing notes for amounts under £5. While the French were wrestling with *assignats* and *mandats*, British provincial banks came and went with astonishing rapidity. Over a hundred of them crashed in 1793 alone.

The Crisis of 1825–6

In that year the Bank of England issued its first £5 notes and four years later the Act of 1777 was repealed in order that the Bank could issue £1 and £2 notes. Because of the wars with France, gold was in short supply and paper money became increasingly necessary. During this period the provincial banks enjoyed new prosperity, and there were more than 700 of them in existence by 1810, issuing a staggering total of some £30 millions each year. The wartime boom was followed inevitably by a slump. In the decade after the Battle of Waterloo, many of the smaller banks either vanished overnight or were taken over by their larger competitors. Most of these banks had been tempted into issuing far too many notes without the assets to cover them. So long as the country's prosperity was increasing rapidly, public confidence was maintained but when the slump began in 1821 more and more of these little banks went out of business. The situation deteriorated rapidly. In November 1825 a large number of companies went bankrupt after a wave of speculation in shares. This crisis caused a run on the banks, as people tried to withdraw their savings in gold and silver.

The situation became worse when the provincial banks could not get at the funds which they, in turn, had deposited with the major London banks, either because of the slow communications of the time or because the big London banks were themselves under pressure. When one of the big banks failed in December 1825 no fewer than 44 provincial banks crashed as a result. By 17 December, four of the biggest London banks had ceased payment and the Bank of England's gold reserve was down to about a million pounds. To alleviate the situation the Bank hastily issued a large quantity of £1 notes which had been partially prepared for release in 1821 but had never been put into circulation. These notes bore the date 1821 at the top, but were dated 20 December 1825 at the foot. They circulated for a few months, until the Bank of England had been able to replenish its stocks of gold with the assistance of Rothschilds, the French merchant bankers. From then until 1928 the Bank of England did not issue notes below £5 in face value.

In the economic crisis of 1825–6, hundreds of country banks went out of business. They are remembered today solely by the interesting notes which they issued, not wisely but too well. They were produced at a time when new processes such as lithography and typography were being developed and improvements were being made in the more traditional copper-plate or recess technique. Fine artists and engravers were readily available and they combined to produce some very attractive bank notes. Every town and city of any importance could boast at least one bank and its notes often reproduced the civic coat of arms or some outstanding local landmark. The Shrewsbury Bank featured the city's ancient gate-way on its notes, while the Torquay Bank depicted a fine view of the port. The banks of Nottingham, Bolton and Richmond showed the castles which dominate these towns. Many of the county banks featured agricultural subjects, as befitted enterprises serving farming communities. Others depicted coal-mines or new-fangled means of transport such as paddle-steamers and railway trains.

The notes of the 'broken' banks are interesting because of the marks stamped on them which indicate that they were produced as evidence in the bankruptcy courts. Many of them also have marks on them indicating how much was actually paid out to creditors in the end. Some notes have as many as four or five of these stamps showing that creditors were often paid almost the full amount eventually, after the banks liquidated their assets.

The Bank Charter Act of 1844 limited the number of banks which could issue their own notes to 72 joint stock banks and 207 others. Their total note

Aberystwyth and Tregaron Bank, £1, 1814.

Huddersfield Bank, £1, 1816.

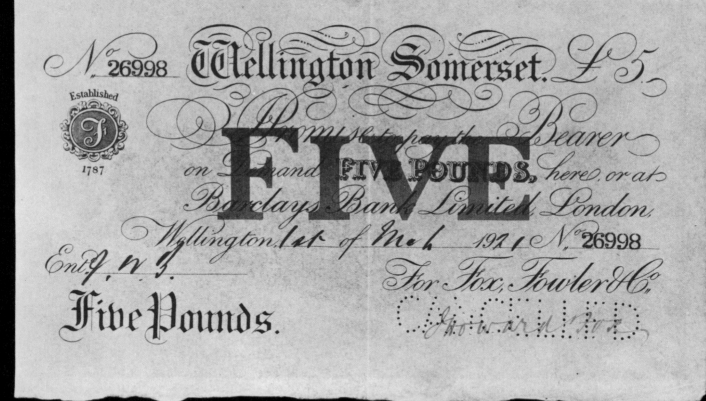

Wellington Somerset £5 note of March 1921—one of the last of the private banknote issues in England. The decorative pattern on the back is inscribed with the names of the towns in which the bank operated.

The £1, £5, £10, £20 and £100 notes of the Royal Bank of Scotland's issue of 1972.

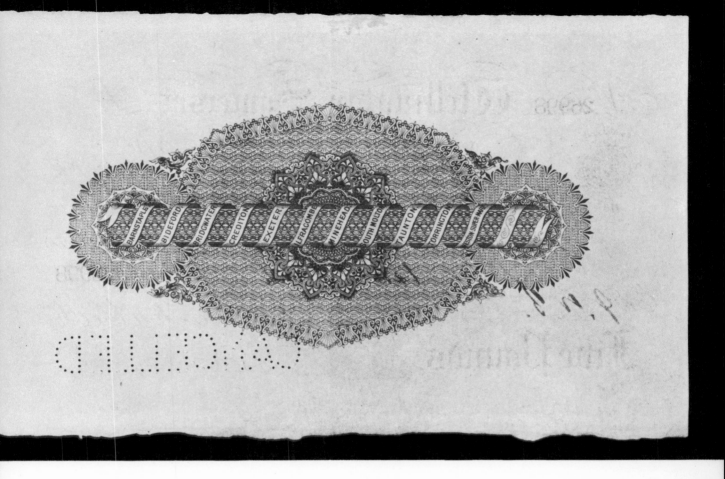

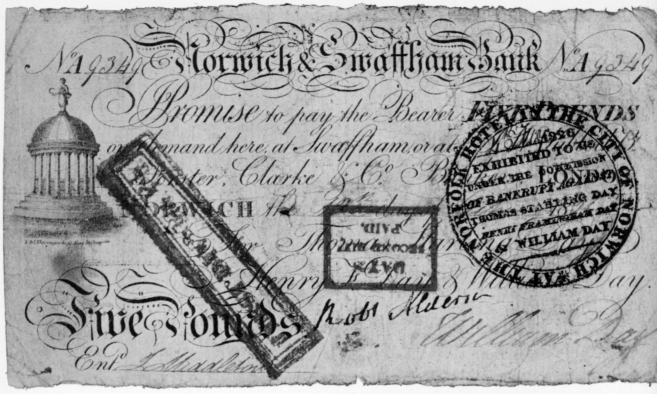

Norwich and Swaffham Bank, £5 of 1824. Note the marks struck across the face to indicate that the bank crashed in 1826 and subsequently paid out two dividends to its creditors.

issue was limited to £8,500,000. During the rest of the nineteenth century, the number of note-issuing banks gradually dwindled. Under the terms of the 1844 Act, no bank with offices in London could issue its own notes. As more and more of the provincial banks were taken over by London-based banks their privilege of issuing bank notes was curtailed. The last of the independent note-issuing banks was Fox, Fowler & Co. of Wellington, Somerset which gave up this privilege in 1921 when it amalgamated with Lloyds Bank.

Private bank notes continued to appear in the Isle of Man until 1961 when the Manx government took over the privilege hitherto enjoyed by the Isle of Man Bank, Lloyds, Martins and Barclays. Since then bank notes have been issued by the Isle of Man Bank under the authority of the Isle of Man Government.

Scotland and Ireland have been issuing their own bank notes since 1696 and 1783 respectively and since the Bank Charter Act of 1844 did not apply to these countries the private banks retain the right to issue their own notes. At the end of the Second World War there were still about a dozen Scottish banks issuing distinctive notes in denominations from £1 upwards, but as a result of mergers and take-overs the number has now fallen to three banks producing up to six denominations each. In

Northern Ireland six banks still issue their own notes. In the Channel Islands, bank notes have been produced by the private banks since 1797, while the States of Guernsey issued the first government notes in 1826. Of particular interest are the set of notes, ranging from sixpence to £5, issued by Guernsey and Jersey during the German occupation of the Second World War. Attractive bank notes are produced to this day by the State banks in both bailiwicks.

Throughout much of the nineteenth century, gold was fairly plentiful, largely as a result of the exploitation of the goldfields in Australia and South Africa. Britain returned to the gold standard in 1816 (when the sovereign of 20 shillings replaced the guinea of 21 shillings as the standard unit of currency) and while gold was plentiful there was little incentive or desire for paper money in everyday transactions.

Treasury Notes

The entry of Britain into the First World War almost caused a financial crisis. Fortunately the declaration of war, on 4 August 1914, coincided with the August Bank Holiday and to avert the crisis the government merely extended the holiday by a further two days. When the banks re-opened on 7 August, they found that gold sovereigns and half sovereigns had been replaced by an issue of paper money arranged by the Treasury, £1 notes, in black, were released on 7 August and 10 shilling notes, in red, appeared a week later. They bore the portrait of King George V on the left and the value in figures on the right. The value, in words, appeared across the centre. At the top was a five-line inscription in Gothic script: "These Notes are a Legal Tender for a payment of any amount. Issued by the Lords Commissioners of His Majesty's Treasury under Authority of Act of Parliament." The serial number occupied the lower left of the notes while a facsimile of the signature of John Bradbury, Secretary to the Treasury, appeared in the bottom right-hand corner. These notes were distributed by the Bank of England and the other banks throughout the British Isles on behalf of the Treasury and were officially known as Treasury notes. Unofficially they were quickly nicknamed 'Bradburys', after the man whose signature they bore.

The Treasury notes were typographed by Waterlow and Sons, a firm of security printers which had been engaged in the production of bank notes, postage stamps and security documents for many years. Because of the sudden decision to print these notes suitable bank note paper was not available and therefore the first series of £1 and 10s notes had to be printed on paper normally used for postage stamps. This accounts for the curious all-over watermark of the royal monogram, usually employed on British stamps of that period. This paper was quite unsatisfactory for bank notes and a second series, printed on proper bank note paper, was speedily ordered. The second series had entirely new designs; the name of the country appeared for the first time and was rendered as UNITED KINGDOM OF GREAT BRITAIN AND IRELAND. In the upper left-hand corner there was a profile of King George V, while an oval badge showing St George and the Dragon appeared in the upper right-hand corner. The inscription on these notes was altered to read: "Ten shillings (or one pound) currency notes are legal tender for the payment of any amount." Below came the authority for the issue of the notes, and the signature of John Bradbury as before.

New £1 notes were introduced in February 1917 and 10s notes in November 1918. Both designs had a much larger profile of King George V on the right while the 10s featured Britannia and the £1 had St George and the Dragon on the left. The 10s note had a plain back, bearing the value, but the £1

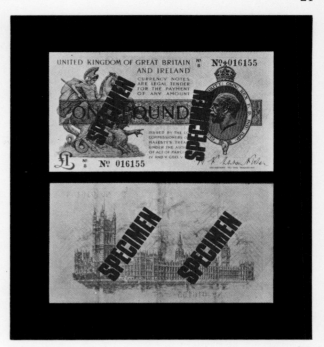

British £1 note of the same series, portraying King George V and St George slaying the Dragon. The back depicts the Houses of Parliament at Westminster.

Isle of Man 50p note, showing a Viking long-ship on the reverse.

depicted the Houses of Parliament on the reverse side. In October 1919 notes began to appear with the signature of N. K. Warren Fisher in place of that of John Bradbury, though the old nickname persisted well into the 1920s.

After the First World War there were several subtle changes in the Treasury notes. First the

Manx £5 note, 1973. The reverse shows Castle Rushen, ancient seat of
the Manx government.

British £5 note issued in 1963, using a full-face portrait of the Queen.

The reverse side of the current British £5 note, portraying the Duke of
Wellington and a scene from the Battle of Waterloo.

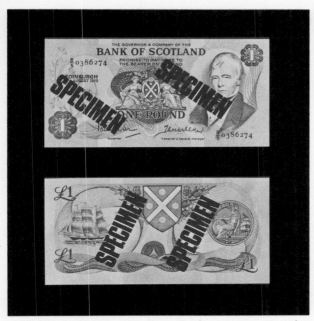

Bank of Scotland £1, issued in 1970. The front portrays Sir Walter Scott, while the reverse features Britannia and a sailing ship.

British 10 shilling note, issued after the Second World War. The seated full-face portrait of Britannia was a traditional feature of Bank of England notes from the eighteenth century.

Sir John Lavery, 1869–1944, designed the first banknotes for the Irish Free State in 1928.

British 10 shilling note, introduced during the First World War. Note the inscription UNITED KINGDOM OF GREAT BRITAIN AND IRELAND. After 1921 this was changed to NORTHERN IRELAND.

Isle of Man 10 shilling note. A similar design, in different colours, was used for the decimal 50 pence note introduced in 1971.

Leith Banking Company, 20 shillings, 1837. The date, serial numbers and signatures were entered in manuscript.

watermark was slightly altered on the pound notes, then the abbreviation "No." in front of the serial number on the 10s notes was omitted. Early in 1928 the name of the country was changed on the notes and the word NORTHERN inserted in front of IRELAND. This took into account the fact that, since December 1921, the United Kingdom had included only Northern Ireland and not the whole of Ireland as before. Notes with this inscription had a fairly short life as they ceased production in November 1928, when the Bank of England took over responsibility for £1 and 10s notes from the Treasury. The Treasury notes continued to circulate until the end of July 1933, when they were called in and ceased to be legal tender.

Later Bank of England Notes

After the economic crisis of 1825–6 and the collapse of so many provincial banks, the Bank of England decided to open branches in the major cities of England and Wales. The first branches opened in Gloucester, Manchester and Swansea in 1826, while branches were opened in Birmingham, Bristol, Exeter, Leeds and Liverpool the following year. In 1834 the Exeter branch was closed and transferred to Plymouth. Subsequent branches were established at Portsmouth, Cardiff, Leicester, Hull, Norwich, Newcastle and Southampton, and a branch was also opened at Belfast in Ireland. These branches issued their own bank notes, similar to the London issues, but with the name of the respective city inscribed. These notes could be cashed at the branch of origin or at the Bank of England in London, but not at other branches. Branch bank notes continued to appear in denominations up to £500 throughout the nineteenth century and, in some cases, they survived as late as the outbreak of the Second World War. During this period, however, many of the branches were closed down and at the present time only the branches in Birmingham, Bristol, Leeds, Liverpool, Manchester, Newcastle and Southampton are still open.

After 1854 both London and branch issues of Bank of England notes bore the same signature of

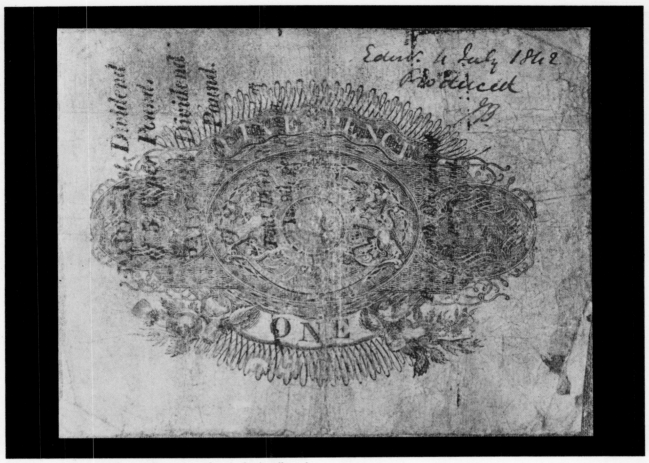

The reverse side of a Leith 20 shilling note. After the bank collapsed various dividends were paid out to holders of these notes, and the amounts were stamped on the back of the notes.

the Chief Cashier, while the name of the Cashier as payee was dropped and the phrase "the Bearer on demand" was substituted. In 1855 the full-face portrait of Britannia was redesigned by Daniel MacLise. The MacLise portrait of the seated Britannia continued to appear on £5 notes until 1956 and on the £1 and 10s notes until 1960 and 1961 respectively.

In November 1928 the Bank of England took over responsibility for issuing £1 and 10s notes, but discontinued notes with a face value above £100. While the notes of £5 and above continued the tradition of black on white, the new £1 notes were printed in green and the 10s notes appeared in brown. In 1940 the colours of these notes were altered to blue and mauve respectively and, at the same time, a thin metal strip was incorporated in the paper as a security device. The Bank's printing works in London were bombed during the Blitz of September 1940 and production had to be shifted to emergency premises at Overton and Whitchurch in Hampshire. The wartime bank notes were pro-

duced by offset-lithography instead of recess-printing and differ from pre-Blitz printings in minor details and shades.

Heinrich Himmler, head of the Gestapo and one of the chief Nazis in wartime Germany, initiated a plan to destroy the British economy by forging Bank of England notes. With typical German thoroughness the project went ahead in 1940–1. A mill at Spechthausen near Berlin was given the task of producing the special paper used for the £5 and higher value notes. A team of former bankers, printers and forgers was recruited from the prisons and concentration camps of Germany and installed at special premises in Sachsenhausen concentration camp where forgeries of a very high quality were eventually produced. Notes from £5 to £50 were produced with authentic signatures, branch marks and serial numbers. Even post office marks, branch endorsements and the names and addresses of "customers" were added to these notes to lend them authenticity. Comparatively few of these forgeries got into circulation. One man who

Promissory note of the Chief Treasury of Wales (Black Sheep Bank), 1971, featuring a view of Snowdonia.

Bank of Scotland, £5, issued in 1970.

Manx £10 note, 1973, featuring a view of Peel Castle painted about 1830.

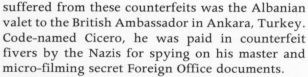

Clydesdale Bank, Scotland, series of 1971. The front of each note portrays a famous person, while scenes from their life appear on the reverse. The £1 note portrays King Robert Bruce and a scene from the Battle of Bannockburn, 1314.

British 10 shilling note of the last issue. Banknotes of this denomination were superseded in 1969 by the decimal 50 pence coin.

suffered from these counterfeits was the Albanian valet to the British Ambassador in Ankara, Turkey. Code-named Cicero, he was paid in counterfeit fivers by the Nazis for spying on his master and micro-filming secret Foreign Office documents.

As soon as it was realised that forged bank notes were in circulation the Bank of England promptly withdrew all notes of £10 and above from circulation in 1943 and changed the type of paper used for the £5 notes in 1944. £5 notes with a metal strip were introduced in 1945. In May 1945 notes from £10 to £1,000 ceased to be legal tender—shortly before the discovery of millions of German counterfeits in the Austrian Tyrol. In 1948 the prewar

colours of the £1 and 10s notes were re-introduced. The postwar notes may be identified by the inclusion of the metal strip, apart from the different signatures found on these notes.

An entirely new £5 note, predominantly blue in colour and only slightly larger than the £1 note, was designed by Stephen Gooden and introduced in 1957. The helmeted profile of Britannia and a lion guarding a key were featured on the front and back respectively. The design of the £5 symbol on the back was slightly altered in 1961 and two years later a new £5 note, bearing a portrait of Queen Elizabeth, was released. The Queen's portrait appeared on green £1 notes introduced on 3 March

Peel Castle, Isle of Man.

1960 and on brown 10s notes issued on 12 November 1961. For the first time in over twenty years, notes of higher value were put into circulation when, in February 1964, a large purple-brown £10 note appeared.

A £20 in purple, with green, blue and gold tints, was introduced on 9 July 1970 and was the first of an entirely new series. A new portrait of the Queen appeared on the front while the back showed the statue of William Shakespeare from the Kent Memorial in Westminster Abbey. Early in 1972 a new £5 note, predominantly blue in colour, was issued; the front of the note was similar to the £20 in design but the Duke of Wellington, Commander

in Chief of the British Army at the Battle of Waterloo, was portrayed on the back. The 10s note was discontinued in 1970, with the approach of decimal currency, and its place has since been taken by the seven-sided 50 pence coin. New £1 and £10 notes have not yet appeared, at the time of writing, but may be released in 1976 and 1975 respectively.

With the release of the new £20 and £5 notes, we can expect more interesting and artistic designs in Bank of England notes than has hitherto been the case. For many years the Treasury and Bank of England notes were rather insipid in their designs and very conservative in the subjects depicted—St George, Britannia, the Houses of Parliament and the

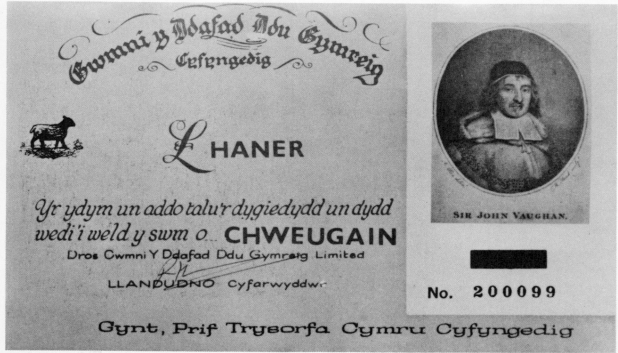

The *Chwarter Bunt* or *Goron*, *Haner Bunt* or *Chweugain*, *Bunt* and *Dwy Bunt* notes of the Welsh Black Sheep Company. In English, these are 25p, 50p, £1 and £2. They are from the 1971 issue.

reigning sovereign. It was left to the Scottish banks to introduce more colourful and varied subjects. Apart from the Bank of Scotland itself, whose notes were rather dull, comparatively crudely printed and in a wishy-washy shade of yellow-brown, the Scottish banks vied with each other in the richness of the colours on their banknotes and the variety of subjects shown. Busy shipyard scenes on the Clyde contrasted with forests and mountain streams, St Giles Cathedral in Edinburgh and the road and

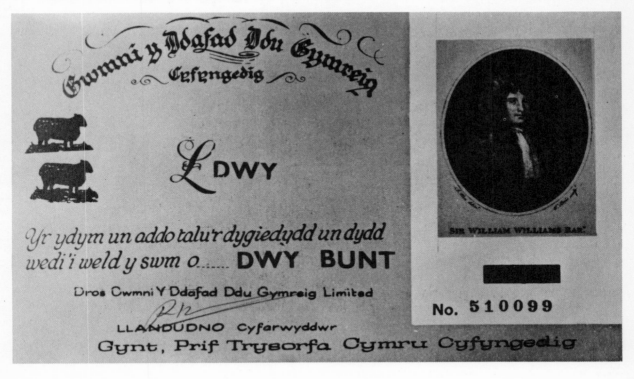

railway bridges of the Firth of Forth contrasted with the portraits of famous Scots such as Robert Burns, Sir Walter Scott, King Robert the Bruce and the industrialist David Dale. Lions, thistles and other symbolic elements were represented.

The Irish banks have also produced some very attractive designs. Among the more recent issues is the £5 of the Northern Bank, which shows a Belfast shipyard scene, flanked by pictures of dairy cattle and a flax mill, representing the main indus-

British £20 note, introduced in 1971, portraying Queen Elizabeth in state robes. St George slaying the dragon and a 'medallion' portrait of

Britannia also appear on the front. The reverse portrays William Shakespeare and the famous balcony scene from *Romeo and Juliet*.

Isle of Man £1, featuring the Annigoni portrait of Queen Elizabeth.

The reverse side of the British £10 note, featuring a stylised lion against a background of *guilloche* engraving—a popular device to defeat forgery.

tries of Ulster. The notes, issued by the Bank of Ireland in Dublin, range from 10s to £100 and feature the heads of mythical figures from the Tontine Building in Dublin, on the back. The colleen with a harp, featured on the front of these notes, is actually the wife of the late Sir John Lavery, the famous portrait painter, who was responsible for the design of the series in 1928 after the foundation of the Irish Free State. The Irish notes have drawn on the ancient monastic art of Ireland for inspiration and the use of inscriptions

in Gaelic as well as English gives them a somewhat outlandish appearance. It is interesting to note that the notes of the Bank of England and the Irish banks are accepted in the Irish Republic, and republican banknotes circulate freely in Ulster. Scottish, English and Irish notes are used in the Isle of Man, which also has its own notes, but in England Irish and Manx notes are not permitted, and the notes of the Scottish banks, though legal tender, are often accepted with a bad grace!

Deal Bank, £5.

Whitby Old Bank, 1 guinea (£1.05) unissued blanks. The dates, serial
numbers and signatures would have been entered in manuscript before
issue to the public.

Welsh Banknotes

In the nineteenth century there were several
provincial banks operating in Wales, but, like their
counterparts in England, they gradually died out,
went bankrupt or amalgamated with London-based
banks, and thus their distinctive notes came to an
end. On 6 September 1969, however, the banking
enterprise *Cwmni y Ddafad Ddu Cymreig* (Welsh
Black Sheep Company) of Llandudno began issuing
promissory notes in denominations of 5s, 10s, £1,
£5 and £10. These handsome notes feature a painting of Caernarvon Castle on the back and portray

various famous Welshmen on the front. The
inscriptions are given in Welsh—*bunt* (pound),
chweugain or *haner bunt* (ten shillings or half
pound) and *goron* or *chwarter bunt* (crown or
quarter pound). The design of these notes was
modified in 1971, following the abolition of the
stamp duty by which a tax of twopence was levied
on each note. At the same time the £10 and £5 notes
were withdrawn and a £2 (*dwy bunt*) note was
introduced. The Welsh Black Sheep notes make a
colourful and unusual addition to any banknote
collection.

3 AMERICAN PAPER MONEY

The American Continent is a rich field for the collector of paper money. The colourful notes of many Latin American countries sadly reflect the political and economic upheavals of that part of the world. As governments toppled and banks crashed, paper money became worthless. Consequently many of the attractive banknotes of South and Central America are still reasonably plentiful at low cost. At the other extreme is the paper money issued under the authority of the United States since 1861, all of which is still legal tender at its face value. Some United States notes, in fact, are worth more than their face value because they bear interest. Old American notes are, of course, invariably worth very much more than their face value, because of their popularity with collectors.

The United States is the only country in the world which has never called in and demonetised obsolete paper money issued under government authority. In this sense a collection of United States notes is unique, since it is protected against changing fashions in collecting. If the worst comes to the worst the collector can always redeem his collection at face value, thanks to the policy of the United States government and its Treasury Department.

Colonial Currency

Long before the crisis of the Civil War compelled the United States government to issue paper money in 1861, there had been various types of non-metallic currency in what is now the United States.

A Red Indian Chief in full tribal regalia.

The original thirteen colonies had paper money, some of which dated back to the late seventeenth century. The earliest example of paper money was produced by the Massachusetts Bay Colony in December 1690, mainly for the payment of troops recruited for the expedition against the Jacobites in Canada. Gold and silver coins, mostly from the Spanish mints in Central and South America, circulated in the British colonies in the eighteenth century, but paper money was used from time to time, for the payment of soldiers on colonial wars and campaigns. Thus South Carolina issued paper money in connection with the campaigns against the Spaniards and the Indians in Florida. Connecticut, New Hampshire, New Jersey and New York all issued paper money in 1709 for the payment of troops fighting the French in the American campaigns of the War of the Austrian Succession. The governors of the British colonies had strict instructions to limit the issue of paper money to times of military emergency. These early examples of colonial currency are extremely scarce.

More common are the colonial notes issued during the American War of Independence (1776–83). The Continental Congress, which met at Philadelphia in 1775, authorised an issue of paper money inscribed "The United Colonies". The so-called continental currency was redesignated by a resolution of Congress in April 1778 and the inscription changed to "The United States". The denominations found on these notes ranged from sterling (sixpence and upwards) to Spanish milled dollars. To make the notes more acceptable to the

An American colonial note for 4 shillings, issued in January 1776 shortly before the Declaration of Independence.

Reverse of the above, showing a wheat-sheaf and the warning "To Counterfeit is Death".

colonists, they were actually signed by leading political personalities of the day; collectors are particularly keen on those notes bearing the signatures of the men who signed the Declaration of Independence, the Articles of Confederation or the United States Constitution. Despite the turbulent conditions under which these notes were produced they were often well produced and sometimes quite artistic in appearance. Among the artists responsible for these early notes was Paul Revere, the famous silversmith, who commanded the colonial militia known as the Minute Men and who took a prominent part in American politics during the War.

From 1775 onwards, the individual colonies, and later the states, issued their own paper money, often in odd amounts. Paul Revere designed and engraved notes for Massachusetts and New Hampshire. His 'man with sword' notes showed a colonist brandishing a sabre in one hand and holding a copy of Magna Charta [sic] in the other. These notes were inscribed "Issued in defence of American Liberty" and also bore lengthy mottoes in Latin. Other notes of the revolutionary period bore such slogans as "Either death or an honourable life" and "Driven by hostile force".

The confused state of American politics at the beginning of the War of Independence is reflected in the notes, issued by Delaware, New Jersey and Pennsylvania among others, which claimed to be made under the authority of King George III. Georgia even had a five shilling note embellished with the British crown, but this was soon dropped from the design! Typical of the inscriptions on the colonial notes of this transitional period is "This bill . . . is emitted by a Law of the Colony of New Jersey, passed in the fourteenth Year of the Reign of His Majesty King George the Third, Dated March 25, 1776."

As the war progressed metallic currency became scarce and paper money was issued in vast quantities, particularly for the payment of the troops serving under George Washington. The inscriptions on these notes are very interesting, they promised to pay the bearer in Spanish dollars at the rate of six shillings each at the end of the war. The notes issued by Connecticut were more explicit, they promised to pay the bearer in gold or silver coin, "at or before the End of one Year after the Expiration of the present War, or a Cessation of Hostilities between Great Britain and these United States, with the Interest at Six per Cent per Annum . . .". The Connecticut notes were the only

Confederate States of America, $20 note issued at Richmond, 1862.
Note the promise to pay the bearer "six months after the ratification
of a treaty of peace".

ones to make actual reference to the enemy country. The colonies were not above using their paper money for propaganda purposes, sometimes depicting the wicked King George trampling on Magna Carta or setting fire to American villages.

State Banknotes

Although the United States government did not feel the necessity to issue paper money before 1861, the individual states thought otherwise. After the War of Independence and the foundation of the United States, the country made rapid economic progress. As there was not enough currency in the form of gold and silver coins to go round, the states filled the gap by authorising banks to issue paper money. Charters were granted by the states to private banks within their territory and these banks were authorised to print and circulate their own dollar notes. Theoretically the backing for this paper currency was the amount of gold and silver on deposit in the bank. Unfortunately this rule was seldom observed, and within a short space of time these banks were churning out paper money as fast as the printing press could produce it.

Whenever there was a financial crisis (and this seemed to happen quite often) and people took their gold and silver out of the banks, these banks had no alternative but to close their doors and go broke. When this happened the paper money of the broken banks became worthless. This happened so often that today collectors use the term 'broken banknotes' to denote the issues of the old-time state banks. Because they were worthless in terms of actual face value, these notes were at one time very common; even now, when the number of collectors is rising rapidly, they can still be picked up for a small sum. They were usually artistically designed and beautifully printed. Like the country banks of Britain, they often allude to local land-marks, historical events and personalities or depict aspects of agriculture, mining and industry of particular significance to that area. Several thous-and different notes are thought to exist. It has been estimated that there were over 1,600 different banks in 34 states, at the outbreak of the Civil War in 1861. With their portraits of Washington, Jefferson and other outstanding national figures, local celebrities, Indian chiefs, negro slaves, cow-boys, miners and cotton-planters, early locomotives and river steam-boats, they provide a fascinating illustration of the American way of life in the pioneer days of that great country.

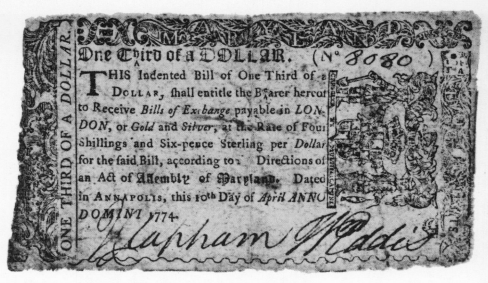

Three American banknotes of the colonial era: third, one and half dollar notes issued by Maryland, 1767–74.

The Confederate States

Both sides in the American Civil War of 1861–5 quickly found themselves desperately short of gold, silver and even copper coins and both had recourse to interesting makeshifts (discussed below in Chapter 8). Inevitably both sides turned to paper money as a way out of their difficulties but, whereas the Union's paper money retained its value as it does to this day, the Confederacy was forced by mounting inflation to issue more and more paper which plunged in value as the war progressed. By 1865 when the Confederate States were forced to surrender, their paper money was declared to be valueless. Many Southern fortunes were lost overnight and for a very long time Confederate money was regarded as a joke. Nowadays, however, collectors take it very seriously. A Confederate dollar is now worth about two dollars in contemporary United States money and the demand for Confederate notes has encouraged unscrupulous people to forge them. Higher denominations, which were once quite worthless, have also risen in value, though the Stonewall Jackson $500 bill now has a collectors' value of about £20 in crisp condition.

The first Confederate currency, totalling $1,000,000, was authorised at Montgomery, Alabama in March 1861, the notes to be redeemed twelve months after issue and to bear interest. The notes ranged in face value from 50 cents to $1,000. The individual state banks, local chambers of commerce and savings banks also continued to issue their own notes in even greater profusion than before. The standards of design and production deteriorated as the war progressed and this encouraged counterfeiting on a grand scale. In addition many Confederate notes were imitated in the North, originally as curios or souvenirs of the war, but perhaps also with the deliberate intention of sabotaging the Southern economy, since many of these Northern counterfeits found their way to the Confederacy and circulated widely in the Southern states.

The Confederate State dollar notes portrayed Andrew Jackson, the famous general of the 1812–14 War who later became seventh president of the United States, and Confederate personalities such as President Jefferson Davis, John C. Calhoun and General Stonewall Jackson. The flag and great seal of the Confederacy and the capitol building in Richmond, Virginia were also featured. As the war dragged on the maturity dates on the notes were extended to two years "after the Ratification of a

George Washington, 1732–99, 1st President of the United States of America.

General Ulysses S. Grant, the Union General, and his staff in the field.

Treaty of Peace between the Confederate States and United States''. Unfortunately the Confederacy lost the war and the notes were never redeemed. The victorious Federal government repudiated all the financial obligations of the Confederacy by passing the Fourteenth Amendment to the Constitution, Section Four of which stated, ''But neither shall the United States, nor any State assume or pay any debt or obligation incurred in aid of insurrection or rebellion against the United States, or any claim for the loss or emancipation of any slave, but all such debts, obligations and claims shall be held illegal and void.''

After the war a young Northern girl, Anna Rush, came to Virginia with her parents on a family visit to their Southern relations. They stayed at the Powhatan Hotel where Anna got hold of some examples of the Confederate money. As a memento of her visit she asked some Confederate officers, who happened to be in the hotel, to autograph the notes. One of them, Major Jonas, wrote the following lines on the back of a note: They have since become famous, and provide a fitting epitaph to the Confederacy, its cause and its paper money:

*Representing nothing on God's
    earth now,
And naught in the waters below it,
As the pledge of a nation that's
    dead and gone,
Keep it, dear friend, and show it.*

*Show it to those who will lend an ear,
To the tale that this scrip can tell
Of liberty born of a patriot's dream,
Of a storm-cradled nation that fell.*

*Too poor to possess the precious ores,
And too much of a stranger to borrow,
We issued today our promise to pay.
And hoped to redeem on the morrow.*

*The days rolled by, and the weeks
    became years;
But our coffers were empty still;
Coin was so rare that the Treasury'd
    quake
If a dollar dropped in the till.*

A battlefield of the American Civil War 1861–5.

But the faith that was in us was strong, indeed;
And our poverty well we discerned;
And this little check represented the pay
That our suffering veterans earned.

We knew it was hardly a value in gold,
Yet as gold each soldier received it;
It gazed in our eyes with a promise to pay,
And each Southern patriot believed it.

But our boys thought little of price or of pay;
Or of bills that were overdue;
We knew that it brought us our bread today;
'Twas the best our poor country could do.

Keep it to tell our history over;
From the birth of the dream to the last;
Modest, and born of the angel Hope,
Like our hopes of success—it passed.

Among the more interesting of the private issues of the Confederacy may be mentioned the dollar note of 1862, issued by the Cherokee Nation at Tahlequan in what is now the state of Oklahoma.

The United States

Although Congress passed an Act on 17 July 1861 authorising the Treasury Department to issue paper money, there were several previous occasions on which the United States had adopted a similar expedient. Promissory notes issued by the Treasury were circulated during the War of 1812–14, the Mexican War of 1846, the 'Hard Times' of 1837–43, the great bank panic of 1857 and the unsettled economic period of 1860 immediately before the outbreak of the Civil War. These promissory notes were of temporary validity and were not intended to circulate widely in the sense that banknotes usually do. They bore interest and were redeemed by the government as soon as the emergency was over.

After the war between the states broke out, the government suspended specie (i.e. coin and bullion) payments and silver, gold and even copper coins rapidly disappeared from the scene. A total of $60 million in paper money was authorised. The first issue is known to collectors as the 'Demand Notes',

Augusta Insurance and Banking Co, 10 dollars.

since their inscription included the words "Promise to pay . . . on Demand". The Demand Notes were the original Greenbacks, so-called because of the predominantly green colouring of the back. They were unique in several respects. They were the only U.S. notes which bore neither the Treasury Seal nor the actual names of the Treasurer and the Register of the Treasury. They bore one set of serial numbers, whereas all later issues have had two, at opposite ends of the note.

Originally it was intended that the Treasurer and the Register should sign the notes in actual hand-writing, but as these busy gentlemen could not find the time to do this the task was delegated to a large team of clerks in the Treasury Department. The inscription was worded in such a way that each clerk had also to insert the words "For the" in addition to their own names. This, in itself, was a waste of time, so new plates were made with the inscriptions "For the Treasurer" and "For the Register". Demand notes with the original inscription are comparatively rare.

The Demand Notes were followed by the 'Legal Tender Notes', first released in 1862. They derive their name from the inscription "This note is a legal tender for all debts . . .". Between 1862 and 1923 there were five issues of Legal Tender Notes, with several sub-varieties. They were issued in denominations from $1 to $10,000 and rank among the most handsome of all American banknotes with attractive pictures of pioneers, Columbus sighting land, the American bison and other typically American subjects. All known examples of the $5,000 and $10,000 bills have been redeemed so none are in the hands of collectors. The Bureau of Engraving and Printing in Washington has specimens of these notes in its archives.

The 'Compound Interest Treasury Notes' are the second rarest category of United States paper money. They earned interest at six per cent, compounded twice a year for a period of three years. They were authorised in 1863 and 1864 at a time when the Civil War was going badly and the Federal government was on the verge of bankruptcy. They were issued in denominations from $10 to S1,000. The back of each note carries a table showing the rates of interest due after certain periods. They were only issued during the Civil War.

'Interest Bearing Notes' are the rarest form of United States paper money; so rare that many ardent collectors of American paper money may never see them in a lifetime of study. They were another wartime expedient and were issued with

Augusta Insurance and Banking Co., 50 dollars.

coupons attached which gave the rates of interest due. 'Refunding Certificates' were introduced in 1879 in $10 denominations earning interest at four per cent. The intention was that holders of these certificates should hang on to them indefinitely but, in 1907, Congress terminated the interest due on them. By that time the certificates, with accrued interest, would have been worth more than twice their face value. Only two or three examples are now believed to be in private hands.

The 'Silver Certificates' are more extensive and offer considerable scope for study. They first appeared in denominations from $10 to $1,000 in 1878 and continued until 1923. They were to be redeemed in silver dollars, hence their name. Altogether there were five issues of Silver Certificates; the second and all subsequent issues included lower denominations of 1, 2 and 5 dollars. The Silver Certificates had finely engraved vignettes on the back printed in black, unlike other forms of paper money which were in green. These notes were extremely interesting in the subjects they depicted. The third issue (1896), for example, is known as the 'Educational Set', since it has vignettes of History instructing Youth, Science presenting Steam and Electricity to Commerce and Electricity as the dominant force.

The 'Treasury' or 'Coin Notes' were issued as a result of the Legal Tender Act of 1890, authorising the Treasury to produce notes backed by silver bullion set aside for the purpose. To this day anyone presenting one of these notes for redemption has to be paid in silver dollars, though they are now of such a rarity that they are worth many times their face value to a collector. They were noted for the delicate engraving of the designs on their backs.

The largest and most popular category consists of 'National Bank Notes', which were issued between 1863 and 1929 in three different charter periods. They came into being as a result of the National Banking Act of 1863 which regulated the note-issuing activities of the numerous state banks. Henceforward the government granted charters to banks, permitted them to issue paper money up to 90 per cent of the value of the U.S. government bonds which the banks had previously deposited with the government as security for the notes about to be issued. Each bank had its own charter number, which appeared on all notes released after 1875. These notes were produced by the Bureau of Engraving and Printing under the same conditions as the regular Treasury series. The basic designs were the same for all banks, the only differences

Peru, 5 soles note of 1970. The front portrays the Inca chief Pachacutec and pre-Colombian artifacts, while the back shows the ruins of the fortress of Sacsahuaman.

being in the name of the bank, the bank charter number, the bank signatures and the coat of arms of the state in which the bank was located.

These notes were issued in three charter periods. The notes of the issues of 1863 and 1875 formed the first period. The fronts of these notes featured personalities and events from American history, while the backs reproduced famous American paintings in the Capitol in Washington. The notes of the second period are known as the series of 1882. The first notes of this series included the 'Brownbacks', which were produced for many of the newly chartered banks. The later issues reverted to the traditional green colouring on the back. Notes of the third period are known as the

series of 1902 and were issued to newly chartered banks and older banks renewing their charters. The National Bank Notes were released in denominations from $1 to $1,000.

The Federal Reserve Act of 1913 introduced a new kind of currency, the 'Federal Reserve Bank notes' and the 'Federal Reserve Notes'. The United States experienced a financial crisis in 1907 which led to a run on the banks. This showed up a number of weaknesses in the national banking system and in order to remedy these defects the Federal Reserve system was established. The country was divided into twelve Federal Reserve districts and the national banks were compelled to submit to district control. The Federal Reserve

Bank Notes were issued to the public through the banks which were obliged to redeem them when necessary. The Federal Reserve Notes, on the other hand, were to be redeemed by the government and not by the banks, hence the difference in their inscription. There were two issues of Bank Notes (1913 and 1918) and three of the Reserve Notes (1913, 1914 and 1918). The attractive vignettes of these notes included farm and industrial scenes, methods of transportation and, striking an appropriate note for the First World War, a modern battleship.

As an economy measure the size of paper money was reduced in 1929. The notes issued since that date are therefore known to collectors as the 'Small-sized Notes' and include those still current. The Small-sized Notes include several of the previous categories—Legal Tender Notes, Silver Certificates, Federal Reserve Bank Notes, Federal Reserve Notes and National Bank Notes—but it is customary to group them together because of their size and the fact that they all date from 1929 onwards and are therefore within the scope of most newcomers to the hobby. This is a very large field as there are innumerable combinations of bank charter number, state arms, types of serial numbers, bank signatures and minute differences in the engraving.

In addition there are 'Gold Certificates', which first appeared at the end of the Civil War. They were printed in bright orange to simulate gold, and were redeemable in gold coin. In recent times, however, the United States authorities have relinquished the use of gold and repayment is now made in silver or paper money. A special category of gold notes was that produced in 1848 at the time of the California gold rush. The 'National Gold Bank Notes' of California depicted gold coins and were printed in shades of yellow ink. These gold notes and certificates are now extremely rare. The fractional currency notes, postage currency and encased postage stamps, used during and after the Civil War, are dealt with in Chapter 8.

Canada

Canada has a long and interesting history of paper money; indeed its paper money is slightly older than the earliest from the United States. In 1685, the French authorities failed to send a supply of coined money to pay their troops stationed in Canada and the governor hit upon the idea of using a quantity of playing cards, on which he signed a promise to pay the bearer a sum of money in coin when the supply of specie arrived. Examples of the very

Simon Bolivar, leader of independence movements in South America.

early card money are extremely rare, though specimens dating from the early eighteenth century are preserved in various museum collections. The idea, born of an emergency, caught on and was used by the French authorities in Canada until the British occupied Canada in 1759. Although actual playing cards were often used, latterly ordinary pieces of plain card were utilised, with suitable inscriptions printed or written on them. Confidence tricksters, however, frequently circulated their own card money, bearing an inscription promising that the King's treasury would redeem them. Back in France, King Louis XV was blissfully unaware of the fact that his name was being used in this way.

Under the British rule, Canada continued to use

Mexico, 2 pesos note, issued by the rebel ''Provisional Government''
at Vera Cruz during the Revolution of 1914.

Brazil, 5 cruzeiros, reproducing a painting entitled ''Conquista do
Amazonas''.

Chile, 100 pesos, subsequently revalued as 10 centésimos de escudo
as a result of currency reform.

Uruguay, 1 peso featuring the *Santa Maria*, flagship of Christopher
Columbus.

Bolivia, 100 bolivianos note of the Central Bank depicting a petroleum refinery.

Paraguay, 1 guarani issued in 1952, featuring a soldier in the uniform of the Chaco War.

card and paper money. The history of paper money in Canada in the late eighteenth and early nineteenth centuries is similar to that of the United States. Numerous small private banks poured forth a vast quantity of paper money which became worthless when the banks crashed. Apart from these banknotes, there were numerous paper tokens issued by traders, manufacturers, the railway and steamship companies, local councils and even the police. These tokens may be recognised by the inclusion of the words "good for" or "*Bon pour*" in their inscriptions.

It was not until 1870 that the Canadian government took steps to reform the currency of the Confederation. At that time paper money, tokens, Indian wampum, United States and Mexican coins circulated freely, but in that year the government declared that only Canadian coins would henceforward be legal tender. Silver coins were struck and put into circulation, but they failed to meet the enormous demand. Accordingly an issue of small-denomination notes was made. These little cents notes are known familiarly as 'shin-plasters' on account of their small size. New designs were introduced in 1900 and 1923 and they were finally discontinued in 1935. During the long period in which they were current, over 300 different varieties of shin-plasters were produced.

Latin America

Since the late nineteenth century, the countries of Latin America have adopted paper money with enthusiasm. Many of the notes issued by these countries were produced by the great international security printers, such as De La Rue and Waterlow in England and the American Bank Note Co. in the United States. Among the many fine portraits to be found on these notes, Marshal Sucre, General San Martin and Simon Bolivar are the most popular subjects. Wildlife is depicted in great profusion from the llama on the notes of Ecuador to the donkey on the early issue of Paraguay. Native types

in some districts as late as 1922, resulted in a multitude of interesting notes issued by the Federalists, their opponents—the Constitutionalists, by various provisional governments, by different Mexican states, by army commanders and by individual revolutionaries such as Pancho Villa. The Mexican notes of the Revolution are a fascinating group in themselves and many of them are still available for a modest outlay.

Colourful banknotes are also issued by many of the island territories of the Caribbean. Apart from the prolific issues of Cuba, Haiti and the Dominican Republic there are attractive notes from Jamaica, Trinidad, the Bahamas and other islands of the British West Indies. Distinctive notes have also been produced in the French territories of Martinique and Guadeloupe and by the Netherlands Antilles. Even the remote Falkland Islands, in the South Atlantic, have had their own paper money

Brazil, 100 cruzeiros of the United States of Brazil portraying Dom Pedro II—a rare instance of a republic featuring its last monarch on its banknotes.

are also a popular subject. More intriguing is the appearance of the *Mona Lisa* of Leonardo da Vinci on banknotes of Costa Rica.

The political upheavals and frequent changes of government in Latin American countries account for the fact that the paper money of obsolete issues is often demonetised and therefore becomes available to collectors at a fraction of its face value. This does not detract from the interest of these notes and, because of their availability, they have long been popular with collectors. The lengthy Mexican Revolution, which began in 1911 and dragged on

for many years. The first issue consisted of peso notes, produced by the Argentinians in 1829 when *Las Malvinas* were under the control of Buenos Aires, but sterling banknotes have been issued since 1899.

4 EUROPEAN PAPER MONEY

In spite of (or because of) the examples set by the *kreditivsedlar* of Sweden and the *mandats* and *assignats* of revolutionary France, paper money was slow to catch on in Europe. Most banks issued notes of relatively high face value, but these were used mainly in internal accounting and tended not to circulate very widely. For all practical purposes and normal daily transactions gold and silver coins were found to be quite adequate. Nevertheless some governments resorted to the issue of paper money when faced with difficulties in time of war or economic upheaval, with the usual result. Too much paper money was issued, its value fell rapidly in relation to metallic currency and finally it was withdrawn and demonetised, to the benefit of future generations of collectors who were thus able to pick up examples of fine engraving and security printing at a fraction of the nominal face value of the notes. In the present century, every country in Europe has issued paper money regularly, and in some cases notes have circulated at times when no metal coins were available at all. Thus examples of notes of very low face value are not uncommon. Space does not permit an account of each country, but a few of the more interesting have been selected.

Russia

Foremost among the paper money of Europe are the notes issued by Russia from the eighteenth century to the present day. There is a tradition that Prince Potemkin, Minister of War and a personal favourite

Tsarist Russia, 5 rouble note of 1909, depicting the Imperial arms.

of Catherine the Great, had quantities of 1,000 rouble notes bound up to look like books and that these books were discovered in his library after his death. No notes of such a high denomination are known to have been issued prior to 1886 and, if such notes had been in existence at the time of Potemkin's death in the mid eighteenth century, they would surely have come to light long before now.

Catherine the Great certainly authorised the issue of paper money and notes exist which bear the date 1769. Catherine was careful to control the issue of paper money, but her son, Tsar Paul I, succumbed to the temptation of issuing enormous quantities of paper roubles to pay for the conduct of the war with Napoleon. By 1812 there were 840 million paper roubles in circulation and they changed hands at the rate of four paper roubles to one silver rouble. Paper money continued to appear during the early nineteenth century, though it lost the respect and trust of both peasantry and the rising commercial classes. In 1841, under Tsar Nicholas I, a new issue called 'credit notes' was introduced and the worthless and discredited paper roubles were withdrawn.

This measure succeeded for a short time only. First the Crimean War (1854–6) and then the Russo–Turkish War (1877–8) stimulated the increased output of paper money. By 1878 there were well over 1,000 million paper roubles in circulation. On the eve of the First World War, in 1914, the amount of paper money in use had risen to almost 2,500 million roubles. At the beginning of the war,

all bank accounts of more than 100 roubles were
frozen and depositors were permitted to withdraw
no more than five per cent of the balance each
month. Enormous quantities of paper money were
printed during the war, and the mounting inflation
of 1916–17 undoubtedly helped to bring about the
revolution of March 1917 and the overthrow of
Tsar Nicholas II. The Tsarist notes were exceedingly
beautiful, ranging from the humble 3-rouble note
to the enormous 'horseblanket' 500 rouble note.
They had beautiful colouring and intricate engraving and portrayed the Tsar and his famous ancestors
right back to Peter the Great. Oddly enough, these
notes continued to circulate after the Revolution
and were reprinted from the original plates by both
the Provisional Government of Alexander Kerensky
and by the Bolsheviks after they seized power in
October 1917. Experts can distinguish the Provisional and Bolshevik re-issues from the Tsarist
originals by minute differences in serial numbers
and the signatures of the cashiers.

Apart from re-issuing the Tsarist notes, the
Kerensky regime introduced a 1,000 rouble note
which depicted the Duma or parliament building.
The Provisional government also placed an order
for republican notes with the American Bank Note
Co. These notes, ranging from 50 kopeks to 100
roubles, were not shipped out to Russia until after
the Bolsheviks had come to power and the notes
were eventually delivered to the White Russian
forces. The 50 kopek notes were used by the White
troops under Admiral Kolchak at Vladivostock, but
the other denominations were used by both White
and Red forces indiscriminately, with or without
distinctive overprints.

In 1918 the Russian Socialist Federated Soviet
Republic introduced a series of rather austere notes,
from 1 to 10,000 roubles in value. These notes were
without any Soviet emblems, but they are sometimes found overprinted with anti-Soviet slogans.
These notes were captured by White troops and
then re-issued in the areas they controlled. In 1919
the Bolshevik authorities released tiny 'settlement
notes' in denominations from 1 to 5 roubles. They
came to be nicknamed 'beer stamps', from their
small size and the fact that their purchasing power
was virtually limited to a glass of beer! Higher
values, from 15 to 10,000 roubles, were nicknamed
'Babel notes' because they carried the slogan
"Workers of the World Unite" in English,

Back and front of the 500 rouble note of the State Credit Bank, Russia,
1912. These handsome banknotes portrayed members of the Romanov
Dynasty.

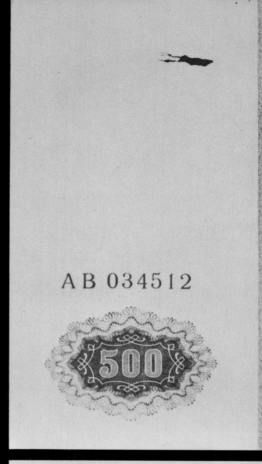

ГОСУДАРСТВЕННЫЙ
КРЕДИТНЫЙ БИЛЕТЪ

ПЯТЬСОТЪ
РУБЛЕЙ

ГОСУДАРСТВЕННЫЙ БАНКЪ РАЗМѢНИВАЕТЪ КРЕ-
ДИТНЫЕ БИЛЕТЫ НА ЗОЛОТУЮ МОНЕТУ БЕЗЪ
ОГРАНИЧЕНІЯ СУММЫ (1 РУБЛЬ=1/15 ИМПЕРІАЛА,
СОДЕРЖИТЪ 17,424 ДОЛЕЙ ЧИСТАГО ЗОЛОТА.)

500
1912

Управляющій

Кассиръ

АВ 034512

Soviet Russia 500 rouble note of 1919, popularly known as a 'Babel'
note, because it bore the slogan "Workers of the World unite!" in
seven languages.

Greece, 5,000 drachmae, issued in 1942 during the German occupation.
Ironically the note depicts the headless statue known as the Victory of
Samothrace.

White Russian 500 rouble note, issued in 1920, during the Civil War,
by the anti-Bolshevist forces operating in South Russia.

Hungary, 10 forint note of 1962, portraying the national poet, Sandor
Petöfi.

Catherine II, Empress of Russia, 1729–96.

French, German, Italian, Arabic and Chinese as well as Russian.

Inflation overtook the Soviet economy in 1921 and notes with a face value of up to 100,000 roubles had to be issued. In 1922 these notes were recalled as part of the currency reform by which one new rouble was equal to 10,000 old roubles. This measure did not halt the inflation and the following year a system of 1923 roubles—one of which equalled a million 1922 roubles—was adopted. Small tickets bearing the impression of non-existent silver kopeks dated 1923 were also issued at the same time and can be classed as a form of paper money. At that time there were no actual coins in circulation. In 1924 the gold rouble, equal to 5,000 roubles of 1923, was introduced. Ten gold roubles was equal to one *chervonetz* (plural *chervontzev*) and various denominations in *chervonetz* currency were produced as paper money from 1924 to 1947.

Like the Tsarist notes, the later issues of the Soviets have been very attractive in design. Symbolic portraits of a coalminer, infantryman and fighter pilot were used on the rouble State Treasury notes issued from 1937 onwards, while the *chervonetz* State Bank Notes of the same period bore a portrait of Lenin on the front. These notes were inscribed in as many as fifteen different languages, reflecting the multi-national character of the Soviet Union. After the Second World War the *chervonetz* notes were replaced by rouble notes ranging from 10 to 100 roubles. Sixteen different languages appeared on the 1947 series of notes, but Finnish was dropped from the notes of 1956 when the Karelo-Finnish Soviet Socialist Republic was downgraded to an autonomous republic. The last of the currency reforms came in 1961 when one new rouble was the equivalent of 10 old roubles. The notes of the Treasury (low values) and State Bank (high values) are much smaller than the pre-1961 issues but follow the same general design and layout of inscriptions.

During the period of the Civil War (1918–23) and the economic crises, no fewer than 130 different notes were issued by the Soviet authorities. In addition emergency issues were made by local councils, trade unions, shopkeepers and innkeepers. In Kharkhov alone, more than sixty different organisations and individuals issued their own paper money. Paper money was also produced by the short-lived independent countries which appeared at this time: the Ukraine, Armenia, Azerbaijan, Georgia, the Trans-Caucasian Federation, the khanates of Khiva and Bokhara and the regimes of the White generals, such as Wrangel,

Germany, 1,000 marks note of the Reichsbank, issued in 1910, the
highest denomination issued before the First World War.

Germany, 1 reichsmark of the *Reichskreditkasse*, for the use of German
troops on active service during the Second World War.

Yudenitch and Denikin. Various adventurers, from Colonel Avalov-Bermondt in the Baltic area to the Cossack Ataman Semyonoff in Siberia, issued their own paper money. Incidentally uncut sheets of Avalov-Bermondt banknotes were captured by the Latvians and used in the printing of some stamps in 1920, during a shortage of plain paper. The stamps have portions of the banknotes printed on the back. Earlier stamps of Latvia were printed on paper bearing the designs of the five rouble notes of the Riga Workers' and Soldiers' Soviet. Thus the early stamps of Latvia are of interest to stamp and paper money collectors alike.

Germany

A certain amount of paper money was produced in the kingdoms, grand duchies, principalities and free cities which comprised the German Empire. Gradually they surrendered their rights to the Bank of Prussia which became the *Reichsbank* (Imperial Bank) in 1876. Nevertheless the state

German Democratic Republic, 10 marks of 1964 portraying the poet Friedrich Schiller.

banks in the larger states of the Empire held on to their rights of issuing distinctive notes as late as 1935 when they were suppressed by the Nazis. The state banks in Baden, Bavaria, Saxony and Württemberg continued to issue their own notes well into the present century.

Shortly after the outbreak of the First World War, coins began to disappear from circulation and the government, faced with an acute shortage of metal which was required for the war effort, was

Series of German notgeld featuring country scenes proverbial sayings in dialect.

forced to issue low-denomination paper money. The first paper money of the war was unofficial and was issued by business and shopkeepers all over the country. This money, known to collectors as the *kleine Notgeld* (small Emergency money), consisted mainly of low denominations, usually of 10, 25 and 50 pfennigs. These local issues, of which there were many different varieties, were superseded by an official issue known as *Darlehnskassen* (state loan notes). This failed to meet the demand and local

issues of *kleine Notgeld* had been resumed by 1916. Every town and village in Germany produced these notes; they were issued by factories, co-operatives and institutions, by chambers of commerce, shopkeepers and hotels. The wartime issues are comparatively scarce but the notes of 1920–2 are still very common. Latterly they were even produced in sets featuring different views of a locality and replaced pictured postcards as popular tourist souvenirs for a time. The *Reichsbank* prohibited

them by a regulation of 17 September 1922, but this did little to stem the flood. As many as 50,000 different types of *kleine Notgeld* have been recorded.

Germany's economic troubles became very serious after the war had ended. In 1921 the reichsmark suddenly plunged to a thousandth of its 1918 value. The *Reichsbank*'s highest denomination before this period was the 1,000 mark note of 1910; in January 1922 it was found necessary to issue 10,000 mark notes and within ten months 50,000 mark notes had been released. On 1 February 1923, a 100,000 mark note went into circulation, followed by a million mark note within three weeks. The following summary of the higher denominations and their dates of issue will give some idea of the astonishing inflation which overtook Germany from the summer of 1923 to the spring of 1924:

1923	1 June	5,000,000 marks
	25 July	50,000,000 marks
	22 August	100,000,000 marks
	1 September	500,000,000 marks
	5 September	1 milliard marks (milliard = American billion = 1,000,000,000)
	10 September	5 milliard marks
	15 September	10 milliard marks
	1 October	20 milliard marks
	10 October	50 milliard marks
	15 October	200 milliard marks
	26 October	500 milliard marks
	1 November	10 billion marks (billion = American trillion = 1,000,000,000,000)
1924	5 February	20 billion marks
	10 February	50 billion marks
	15 February	100 billion marks

Before the inflation came to an end early in 1924 when Germany repudiated her National Debt and started again with a clean slate, a new system of paper money, guaranteed by mortgage bonds funded in real estate, was introduced. These *rentenmarks* were secured by interest-bearing bonds into which they could be automatically converted. The government succeeded, almost miraculously, in floating a gold loan which gave it breathing space and enabled the work of stabilising the currency to be carried out successfully. The enormously high denomination Reichsbank notes of 1923–4 can still be purchased for less than a pound each, although some of the last issues, which

Germany, 50 marks of the Reichsbank issued in 1919.

Germany, Reichsbank note for a billion (1,000,000,000,000) marks, 1923.

were quickly superseded by the *rentenmark*, are scarce and rather expensive nowadays.

At the height of the crisis it cost millions of marks to post a letter or buy a box of matches. Workmen were paid their wages twice daily and took laundry baskets with them in which to place the huge bundles of notes. Paper money became worthless almost before the ink of the printing press was dry. The value of the mark dropped almost by the hour. In the end people dispensed with money altogether and reverted to a primitive system of barter, especially in country areas where farmers and peasants could use potatoes, eggs and butter as a form of currency.

With the beginning of the postwar inflation, the group of emergency paper money known to collectors as the 'large *Notgeld* (first series)' came into being. These notes are found in denominations of 1 to 50 marks and the majority of the 4,000 types recorded are dated 1918. The last category, known as 'large *Notgeld* (second series)' appeared in 1922–3 to fill the gap which even the prolific issues of the *Reichsbank* could not close at this time. Some 3,600 types appeared in 1922, but more than 60,000 in 1923. Great ingenuity and artistry was shown by the issuing authorities in making their notes as colourful and interesting as possible; often they commemorated local events and honoured historic personages. Before long these notes, particularly those rendered obsolete or invalid by the rising inflation, were being avidly collected and many towns and cities pandered to the collectors by providing long pictorial sets. Special albums were manufactured by Schaubek and other leading stationers to house collections of *Notgeld* and many a provincial *rathaus* or village *handelskammer* made a tidy profit from sales of their notes to dealers and collectors. This business rapidly got out of hand, and the *Reichsbank* regulations failed to stem the flood. *Notgeld* was responsible for bringing more people into the hobby of paper money collecting than any other kind of paper money and to this day the hobby is at its strongest in Germany. Even now the colourful and quaint notes of the German Inflation period are to be found in most collections.

The reichsmark notes of the Nazi period (1933–45) are also quite plentiful since many of them were 'liberated' by Allied servicemen at the end of the war when the Nazi money became worthless. Since the war separate issues of paper money have been made in West Germany (the Federal Republic) and East Germany (the Democratic Republic). Both the *Bundesbank* (west) and

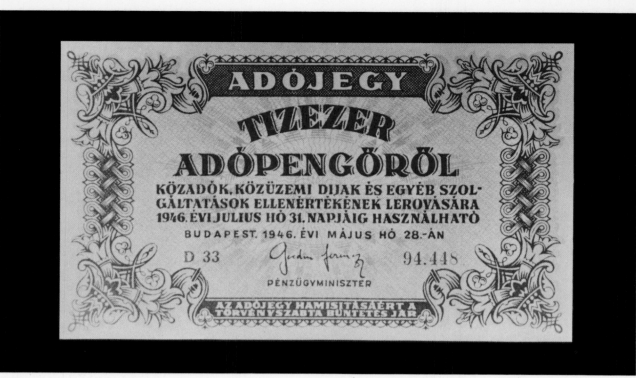

Hungary, 100,000 adöpengö note issued in 1946 during the hyper-inflation.

Austro-Hungarian Empire, 1 crown note inscribed in Magyar and German for use in both parts of the Dual Monarchy. The note was overprinted *Deutschösterreich* (German Austria) at the end of the First World War when there was a short-lived attempt to unify Austria and Germany.

Hungary, 100 forint, reproducing on the reverse a painting by Karoly
Lotz.

Hungary, 20 forint note of 1965, featuring an allegory of industry and
agriculture on the reverse.

Spain, 50 centimos note issued by the Republican faction during the Spanish Civil War.

Garibaldi, the great Italian patriot, is portrayed on his country's notes.

the *Notenbank* (east) have produced attractive examples of paper money, portraying famous German scientists, artists, poets and writers, as well as views, landmarks and industrial scenes.

Other Countries

Germany was not the only country to experience high inflation in the early 1920s. Neighbouring countries, such as Austria, Hungary and Poland, and Czechoslovakia to a lesser extent, also experienced high inflation and were forced to issue vast quantities of paper money which rapidly became worthless and now provides the collector with some excellent material at a low cost. Hungary had the misfortune to experience inflation on two occasions during this century. The second period came after the Second World War when Hungary was engulfed by the worst inflation of all time. The pengo fell so far in value that the government was forced to issue paper money up to the denomination of one quintillion pengos (1,000,000,000,000,-000,000). When even this was found to be insufficient the authorities released *Adopengo* notes in 1946. The highest denomination was a thousand million *adopengos*, equal at that time to 20,000,000,-000,000,000,000,000,000,000 pengos. Today this astronomical note is worth about £5 to collectors. Greece also had a postwar inflation, accompanied by large quantities of paper money, but in 1954 the currency was reformed and one new drachma was exchanged for 1,000 old drachmae.

Other countries which suffered lesser inflation had to make do with paper money for quite long periods. At the end of the Second World War the value of the French franc fell sharply and there were no coins in circulation for several years. Visitors to France in the immediate postwar years will recall with distaste the bundles of grubby banknotes which were required for even small transactions. Coins gradually replaced the small franc denominations but the currency was not reformed until 1960 when one new or heavy franc equalled 100 old francs. Italy's currency unit, the lira, was worth a few pence before the Second World War but afterwards rapidly depreciated but not to such an extent that it has been felt necessary to reform the currency. At the present time, therefore, coins are issued in denominations up to 500 lire while banknotes range from 500 lire upwards. The current series portrays famous Italians including Christopher Columbus, the Genoese seaman who discovered America. Columbus has appeared so often on the paper money of the United States and the Latin American countries that his Italian

France, assignat for 25 livres issued during the Revolution. Note the
fasces, cap of liberty and other republican symbols in the side panels.

France, 5 francs issued in 1922, with an Art Deco portrait of Marianne,
symbol of the French republic.

France, 5 francs issued in 1943. Members of the Resistance movement often sketched in a profile of Marshal Petain, the Vichy leader, above the fist of the farmer shown on this note, so that it appeared as if Petain was being throttled. The penalty for possessing such notes was death.

Yugoslavia, 1 dinar of 1944 depicting a partisan soldier. Note the names of the Yugoslav federative republics and the inscriptions in Serb, Croat, Slovene and Macedonian warning against counterfeiting.

Italy, 1,000 lire note of 1968 portraying the composer, Giuseppe Verdi.

Yugoslavia, 100 dinars note of the National Bank, showing a girl in national costume and a view of the Adriatic coast.

Belgium, 20 francs of 1964, featuring the Atomium from the Brussels World Fair of 1958.

Bulgaria, 3 leva of 1951, featuring the hammer and sickle emblem of communism.

Russia, 50 kopeks note of the Russian-Asiatic Bank, showing a locomotive.

Bulgaria, 10 leva of 1951, portraying Georgi Dmitrov on the front and a combine harvester on the reverse.

origins are often forgotten.

Currency reforms, following periods of inflation, are the most fruitful sources of paper money for the collector, since the old notes are called in, demonetised and often sold off to dealers at a fraction of their nominal face value. In many countries of the Communist bloc, the paper money is changed at regular intervals and the obsolete notes are demonetised to foil black marketeers and speculators who may have hoarded paper money from illegal transactions. The obsolete notes are often sold to dealers and thus provide collectors with interesting and attractive notes for a modest sum. In Bulgaria, for example, the state banknotes of 1951 were withdrawn in 1962 when the current series was introduced. The notes follow the same basic designs, but the colours have been altered and the date appears prominently in the design.

The banknotes of postwar Yugoslavia are interesting on account of their inscriptions in four languages and two different alphabets, reflecting the jealousies of the seven republics which make up the Federative People's Republic of Yugoslavia. The names of the seven countries also appear on each note—Serbia, Croatia, Slovenia, Bosnia and Herzegovina, Macedonia and Montenegro. The immediate postwar issues had stern portraits of partisan fighters but more recent notes have portrayed peasant women or feature some of the scenery which is such a popular tourist attraction these days.

The paper money of Belgium and the Netherlands is notable for the high quality of its production and also for the beautiful reproductions of Old Master paintings, both portraits and typical Dutch landscapes of canals and windmills. The Scandinavian countries make use of traditional Viking ornament in the borders of their notes. Quite an interesting collection could be devoted to paper money illustrating various artistic styles. Spain and Portugal also draw on their Old Masters for inspiration, reproducing portraits of historical personalities and famous events in history.

The smaller countries of Europe should not be overlooked. Attractive notes have been issued by San Marino and the tiny principality of Liechtenstein, tucked between Austria and Switzerland. Monaco and the Vatican issue their own francs and lire notes with beautiful pictorial or religious themes. Gibraltar began issuing paper money in 1914 at the time when the British Treasury notes first appeared, and since then the Rock has been featured on the notes issued by the Gibraltar government. Gibraltar even had a two shilling note, prepared in 1938 in anticipation of the Second World War. These notes were never issued and most of them were destroyed in 1968, so very few of them are in the hands of collectors.

5
ASIAN
PAPER MONEY

Although the Chinese invented paper money and used it for almost eight hundred years, they then abandoned it completely and did not re-introduce it until the middle of the nineteenth century. Many scholars, in fact, doubted the truth of Marco Polo's description of Chinese paper money which he witnessed in the thirteenth century, even though other medieval writers had also mentioned it. The first actual notes, of the Ming Dynasty, only came to light in 1900 when British troops sacked Peking at the end of the Boxer Rebellion. A quantity of Ming notes was unearthed below a statue of Buddha where they had been placed in much the same way as coins are buried in the foundations of western buildings. These notes, dating from the middle of the fourteenth century, caused a great stir and fetched very large sums when they were first auctioned. Subsequently more of these large notes were found and the price dropped rapidly. Today a Ming note in fine condition would be worth £200 to £500.

Following the Opium War of 1841, Britain was permitted to open trading posts in several major seaports of China (the so-called Treaty Ports) and the island of Hong Kong became a British colony. Trade was carried on by the Honourable East India Company and a number of commercial concerns with their headquarters in Britain or India. In the wake of the traders came the bankers. The Bank of Western India established an office in Hong Kong in 1842, later it changed its name to the Oriental

Bank and issued banknotes thus inscribed. The Commercial Bank of India opened branches in Canton (1851) and Shanghai (1855) and also issued notes for use in China. Soon other European powers became interested in the lucrative trade with China and inevitably opened banks in the Treaty Ports. By the turn of the century there was a large number of banks in Amoy, Canton, Chefoo, Foochow, Hankow, Ningpo, Shanghai and other major Chinese cities. Belgium, France, Germany, Italy, the Netherlands, Russia and Britain operated these banks. Both Japan and the United States also opened banks in China. All of these banks issued attractive notes designed on western lines, with vignettes of steamships and trains, or pictures of the banks and prominent buildings in the international sections of the cities. The currency in which these notes was issued consisted of Chinese dollars.

The Chinese themselves resorted to paper money in the 1850s. The Imperial government suffered a severe economic crisis as a result of the T'ai-ping Rebellion which lasted for almost eleven years (1853–64). At first paper money was issued in denominations from 500 to 100,000 cash (copper) and 50 taels (silver), but the paper money quickly dropped to a thirtieth of its face value and was then discontinued altogether. The *Hsien Feng* notes of the 1850s resembled the earlier notes in their exclusive use of Chinese characters and traditional forms of decoration.

By contrast, the notes issued by the Chinese banks which began to appear at the turn of the century were thoroughly westernised in appear-

The north gate of the Sanchi stupa in India.

Central Bank of China, 5 yüan of 1936 featuring a pagoda on the reverse.
The front of these notes portrayed Dr Sun Yat-sen and was inscribed
entirely in Chinese.

ance. The first of these banks was the Imperial Bank of China, founded in 1897. Eight years later the Hu Pu Bank (later known as the Ta Ching Government Bank) was established. The Bank of Communications was formed in 1907 and, as its name suggests, was prominent in the development of the railway network in China in the early years of this century. These Chinese banks issued notes with values in dollars or yüan; the notes were mostly printed in America or Europe, though they often had suitable oriental themes such as dragons, junks and portraits of Confucius.

The republican movement, headed by Dr Sun Yat-sen and based initially in Japan, issued bonds in the name of the "Chinese Revolutionary Government" which promised to pay the bearer on demand "after one year of its establishment in China". These notes were used to pay troops of the revolutionary armies which finally overthrew the Manchu Dynasty in 1912, though curiously enough it was not until the currency reform of 1935 that the Chinese republican government actually redeemed these bonds. Other bonds, in denominations from $10 to $1,000, were issued under the authority of Sun Yat-sen in San Francisco in 1911.

Shortly after the overthrow of the Manchu

Dynasty, the infant republic disintegrated; age-old quarrels between North and South, intrigue by European, American and Japanese business interests and the struggle for power by numerous war-lords and bandit chiefs resulted in the anarchy and disorder which did not come to an end until the 1930s when General Chiang Kai-shek came to power. Even then Chiang had to contend with the Communists, who were virtually independent in north-western China from 1935 onwards, and the growing menace of the Japanese who seized Manchuria in 1931 and invaded China proper in 1937. The troubled events are reflected in the numerous War-lord notes of the 1920s and the inflationary money of the 1930s and 1940s.

The European and American printers had a field-day during the period of the civil wars up to 1929. The War-lords relied very heavily on paper money to finance their campaigns and the only way that they could persuade the luckless peasants to accept it was to make sure that it was as colourful and beautifully designed as possible. When the latest issue of paper money turned out to be just as worthless as its predecessors, the War-lord would close the bank (occasionally executing the manager as a gesture of goodwill towards the depositors),

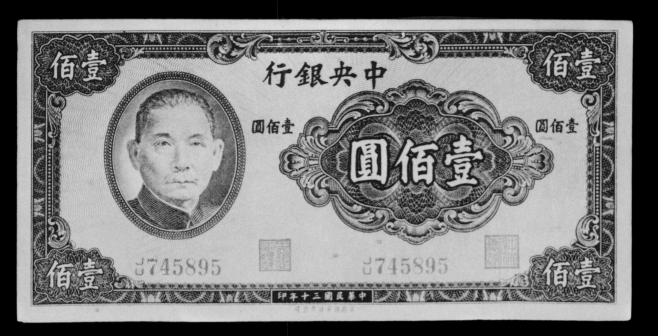

Central Bank of China, 100 yüan note of 1941, portraying Dr Sun Yat-sen.

re-open it under a new name and issue another brand of banknote. As the tide of war ebbed and flowed across China and districts changed hands, War-lords would foist their paper money on the people at bayonet-point, or execute those on whom the banknotes of rival War-lords were found.

Among the more famous notes were those depicting a blown-up railway line, issued by Feng Yün-hsiang, the Christian general of North China who once baptised his entire army with a garden hose as they paraded past him! The War-lord notes seldom bothered with such formalities as an inscription promising to pay the bearer on demand. The bandits of Kirin went a stage farther and issued notes which were inscribed in Chinese "Not payable to lamplight". This and similar inscriptions were intended as a warning to the customer not to change notes in artificial light because of the many forgeries which were going around. Some notes even had the inscription quaintly rendered in English as "No pay tonight", an example of unconscious humour or disarming frankness.

In an effort to bring some order to the country's finances, the Kuomintang government established the Central Bank of China in 1928. Other government banks included the Farmers Bank, which began issuing notes in 1935. In a bid to overcome chronic inflation the government of Chiang Kai-shek introduced 'Customs Gold Units' in 1930. Originally these notes were intended for the payment of customs dues but they were widely accepted as currency. Like the other Chinese currency, however, they suffered from inflation and eventually there were notes for 250,000 Gold Units. The last issues appeared during and after the Second World War and were deliberately back-dated by the authorities to give them greater respectability.

As the Communists advanced and the Nationalists of Chiang Kai-shek retreated a new currency was introduced in August 1948. The gold yüan of 100 cents depreciated even more rapidly and within a few months notes for denominations up to a million gold yüan were being issued. In desperation the Nationalists reformed the currency again, and introduced the silver yüan, but it fared no better than its 'gold' predecessor. The currency was only established when the Communists drove the Nationalists from the mainland in 1949. Communist China's unit of currency is the yüan and paper money is now used exclusively, even for the smallest amounts. Since 1949 the Nationalist

The beautiful and sacred mountain Fujiyama which stands near Tokyo.

Laos, 20 kip note of the National Bank, showing a temple, and featuring
Apsaras (dancing nymphs) in the decorative panels.

A Japanese painting of travellers on the road.

Japan, 1 yen. Note the chrysanthemum emblem and agricultural symbols.

Bank of China 10 yüan note of 1940, depicting the Temple of Heaven, Peking.

government on Formosa, with immense American financial backing, has succeeded in keeping its currency stable. Coins in aluminium and brass are now used for the smaller denominations and paper money for the dollar denominations.

The paper money of the Chinese government banks, the provincial banks, the large number of former foreign banks and the numerous War-lord banks adds up to a formidable volume. It has been estimated that over 60,000 different Chinese banknotes have been issued in the past 120 years, and this is another field which offers considerable scope to the collector of modest means.

Attractive notes are issued by the Portuguese colony of Macao and the British colony of Hong Kong. The latter even includes the world's lowest denomination in current use—a one cent banknote which can only be used for the payment of electricity bills which include the odd 1 cent amount. The Hong Kong dollar is currently worth about 8p in British currency and even the cheapest Hong Kong postage stamp has a face value of 5 cents.

Japan

Like China, Japan was using paper money long before the idea was adopted in Europe. Notes are known to have been used since the first year of the Kemmu era (1334 A.D.), in the reign of the Emperor Daigo (1318–38), and circulated among the merchants in what is now the Ginza district of Tokyo. Japanese notes were long and narrow, hence the nickname 'bookmarks' given to them by collectors. They were block-printed and often had attractive flower designs or pictures of merchants and country scenes. The native paper money was often forged and for that reason the Japanese authorities introduced a series of notes in 1811 that had been printed in Germany; they were the first European-style banknotes to circulate in the Far East. At that time there were no banks in the Western sense, but most cities had several money-changers who also issued notes with values equivalent to gold, silver and copper coins.

After the Meiji revolution of 1868, when the emperor Meiji seized control from the powerful Shoguns (Japan's military dictators) and moved his capital from Kyoto to Tokyo, the currency was reformed. The old system of *mon* was replaced by a decimal currency based on the yen of 100 sen (cents) and a federal reserve fund was established to ensure that no paper money would be issued without proper metallic backing. Since then

Marco Polo and his companions were the first Europeans ever to see paper money.

The Dalai Lama of Tibet.

Japanese paper money has been issued on a sound footing and, like American dollars, tends to be rather expensive to purchase. On the other hand the paper money printed for use in China, Malaya, the Dutch East Indies, the Philippines and other territories occupied by the Japanese between 1937 and 1945 is still quite plentiful and usually very cheap. The occupation money issued by Japan is discussed more fully in Chapter 8.

Other Countries

Both Tibet and Korea followed the pattern set by China in issuing paper money at a very early date. Paper was made from the pulp of the mulberry tree and printed with blocks made from birchwood slabs. Tibetan notes were produced by the lamas and often depicted the Lord Buddha and other religious emblems. Primitive notes of this type continued to be used in Tibet until the Chinese Communists seized control in the 1950s. Since then it is presumed that Chinese Communist paper money has been used in that remote country.

The idea of using paper money was first mooted in Korea in 1391 but, because the printing works was burned down, a further ten years elapsed before the first paper money was actually put into circulation, under the authority of King Taejong. At various times in the fifteenth century, paper money was issued when coins were in short supply but it had died out by 1445. Four centuries later the Japanese established branches of the National Bank of Japan at Pusan and Inchon and issued notes which were primarily intended for the payment of customs dues, though they began to circulate freely in normal business transactions. The Russians opened a bank in Seoul, the Korean capital, at the end of the century to promote Russian commercial interests in the country. Growing commercial rivalry between Russia and Japan over Korea led to the war of 1904–5 in which the Japanese decisively defeated the Russians. From then onwards, the Japanese control over Korea was gradually tightened; the Bank of Korea was founded in 1909 and was nominally the country's state bank though, in fact, it was entirely under Japanese management. The following year Korea was annexed by Japan and the bank changed its name to the Central Bank of Chosen (the Japanese name for Korea). *Chosen* banknotes circulated widely not only in Korea but also in Manchuria and other districts of China which came under Japanese occupation in the 1930s.

Indonesia, 25 rupiah note of 1964 depicting a soldier.

Indonesia, 5 rupiah banknote showing a ruined temple. The inscription
at the foot contains a warning against forgery.

Nepal, 10 rupees banknote, current issue.

Following the liberation of Korea in 1945, the paper money of the Bank of Chosen continued in circulation until 1950 when it was superseded by the Bank of Korea. North of the 38th Parallel, paper money of the People's Bank of the Korean Democratic Republic was used. During the North Korean occupation of Seoul and other towns in South Korea, the Communist notes circulated in those areas and, in addition, the Communists forged and issued the South Korean notes in an attempt to cripple the Southern economy. The South Korean government was forced to recall its won currency and substitute new hwan currency. The notes of South Korea portrayed President Syngman Rhee but, after he was deposed in 1960, his portrait was replaced by that of the fifteenth century King Sejong. Because of mounting inflation a new system based on the won was adopted in 1962 and notes in denominations from 10 cheon to 500 won were printed by the English firm of De La Rue.

The paper money of India is another fertile field for the collector. Many of the princely states issued their own notes under the British Raj. Many of these were crudely printed on hand-made native paper with Hindu symbolism and strange scripts; others were printed by De La Rue, Perkins Bacon or Waterlow and Sons in England and were thoroughly British in appearance, apart from the fine portraits of the maharajahs. Several commercial banks issued their own notes in British India, while

Laos, 1 kip note of the National Bank with motifs inspired by traditional Laotian art.

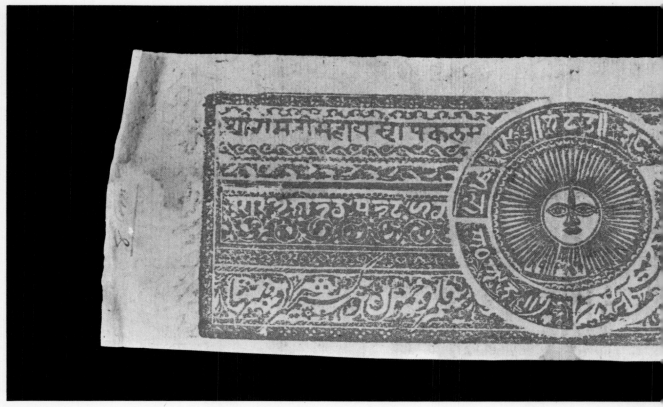

A primitive banknote from one of the Indian native states, late nineteenth century.

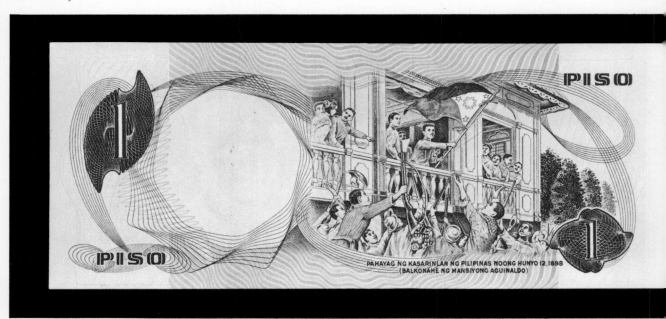

Philippenes, 1 peso banknote issued in 1971, showing a scene from the
history of the islands.

of native manufacture. Persia's paper money, on the other hand, was mostly printed in Europe and various security printers had a hand in its production.

Paper money in Indonesia dates back to the issues of the Dutch East India Company in Java and Sumatra and many of the later issues, produced in this century, are picturesque examples of the engraver's art. Since 1945, paper money has been issued in great profusion by Indonesia. The political upheavals which culminated in the overthrow of Dr Sukarno and chronic inflation have resulted in several issues of paper money which have been demonetised and subsequently become available to collectors at a nominal price. With their exotic designs of temples, animals and mythological figures, these notes are very popular with collectors.

Thailand (Siam) has issued paper money since the latter years of the nineteenth century and most of it was printed in Europe, with a high standard of design and execution. Indochina, and the countries which succeeded it—Vietnam, Laos and Cambodia —have issued notes decorated with temples and native art. Both Burma and Malaysia have also produced interesting notes, printed in Britain but faithfully depicting native folk-lore, scenery and

Qatar, the current 5 riyals banknote.

rupee notes were also issued on behalf of the Indian government. Since 1947 attractive notes have been released by India and Pakistan. To the north of India, both Nepal and Afghanistan have issued paper money since the nineteenth century, mostly

artistic motifs. The Philippines National Bank, under American auspices, was founded in 1916 and since then has issued many attractive peso banknotes, blending traditional art with western-style vignettes.

6 AFRICAN PAPER MONEY

Although it was one of the last continents to adopt paper money, Africa has produced some of the world's most interesting issues, while the emergence of many new countries in recent years has given new possibilities to the paper money collector. Until recently the majority of the issues were made by European controlled banks, which operated in the various colonies, and by state banking organisations whose notes were circulated in a group of territories which were linked economically. Attractive banknotes were issued by the independent countries—Liberia, Ethiopia and Egypt—but elsewhere the European influence was very strong.

South Africa

The earliest paper money of Africa appeared in the latter half of the eighteenth century and, as is so often the case, was issued in time of war. In 1781, war broke out between Britain and the Netherlands, the latter country supporting the alliance of France and Spain with the American colonies in their struggle for independence against the mother country. The British naval blockade of the sea route to the Dutch East Indies caused considerable hardship to the Dutch colony at the Cape of Good Hope. There was an acute shortage of gold and silver coins and the governor of the colony was forced to issue paper money. The emergency notes appeared in 1782 and were entirely hand-written, there being no printing press at the Cape at that time. Because they were easy to imitate, these notes

The Umtata Falls in the Transkei, South Africa.

were frequently changed. Although it was primarily a wartime measure, paper money swiftly became popular with the Dutch settlers and was retained after the war ended.

After Napoleon occupied the Netherlands and formed it into the Batavian Republic, the British invaded the Cape and occupied it until 1803 when it was handed back to the Batavian Republic under the terms of the Treaty of Amiens. A new issue of paper money was made in 1804 under the authority of the Batavian Republic. In addition many businessmen issued their own *goed voor* notes which enjoyed a limited local circulation during temporary shortages of government paper money. Early in 1806 the British again reoccupied the Cape and from then on it became a British colony. At first the Batavian paper rix-dollars were allowed to circulate as before, but in 1810 a new issue of notes, featuring Britannia, was released. British currency was introduced in 1831 and the existing Cape currency withdrawn though promissory notes, in denominations from £1 to £100, were permitted.

At first banking was carried on by the Lombard Bank on behalf of the colonial government but, in 1837, the first private banks were permitted to issue their own paper money and, by the middle of the century, there were no fewer than forty different banks issuing notes in Cape Colony, not to mention a number of large commercial organisations such as the Namaqua Mining Company and Mosenthal Brothers of Cape Town. Many of these banks, however, suffered the fate of over-issuing and went out of business. The Bank Act of 1891

Some African states feature native art on their notes.

was designed to stamp out this problem and hence-forward banks were limited to issuing notes up to the amount of securities which they were obliged to deposit with the state bank. By 1893, therefore, only four private banks were still issuing their own notes. Like the private banknotes of Britain and the United States, the issues of South Africa are exceptionally interesting for their quaint vignettes of scenery, wildlife, industry and agriculture in the mid nineteenth century and many of them can still be picked up fairly cheaply. A curious feature of Cape notes, prior to 1891, was that they were not issued in denominations below £4 because of a government ordinance decreeing that notes had to be worth at least 50 rix-dollars (£3.75).

There were nine private banks in Natal and three in the Orange Free State, as well as the branches of Cape banks which, in some instances, issued local varieties of paper money. The Transvaal, or South African Republic as it was officially known, had a long and chequered history of paper money, as the state lurched from bankruptcy to financial crisis with monotonous regularity. In addition to the old Dutch rix-dollar notes of the Cape which the Boers took north with them on the Great Trek of 1838, the Boers issued treasury notes known as *mandaten* (1857) and interest-bearing notes in denominations of 5 and 10 rix-dollars (1865). The pound sterling was adopted in 1866 and handsome notes, em-bellished with the republic's coat of arms, were issued. Several issues appeared up to 1891, many of the notes being personally signed by President Kruger in an effort to get people to accept them. Several commercial banks, mainly of Dutch origin, issued notes in this period. In 1890 the National Bank of the South African Republic was founded, with the backing of British, Dutch and German businessmen, and its attractive notes, bearing a finely engraved portrait of Paul Kruger, rapidly became popular. During the Boer War several issues of paper money were made at Pretoria, Pietersburg and Pilgrim's Rest, the last of these being a 'commando' issue printed on pages of ruled paper ripped from exercise books. Several emergency issues were made on the British side during the war and are mentioned in greater detail in Chapter 8.

Paper money for use throughout the Union of South Africa was adopted in 1910 and was issued in sterling denominations on behalf of the govern-ment. The Republic of South Africa changed to a decimal system based on the rand of 100 cents in 1961. The unit of currency takes its name from the Witwatersrand goldfields where so much of the country's wealth has been mined. The paper money

Nigeria, £1 note of the Central Bank. This series depicted the bank on the front and agricultural scenes on the reverse.

of South Africa since 1910 is among the most colourful in the world, with fine portraiture, scenery and exotic wildlife.

East Africa

Paper money was issued in the territories of East Africa under the auspices of the Imperial British East Africa Company in Kenya and the German East African Bank in Tanganyika. The latter notes, issued at Dar es Salaam between 1905 and 1915, bore a suitably warlike portrait of Kaiser Wilhelm II. The German forces, under the command of General von Lettow-Vorbeck, produced a crude series of 'Bush Notes' in 1916–17. These notes were printed by means of a rubber printing outfit and were hand-signed. After the First World War economic crises led to the substitution of the florin for the rupee, and this, in turn, was quickly superseded by the shilling as the standard unit of currency. There were 100 cents to the shilling and 20 shillings to the East African pound. Notes were issued under the authority of the East African Currency Board for use in Kenya, Uganda and Tanganyika. Since attaining independence in the early 1960s these countries have issued their own distinctive notes, portraying their presidents and

featuring agricultural produce, industry and wildlife.

West Africa

Apart from the colourful issues of Liberia, paper money was issued in West Africa by the British and French authorities for use in the various territories under their control. Since independence the territories of the French Community and associated countries have continued to pool their financial resources and issue notes which are uniform to former French West Africa or French Equatorial Africa. The particular country of issue can only be determined from the serial numbers; different series being used for such countries as Dahomey, Ivory Coast, Chad and Cameroun. The vignettes on these notes strike a nice balance between the scenery, landmarks and native types of the countries concerned.

Prior to 1958, sterling notes of the West African Currency Board were in use in the four British territories of the Gambia, the Gold Coast, Nigeria and Sierra Leone. As they gradually became independent, however, these countries adopted their own distinctive currency systems and introduced their own paper money. The first to do so

State Bank of Morocco, 10 franc note of 1943.

was Ghana (formerly known as the Gold Coast) which became independent in 1957 and introduced distinctive notes in July 1958. Sterling was abandoned in favour of a decimal system based on the cedi of 100 pesawas which was introduced in 1965. Banknotes of the Bank of Ghana, in denominations from 1 to 100 cedis, were issued with the profile of Dr Nkrumah, president of the republic. Dr Nkrumah was deposed in February 1966, while absent from the country on a visit to Peking, and the new military government decided to withdraw the cedi banknotes from circulation and replace them with an issue featuring traditional art forms instead of the president's portrait. At the same time the currency was reformed so that one new cedi (equal to ten shillings sterling) was worth 1.20 old cedis. Between 1967 and 1969, notes in denominations of 1, 5 and 10 new cedis were issued.

Nigeria replaced the notes of the West African Currency Board in June 1959 by an issue of the Central Bank of Nigeria in denominations of 5s, 10s, £1 and £5. The five shilling note was a new idea, designed to take the place of many of the old West African Currency Board coins which were gradually withdrawn from circulation at this time. The Nigerian banknotes followed the same colours and

Egypt, £1 note of 1940.

designs as their WACB predecessors, featuring a river scene on the front and various aspects of agriculture on the back. Nigeria became a federal republic in October 1963, but it was not until July 1965 that new banknotes, inscribed "Federal Republic of Nigeria", were issued. These notes had a common design on the front, a view of the Central Bank in Lagos, and various agricultural scenes on the backs.

At the end of May 1967, the eastern region of Nigeria broke away from the rest of the country under the name of the Republic of Biafra. The Biafran authorities seized all the Nigerian currency, to pay for essential imports, and replaced it with an issue of Biafran currency. To forestall this the Nigerian government recalled all banknotes of the previous issue and introduced a third series, similar to the second in general design, but in new colours and with variation in the background scrollwork. The first series of Biafran notes, ranging from 5s to £10, was printed in Portugal and featured a palm tree and rising sun, symbolising the new republic. A second series, printed in Switzerland, was released in 1969 in the same denominations as before. The palm tree emblem appeared on the front, but various industries and occupations of

Biafra were shown on the back of the notes. Biafran resistance was finally crushed in January 1970 and the federal government immediately repudiated all debts of the Biafran regime. The paper money of the erstwhile republic, like that of the Confederate States of America, became valueless overnight. Large quantities of uncirculated Biafran notes have since come on to the market and are still available for much less than their face value, pathetic mementoes of a grim civil war.

Both the Gambia and Sierra Leone have issued their own paper money within the past decade, the latter country introducing a new currency system based on the leone of 100 cents in 1964. The Gambia changed to the dalasi of 100 butbuts in 1971.

Central Africa

Paper money was issued under the authority of the British South Africa Company for use in Mashonaland and Matabeleland at the turn of the century. From the 1920s onwards, distinctive notes were released in Northern and Southern Rhodesia, and Nyasaland. The short-lived Federation of Rhodesia and Nyasaland, which existed from 1954 to 1964, also issued sterling banknotes. Since then paper

10 francs note of the Central Bank of the Belgian Congo and Ruanda-Urundi showing an okapi on the reverse.

money has been issued for Rhodesia, Zambia and Malawi, as Southern Rhodesia, Northern Rhodesia and Nyasaland are now known. Zambia went decimal in 1968, the unit being the kwacha; Malawi also has the kwacha, divided into 100 tambala.

The Portuguese territories in Central Africa— Mozambique in the east and Angola in the west— have also issued their own paper money for many years. At one time, these territories used notes which were similar to those circulating in the mother country, but with distinctive serial numbers.This practice gave rise to an unfortunate swindle perpetrated against the firm of Waterlow and Sons, who were duped into printing duplicate sets of banknotes in the 1920s. The latter were ostensibly for release in Angola but, in fact, were put into circulation in Portugal itself where they almost bankrupted the economy, toppled the moderate republican government and brought the dictator Salazar to power in 1926. Though several of the swindlers were prosecuted for this crime, the main burden of responsibility was borne by Waterlows who had to compensate the Portuguese government for the losses they incurred.

The former Belgian Congo issued paper money with a strong Belgian influence in its design. After

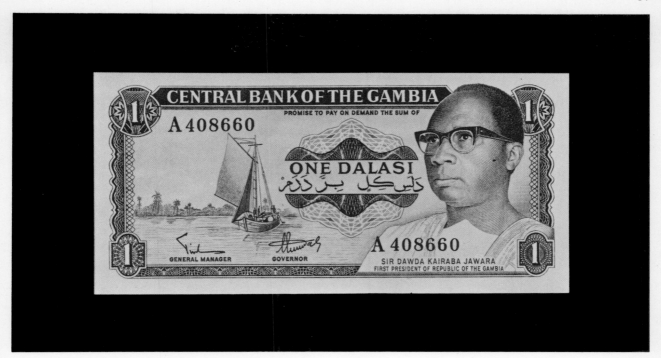

The Gambia, 1 delasi banknote showing the first president of the Gambia, Sir Dawda Kairaba Jawara.

the Belgians withdrew from the area in 1960, paper money was issued not only by the Congolese Republic (now renamed Zaire), but by the break-away regimes of Moishe Tshombe in the copper state of Katanga and by 'King' Albert Kalonji in South Kasai. At the same time the former mandated territory of Ruanda-Urundi split up to form the republic of Rwanda and the kingdom of Burundi, both of which speedily began issuing distinctive banknotes. The paper money of the latter was changed in 1967 as a result of a military coup which overthrew the monarchy, and in the same year the Congolese Republic stabilised its currency after a period of inflation by introducing the zaire divided into 100 makuta each worth 100 sengi, thereby requiring another series of banknotes. The paper money of the emergent nations is nothing if not colourful and interesting, reflecting the dramatic history and economic crises of these countries.

North Africa

The pattern of paper money in North Africa is rather similar to that of South Africa. Banking was under the control of European commercial interests until very recently and reflected the struggle by the various European powers to gain the ascendancy in that area. Spanish pesetas and colonial currency circulated in the Sahara and the Spanish zone of Morocco; French franc denominations circulated in French Morocco, Algeria and Tunisia; Italian colonial lira banknotes were used in Tripolitania and Cyrenaica while piastres of British design and manufacture circulated in the Sudan. Only in Egypt and Ethiopia were distinctive bank-notes used, in deference to the sovereignty of these countries, but even there British, French and Italian banking influence was strong. Morocco began issuing distinctive notes in 1959, with a currency based on the dirham of 100 francs. In the same year the Central Bank of Tunisia was founded and began issuing notes in a currency based on the dinar of 1,000 milliemes. The British firm of Bradbury Wilkinson began printing notes for the United Kingdom of Libya in 1952, with the emblems of the Senussi royal family. A new republican series of banknotes was issued in 1971, following the over-throw of the monarchy and the establishment of the Libyan Arab Republic; it consists of dinars divided into 1,000 dirham.

Inflation, currency reform, political changes and revolution have all combined to make the paper money of modern Africa as interesting and varied as that of Latin America in the late nineteenth and early twentieth centuries.

7
AUSTRALASIAN PAPER MONEY

The history of currency in Australia is not unlike that of the early United States, with various make-shifts preceding the government issues. A fantastic variety of coins of many different countries, from Britain and Spain to the Mogul Empire of India and the Dutch East Indies circulated among the early colonists of New South Wales. These coins were supplemented by tokens of local origin and a number of different forms of paper money. Among the latter the most acceptable were the receipts for meat, grain and other foodstuffs issued by the Official Commissariat Store at Sydney. Military payment warrants and vouchers also circulated freely in place of paper money and several merchants and traders in Sydney issued paper or card 'good fors'. A similar situation developed in Tasmania.

Governor Lachlan Macquarie tried to suppress these various unofficial issues of paper money by introducing Spanish silver dollars which were divided into two parts—the central 'dump' and the outer ring, known as a 'holey dollar'. The businessmen of Sydney, however, continued to issue their own paper money, foremost among them being Garnham Blaxcell who produced a £1 note in 1814. To stem the flood of private notes, Macquarie founded the Bank of New South Wales

Van Diemen's Land (Tasmania), sixpence notes issued at Hobart in 1825 and 1826. Note the promise to pay the bearer "In Spanish Dollars"—the only regular form of currency then used in the colony.

in 1817 and issued banknotes in dollar denominations, since the Spanish dollar was the commonest form of currency at that time. Sterling banknotes began appearing in 1829 and there was a spate of private banks which flourished briefly in all six colonies of Australia, as well as the state banks of Victoria, Queensland, South and Western Australia and Tasmania. The depression of the 1840s led to the closure of many of these banks, and their notes are now quite scarce. There was a revival of private banks following the discovery of gold in 1851 and within a few years many traders, innkeepers and pioneer industrialists were issuing their own notes. The paper money of the private and state banks gradually died out by the end of the nineteenth century and was replaced by the issues of the Commonwealth of Australia. In 1966, Australia abandoned sterling in favour of a dollar currency. Notes in denominations from 1 to 10 dollars were introduced that year and feature famous Australians and Aboriginal art.

The same pattern was repeated in New Zealand, the issues of traders and private banks giving way to the notes of the large commercial banks, such as the Union Bank of Australia, and then to the notes of the New Zealand government. These have always had a high standard of design, drawing on traditional Maori art for inspiration. Other subjects depicted on New Zealand banknotes have included the female figure of Zealandia, Maori warriors,

Hong Kong: small notes for small denominations—1, 5 and 10 cents.
The 1 cent note has probably the lowest value of any banknote in
current use.

New Zealand $2 of the same series, depicting mistletoe and a rifleman hummingbird.

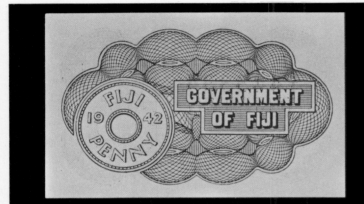

Obverse and reverse of the Government of Fiji 1 penny note, issued in 1942.

New Zealand $1 of 1967, featuring clematis and a fantail. The front bears a portrait of Queen Elizabeth by Anthony Buckley.

The Kiwi is the New Zealand national bird.

West Samoa, 2 talas banknote showing a native hut.

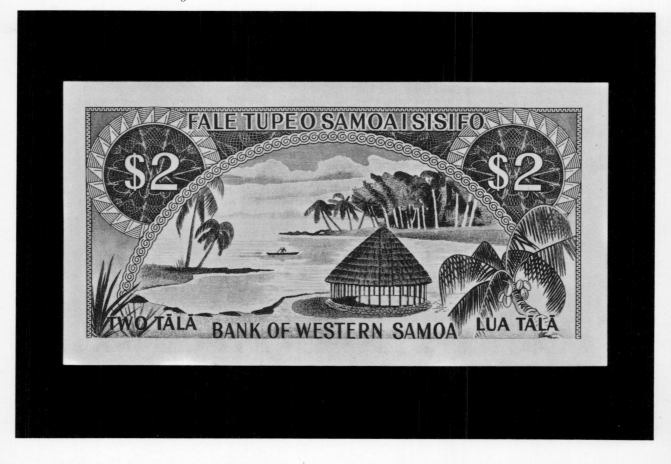

Bank of Indochina 20 franc note, issued at Papeete in French Polynesia. Note the inscription, bottom right, threatening punishment to counterfeiters.

birds, flowers and scenery, as well as some of the finest portraits of the reigning monarch used on any banknotes of the British Commonwealth. Like Australia, New Zealand adopted a decimal currency in 1967 and since then has issued banknotes in denominations from $1 upwards.

Australian or New Zealand currency circulates in many of the British island territories of the Pacific, but on certain occasions local issues of paper money have also been made. The tiny island in the Gilbert and Ellice group, Fanning Island, had its own £1 notes during the Second World War when the Japanese naval blockade prevented supplies of currency arriving from Australia. The notes were printed in Hawaii on behalf of the Fanning Island

Plantations Ltd. After the war the notes were cut in half, surcharged 1s or 2s with blue pencil, and used as cinema tickets! Examples of whole notes are exceedingly rare.

The currency used in the French colonies of New Caledonia, Polynesia and the condominium of the New Hebrides is not often seen and is worth collecting. The New Hebrides has notes inscribed bilingually, in English and French, in denominations of *francs d'or* (gold francs). In French Polynesia, currency is supplied by the Bank of Indochina which has a branch in Papeete and issues franc notes with attractive Polynesian scenery, flowers and native types featured on them.

Australia dollar, introduced in 1965. The reverse depicts aboriginal rock paintings of hunting and domestic scenes.

8
EMERGENCY PAPER MONEY

All paper money, in a sense, is a substitute for gold and silver coinage and had its origins in times when specie was in short supply. But there have been times when even paper money was scarce or unobtainable, or when even the lowest denomination of coins has been unavailable. In these circumstances, various forms of emergency money have become necessary. During the Second World War the Fijian authorities were forced to issue a penny note, because servicemen stationed in the colony had snapped up all the low-value coins as souvenirs.

Even older than paper as a form of substitute money were pieces of fur (used in medieval Russia) or leather. Strips of leather, suitably inscribed, engraved, embroidered or embossed, were used as emergency money in the Greek state of Sparta as long ago as 890 B.C. and also by the Romans, Carthaginians and Chinese in the pre-Christian era. Leather 'coins' were used in England on several occasions: in 970, at the end of the twelfth century, in 1280 and in the early nineteenth century. During the siege of Leyden by the Spaniards in 1572 the burghers cut up the leather bindings of books, embossed them with an official seal, and used the pieces as money. Other countries in which leather money has been used include Russia (1655), France (1250), Serbia (during the Turkish siege of Belgrade, 1688) and Denmark (during the siege of Oslo by the Swedes, 1716). The North American Indians made use of leather money, strips of this material being issued as

D-Day—troops coming ashore in France.

currency by Pontiac in Canada (1762) and Sitting Bull during the Sioux rebellion of 1875.

Before the passage of the Truck Act in 1831, many industrialists paid their workmen in token currency which could only be spent at the company's shop. Though most of these tokens were made of pewter or bronze, a few were made of cardboard including the fourpence, shilling and halfcrown tokens issued by the Malcolmson Brothers for the use of the flax-spinners of Waterford. Although they were illegal, these tokens were quite popular with the Malcolmsons' employees and they continued in use as late as 1876. Some were circular, like coins, while others were eight-sided.

Postage Stamp Money

The shortage of coins during the American Civil War has already been mentioned in Chapter 3. Shopkeepers were unable to give small change to their customers and inevitably a system of barter arose which was highly impracticable. Postage stamps, however, were a handy substitute for cents, nickels and dimes and they circulated for a time in place of coins—until they became so grubby and dog-eared that they were almost unrecognisable. In New York City alone the sale of stamps rose from $3,000 daily to $16,000. It was then that John Gault, a Boston sewing-machine salesman, came up with the brilliant idea of encasing stamps in small circular metal discs, rather like coins, but with a transparent mica front through which the face of

Russian stamps of the Romanov Tercentenary series of 1913, were re-
issued in 1915–16 printed on cardboard, with an inscription on the
back to signify their usage as money, following a shortage of low
denomination coins. In some cases the stamps were also overprinted
with a large numeral on the face to denote their value.

the stamp would be visible. Gault's idea spread like
wildfire; at last the public had something which
looked and felt like a coin, and a handful of them
even had something of the jingle of the coins which
were so sadly missed.

The encased stamps had the added advantage
over the former coins in that they provided space
for enterprising merchants—and the American
ad-man of a century ago was just as enterprising as
his present-day counterpart, judging from the
numerous varieties of advertisements found
stamped or engraved on the backs of these discs.
The stamps used were the definitive series of 1861
and denominations ranging from 1 to 90 cents were
used. An unusual multiple token was the rectangle
enclosing a strip of three 3 cents stamps to make a
9 cents 'coin'. It is estimated that over 200 different
varieties of encased postage stamps were produced,
with many combinations of advertisement ranging
from patent medicines to life assurance.

The use of encased postage stamps was short-
lived and they were soon eclipsed by the government issues known as 'Postage Currency'. In
August 1862, the federal government introduced
small notes in denominations of 5, 10, 25 and 50

A shortage of Austrian coins after the First World War was met by
issuing stamps on thick card, so that they could be used as either coins
or stamps.

The obverse of a Tibetan note of low denomination.   5 peso note of the Bank of Guatemala, obverse, 1919 series.   50 cent or half-dollar note of the Bahamas Monetary Authority, reverse, 1968 series.   The obverse of a 100 drachmae note issued by a Greek farmers' bank in 1945.

5 dollar note of Vietnam, reverse. The reverse of the 500 kronor note of Denmark, 1961 series. 10 rupee note of the Bank of Ceylon, now Sri Lanka, 1970·series. The·obverse of the 1 baht note of Thailand, 1936 series.

Group of four Latvian postage stamps, issued in 1920, and printed on the backs of unissued banknotes produced by Colonel von Avalov-Bermondt commander of the Baltic Landeswehr fighting the Bolsheviks. Portions of these banknotes may be seen on the backs of the stamps.

stamps was strengthened by the fact that the earliest issues had reproductions of stamps engraved on them—five 5 cent stamps on the 25c notes and five 10c stamps on the 50c notes. The allusion to stamps was taken a stage further by perforating the notes in the manner of stamps, though this unnecessary device was soon done away with. The pretence of postage stamps was dropped in 1863 when small notes in denominations from 3c to 50c were issued as 'Fractional Currency'. The pictures of stamps were replaced by handsome portraits of George Washington, but the notes bore the inscription "Receivable for all U.S. stamps", thus retaining a link with the earlier Postage Currency.

Encased stamps were used as currency at the end of the First World War. Prior to the inflation period of 1922–3 in Germany and Austria, the shortage of coins was met by encasing stamps in a similar fashion to the American tokens of sixty years earlier. These mica-faced discs are larger than the American type, and were backed by either aluminium or plastic. Likewise they carried a wide range of advertisements. The practice spread to France who was also experiencing an acute shortage of specie. The French discs sometimes have a numeral on the reverse indicating their value. The use of such makeshifts even extended to former neutrals, such as Norway, Denmark and Argentina, while Belgium, Greece and Italy also used them to some extent. Examples from countries other than Germany, Austria and France are extremely scarce. Postage stamps were declared legal tender in Britain in both world wars, but on neither occasion were they encased for the purposes of circulation.

Stamps have also been circulated in place of coins, by sticking them on special cards. The British South Africa Company adopted this measure to fill the gap during the Boer War; small cards were issued in 1900 by the Civil Commissioners at Bulawayo. They bore the statement: "Please pay in cash to the person producing this card the face value of the stamp affixed thereto, if presented on or after the 1st August 1900. This card must be produced for redemption not later than 1st October 1900."

These cards were printed at the Chronicle Printing Works in Bulawayo and a great variety of rubber stamps was used to authenticate the signature of the Company Secretary, H. Marshall Hole. On the back of the cards, stamps of the

98

Siege of Mafeking, 10 shillings and £1 notes, designed by Baden-Powell himself.

British South Africa Company were affixed. They ranged in value from threepence to ten shillings. Of the £20,000 worth issued, about £1,000 were never redeemed and it must be presumed that the quantity of stamped cards in the hands of collectors is fairly small.

An extension of this idea was the re-issue in 1915 of three of the Romanov commemorative stamps of Russia, printed on stout card and inscribed on the back "On par with silver currency". The stamps were the 10, 15 and 20 kopek denominations and, though they were mainly intended to be used as money, they could be and sometimes were used for postage on letters. In 1917, the Kerensky government treated the 1, 2 and 3 kopek stamps in similar fashion, some of the 1 and 2 kopek values being surcharged "1" or "2" across the face of the stamp as well. Stamps printed on card for use as currency appeared at the end of the First World War in some of the fragments of the former Russian Empire. The shortlived governments of the Don Cossacks, Armenia, the Crimea and the Ukraine produced various stamps in 1918–20 printed on ungummed paper or thick card with inscriptions on the reverse authorising their use as coins. As an alternative to encased postage stamps, Austria also produced cardboard stamps in 1919–20 for use as money. During the Second World War, Ceylon and the Indian state of Bundi issued small cards with contemporary stamps printed on them, for use as small currency.

Stamps mounted on cards in the Rhodesian manner were used in Madagascar during the First World War and were issued officially by the *Bureau des Postes*, in denominations from 5 centimes to 2 francs. Turkey used postage, revenue and railway stamps backed by yellowish paper for a time at the end of the First World War in place of metal coins. During the Spanish Civil War, a shortage of small coins was met by the republican government who issued the definitive stamps affixed to cardboard discs bearing the Spanish coat of arms on the reverse. Filipino guerrillas operating against the Japanese in 1942 produced 5 peso notes to which revenue stamps of the appropriate amount were stuck.

Siege Money

There are numerous examples of paper money having been produced in towns and districts besieged by the enemy in time of war. Indeed, the earliest example of paper money in Europe may well have arisen in this way. In 1483, the Moors besieged the town of Alhama in Granada and, in order to pay his soldiers, the Spanish commander, the Conde de Tendilla, produced notes in the name of the King of Aragon promising to pay the bearer the equivalent sum in gold or silver coins at the end of the siege. None of these notes has ever been found, although references to them appear in the writings of contemporary historians. If they actually existed—and there is no good reason to doubt it—they preceded the *kreditivsedlar* of Sweden by almost two hundred years. This was a wartime expedient, however, and a further three centuries elapsed before Spain adopted paper money for general use.

In 1793, the French royalists in Lyons rose in revolt against the new-born republic and held the city against the republicans for two months. During that period the defenders of Lyons used paper money inscribed in French "Lyons besieged— Resistance to Oppression". Later the same year republican troops, penned up in the city of Mayence (Mainz) by the advancing Prussian army, used paper money in denominations from 5 sous to 50 livres. In 1807 the Prussians were besieged by the French at Colberg and had to use paper money for a short time. Two types of note were issued: commission coupons authorised by a coinage commission, and Meinecke coupons, named after the Counsellor for War and Crown Lands. Both issues were in denominations of 2, 4 and 8 groschen. In 1813 the French were besieged in the Thuringian city of Erfurt by the Prussians. The commander of the French garrison authorised an issue of siege notes, printed in German in denominations from 2 groschen to 5 thalers.

During 1848, revolutions and rebellions broke out all over Europe—in France, Germany, Italy, Hungary, Poland and elsewhere. Rebels held out for several months in a number of cities and issued their own paper money under siege. The most prolific issues appeared in Hungary which was in

A group of Boers keeping watch at Magersfontein, scene of an important battle during the Boer War.

a state of revolt against the Habsburg rulers of Austria. The Hungarian Uprising was eventually suppressed in 1849, when the Habsburg emperor called on his ally, the Tsar of Russia, to send troops into Hungary, they quelled the revolt with great brutality. The Austrian garrison in Arad used temporary paper money while the town was besieged by the Hungarian rebels, while the Hungarians issued paper money in various krajczar denominations in Esseg, Komarom and Temesvar while they held out against the armies of Austria and Russia.

The Italians of Lombardo-Venezia also rebelled against their Austrian overlords. For a short time Venice flourished as the Republic of St Mark and issued paper money inscribed *Moneta Patriottica* (patriotic money) in denominations from 1 to 100 lire. The Venetian notes are among the most artistic of all siege money, with allegorical figures of Neptune and the goddess of Justice. These notes were current during the siege of Venice which came to an end in August 1849 when the Italians were compelled to surrender to the Austrians. Several Italian fortresses issued paper money while they were besieged by the Austrians. The notes of Osopo, in denominations from 50 centesimi to 6 lire, were entirely hand-written, whereas those of Palmanova were properly printed, though hand-signed and numbered.

Both Belfort and Langres used paper money during the sieges of the Franco-Prussian War in 1870. When the Sudanese capital of Khartoum was besieged by the army of the Mahdi in 1884–5 General Gordon issued paper money, in denominations from 5 piastres to 50 Egyptian pounds. The notes were entirely inscribed in Arabic signifying "This sum is accepted and will be paid at the Treasury in Khartoum or Cairo six months from the present date . . .". The lower values bore a facsimile of Gordon's signature but the higher denominations were personally signed by the general. It is thought that a total of £168,500 worth of notes were issued, but most of them were destroyed by the Mahdi's followers when they sacked and looted Khartoum at the end of January 1885.

Fifteen years later, Africa was again the scene of a famous siege which resulted in some attractive mementoes for the paper money collector. The town of Mafeking was besieged by the Boers from 16 October 1899 to 17 May 1900. The small British garrison was commanded by Brevet-Colonel Robert Baden-Powell, whose gallant defence of the town won him promotion to Major-General. Seven years later he founded the Boy Scout movement. During the siege Baden-Powell was responsible for a temporary issue of paper money. The Standard Bank began to run short of coins, as people were hoarding them, and an issue of notes, in denominations of 1, 2 and 3 shillings, was made in January 1900. The notes bore the signatures of R. Urry, manager of the Standard Bank, and Captain H. Greener, the Command Paymaster. A total of £1,045 was issued

Siege of Mafeking, voucher for 1 shilling, issued under the authority of Colonel Baden-Powell, January 1900.

Back and front of a half-crown currency card, issued in Rhodesia in 1900 to meet a shortage of silver coins caused by the Boer War.

in these low value notes. Subsequently higher denominations were felt to be necessary and ten-shilling and one pound notes were introduced in March 1900. These notes were quite interesting in appearance, bearing designs by Baden-Powell himself. The 10s note featured soldiers manning a field gun and a maxim machine gun. The design and production of this note was later described by

Baden-Powell: "We tried various dodges, drew a design on copper, bit it out with acid all right, but could not get sufficient pressure to print it, though we tried it through a mangle. Then we cut a croquet mallet head in half and made wood-cuts." The wood-cuts were engraved by C. Riesle whose initials appear on the right-hand side of the note.

The £1 note, also designed by Baden-Powell,

A 1916 cartoon of a British general eating out in France.

showed a group of defenders round the garrison's home-made gun, the Wolf. The original drawing was photographed and a printing plate made from it by the ferro-prussiate process—a novel and surprisingly modern technique which was also adopted for the Mafeking postage stamps. Only 638 of these £1 notes were printed. It is interesting to note that a high proportion of the Mafeking siege notes (some £4,590 worth) were never redeemed, yet the number of notes known to be in the hands of collectors is very small, a total of fewer than 500. Many notes are probably still lying around in old family correspondence undetected and unconsidered.

Paper money of a rather different kind was issued in the town of Kimberley while it was besieged by the Boers. These notes did not bear denominations in money, but were worth certain amounts of food, for which they could be exchanged. Five pound notes were issued at Koffyfontein, in the Orange Free State, while it was under siege, but they are extremely rare and very little is known about them.

During the Second World War, notes in denominations of 1, 5 and 10 cents were issued in Hong Kong during the siege of December 1941 before the colony surrendered to the Japanese. During the blockade of Malta in 1941–2 a stock of George V two-shilling notes dated November 1918 was unearthed, surcharged for use as 1 shilling notes and pressed into service, until a fresh supply of money could be sent out from Britain.

Promissory notes were issued by Major-General Steffens, commander of the Norwegian garrison besieged by the Germans at Voss in 1940. Steffens issued these notes with the full authority of the Norges Bank and used them to pay his troops. These notes are now very scarce and highly prized as souvenirs of the gallant last stand of the Norwegian army against the Nazi invaders.

Invasion and Occupation Money

One of the problems facing troops when they invade a country is how to pay for food and goods. The old answer was quite simple: you did not pay, you merely seized what you wanted as part of the spoils of war. Nevertheless, by the time of the First World War, it was customary to issue special paper money to troops immediately before an invasion took place. One of the earliest examples of this occurred in 1915 when British troops destined for the beaches of Gallipoli were paid on embarkation with British Treasury notes overprinted in Arabic to signify their value in Turkish piastres. The 10s note was worth 60 piastres and the £1 note was worth 120 piastres. Unfortunately the expedition never got beyond the bullet-riddled beaches of Gallipoli and never got the opportunity to spend this money. Most of the issue was later recalled, though a few examples of this invasion money survived and were kept by soldiers as souvenirs of the ill-fated campaign.

During the Second World War, invasion and occupation notes were produced by both sides. At first the Germans used the money of Czechoslovakia and Poland, suitably overprinted, after invading these countries in 1939. Later they issued three kinds of paper money for use in the occupied territories of Europe. *Reichskreditkassen* (state credit bank) notes were introduced in September 1939 for the use of the civil population. Auxiliary payment certificates (*Behelfszahlungsmittel*) bore denominations in pfennigs and marks and were issued to German troops at a value ten times greater than that printed on them. When civilians came to redeem them, of course, they only got the nominal value for them. The British produced excellent forgeries of these notes, with a German rhyme on the back which meant "50 pfennig is my name—I'll cheat everyone of 4.50 marks who thinks Hitler gives him something". These notes were dropped over occupied territory by British aircraft. Reckoning notes (*Verrechnungsscheine*) were issued to German forces immediately before the invasion of a country took place. They were then exchanged for currency of the country after the invasion began.

In many cases the Germans took over the banking facilities of the countries they occupied and issued notes under their authority, often incorporating the German eagle and Nazi swastika emblem in the design. Among the rarest issues are those prepared for use in the Ukraine in 1941, following the German invasion of Russia. These notes were to have been distributed through the Kiev State Bank but were never put into circulation and examples of them are now extremely scarce.

The Japanese had a prolific series of invasion and occupation money which they used in 1941–5 in those areas of South-east Asia and the Pacific which they conquered. The notes were inscribed in English and featured scenes of South-east Asia, native huts and bullocks. They were issued in denominations up to 1,000 dollars. The same basic designs were used throughout most of the occupied territories but the notes can be identified by the code letter prefixing the serial numbers: B (Burma), M (Malaya), O (Oceania), P (Philippines) and S (Sumatra). The Philippines subsequently had dis-

A drawing of Colonel Robert Baden-Powell, founder of the Boy Scout Movement and commander of Mafeking during the siege.

Japanese military occupation note for 10 dollars, derisively known as 'banana money' because of the principal motif. The code-letters MP indicate that this note was issued in Malaya.

Japanese occupation 10 centavos note, for use in the Philippines.

A Japanese machine-gun post.

tinctive notes portraying Dr José P. Laurel or José Rizal, after the Japanese established a puppet government at Manila. The Filipino guerrillas retaliated by issuing their own paper money, possession of which could mean death for anyone caught by the Japanese. The Sumatra notes were printed in Dutch and circulated throughout the former Dutch East Indies. The Oceania notes, intended for use in Papua, New Guinea, the Solomon Islands and the Gilbert and Ellice Islands, were valued in Australian pence, shillings and pounds. In Java and Burma, notes inscribed in native languages appeared later in the war, after the Japanese installed governments ready to obey their orders.

The Allies also produced many issues of invasion and occupation money. First of all there were the forgeries of Japanese notes which had various propaganda messages and slogans printed on them. Those dropped over the Philippines bore the legend "The Co-Prosperity Sphere—What is it Worth?" The Malayan 10 dollar note was forged with a message, in Malay, Burmese and Chinese, on the back: "At present in Malaya Japanese money is not recognised and the original notes are the only legal tender. When the British return to Malaya their notes will be used as before. Japanese notes will disappear together with the Japanese, forever, and

Emergency money used in French Somaliland, issued by the Franco-Ethiopian Railway Company.

United States military payment certificate for 5 cents.

United States military payment certificate for 5 cents, showing the head of the Statue of Liberty.

Allied invasion money: 1 lira note issued for use in Italy, 1943. The back of this note is inscribed with the Four Freedoms.

British 5 franc note issued in France after the Normandy landings in 1944.

A cartoon of General Gordon by Spy.

the original British money will be used forever."

The British and the Americans produced lira notes for the invasion of Sicily and Italy in 1943 and franc notes for the D-Day landings in Normandy in June 1944. The D-Day notes depicted the French tricolour flag and were inscribed *Emis en France*. General De Gaulle, leader of the Free French forces, objected strongly to the design of these notes, saying that no one but the French themselves had the right to display the tricolour. He also objected to the words *Emis en* (issued in) and subsequent issues of the franc notes were inscribed merely

"France" and omitted the tricolour. Invasion currency was also produced for use in Belgium and the Netherlands. The latter objected to the design of the Dutch notes and these were withdrawn after a very short time. The Allies printed marks and schillings for use in Germany and Austria after these countries were occupied. The notes issued by each of the four powers (Britain, France, Russia and the United States) may be distinguished by their serial numbers. British Military Authority notes were issued in sterling denominations for use in Somaliland after it was liberated from Italian

Back and front of the 1 franc emergency note of the Franco-Ethiopian Railway Company, bearing a postage stamp as a form of money.

troops in 1942. Later notes in Military Authority Lire (M.A.L.) were produced for circulation in the former Italian colonies of Tripolitania, Cyrenaica and Eritrea.

Indian notes were overprinted for release in Burma under the authority of the British Military Administration in 1945–6, pending the transfer of power to an independent Burmese government. Liberation notes were also circulated in Malaya and Hong Kong after the Japanese surrendered in September 1945.

Other relics of the Second World War include the paper money used by prisoners of war in German and Japanese hands, the notes used in the ghettoes of Warsaw, Litmannstadt (Lodz) and Theresienstadt (Teresin), the paper money of Dachau, Auschwitz and other concentration camps and the money issued by the resistance movements in France, Poland, Czechoslovakia and Yugoslavia. Slovak partisans issued notes emblazoned with a

A contemporary print of the fighting during the Siege of Venice by the Austrians in 1849.

red star and the slogan "Death to Fascism". In Montenegro the partisans issued paper money whose value decreased slightly each month and this novel idea was supposed to ensure that the notes circulated as widely as possible.

After the Allies occupied Japan in September 1945, a type of paper money known as 'Foreign Trade Payment Certificates' was introduced. These certificates bore values in American dollars or British sterling and were used in place of the normal currency at a time when Japanese paper money was discredited.

The activities of speculators and black marketeers caused concern to the Allies after the Second World War. The Americans introduced 'Military Payment Certificates', a form of paper money which were used by servicemen when purchasing goods from the PX or military canteens. From time to time these certificates were suddenly replaced by new issues, all personnel being confined to camp while the changeover took place, so that civilians who had amassed vast quantities of these notes illegally were unable to get rid of the obsolete issues. The British troops used notes known familiarly as 'bafs', from their initials. 'British Armed Forces Vouchers' came into use in 1945 and were employed in many postwar campaigns, from Korea to Suez, as well as in British garrisons and stations all over the world in time of peace. Some of these notes bear an overprint "Issued in H.M. Ships Afloat for use in N.A.A.F.I. canteens only", which clearly explains the purpose for which they were issued.

Russia also produced distinctive paper money for the use of Soviet troops occupying former enemy territory or liberated countries. As well as the American-printed notes for use in Germany, distinguished by a special dash in front of the serial numbers, the Russians printed their own distinctive notes for use in Austria, Czechoslovakia, Hungary, Poland and Roumania, and issued paper money for use in Manchuria and Korea after the Japanese surrender in 1945.

A chapter which has dealt mainly with the emergency issues produced in wartime could not end without a reference to the notes issued in the Philippine island of Leyte in October 1944, after it was liberated from the Japanese by General Douglas MacArthur. The Secretary of National Defence and Communications authorised the overprinting of the word "Victory" on both postage stamps and banknotes to celebrate the landing of the Americans. These notes are now highly prized as mementoes of the defeat of the Japanese in the Second World War.

KRAFT : WENIG REDEN · VIELGESCHAFFT ·

10 Pf

· NOT GIBT · Notgeld der Marienkirche Stadt mit Frankfurt a.O. anno 1921 Das Stadthaus · NOT LEHRT BETEN ·

JOCHEM

WISCH · WARD AUS DER NOT GEBOR'N · ALS UNSER GOLD VERLOR'N ·

25 Pf

· AUCH DIESER NOTGELD · Rathaus Frankfurt a.d.Oder · v. Norden · NOT MACHT ERFINDERISCH ·

JOCHEM

DIE KETTEN REISSEN · UEBER NACHT ·

50 Pf

· O · ERWACHT · Rathaus Frankfurt a.d. Oder Südgiebel · NOT BRICHT EISEN ·

JOCHEM

LIG : EINST BEIM MORGENROT · WIRD · DAS HOFFEN SEI UNS HEI

1 M

NACHT U. NOT VERZEIHLICH · Frankfurt a.O. Marien-Kirche von Süden · NOT KENNT KEIN GEBOT ·

JOCHEM

9
COMMEMORATIVE
PAPER MONEY

Collectors of paper money are more fortunate than their stamp-collecting brethren, in one respect at least. While every country now churns out vast quantities of postage stamps to commemorate every conceivable event and personality under the sun, banks and treasuries have made surprisingly little use of paper money for commemorative purposes. This is all the more surprising when it is realised that nowadays coins are frequently issued for this reason. Very few Eisenhower dollars or Churchill crowns can ever have been used in normal circulation, because they are usually retained by collectors as souvenirs. In the same way paper money, with its much greater scope than postage stamps for artistic treatment, would seem to be ideally suited to a commemorative treatment. But up to now there have been very few issues of commemorative paper money.

Many of the issues of *Notgeld*, referred to in Chapter 4, were commemorative in character and frequently alluded to local events and famous persons. The *Notgeld* of the early 1920s provides numerous fascinating examples, and one would need a very good knowledge of local history to appreciate the significance of the subjects depicted on these notes. Take the *Notgeld* of the town of Bielefeld, for example. The 1 mark note depicted a view of the town as it was in 1760 and bore a riddle, in German: "What have marriage and school slates in common? Bielefeld girls count on both." The note also depicts soldiers playing leap-frog, a reference to Councillor Svering who leap-frogged

Series of notgeld from Frankfurt on the Oder depicting the Marien-kirche (10pf), northern town hall (25pf), southern district town hall (50pf) and southern Marienkirche (1 mark).

over the Lord Mayor to become Minister. The 5 mark note symbolised the 29 countries who fought Germany in the recent war and bore several important dates, including that of Kaiser Wilhelm II's abdication in November 1918. The 20 mark note alludes to the 131st (Bielefeld) Regiment, with the dates of the battles in which it fought. The 50 mark note is a curiosity, mixing history with political propaganda. The back of the note gives the German casualty figures for the Franco-Prussian War of 1870 and the First World War, with slogans urging one to fight hard in the troubled times ahead. This side of the note also makes reference to the statue of Germania which Napoleon's troops looted in 1807 and which was brought back to Germany seven years later, via Bielefeld and erected on the Brandenburg Gate in Berlin. The front of the note sheds an interesting light on the manufacture of paper money from rags. A sausage machine shows cloth being poured in at the top and coming out in the form of banknotes. A girl on the right of the note is depicted in the act of peeling of her knickers for conversion into paper money. The higher denominations bore references to President Woodrow Wilson's peace proposals and the League of Nations depicted as the tormentor of a war-stricken Germany. Incongruously, in the middle of all this propaganda there is an inscription commemorating the 55th anniversary of the firm of Dürkopp. A fascinating collection of *Notgeld* could be formed depicting historic personalities like Martin Luther and the Iron Chancellor Bismarck, or referring to historic anniversaries such as the Battle of Dresden (1813) or the Reformation.

With the exception of German *Notgeld*, all the issues of commemorative paper money which have

Austria, Notgeld, 1919. 75 heller note of Fieberbrunn with a politically inspired cartoon on the back. The frontier sign between Germany and Austria is being pulled down—part of the "German Austria" campaign of that year.

Austria, 10 heller note of Bad Aussee in Styria, 1920.

The notgeld of the German town of Emden featured a view of the town hall on the front and a picture of the famous warship of the same name, on the reverse.

1 peso note of the Bank of Colombia, reverse, 1964 series.   The obverse of a 50 pound note of the Bank of Israel, 1955 series.
Ten shilling note of the Central Bank of Ireland, obverse.   The obverse of a 20 koruny note of Czechoslovakia, 1949 series.

The reverse of a 5 cedi note of Ghana, 1967 series.   The reverse of a 50 rupiah note of the Bank of Indonesia, 1946 series.
The obverse of a 1 dollar note of Singapore.   1,000 peseta note of the Bank of Spain, reverse, issued in Bilbao in 1937.

Austria, 20 heller note of Weissenbach bei Modling, 1920.

Austria, Notgeld (emergency money) for 5 hellers, issued at Wörgl, Tyrol.

Belgard notgeld commemorating the Belgard 'Death's Head' cavalry under Frederick the Great, 1744 (25pf) and showing the civic coat of arms (50pf).

Belgard notgeld: further notes in the series commemorating the Death's Head cavalry—Field Marshal von Mackensen (50pf), cavalryman as a French prisoner of war, 1758 (75pf) and a scene from the battle of Braunsberg in the Napoleonic Wars (1mk).

Naugard in Pomerania notgeld; 25pf, 75pf and 1mk notes portraying Bismarck (provincial deputy for Naugard, 1844) and Schill (general in the Napoleonic Wars), with landmarks and local crafts.

so far appeared have come from the American continent. The earliest of these consisted of 1 and 2 gourde notes issued by the republic of Haiti in 1904 to celebrate the centenary of Haitian independence. They portrayed respectively the patriots Jean-Jacques Dessalines and Nord Alexis. Six years later Mexico's Banco Minero released 5 and 10 peso notes in honour of the centenary of independence. Canada issued a 25 dollar note in 1935 to mark the Silver Jubilee of King George V. In honour of the centenary of Confederation, Canada issued a one dollar note in 1967. This note was novel in that it was not intended for general circulation, although it was strictly legal tender. It bore the date 1867–1967 in place of the usual serial numbers. Collectors could get specimens of this note from the headquarters of the Bank of Ottawa in Ontario for $1.35, the extra amount covering registration and postage. Centennial banknotes, with serial numbers, were circulated normally during 1967 in place of the ordinary dollar note (issued since 1954) which was suspended for that year.

Colombia issued a one peso note in 1938 to commemorate the 400th anniversary of the foundation of Bogota. In 1953 Cuba released a 1 peso note honouring the birth centenary of Jose Marti, the island's national hero. Two years later the Dominican Republic issued a 20 peso note to celebrate the jubilee of the Trujillo regime. The most recent commemorative item is Venezuela's 5 bolivares note of 1967 celebrating the quatercentenary of the city of Caracas.

Although this is, as yet, a small category of paper money it can only be a matter of time before the idea of commemorative notes becomes more acceptable. Now is the time to get hold of the early issues while they are still available.

Austria, 50 heller note of Traunkirchen, 1920.

10
OTHER KINDS
OF
PAPER MONEY

Apart from banknotes there are many other forms of paper money. For the most part these have been overlooked by collectors, though they are not without interest. One of the oldest forms of paper money, the promissory note, has already been mentioned in the first chapter, but there were other kinds of document which were handled as though they were actual money. Military payment warrants were used in the seventeenth and eighteenth centuries as a handy method of arranging the pay for soldiers on campaigns and expeditions. They were issued by the Command Paymaster to the commanders of regiments who used them to draw coined money from local banks. These warrants have been neglected by paper money collectors, but have long been popular with militaria enthusiasts and they are now quite hard to find. Cash warrants of a similar nature have been used right up to the present day for the payment of employees and, because security devices were often incorporated in their printing, they are parallel to paper money and therefore worth studying and collecting.

In the middle of the nineteenth century, the postal services in many countries of Europe and America began a system of money transactions through the post, without the actual coins having to be sent. Britain and the United States pioneered the money order system whereby certificates for certain amounts of money could be sent enclosed in an ordinary letter and cashed by the recipient at a Money Order Office. Money orders are still used, for larger amounts, to the present day, but

A cheque can be written on anything. Here Albert Haddock (Roy Dotrice) pays his income tax to the Inspector (Richard Wattis) written on a cow.

quite small amounts are now transmitted by means of postal orders or postal notes. Every country now uses postal orders and an interesting and varied collection could be formed of these items. At the beginning of both world wars, postal orders were declared legal tender in the United Kingdom. Special consignments of halfcrown and five-shilling postal orders were prepared in 1940 for use as money if Britain had been invaded by the Germans. As the threatened invasion did not take place, these special postal orders were destroyed, though a few of them did get into the hands of collectors and are now highly prized. Incidentally proper banknotes of these denominations were subsequently prepared, but these were never issued either and were all destroyed at the end of the war.

Nowadays banks issue special cheques to their current account holders who can write sums of various amounts for the payment of goods and services instead of actually handling money. In the early days of banking, however, it was usually quite sufficient for the customer to write out a cheque on any piece of paper which happened to be handy. The introduction of stamp duty on small money transactions in the 1690s meant that these pieces of paper had to bear the embossed stamp of the Stamp Office to show that the duty had been paid, and this led to the production of proper cheques by banks. The stamp duty on cheques was abolished in Britain in 1970 but, prior to that date, the upright oval embossed stamp showing the heraldic flowers of the United Kingdom or, more recently, the royal crown, were a familiar sight on cheques.

Bank cheques are a form of security printing,

produced by the same firms that print banknotes and an interesting collection could be formed of the cheques of different banks, showing the imprints of different security printers. These could also be matched with banknotes from the same bank or printing company. Old cheques are not as uncommon as one would think. Used cheques, which have been paid into a bank and bear the cancellation stamp, turn up in old accumulations of family papers and firm's correspondence bought in bulk by scrap and salvage merchants and in this way they gradually filter through to collectors. As a rule the design of cheques is not as colourful or elaborate as that of banknotes, though they usually incorporate special security features, such as the use of fugitive ink, which dissolves in water, or chemical substances impregnated in the paper to defeat the forger. In recent years, however, a number of banks, particularly in the United States and Canada, have begun issuing pictorial cheques to their customers and this practice has now spread to British and European banks. This idea began with some of the banks in the American West who embellished their cheques with cowboys and Indians, stage-coach scenes and prairie landscapes. Some of the recent British designs have featured famous London landmarks and famous beauty spots. Others have flower or animal designs, or psychedelic patterns in many different colours. Already these pictorial cheques are attracting the serious attention of collectors, and this may well stimulate interest in cheque-collecting in general.

The prevalence of counterfeit banknotes in the nineteenth century, when there were numerous private banks, has already been mentioned. The penalties for counterfeiting were very severe. At the best, it was an offence punishable by transportation to the Australian colonies, and at worst it meant death by hanging. Between 1805 and 1818 the Bank of England successfully prosecuted no fewer than 501 persons for counterfeiting its notes alone, and 207 of these were sent to the gallows. Examples of counterfeit banknotes of this period are highly prized by collectors and, ironically, are worth very much more than the genuine notes. At one time counterfeit notes were officially cancelled by the banks and returned to the unlucky persons who tried to pay them in. At other times, however, the mere possession of a counterfeit note was regarded as a crime with stiff penalties. Even now it is against the law in Britain and many other countries to possess counterfeit notes and these are usually confiscated by the authorities. As a result very few of these interesting items ever find their

way into collections, other than official archives. Examples of the Bank of England notes forged by the Nazis during the Second World War still turn up from time to time, since a certain amount of them did get into circulation in Europe and South America at the end of the war.

The savage sentences meted out to counterfeiters in the early nineteenth century led the Society of Arts, in 1809, to produce a report investigating ways of printing a banknote which could not be forged. They pinned their faith on the stereotype process which, in fact, would have been relatively easy to imitate and, fortunately for the Bank of England, was never adopted.

Political reformers urged that the severe laws against counterfeiting should be relaxed. George Cruikshank, the cartoonist and political satirist, even went so far as to design a Bank Restriction Note which was entered at Stationers' Hall and subsequently sold to the public for a shilling (5p). The note was inscribed "Specimen of a Bank Note —not to be imitated. Submitted to the Consideration of the Bank Directors and the inspection of the Public." The note was a close parody on the existing Bank of England notes. The figure of Britannia in the upper left-hand corner was surrounded by skulls and corpses, the £ sign was made of a hangman's rope. The main part of the design showed a gallows on which eleven men and women were hanging. Above this gruesome picture were the words "Promise to Perform", and underneath was the inscription "During the Issue of Bank Notes easily imitated and until the Resumption of Cash Payments or the Abolition of the Punishment of Death". The note was signed on behalf of the Governor and Company of the Bank of England by J. Ketch. Jack Ketch was the notorious public hangman of the period.

As a result of Cruikshank's note, a best-seller which caused rioting on the streets of London, the government was forced to take action. A Royal Commission was appointed in 1818 to investigate ways of producing notes which could not be imitated. The Bank of England was swamped with trial banknotes and designs from inventors, artists and printers. Sir Charles Bagot, the British Minister in Washington, discovered an American firm called Murray, Draper, Fairman & Co which had recently invented several processes which revolutionised banknote printing. These processes were the invention of Jacob Perkins, an employee of the company, whom Sir Charles persuaded to go to London and offer his services to the Bank of England. In 1819 Jacob Perkins crossed the Atlantic and subse-

Counterfeiting banknotes was one of the many crimes punishable by hanging.

quently won a contract to print banknotes using his siderographic transfer process and the rose engine which produced highly complicated background patterns of engraving. In this way the great firm of Perkins Bacon had its beginnings. Twenty years later it was Perkins Bacon who had the honour of printing the world's first postage stamps, the famous Penny Black and Twopence Blue of 1840, and for much of the nineteenth century this company dominated the world stamp and paper money production.

Apart from counterfeits, which were a tremendous problem for the banks, there were pieces of paper which pretended to be banknotes but were, in fact, a form of practical joke. These "skit notes" as they are called, fooled many of the illiterate or semi-literate people who were induced to accept them at markets and fairs and then found, to their cost, that what they had accepted proved to be quite worthless. These notes cannot be regarded as counterfeits though, like Cruikshank's note, they often parodied the designs of existing banknotes. Such notes purported to be issued by the Bank of Fools (an April Fools' Day joke), or the Bank of Hearts (for giving to one's lover on St Valentine's

Day). Others were produced as advertising gimmicks by enterprising tradesmen. The "Bank of Perukes", for example, issued skit notes advertising a Liverpool firm of wig-makers. Imitation paper money is often used, to this day, for advertisement purposes. The coupons given out by soap manufacturers often have the superficial appearance of banknotes, complete with ornate designs and an intricate geometrical background imitating the design of banknotes. Skit notes are still occasionally used for satirical purposes. In 1966, imitations of British £5 notes were produced in Rhodesia at the height of the UDI controversy. In place of Queen Elizabeth's portrait they showed a caricature of the then British Prime Minister, Harold Wilson, complete with pipe and, in place of the usual promise to pay the bearer, a reference to political promises which had been broken. These notes were crudely printed in black on white paper and would never have deceived anybody, but no doubt they served to boost morale in Rhodesia at the time.

The banknotes of many countries, including Belgium, France, Germany, Italy and Yugoslavia, carry stern warnings threatening dire retribution on those who counterfeit or distribute forged notes.

A skit note, produced in connection with St Valentine's Day, and modelled on the contemporary notes of the private banks in England.

Another fringe aspect of paper money which has attracted the attention of some collectors deals with objects which derive their design from banknotes, real or imaginary. Carrier bags, tea-towels, head-scarves and printed handkerchieves have taken paper money as their design. In the United States some years ago, tiny imitations of the one-dollar bill were produced by a novelty manufacturer, to show how the dollar had shrunk in value. As a rule, however, government authorities frown on the use of their paper money in this way, though the manufacturers of such souvenirs are seldom prose-cuted for it. Phantom money includes banknotes for entirely fictitious countries, play money used in Monopoly and other games of chance, toy money printed in connection with children's toy shops and post offices and even funeral money, produced in China and parts of Latin America. Chinese 'hell notes' are buried with the dead so that they may pay for food and services when they pass over to the next world. All of these are interesting facets of paper money in which the collector may special-ise at little cost.

Advanced collectors are not content to get hold of examples of the notes as actually issued. Any-thing connected with the issue of paper money is of interest to them. This includes the original artist's drawings and sketches on which the banknotes are based. These pieces of original artwork are, not surprisingly, very rare. The finished artwork is usually retained either by the bank commissioning the design or by the printers who produced the notes, but occasionally preliminary drawings come to light, perhaps among the private papers of artists after their death. Proofs taken from the die as it is engraved, are another rare category of interest to the specialist. Complete proofs of bank-note designs are seldom seen, for security reasons, but occasionally proofs of the portrait, the vignette decorating the back of a note or other portions of the design may be found. Proofs taken from the die for the complete banknote are usually cut in half, so that the design is incomplete and cannot be easily imitated. In modern banknote printing, several processes are combined to defeat the forger. Recess or intaglio printing is used for the basic design, but background patterns may be applied in various colours by offset lithography or photo-gravure, while serial numbers and parts of the inscription may be applied by letter-press or surface-printing. Theoretically proofs could exist of each colour separation and each printing

A series of notgeld from Neubrandenburg, depicting scenery and landscapes in the locality. By 1921, notgeld sets were being produced mainly for collectors.

operation, but it would be very rare for a complete series of proofs to become available to the collector.

Security printers would often send their representatives on a tour of Latin America or China, in the hope of securing contracts to print banknotes for these areas. For this purpose, therefore, they would print sample notes which were intended to advertise the company and demonstrate the quality of its printing. The American Bank Note Co, De La Rue, Waterlow & Sons, Perkins Bacon and Giesecke & Devrient were among the companies who produced sample notes, often in various languages, with a view to winning contracts. These undenominated notes often portrayed the chairman of the company, the printing works or landscapes. Alternatively they would make use of actual banknotes which they had printed, and these would be distinguished from the issued notes by having zero serial numbers, the words "Cancelled" or "Annule" printed across them or a pattern of holes punched out of them. Banknotes with zero serial numbers and overprinted "Specimen" are used, even now, by banks for publicity purposes. Notes may be found with the equivalent in other languages—"*Müster*" (German), "*Monster*" (Dutch) or "*Saggio*" (Italian).

Stocks and share certificates, government bonds and even lottery tickets are now attracting the attention of paper money collectors, not only because they represent a form of money in one sense, but because they are invariably produced by the same firms of security printers who produce banknotes and, as such, they often incorporate features and motifs in their designs which are also to be found on banknotes. Like the paper money of the nineteenth century broken banks, the share certificates of long defunct and bankrupt companies are reasonably plentiful and are by no means expensive since they have no real monetary value and are only of aesthetic value to the collector. In many cases they served to attract and impress the would-be purchaser and therefore no expense was spared in making them as handsome as possible. They are usually much larger than banknotes and were often beautifully engraved. These relics of goldmines which were worked out long ago or of railway lines which have long ceased to operate, possess great historical interest and form an attractive addition to any paper money collection.

11
COLLECTING
PAPER MONEY

Notaphily—the hobby of collecting paper money —is of very recent growth. The name for the hobby was invented as recently as 1969 and it is not entirely satisfactory since it is partly from the Latin—*nota* (a note) and the Greek—*philos* (love of), when it should preferably have been derived from the same language. That collectors should only recently have got around to coining an expression for their hobby is an indication of its very recent growth. Yet there is evidence to suggest that paper money was being collected 180 years ago, for printed sheets of different *assignats* and *mandats* were produced as souvenirs and must have catered to people who were interested in them as historical documents of the French Revolution, rather than as actual spending money.

It is really only since the First World War that paper money has been universally accepted in place of silver and gold and thus it is within the past fifty years that notaphily has become popular. Many of the notes of the broken banks, or the paper money produced in times of economic upheaval or wartime sieges, were only preserved by chance or by people who laid aside specimens as curiosities. There was no market for obsolete paper money until fairly recently and notes were seldom acquired in large quantities for distribution to dealers and collectors. At the same time, apart from a few eccentric characters who collected paper money, collectors were few and far between, until after the First World War. Some fantastically large collec-

Front and back of the £1 note issued by the erstwhile Republic of Biafra which seceded from the Federation of Nigeria in 1969–71. A good example of interesting notes which can be picked up very cheaply.

tions of banknotes were formed in the last century and formed the nucleus of the present-day knowledge on the subject. Ludwig Clericus of Magdeburg, for example, began collecting paper money in the 1870s. Clericus wrote several important books and many articles about paper money. After his death the German State Printing Works in Berlin purchased his collection but unfortunately it was destroyed in the bombing of Berlin in 1945. Most of the great nineteenth and early twentieth century collections of paper money were formed in Germany or Austria and many of them suffered great losses during the two world wars. The Pflümer collection, amounting to over 10,000 items, was purchased by the Marquess of Bute, who was also noted for his collections of airmail and war stamps, and these collections suffered heavy loss when the London home of the Marquess was destroyed during the London Blitz.

Notaphily received its first great stimulus during and after the First World War with the appearance of the high-denomination German banknotes and the myriads of *Notgeld*. For the first time the hobby captured the imagination of the man in the street as well as the wealthy scholar or historian. Interest waned in the 1930s, but rose again during and after the Second World War and a new generation of collectors was recruited to the hobby by the vast quantities of Japanese occupation currency which flooded Europe and America after the war. As coin and medal collecting boomed in popularity in the 1960s so also did paper money collecting. Hitherto collectors had little opportunity to purchase examples of paper money. Occasionally coin dealers would include a few banknotes in their stock but, generally speaking, they took little interest in this aspect of numismatics and knowledgeable collectors could often pick up rare items for a fraction of their true value. Now there are several important dealers who specialise in paper money and publish detailed catalogues and price lists. Spink's, the oldest-established coin dealer in Britain, and Stanley Gibbons, one of the world's foremost stamp dealers, both opened paper money branches in 1971 and have begun publishing catalogues and other literature connected with this new hobby.

Numismatic magazines on both sides of the Atlantic now give a great deal of space to articles and features on paper money, and carry extensive advertising from dealers who specialise in this field. Collecting is made easier, especially for the beginner, by the attractive packets of mixed notes which are now retailed in many department stores, book-shops and drug-stores. Packs of obsolete banknotes are now given away as premium offers by manufacturers of many different commodities, from cigarettes to shampoo. By saving two or more packets or labels from the appropriate brand, the would-be collector can send up to the manufacturer and receive, in return, a bundle of attractive banknotes with which to start off his collection.

Apart from the dealers, the department stores and the premium offers, all of which have provided the collector with ways of getting specimens, the old, traditional methods still exist. In those happier days, before the Second World War, when there were no currency restrictions, banks and travel agents were a happy hunting ground for the paper money collector and attractive specimens from all over the world could be obtained in this way, by paying the going exchange rates. Even now a friendly bank manager may be able to help you secure interesting examples of notes which may have ceased to be legal tender but which are still valid and are occasionally handed in for redemption. Taxi-drivers, hoteliers and shopkeepers, particularly those catering largely to tourists and foreign visitors, have a good opportunity of receiving a wide range of paper money of all kinds. Conversely foreign travel by friends and relatives can often yield interesting examples of paper money. Servicemen in both world wars, as well as a host of minor campaigns, have had an unrivalled opportunity to secure paper money in large quantities, especially in cases where the paper money has become worthless on account of the downfall of a government or the surrender of a country, as happened with Germany in 1918 and 1945.

Examples of old paper money turn up in the oddest places. Distrust of banks has led many a canny individual to salt away his or her money in the upholstery of furniture or a mattress and little caches of banknotes have often come to light when old bedding or furniture was being broken up. Banknotes have been used as book-markers by absent-minded individuals, turning up many years later perhaps when the books were cleared out and sold to a dealer. Antique dealers have sometimes found bundles of old banknotes secreted in drawers in desks and bureaux and, if the original owner cannot be traced, these notes inevitably come into the hands of collectors. Until the advent of banknote dealers within the past few years, the search for old paper money added a great deal of zest and excitement to the hobby. Part of the fun of collecting can lie in the unusual way in which the prize specimens were obtained.

Condition of paper money

Until recently paper money collectors were quite happy to give space in their collections to notes whose condition was far from perfect. The justification for this was that, since paper money was seldom if ever laid aside at the time of issue for

Series of notgeld from Neubrandenburg showing landmarks of the area.

preservation in a collection, it was bound to show some signs of wear and tear through having been passed from hand to hand. Thus blemishes like creases, pin-holes and dog-eared corners were usually disregarded. In many cases, so few examples of a particular note had been preserved at all that collectors were glad to have them in any condition. Half a note was better than none at all.

With the sudden growth of the hobby in the past few years, however, and the hardening of the market involving dealers and collectors alike, the old free and easy approach to condition is disappearing. Many notes now pass straight from the banks into notaphilic collections and are preserved in impeccable condition. Furthermore a large proportion of the obsolete notes are now turning up in better condition than before, as interest in collecting develops and people search out items which had been hidden away. Consequently, as dealers' price-lists develop into standard guides and catalogues, condition is becoming an important factor in determining the value of paper money.

Nevertheless perfection will not always be possible. When compared to other collectable objects paper money comes off rather badly. Banknotes are made of paper, as are postage stamps, but are expected to endure far rougher usage. Similarly they have to perform the same function as coins, without being of the same hard-wearing material. So used banknotes will always have a place in a paper money collection, though the collector should try always to obtain the finest examples he can find.

There are five factors which may affect the condition, and therefore the value, of a banknote. The first of these is cleanliness. The ideal banknote

The second factor is creasing. A banknote which has been folded in half, but is otherwise in clean, fresh condition, would still be a desirable item. The effect of a fold such as this could be minimised by carefully ironing out the crease between sheets of blotting paper. One or two folds of this sort would not make much difference to the value of a note, but where the note has been folded a number of times, both horizontally and vertically, it would not be such an attractive item. Prolonged folding produces heavy creases which may actually damage the surface of the note, and in these cases it would have to be regarded merely as a space filler until something better turned up.

Surface damage is the third factor to take into account. The mildest form of surface damage would consist of crumpling and, here again, light ironing between sheets of blotting paper can work wonders. Other forms of damage include severe staining, rust marks, scratches, thinning or tears, and as the damage becomes progressively worse so the value of the note diminishes.

The edges of a banknote are prone to damage and this constitutes the fourth factor. Slight nicks in the edges of a banknote or minute creasing across the corners would not have much adverse effect on

should have a fresh appearance, without dirty finger-marks. Slight dirt marks, dust marks or light staining would make it less desirable, but still quite presentable. The value of a note would be halved, however, if it was very dirty, or was disfigured by those squiggles which bank clerks delight in making with ball-point pens or indelible pencils. Very dirty notes would only be worth preserving as space fillers, until better specimens were obtainable.

its value, but extensive tears or chunks of paper actually missing round the edges would not be desirable. If the corners were heavily dog-eared, or one or more corners were actually missing, the note would again have no more than 'space filler' value.

Damage to the body of the note is the fifth factor. Under this heading come pin-holes, slight tears caused by paper clips or any other kind of damage resulting in holes or tears in the note itself. In extreme cases notes may actually have been torn or cut in half and subsequently been repaired with sticky tape. Here again, the advisability of retaining such specimens for the collection will depend largely on whether better examples are likely to turn up or not.

Dealers and collectors use various terms to describe the condition of notes. Unfortunately the hobby is still relatively young and these terms have not been codified to the satisfaction of everyone who uses them. Thus paper money in the finest condition is sometimes described as Crisp—a term which is self-explanatory, or Mint (a term borrowed from stamp collecting), or New, or Uncirculated (the latter being a term used by coin collectors). Notes in descending degrees of perfection are described as Extremely Fine, Very Fine or Fine—all terms which are already used by coin collectors. Below Fine comes Very Good which tends to describe a note in such appallingly bad condition that it is hardly worth bothering with. Surprisingly enough, there are even lower grades such as Fair, Poor and Mediocre, which would be applied to items which were torn, badly creased, heavily stained, excessively dog-eared and rubbed on the surface.

Collectors of paper money apply their own rules regarding the repair of damaged items. Whereas philatelists would regard a repaired postage stamp with horror and repulsion and instinctively reject it, the notaphilist will quite happily re-unite the scattered pieces of a banknote with adhesive tape or completely laminate the note in silk. Actually the differences between philatelists and notaphilists is only one of degree and the passage of time will tend to lessen this difference. The very early stamp collectors were not very fastidious and many of the greatest rarities (the so-called Hawaiian Missionary stamps of 1851, for example) have only survived in heavily repaired condition, while the unique One Cent of British Guiana of 1856 has clipped corners and a badly rubbed surface. Where a note is readily obtainable (e.g. a current issue), the collector should be satisfied with nothing less than Crisp condition and, generally speaking, modern notes are not collected in grades below Very Good. Even the earliest notes of Imperial China have survived in Fine or Extremely Fine condition, so never be content with second best.

Dirty notes *can* be cleaned by washing them gently in warm water but this should be done with caution, and it is best to experiment with a similar note, of little value, if possible. The reason for this is that some modern notes use water-soluble inks for printing part of their design (usually one of the background tints) and immersion in water may damage the note irremediably. Never use soaps or detergents, as the chemicals in them can react unfavourably with the colours of the note and produce some unusual, and uncatalogued, shades! After washing, the notes are laid carefully between clean sheets of blotting paper. A few books placed on top will help to press the note flat and remove all but the most determined creases.

Mounting and Housing the Collection

Certain museum collections and official archives are housed in cabinets with sliding frames in which paper money is mounted between glass panes. While this is a very attractive way of displaying a collection it is also very expensive and takes up a great deal of room. Until recently most notaphilists were content to house their collections in conventional loose-leaf stamp albums or photographic albums. In these albums, the notes were held in place by transparent photographic mounting corners and the relevant data, such as date, bank and country of issue, could be written on the page above each note. The disadvantage of this system was that only one side of the banknote could be examined without actually taking the note out of its mounting corners. As an alternative to this small transparent hinges, like those used by stamp collectors, were used to affix the notes to the album page. By this method the note could be turned over so that the back could be examined. This was more satisfactory, but many collectors felt that stamp hinges would leave an unsightly mark on the backs of notes which would detract from their value.

The solution to these problems is now provided by the special albums which have been produced in recent years. These albums have plastic, acetate or PVC sleeves instead of pages. The notes are inserted into the sleeves, which often have small separate pockets for cards on which the relevant data can be written. These albums are often sold by stamp dealers, since they are also used by philatelists for housing envelopes and postcards.

INDEX